Disability and Shopping

Disability and Shopping: Customers, Markets and the State provides an examination of the diverse experiences and perspectives of disabled customers, industry and civil society. It discusses how the interaction between the three stakeholders should be shaped at aiming to decrease inequality and marginalisation.

Shopping is a part of everyday modern life and yet businesses struggle to adequately meet the needs of 80 million disabled customers in the European Union single market. While there has been extensive research into how individuals engage in customer roles and experience, and how businesses and policies both shape and respond to these, little is known of the same dynamics and practices regarding people with impairments. This book addresses this need by revealing the perspectives, interactions and experiences of disabled customers and their interaction with policy and business.

It will be required reading for all scholars and students of disability studies, sociology, marketing and customer relations.

Ieva Eskytė is a postdoctoral research fellow in the School of Law at the University of Leeds, UK.

Routledge Advances in Disability Studies

The Changing Disability Policy System
Active Citizenship and Disability in Europe Volume 1
Edited by Rune Halvorsen, Bjørn Hvinden, Jerome Bickenbach, Delia Ferri and Ana Marta Guillén Rodriguez

Citizenship Inclusion and Intellectual Disability
Biopolitics Post-Institutionalisation
Niklas Altermark

Intellectual Disability and the Right to a Sexual Life
A Continuation of the Autonomy/Paternalism Debate
Simon Foley

The Changing Disability Policy System
Active Citizenship and Disability in Europe Volume 2
Edited by Rune Halvorsen, Bjørn Hvinden, Jerome Bickenbach, Delia Ferri and Ana Marta Guillén Rodriguez

Cultural Disability Studies in Education
Interdisciplinary Navigations of the Normative Divide
David Bolt

Institutional Violence and Disability
Punishing Conditions
Kate Rossiter and Jen Rinaldi

Disability and Shopping
Customers, Markets and the State
Ieva Eskytė

https://www.routledge.com/Routledge-Advances-in-Disability-Studies/book-series/RADS

Disability and Shopping
Customers, Markets and the State

Ieva Eskytė

LONDON AND NEW YORK

First published 2019
by Routledge
2 Park Square, Milton Park, Abingdon, Oxon OX14 4RN

and by Routledge
52 Vanderbilt Avenue, New York, NY 10017

Routledge is an imprint of the Taylor & Francis Group, an informa business

© 2019 Ieva Eskytė

The right of Ieva Eskytė to be identified as author of this work has been asserted by her in accordance with sections 77 and 78 of the Copyright, Designs and Patents Act 1988.

All rights reserved. No part of this book may be reprinted or reproduced or utilised in any form or by any electronic, mechanical, or other means, now known or hereafter invented, including photocopying and recording, or in any information storage or retrieval system, without permission in writing from the publishers.

Trademark notice: Product or corporate names may be trademarks or registered trademarks, and are used only for identification and explanation without intent to infringe.

British Library Cataloguing-in-Publication Data
A catalogue record for this book is available from the British Library

Library of Congress Cataloging-in-Publication Data
Names: Eskytė, Ieva.
Title: Disability and shopping: customers, markets and the state / Ieva Eskytė.
Description: 1st Edition. | New York: Routledge, 2019. |
Series: Routledge advances in social work | Includes bibliographical references and index.
Identifiers: LCCN 2018043001 | ISBN 9781138105775 (hardback) | ISBN 9781315101750 (ebook)
Subjects: LCSH: People with disabilities—European Union countries. | People with disabilities—Services for. | Stores, Retail—Barrier-free design. | Shopping—European Union countries.
Classification: LCC HV1559.E8 E75 2019 | DDC 381/.1087094—dc23
LC record available at https://lccn.loc.gov/2018043001

ISBN: 978-1-138-10577-5 (hbk)
ISBN: 978-1-315-10175-0 (ebk)

Typeset in Times New Roman
by codeMantra

To my son, Dovydas

Contents

List of figures xi
Acknowledgements xiii
List of abbreviations xv

Introduction 1
Conceptual perspectives 3
  Models of disability 3
  CA theory 5
  Research and data generation strategies 6
  Research strategy and key research questions 7
  Why Lithuania and the United Kingdom? 10
  Policy framework 11
  Mystery shopping 11
  Discussing shopping experience – interviews with customers 13
  Studying business and civil society's perspectives 14
  Analysing the data 16
  Structure of this book 16
Bibliography 20

1 Disabled people in the market 26
Disabled people and markets: historical insights and current practice 27
  Useless eaters 27
  Passive service users 29
  From consumers to producers: example of direct payments 31
  A target for new business 33
  Vulnerable consumers 34
Shopping chain and disabled customers 36
  Customer information 37
  Navigation in retail premises 39
  Interaction in the shop 42

Accessibility and the private market 44
　　Accessibility and user involvement 45
　　Accessibility and a common language 48
　　UD and retail premises 50
Concluding comments 51
Bibliography 53

2　Accessibility in the EU markets　　　　　　　　　　　　　70
Accessibility in the global context 71
　　Accessibility and the CRPD 72
Accessibility in the European single market 77
　　Disabled customers 78
　　Information provision 80
　　Accessibility of retail premises 82
Accessibility in national markets: Lithuania and the United Kingdom 85
　　'Socially vulnerable' consumers in Lithuania 85
　　'Vulnerable consumers' in the United Kingdom 88
　　Accessibility in Lithuania 90
　　Accessibility in the United Kingdom 92
Concluding comments 94
Bibliography 96

3　Communicative action and the EU markets　　　　　　　102
Market accessibility and a lifeworld 104
　　'System' and 'lifeworld' 104
　　EU policies and the lifeworld 107
　　Large business, SMEs and the lifeworld 110
　　Private market, customers and the lifeworld 111
Access to the discourse and power relations 112
　　Communicative action 113
　　Bargaining and arguing 114
　　Bargaining, arguing and international relations 117
　　Communicative rationality and OMC 119
Concluding comments 121
Bibliography 122

4　The chain of an accessible shopping　　　　　　　　　　128
Customer information 129
　　Information about shops 129
　　Information about products 133
　　Information about product accessibility 136

The journey to a shop 140
   Home environment 140
   Public environment 141
   Public and private transport 145
Navigation in retail premises 148
   Entering the shop 148
   Operating in retail premises 151
   Reaching products 154
Interaction in the shop 157
   Interaction with informal assistants 157
   Interaction with shop assistants 158
   Interaction with 'special' shop assistants 162
Concluding comments 164
Bibliography 166

5 The lifeworld of accessible markets   169
   Notions of disabled customers and accessibility 170
      International business and civil society's perspectives
         on disabled customers 170
      National business' perspectives on disabled customers 173
      National civil society's perspectives on disabled customers 176
      International stakeholders' perspectives on accessibility 178
      National stakeholders' perspectives on accessibility 180
   The role of policy discourse 183
      Global regulations 183
      EU instruments 187
      National policies 189
   The role of business practice 193
      Accessibility, expenditures and profit 194
      Corporate social responsibility 197
      Product accessibility information 198
      Trainings 199
   Concluding comments 202
   Bibliography 204

6 Access to the discourse and power relations   206
   Formulating the discourse: internal processes 207
      Stakeholder position: international perspectives 207
      Stakeholder position: national perspectives 212
      Stakeholder position and disabled customers 214
   Formulating the discourse: public sphere 216
      Communication and a common goal 217

Communication and strategic goals 219
Communication and awareness 223
Concluding comments 225
Bibliography 227

7 Summary and conclusions 229
Book overview 230
What are the experiences of disabled people as customers in the mainstream private retail markets and their perspectives towards accessibility? 231
How do stakeholders of the European single market for ICT products perceive disabled people as customers, and what factors shape their knowledge and positions? 233
How do private business and civil society engage into communication and collaborative innovation to create more accessible EU single market and facilitate disabled customers' participation? 236
Way forward 241
Bibliography 245

Index 247

List of figures

1.1 Accessible shopping chain 37
4.1 Delusion of information about accessible products 137

Acknowledgements

This research was made possible by assistance, encouragement, cooperation and support of many great people. My sincere gratitude goes to Mark Priestley and Anna Lawson for their patient and encouraging guidance through the journey of this research. Discussions and idea developments with Rob Imrie, Rannveig Traustadottir, Lisa Waddington, Tom Campbell, Mark Davis and Nick Emmel contributed greatly and made the process challenging yet enjoyable. Thank you to Colin Barnes and Alison Sheldon for an ongoing inspiration and example of academic passion for disability studies. My friends Rima Baranova, Andrea Broderick, Stelios Charitakis, Orla Kelly, Jack Palmer, Benjamin Hirst, Angelica Pessarini, Ema Loja, Catriona Clark, Julia Swallow, Jenny Read, Laura Connelly and many others were there for me when most needed. Support and guidance of Klaus-Dieter Axt and Alejandro Moledo in understanding and navigating Brussels and the EU policy processes was invaluable. I am grateful to my family, who trusted and supported me despite big distance and fast life tempo. A very special thanks goes to Gordon Clubb who saw the birth of this book from the very first steps and was invaluable in clarifying ideas and making me believe in what I do. While I started writing this book as an academic, I finished it as an academic mother. I am truly grateful for my baby son Dovydas who taught me unquestionable love and occasionally slept or played so I can finish writing. And above all, the greatest thank you goes to all disabled people in the United Kingdom and Lithuania, industry and civil society who shared with me their experiences of accessibility and customer participation.

List of abbreviations

ADA	American Disability Act
BSA	British Sociological Association
BSH	Brand-Specific ICT Shop
BSI	British Standard Institute
CA	Communicative action
CESCR	Committee on Economic, Social and Cultural Rights
CRPD	Convention on the Rights of Persons with Disabilities
CSR	Corporate Social Responsibility
Committee	Committee on the Rights of Persons with Disabilities
Council	European Council
DPO	Disabled People's Organisation
DREAM	International Training Network Disability Rights Expanding Accessible Markets
DTCA	Direct to Consumer Advertising
EA	Equality Act
EAA	European Accessibility Act
EC	European Commission
EP	European Parliament
ESC	Economic and Social Council (UN)
ESR	Early Stage Researcher
ESRC	Economic and Social Research Council
ESO	European Standardisation Organisation
EU	European Union
GDP	Gross Domestic Product
GPA	German Psychiatric Association
IBR	International ICT Business Representatives
ICT	Information and Communication Technologies
IDPO	International Disabled People's Organisation
IL	Independent Living
LŽNS	Lietuvos Žmonių su Negalia Sąjunga
MS	Member States
NBSH	Non-Brand-Specific ICT Shop
NSCP	National Strategy for Consumer Protection (LT)

OFT	Office of Fair Trading (UK)
OMC	Open Method of Coordination
PA	Personal Assistant
PACs	Professionals Allied to Community
PAMs	Professionals Allied to Medicine
TRC	Technical Regulations for Construction (LT)
SME	Small and Medium Enterprises
SP	State Parties
UCD	User-Centred Design
UD	Universal Design
UPIAS	the Union of Physically Impaired Against Segregation
US	United States
WHO	World Health Organisation

Introduction

Disabled people and their everyday realities are usually considered in the context of barriers to participation in the labour market, education, health and social care services, independent living and more recently sexuality and family relations. These areas have received attention from the disability movement and academia as well as gained political currency. While their importance is unquestionable, the intensifying link between being a customer and a citizen (Bauman, 1988, 2007, Gabriel and Lang, 1995) positions access to and equal participation in retail market as an important element for full participation in society (Convention on the Rights of Persons with Disabilities (CRPD), 2006). Shopping, being a form of participation in the market, provides individuals with a possibility to exercise choice and control (Bettman et al., 1991), engage with social networks and communities (Miller et al., 1998), is a form of leisure (Graham et al., 1991) and a means of shaping and communicating identity (Andreoli, 1996, Dholakia et al., 1995). While usually non-disabled individuals are relatively free to engage in customer role, people with impairments are often eliminated from barrier-free and equal participation in the shopping process (Baker et al., 2007, Burnett and Paul, 1996, Cheng, 2002, Kaufman-Scarborough, 1999, 2001, MacDonald et al., 1994).

Academic interest in disabled people's customer participation is emerging (Baker, 2006, Burckley et al., 2015, Burnett and Baker, 2001, Cheng, 2002, Kaufman-Scarborough, 1998, 1999, 2001, Ray and Ryder, 2003, Wilton et al., 2018), but the topic remains under-researched. The main focus tends to be on barriers faced by people with a certain type of impairment either in retail premises or when interacting with shop assistants. While some attempts to question deeper roots of disabling practices are present (Kaufman-Scarborough, 1998, 2001, Kaufman-Scarborough and Menzel Baker, 2005), the majority of studies are relatively descriptive and address empirical rather than actual and real domains of reality. This book, therefore, goes beyond actual seller–customer exchange interaction in retail premises. Even though it recognises the growing importance of online shopping (Häubl and Trifts, 2000, Limayem et al., 2000, Wolfinbarger and Gilly, 2001), it focuses on shopping process and experience in retail outlets and treats shopping as a holistic process and a chain that is experienced by each individual in a unique way. In such a context, accessibility of customer information, home and public environment, public and private transport, external and internal shop environments, and shop assistants' awareness of disability and accessibility play a part in shaping accessibility and equality of a disabled customer's participation.

Industry and civil society plays an important part in shaping practices of and dynamics within the retail market. However, their experiences and perspectives regarding disabled people's customer rights and market accessibility remain under-researched. Consequently, this book adopts a multiple perspective approach and brings together experiences and perspectives of disabled people, industry and civil society. It first investigates and describes disabled customers' experiences beyond the market exchange process in the shop. It then detects perspectives, interactions and experiences of the European Union (EU) industry and civil society that shape disabled customers' experiences and which should be considered aiming to introduce greater accessibility to the EU private market.

The necessity to address the aforementioned issues was recognised by the United Nations (UN) CRPD (2006) that positions access to customer goods and services in the private sector as essential for full participation in society. Specifically, article 9.2b requires states 'to ensure that private entities that offer facilities and services which are open or provided to the public take into account all aspects of accessibility for persons with disabilities'. Recalling the focus of the Convention on Information and Communication Technologies (ICT; art.9.2h), this book sheds light on the consumer market for ICT products as an example of the dynamics, although with wider implications for other markets. It positions ICTs as a case study of a product and uses them as an example of purchasing an item, but leaves its technical features aside.

The present study is underpinned by the social model of disability and Habermas' theory of communicative action (CA). Habermas' history of thought and his focus on Europeanisation, political, legal, economic and philosophical relationships between the state, market and an individual allows the use of social model analysis with a materialist approach and multiple justification of different levels of barriers. The chosen theoretical perspective frees disabled people's customer experience from the vacuum of an individual. It sheds light on a variety of barriers and possibilities, shaped by political decisions and processes, and the nature of the capitalist market. This book explores how the ICT industry and civil society's lifeworld, access to the discourse and power relations shape disabled customers' shopping experiences beyond the actual exchange process in a shop and may lead towards more accessibility in the EU private market.

Conceptual perspectives

Models of disability

The individual model of disability that is also known as the 'medical' model, perceives disabled people's experiences as a direct result of their impairments (Oliver, 1983). It portrays disability as a 'personal tragedy' (Barnes et al., 1999, Oliver, 1990) and positions people with impairments as 'abnormal' and weak individuals, who need sympathy (Brisenden, 1986) and have to be 'cured' or 'cared' for (Finkelstein, 1991). It converts disabled people into actors, dependent on non-disabled society members, professionals and the state (Barnes et al., 1999, Oliver, 1990, Stone, 1984). The latter usually responds by providing 'special' provision such as segregated schooling (Barton, 1997, 1995, 2004, Cook et al., 2001, Oliver and Barnes, 2010, Walker, 1993), special labour market (Airhart, 1987, Gleeson, 1999, Thornton and Lunt, 2006) or housing (Clapham and Smith, 1990, Imrie, 2004, Stewart et al., 1999). Such practice often leads to exclusion, segregation and stigma. Retail market also seems to be premised on the individual model, and the first chapter discusses this in more detail. An important point to underline is that both the state and the market locate the problem of market inaccessibility and disabled customers' exclusion within a person rather than within society, state's actions and business' practice.

Language plays an important role in shaping disabling practices (Mallett and Slater, 2014, Oliver, 1996). While Bickenback (1993) notes that using appropriate and exact labels may provide professionals with a possibility to create and share similar vocabularies and to improve communication, usually labels have a negative and disabling effect on people's everyday life (Auslander and Gold, 1999, Blaska, 1993, Foreman, 2005). For instance, Zola (1993) argues that language is not only a personal but also a political issue, enabling more powerful or privileged actors to keep others 'in place' and to take over the control of minorities' lives. Terminologies that are alive in narratives and mindset of policymakers, professionals, media and disabled people often have a negative effect on attitudes towards people with impairments, foster stereotypes and portray them as vulnerable and dependent (Auslander and Gold, 1999, Pierce, 1998). Expressions and abridgements such as 'the disabled' or 'the blind' deny people's individuality and personality (Zola, 1993). Words such as 'unfortunate', 'suffering' and 'difficulty' (Byron et al., 2005) position disabled people as victims, poor or helpless and needing pity (Shakespeare, 2000). Likewise, usage of diagnoses stigmatises and has a negative impact on individuals' participation in community and social networks (Penn and Nowlin-Drummond, 2001), and the term 'patient' often eliminates disabled people's activity and imply passivity (Oliver, 1996, Zola, 1972, 1975, 1977, 1993).

4 Introduction

On the other end of the spectrum is the social model of disability. It positions social structures as the main factor behind disadvantage and disablement of people with impairments. Being inspired by the Independent Living Movement in the United States in the 1970s (Gillinson et al., 2005), the Union of Physically Impaired Against Segregation (UPIAS, United Kingdom) entrenched this alternative approach in the Fundamental Principles of Disability (1976:3–4):

> In our view, it is society which disables ... impaired people. Disability is something imposed on top of our impairments, by the way we are unnecessarily isolated and excluded from full participation in society. Disabled people are therefore an oppressed group in society. To understand this it is necessary to grasp the distinction between the ... impairment and the social situation, called 'disability', of people with such impairment.

In Oliver's terms (1983:23), the social model 'involves nothing more or less fundamental than a switch away from focusing on the physical limitations of particular individuals to the way the physical and social environments impose limitations upon certain groups or categories of people'. In such a context, while an impairment is a physical feature of an individual, society's reaction to impairment (Morris, 1993), unequal power relations between disabled and non-disabled people (Barnes and Mercer, 2003, Campbell and Oliver, 1996) and social barriers and prejudice (Shakespeare, 1996) are the factors that exclude, marginalise, oppress and disable people with impairments. The social model positions people with impairments as a socially oppressed group (Barnes and Mercer, 2003) and as 'collective victims of an uncaring or unknowing society rather than individual victims of circumstance' (Oliver, 1990:2). Hence, it provides a political and conceptual framework which enables to tackle collective oppression, rather than to fix, cure or adjust separate individuals.

Despite the recognised importance, the social model is widely problematised by actors within and outside the disability movement (Abberley, 1996, Crow, 1996, French, 1993, Terzi, 2004). While there is no room here for a discussion of the raised concerns, for the purpose of this book, it is worth noting that similar to the individual model, in the social model context, language plays an important role in shaping disabled people's representation and experiences. Some scholars advocate for 'people first language' (Auslander and Gold, 1999, Blaska, 1993, Foreman, 2005, Penn and Nowlin-Drummond, 2001, Zola, 1993) and the term 'people with disabilities'. As an example, Blaska (1993:27) notes that such phrasing 'demonstrates respect for people with disabilities by referring to them first as individuals, and then referring to their disability when it is needed'. In a similar vein, La Forge (1991) argues that such expressions secure one's individuality and personhood, and Zola (1993) emphasises that the preposition 'with' reflects ideology of the social model of disability and establishes a clear grammatical and figurative distinction between an individual and his/her disablement experiences. While the scholars make a valid point, the terms 'disabled people' and 'people with impairments' are used in this book. First, as Oliver and Barnes (1998:18) assert, 'the use of phrase "people with disabilities" is unacceptable because it blurs the crucial distinction between impairment and disability'. Second, among a number of people criticising the 'people with disabilities' term, Titchkosky (2001) notes that it disconnects disability from social and political contexts and supports measurement of conditions of limitation and lack. She goes further and argues that 'disability is something that individuals have to deal with, but *only as individuals*. Disability is not something that individuals *are*, and no one needs to deal with people who have an identity as "disabled people" – an oppressed minority group' (Titchkosky, 2001:136).

This book documents a variety of barriers that prevent people with impairments from accessible and equal participation as customers and argues that their exclusion from the mainstream private market is shaped by external factors and structures. Hence, it seems legitimate to use the term 'people with impairments' and so to identify a variety of barriers and potentials and to refer to them collectively as 'disabled people' as an oppressed customer minority group in the EU market. The chosen phrasing neither negates people's abilities nor positions impairments in front of the person. Indeed, it allows achieving more clarity in terms of identifying barriers and opportunities for exercising customer rights. This is important, as such employment of language enables shaping and challenging the validity claims discussed by Habermas (1976, 1984, 1985) in a way which is more 'understandable' to the stakeholders involved in the process.

CA theory

The decision to adapt Habermas' theory of CA is premised on several interrelated strands. First, since this book explores disabled customers' experiences within the EU single market, Habermas' history of thought on the Union is particularly useful. His discussions are premised on specific historical events, policy developments and various time periods (Verovšek, 2012). He critically evaluates challenges and opportunities and links these with national governments and EU citizens (Habermas, 2001). Despite awareness of the weaknesses of the EU, Habermas believes in the Union. He notes that political processes and developments that started after the ratification of the Treaty on EU (1992) positioned the Union as an 'exemplary case' of 'democratic politics beyond the nation-state' (Habermas, 2001:88) and acts as a vehicle for social integration and common political culture (Habermas, 1999, 2001). Most importantly, he treats the EU as a tool that may provide citizens with an opportunity to 'assume influence upon the development of worldwide systematic operations through their own political public spheres and their own democratic content' (Habermas, 1994:165). This is particularly important to this research as such perspective recalls general principles of the CRPD and provides a framework for disabled people's participation and leadership as citizens and customers in the EU policy and market processes to emerge. The adaption of the theory enables identifying potential roots of customers' disablement and exclusion, laying in regional and national policy instruments and mechanisms as well as detecting EU policy potentials in shaping an accessible EU single market.

Second, in the theory of CA, Habermas interlinks state, market and individuals. This may be linked to Bhaskar's (1975) critical realist perspective, suggesting that reality is composed of three overlapping domains: empirical, actual and real. While the empirical domain is experienced and observed by an individual directly (Bhaskar, 1975) in the actual domain, the observed events occur with an individual having no knowledge of them (Tsoukas, 1989). The real domain of reality is identified with 'underlying tendencies or mechanisms which may in a given situation give rise to events' (Partington, 2000:98). Hence, linking Habermas' work with the critical realist ontological position enables me to shed light on how market structures and procedures (real domain) shape accessibility practices and policies, attitudes and interaction patterns between state, market and disabled people (actual domain), which are directly experienced by customers with impairments (empirical domain).

Adapting Habermas' CA theory allows holding on to the social model and its materialist approach. It enables focusing on multiple levels (global, regional and national) of social, cultural, political and attitudinal factors that shape business, civil society and disabled customers' experiences and realities. The theory is seen as an appropriate way to negotiate barriers and tensions between key stakeholders and disabled customers. It provides a framework within which they can share experiences, concerns and perspectives, shape common language and knowledge, establish and maintain social relationships and negotiate the common goal of accessibility and strategies for its achievement.

Research and data generation strategies

One way of understanding the tensions and the potential for reconciliation in the European policy process and market practice is to build a knowledge set about all stakeholders' experiences and the processes that may affect their perspectives. Drawing on Habermas' theory of CA, this book brings all parties, including disabled people, into one academic space as equal partners and informants. It invites them to share experiences, knowledge, norms, values and perspectives. The employment of qualitative methodology provides an opportunity to indirectly shape common language and knowledge, to engage in communication, and hopefully CA, regarding an accessible EU single market. Global, regional and national instruments, addressing customer rights and protection and accessibility of public and private spaces, as well as insights from previous studies are employed as a framework to better understand stakeholders' actions, positions and potential for collaboration and knowledge innovation.

Research strategy and key research questions

Research design, implementation and data dissemination strategies and practices receive great attention in disability research. Due to a long history of disabled people's exclusion, oppression and unequal power relations in the research field (Kitchin, 2000, Oliver, 1992, Stone and Priestley, 1996), an emancipatory research approach has been introduced (Kitchin, 2000, Oliver, 1992). Although it has been debated by the scholars, the UK Disabled People's Coalition (UKDPC; 2005) distinguishes seven core principles that should be implemented when adopting the approach. These are as follows: disabled people should be in control of the research, the researcher should be accountable and explain the intentions of the research as well as use appropriate methods for findings dissemination, the research should be based on the philosophy of empowerment and the improvement of disabled people's lives, the rigour of the research should be achieved through the applied methods and the research itself should be open to detailed examination, applied methods should be appropriate for the research as well as for the informants involved in it, the focus should be on the disabling practices in the society and all this should fit with the social model of disability. Initially, this book aimed to adopt all principles of the emancipatory research. However, its pure adoption was impossible. Nevertheless, several aspects have been implemented. The initial objective was to reveal disabled people's customer experience and to identify structures and processes that prevent them from equal access to and participation in the mainstream private market. It was aimed to do this through their perspectives and the identification of the experiences of key stakeholders who are involved in the process. Furthermore, adoption of the social model and used methods and strategies for research findings dissemination bring the research closer to the emancipatory approach.

As it has been already suggested, the research holds the position that aiming to facilitate disabled people's participation in the mainstream private market as customers, the revelation of customers and key stakeholders' (civil society and business) experiences is essential. Hence, the research investigates accessibility of the private retail market for people with different types of impairment beyond the exchange process in the shop. It explores how contradictions in the public discourse surrounding disability, accessibility and retail customers manifest at an empirical level and shape stakeholders' experiences. With this in mind, the main research question addressed in this book inquires,

> What are disabled customers, EU industry and civil society's perspectives and experiences that should be considered, aiming to facilitate disabled people's participation in the mainstream private market?

8 *Introduction*

Subordinate research questions explore various dimensions of the topic. For instance, the first secondary question asks,

> What are the experiences of disabled people as customers in the mainstream private retail markets and their perspectives toward accessibility?

It aims to provide insights into empirical customer experiences in different stages of the shopping chain. It sheds light on faced barriers, potentials, coping strategies and resilience practices. This requires detailed disabled customers' experiential perspectives gathered through mystery shopping and semi-structured interviews.

In addition, EU industry and civil society's perceptions of market accessibility and disabled customers are targeted, and factors potentially shaping this knowledge and positions are addressed:

> How do stakeholders of the European single market for Information and Communication Technology products perceive disabled people as customers, and what factors shape their knowledge and positions?

Finally, some insights into the way private business players and civil society may engage in communication, aiming to innovate and produce knowledge regarding what would work for creating accessible EU single market are provided:

> How do private business and civil society engage into communication and collaborative innovation to create more accessible EU single market?

This book adopts a retroductive perspective. It aims to 'discover underlying mechanisms that, in particular contexts, explain observed regularities' (Blaikie, 2010:87). Being tightly linked to Bhaskar's (1975) work on reality domains, this strategy suggests that while on the empirical level experiences can be detected, the actual domain consists of events that not necessarily can be observed. Either way, behind the two types of reality are structures and processes, making reality to produce events (Proctor, 1998). In other words, social structures within which an individual is located cause and affect the behaviour. With this in mind, this book first provides an adequate description (Blaikie, 2010) of disabled customers' experiences. It addresses these beyond the actual market exchange practice and sheds light on shopping process as an accessible chain. It holds the position that disabled customers' exclusion, vulnerability and markets inaccessibility is a result of contradictions in the public discourse surrounding disability, accessibility and retail customers. Hence, the second part of this book reveals ICT manufacturers; ICT business representatives; sellers; and disabled people organisations' (DPO) attitudes, norms and values towards the issue of international and national.

Epistemologically, aiming to answer the main research question, it was important to examine barriers and potentials through disabled customers, ICT industry players and civil society's experiences. The study took the position that while the actors can represent social reality within which they operate (Blaikie, 2010), the employment of various methods is essential in order to allow the informants to engage in a 'dialogic' process, revealing underlying realities and social structures (Habermas, 1970). A combination of qualitative methods provided insights into the setting of a phenomenon and allowed gaining understanding of underlying reasons and motivations (Blaikie, 1993). It also contributed to uncovering new and under-researched trends in thought, responses to the EU policies and dimensions of the lifeworld and communicative practice. The main empirical sources involved mystery shopping and semi-structured interviews with disabled customers and semi-structured interviews with and observations of ICT industry and civil society. While applied methods and the rationale of the research are qualitative, in aiming to either provide a background or to support the data some explanations are of a quantitative nature.

Triangulation was another important element of the research strategy that ensured a multidimensional perspective of the phenomenon (Foster, 1997) and increased validity, reliability and strength of the study (Denzin, 1970). Data source, methodologic and theoretical triangulation approaches were employed. With regard to data source triangulation, the data were collected from disabled customers, ICT manufacturers, regional representatives of ICT products industry and civil society, national DPOs and ICT shop assistants and managers in Lithuania and the United Kingdom. In terms of methodologic triangulation, within-method triangulation (Kimchi et al., 1991) was adopted. Specifically, when gauging disabled customers' experiences, mystery shopping was combined with semi-structured interviews. Aiming to reveal industry and civil society's perspectives, semi-structured interviews were combined with observations. With regard to theoretical triangulation, although Denzin (1970) refers to the employment of multiple theories, this book uses literature on disability; markets; international relations; the EU; the social model of disability; Habermas' theory of CA; and specific global, regional and national soft and binding policy instruments. This assisted in increasing alternative explanations of EU markets accessibility and enabled looking beyond retail practice. The sum of the three types of triangulation allowed to provide rich, multi-perspective and unbiased data (Thurmond, 2001), which are currently insufficient in the field.

The research has been carried out by a non-disabled researcher. Kitchin (2000) argues that non-disabled researchers may approach the project from a subjective and biased position and promote predetermined agendas. This, in return, may have a negative impact on applying research results in an empowering way (Branfield, 1998), continue limited representation of disabled people's knowledge and experience (Shakespeare, 1996) and maintain their marginalisation and oppression (Barnes and Mercer, 1997). Faulkner and Thomas (2002) suggest that research carried out by individuals representing the researched group have more potential to gain deeper knowledge and provide more meaningful outcomes. Although the authors make a valid point, Barnes (1992) notes that having an impairment does not ensure a high quality and implementation of emancipatory research, and that non-disabled researchers may also positively contribute to the field. Indeed, 'the cultural gulf between researchers and researched has as much to do with social indicators like class, education, employment and general life experiences as with impairments' (Barnes, 1992:121–122). Hence, it was important to be aware of how my and research participants' personal, social and cultural characteristics may affect our interaction and research processes. While professional social work experience and scholarship in disability studies helped me to identify strategies for dealing with the outlined challenges regarding disabled customers, internships at the international ICT industry representatives and international DPO assisted me in relating to the informants of industry and civil society.

Having established research strategy and ontological and epistemological positions, the following section sheds light on sampling strategies and techniques that were chosen to identify and involve the participants.

Why Lithuania and the United Kingdom?

The research selected countries that share differences and similarities in terms of generic political developments, market economy, retail practice, social policy and disabled people's history and current position. It was aimed to look at the EU members, which in one way or another reflect processes and experiences that are typical to disabled customers, industry and civil society in other EU countries. Hence, intensity sampling technique has been chosen (Patton, 1990:171), and Lithuania and the United Kingdom were selected as they meet the criteria of the technique, and I am fluent in both languages.

Regarding generic political developments, both countries are members of the EU. The United Kingdom entered the Union in 1973, and Lithuania joined the Union in 2004. Both countries act in the EU economic area under the EU Single Market framework and legislations and seek to guarantee the fundamental freedoms of the Union: free movement of goods, services, capital and people. Furthermore, they have ratified the CRPD and the Optional Protocol (26/02/2009; 07/08/2009 and 30/03/2007; 18/08/2010, respectively) and are obliged to transfer the duties into national legislations.

In terms of general and disability-related characteristics, Lithuania is an Eastern European country with 2.9 million inhabitants (Lietuvos Statistikos Departamentas, 2014) and the United Kingdom is a Western European country with 64.1 million inhabitants (Office for National Statistics, 2014). While 8.03% of Lithuanians are identified as having impairments (Bringing Neighbours Closer, 2012), the number in the United Kingdom reaches 16% of total population (Department for Work and Pensions, 2014).

Regarding market history and relations, the two countries share more differences than similarities. To begin with, as a post-Soviet Union country, Lithuania has a short history of a small, still developing market. The 'rebirth' after regaining independence in 1990 (Vebra, 1994) brought challenges such as unbalanced economy, fragmented and unevenly developed market sectors, blurry import/ export patterns, lack of legal instruments, regulating market relations (Bertelsmann Stiftung BTI, 2010, Hohnen, 2003) as well as limited trading traditions and market economy skills (Bouloff, 1991). At the other end of the spectrum is the United Kingdom, having long-time domination in the European and world economy (Aldcroft, 1964), leadership in international and domestic banking (Collins, 1988) and international commerce and finance (Rota and Schettino, 2011, Mollan and Michie, 2012). Thatcher's era (1979–1990) and the new approach to economic policy introduced privatisation, tax changes and reformed industrial relations (Crafts, 2002) that played a part in positioning the United Kingdom as a long-term competitive economy.

The research activities have been carried out in city A in Lithuania and city B in the United Kingdom. While due to confidentiality the names of the cities are not revealed, it is important to note that the locations are similar in terms of inhabitants' consistency, retail market, shopping facilities and accessibility of public spaces.

Policy framework

Due to ontological and epistemological positions and the knowledge acquired through literature review, global (CRPD, United States), regional (EU) and national (Lithuania, United Kingdom) policy instruments, addressing customer rights protection, accessibility of public spaces and shops, were examined. The analysis of the discourse of policy instruments enabled detecting potential roots of the disablement (Barnes, 1991) and underlying legal norms and rules (Henn et al., 2006) that may impact stakeholders' obligations and interactions and disabled customers' experiences. Since EU negotiating settings are distinguished by high levels of institutionalisation and socialisation (Lewis, 1998) that shape a framework for a common lifeworld to emerge (Risse, 2000) and may lay preconditions for engaging into communication and collaborative innovation regarding an accessible EU single market, the analysis of the aforementioned instruments became an important part of the research.

Mystery shopping

The research aimed to reveal a range of different experiences and not to purely focus on barriers encountered in the retail premises by people with a certain type of impairment. In addition, although shopping is a natural activity of everyday life (Baker, 2006), ICT shopping is not so common.

Therefore, it was decided to use methods which stimulate participants' experiences and enable them to negotiate these experiences as they unfold and not just narrating afterwards. With this in mind, prior to describing ICT shopping experiences via qualitative interviews, the informants were invited to participate in mystery shopping (Hudson et al., 2001, Miller, 1998).

In Lithuania, the majority of the participants were contacted through local DPOs who acted as gatekeepers. Potential participants were personally provided with information about the research either by the organisations or by me and the standard procedure of informing about social study was followed (Barnes, 1992, Barnes and Mercer, 1997, Stone and Priestley, 1996). In the United Kingdom, such practice did not work, because due to financial cuts and shortage in human resources at the time, they were unable to assist in recruiting research participants. Instead, the organisations shared short invitations on their website pages, emailing lists or Facebook profiles. British and Lithuanian participants were provided with identical information and, if needed and preferred, in different accessible formats. Research-related travel expenses were covered and a thank-you gift for taking part in the study (£10 in the United Kingdom and LT50 in Lithuania) was provided to each informant prior to engaging into the research activities.

Before starting mystery shopping, I highlighted that the focus of the inquiry is on barriers and potentials in the public environment, transport infrastructure and retail premises and not on individuals' 'performance'. People who agreed to participate decided on the meeting location, time, visited shops and the location for the interview. This provided them with more control over and power in the research process (Barnes, 1992). With all but three participants, we met either outside their home or in public places and travelled to their chosen shop together. Vakare (Lithuania, age 41–64), Povile (Lithuania, age 41–64) and Chris (United Kingdom, age 18–40) expressed the preference to visit shops individually and to meet straight after that for the interview.

The duration of the trip to the shop and of the mystery shopping varied. While some participants reached the shop in 5 or 7 minutes, others spent from 10 to 45 minutes travelling. Similarly, while some informants spent 5–10 minutes in the shop and looked around without communicating with shop assistants, others spent more than an hour and interacted with salespeople. Around half of the informants expressed the will to visit grocery or cloth shops, instead of ICT retailers. The majority of the participants possessed some products. Four customers bought different ICTs and others bought food, clothes, presents or home appliances. It is important to highlight that all informants who have bought the items perceived me as a source of assistance. As an example, Ramune (Lithuania, age 18–40) asked me to describe a coat colour; Katrina (Lithuania, age 18–40) asked me to reach some products in the pharmacy; Rolandas (Lithuania, age 41–64) – to accompany him to a bank and an ICT shop; Hilda (Lithuania, age 65+), Barbora (Lithuania, age 41–64) and

Daphne (United Kingdom, 18–40) asked me for some assistance in grocery shopping; and Rachel (United Kingdom, age 41–64), Alison (United Kingdom, age 18–40), Jack (United Kingdom, age 41–64) and Peter (United Kingdom, age 18–40) asked me to assist in other shopping process stages. None of the participants asked for assistance in making actual customer choices. On the contrary, my role was to assist in overcoming barriers such as climbing steps, finding products, reading information about products, and describing colours and shapes.

Mystery shopping also involved shop assistants, who neither knew about the research nor were interviewed. While one can question the ethics of such kind of observation (Herrera, 1999, Homan, 1980), it provided insight into salespeople's natural behaviour (Gray, 2009) and enabled collecting objective data (Petticrew et al., 2007) about their interaction with disabled customers. Being aware of the existing ethical challenges, professionals' confidentiality is respected. Neither their names, shop locations nor any other information that could break the principle of confidentiality and have a harmful impact are identified. Although some of their phrases said during the mystery shopping are used, the same principle and practice of ensuring confidentiality and anonymity have been used when presenting the accounts.

Discussing shopping experience – interviews with customers

Semi-structured interviews followed the mystery shopping. Since Habermas' theory of CA and the social model of disability are related with interactional, contextual or situational factors, the interviews were conducted in the context of the private market realm. Methodologically such an approach enables detecting and linking social experiences and processes that affect the researched phenomenon (Mason, 2002). With an exception of Lisa (United Kingdom, age 18–40), who was interviewed in the day care centre; Herbertas (Lithuania, age 65+), who was interviewed at his home; and Chris (United Kingdom, age 18–40) and Lukas (Lithuania, age 18–40), who were interviewed via Skype, the interviews were conducted in coffeehouses and pizzerias. Discussing shopping experiences in another area of the private market enabled expanding on customer experience–related issues that may have been neglected if the interviews were conducted in participants' home or meeting rooms. Second, while conducting interviews in a non-business place would have saved my funds, it may have prevented the participants from comparing this type of private service delivery with retail customer experience and to reflect while experiencing.

A great care was taken to use accessible research tools and communication means. For example, interviewing techniques such as simple words and pictures, short sentences, asking one question at a time and rephrasing questions were used and enabled achieving accuracy (Finlay and Lyons, 2001). Self-directed reflections by the interviewee (Rodgers, 1999) were also encouraged. As a result, some participants with cognitive impairments changed the path and the format of the interview. For instance, Andrius (Lithuania, age 18–49) talked about customer experiences while showing some pictures on the mobile phone. Ignas (Lithuania, age 18–40) shared shopping experiences linking these to his personal experience of selling cigarettes. The greatest example of the benefits brought by self-directed reflections was demonstrated in the interview with Sarunas (Lithuania, age 41–64). During the mystery shopping, he collected leaflets from the majority of shops in the visited shopping mall. While he collected the materials aiming to prove to his family members that he visited a shop without them, during the interview, the leaflets served as a stimulation to tell shopping-related and product usage–related stories.

Semi-structured interviews captured participants' opinions about customer experience not only in the visited ICT shop but also revealed general shopping-related experiences and insights. Narrating the experiences right after the visit to the shop allowed identifying meanings that people ascribe to the shopping process and outcomes (Gray, 2009). Opportunity to articulate and reflect on recent events enabled the gathering of more detailed responses, clarifications, perceptions, feelings (Arksey and Knight, 1999), knowledge and attitudes (Cohen and Manion, 2000) that occur in the private market.

Having detected disabled customers' experiences at the empirical level (Bhaskar, 1975) and having provided an adequate description of these experiences (Blaikie, 2010), the research shifted towards the identification of market practices and events that not necessarily can be observed but play a part in shaping accessibility of the EU single market. With this in mind, the following discussion addresses methods and data generation strategies employed to gather accounts of the EU ICT industry and civil society.

Studying business and civil society's perspectives

This stage of the research aimed to explore social, political and market structures that shape the stakeholders' lifeworld and the patterns of their involvement in communication and collaborative innovation regarding markets accessibility. Light was shed on the lifeworld, access to the discourse and power relations. The enquiry included semi-structured interviews with ICT manufacturers, international representatives of ICT industry and civil society, national DPOs as well as ICT product shops in Lithuania and the United Kingdom. The content of the questionnaires for each group was founded on the analysis of global, regional and national instruments and insights from the literature discussed in the first chapter and were framed within the three key dimensions of Habermas' theory of CA. Despite the ideological unity, questionnaires for each group were constructed to fit the informants' professional experiences and contexts within which they operate. Hence, as advocated by Niemann (2004), the interviews employed a similar protocol of asking questions concerning stakeholders' lifeworld, access to the discourse and power relations, but the provided questions were not identical and paralleled one another. Such approach revealed disparities and similarities among the informants (Pahl, 1995) and increased validity of the analysed phenomenon (Huffcutt and Arthur, 1994). The wording and the contexts were adjusted to specific stakeholders. The employment of conceptually and technically similar questionnaires, which are sensitive in the used language, contexts, translational differences and ethics (Bryman, 2012, Mason, 2002, Turner, 2010), enabled indirectly bringing all actors into one room. It provided them with a possibility to express positions toward issues concerning disabled customers and market accessibility in the most familiar language.

Similar to disabled customers, in aiming to gauge stakeholders' perspectives, positions and experiences, semi-structured interviews were adopted. Being relatively informal and interactional exchange of dialogue (Mason, 2002), this type of interviewing allowed addressing a range of themes, issues and perspectives without rigidness and a sense of being official (Blaikie, 2010, Mason, 2002). It enabled gauging informants' meanings and interpretations of disabled customers and accessibility (Blaikie, 2010), experiences of operating under various legal requirements and communicating with actors involved in the process.

Regional ICT industry experiences and perspectives are represented by a company producing ICT products and having a strong focus on accessibility and an organisation representing EU ICT industry at an international level. An organisation representing disabled people from across Europe represented regional position of the disability movement.

While it was relatively easy to identify and recruit international actors, this was not the case with national informants. Several approached national DPOs in both countries noted that retail market accessibility is not a part of their agenda and activities. Consequently, accounts shared in this book are by informants, who work at DPOs working on different aspects of accessibility that are indirectly linked to customer participation. Similarly, none of the approached Lithuanian and British ICT industry representatives agreed to be a part of the project. The refusal was based either on political or on internal policy-related reasons.

Responding to the accounts shared by customers, I decided to involve two types of retailers: brand-specific ICT shops that sell products produced by one manufacturer and shops that sell ICTs produced by different companies. While this goal has been achieved in Lithuania, none of the approached British shop assistants or managers agreed to be a part of the project. Some British professionals agreed to share their accounts 'off the record', and the majority noted that they do not specialise in accessible technologies and consequently refused to be interviewed.

Interviews and 'off record' conversations were complemented by observations of international industry and civil society actors and policymakers. During my PhD studies, I worked as an intern for the international representatives of the ICT industry and civil society. This provided with the opportunity to gain background knowledge that allowed a better understanding of shared accounts and dynamics at the regional level.

Analysing the data

Data analysis was thematic. With regard to disabled customers, it was related to their experiences throughout the shopping chain. In terms of industry accounts, the analysis related primarily to the three dimensions of Habermas' theory of CA. In both cases, the data analysis process involved 'careful reading and re-reading' (Rice and Ezzy, 1999:258) of research material aiming to identify the main themes. Alongside the pattern identification within the data (Fereday and Muir-Cochrane, 2008), individual or unique cases were noted down. The interviews were repeatedly read, aiming to find commonalities or contradictions among these unique cases. Although the analysis started by looking either at shopping stages or CA dimensions, the analysis process overstepped the initial themes and have developed additional themes, that were coded prior the interpretation (Boyatzis, 1998). For instance, one of the anticipated themes was accessibility of home environment and its relation to customer experience. The analysis of industry players' accounts revealed additional factors shaping their knowledge about and lifeworld regarding disabled customers and accessibility. Differences in experiencing accessibility were also identified, showing that while some artefacts and relations within the private market can be experienced as barriers by informants with certain impairments, for individuals with other types of impairment, the same objects may be accessible.

Structure of this book

The following chapters are structured in a way so as to answer the outlined research questions and to reveal perspectives, interactions and experiences of disabled customers, European industry and civil society that should be considered in aiming to create a more accessible mainstream private market.

This book starts by framing disabled customers' experience in the European single market and their perspectives towards accessibility. The first chapter provides an overview of people with impairments customer experiences and suggests that state and the market restrict and suspend disabled individuals' agency, independency and freedom. They are excluded from equal participation in retail market and are perceived as 'vulnerable' consumers. This chapter then adapts the concept 'travel chain' from Scandinavian disability and transport studies and introduces the notion 'accessible shopping chain', consisting of four stages: customer information, journey to a shop, navigation in retail premises and interaction in a shop. It disconnects faced obstacles and customer vulnerability from individuals' impairments and suggests that state and market's actions and ontology premised on ableism and the focus on non-disabled citizens and customers are important factors in shaping disabled customers' exclusion and inequality. It then suggests that discrepancies in professionals who are involved in different stages of an accessible shopping chain, professional ontologies and insufficient knowledge about and awareness of accessibility and disability contribute to shaping barriers and customer exclusion. It then proposes that disabled people's involvement as co-designers in all shopping chain stages and positioning universal design (UD) as a founding conception behind the practice may lead retail market towards more accessibility and transform disabled people from 'vulnerable' into equal customers.

The second chapter sheds light on the framework provided in global, regional and national policy instruments for more accessible retail market to emerge. It suggests that public movements and public policy developments in the area of accessibility and rights via social claims brought the private market into the public sphere. Therefore, it demonstrates how law and public policy frames public discourse on private market as they relate to disabled customers and the EU and so provides a platform for the accessible shopping chain to emerge. It suggests that even though global instruments introduce the discourse on rights and accessibility and aims to reconstruct disabled people from 'vulnerable' consumers to equal customers, the practice is not consistent across global, regional and national levels. Indeed, some tensions are present in these policy discourses. The chapter first sheds light on the CRPD, concepts of accessibility and requirements for member states to provide a framework, within which private providers would take into account all aspects of accessibility. It then moves on to explore the way the EU responds to such obligations and notes that contrary to the Convention, at the regional level, disabled people are constructed as 'vulnerable' customers and certain measures for market accessibility are premised on the individual model. The chapter then looks at national perspectives in Lithuania and the United Kingdom and suggests that the perspectives are similar to the regional practice.

Responding to the discussion in the first two chapters, the third chapter argues that in aiming to facilitate disabled people's participation in the mainstream private market, cooperative action is needed. It draws on Habermas' theory of CA and suggests that it can provide a useful insight and understanding to inform the way market accessibility and customer rights should be ensured. It sheds light on three elements of the theory: lifeworld, access to the discourse and power relations. It builds on previous studies analysing the EU and the private market. It suggests that the EU may either provide a framework for more accessibility to emerge or may act as a system that prevents member states and business from creating common language and accessible customer experience. The chapter concludes with an overview of an open method of coordination (OMC). It suggests that located within a deliberative democracy framework, OMC may be employed as a tool, enabling stakeholders to access formation of the discourse in the public sphere and getting closer to meeting CRPD requirements.

18 *Introduction*

The fourth chapter begins the empirical journey of this book. It explores a micro level of disabled customers' experiences of and perspectives towards accessibility. These were gauged through mystery shopping and interviews with shoppers with different impairments in the United Kingdom and Lithuania. The analysis is framed within the concept of the 'accessible shopping chain', identified in the first chapter. The discussion suggests that despite differences in individual experiences, customers with impairments usually go through all stages but face different obstacles. A variety of attitudinal and physical barriers are outlined showing how they impede customer participation and shape their exclusion and vulnerability. The chapter expands the discussion started in the first chapter and provides empirical evidence, supporting the claim that disabled customers' exclusion, vulnerability and inequality are shaped by ableism that, respectively, informs the state and markets' focus on non-disabled citizens and customers. In addition, a number of resilience practices and coping strategies of customers with impairments are presented. This suggests that people with impairments are not passive victims of market inaccessibility and that their customer vulnerability and exclusion should be detached from their impairments and positioned as a result of oppressive practices of the state and the market.

The fifth chapter begins developing some explanations for underlying mechanisms and processes that are potentially causing disabled customers' experiences outlined in the previous chapter. Drawing on Habermas' theory of CA, in particular on the lifeworld, and on the data gathered through observations of and interviews with regional and national ICT industry and civil society, it starts the discussion by outlining stakeholders' understandings and perspectives of disabled people as ICT customers and their 'accessibility needs'. It suggests that despite some ontological differences and tensions, all stakeholders acknowledge the need for more accessibility in the EU private market. It suggests that notions, positions, values, norms and other elements constituting their lifeworld are often shaped by global, regional and national policies and business practices that either deconstruct or strengthen disabled customers exclusion and vulnerability. The chapter provides unique and under-researched insights into empirically unobservable structures, potentially shaping accessibility of the EU single market.

The sixth chapter suggests that even though sometimes stakeholders inhabit the same lifeworld and position accessibility as a common goal, their access to the formulation of the discourse in the public sphere differs. Unequal power relations and frequent elimination from shaping the discourse are some of the factors that prevent them from creating comprehensive knowledge about market accessibility. The chapter first suggests that since business and civil society acknowledge the need for a more accessible private market, the majority of the stakeholders engage into communication to achieve this common goal. The chapter demonstrates that before engaging into communication with each other, the actors usually shape a unified position within a setting. It then discusses how they engage into communication with each other, what the interactions and communication strategies are and how the process is related with the achievement of common or strategic goals. It also links communication with awareness raising of accessibility and other stakeholders' realities. The chapter suggests that while international stakeholders have better opportunities to engage into innovative cooperation, national actors and disabled customers usually access the formulation of the discourse and knowledge creation through participation in different organisations' activities. However, their involvement is insufficient and often suppressed by power relations in industry and policy mechanisms and structures.

The concluding chapter summarises the findings and provides key insights. It first recapitulates disabled customers' experiences in the mainstream private market and their perspectives towards accessibility. It highlights the role played by ableism and the state and market's focus on non-disabled citizens and customers. It then discusses the way stakeholders of the European single market for ICT products perceive disabled people as customers and what factors shape their knowledge and positions. It provides some insights into legal and market structures that through shaping stakeholders' lifeworld, potentially mould disabled customers' realities. The chapter concludes by shedding the light on the way private business and civil society engage into communication and collaborative innovation to create more accessible markets and more effective customer policies in the EU. The discussion demonstrates that despite potential inhabitation of the same lifeworld, due to unequal power relations and focus on the achievement of strategic goals, stakeholders do not exploit the full potential to innovate knowledge on accessibility and do not engage into CA in the Habermasian way. It suggests that regional and national policy bodies should employ various incentives, founded on CRPD and encouraging stakeholders to engage into trans-regional and trans-sectorial communicative practice on accessibility, positioning disabled people as equally important stakeholders. The chapter concludes by suggesting the way forward aiming to ensure equal opportunities for all EU customers and society members.

Overall, this book demonstrates that disabled people do experience exclusion and vulnerability as customers of mainstream goods and services. Usually, these experiences are moulded by external factors that are neither caused by nor depend on an individual. It also demonstrates that key stakeholders of the European single market acknowledge the need for more accessibility and position it as a common goal. However, their perspectives and actions are oriented towards the achievement of strategic goals, dominate in current practices and prevent the actors from engaging into CA, as suggested by Habermas. However, even if the ideal speech situation remains utopic, stakeholders, including disabled people, should continue their present communication and knowledge innovation practice, and the EU and national governments should provide a stronger framework for such interactions to occur.

Bibliography

Abberley, P. 1996. Work, utopia and impairment. *Disability and society: Emerging Issues and Insights*, 11, 61–79.

Airhart, D. L. 1987. Horticultural training for adolescent special education students. *Journal of Therapeutic Horticulture*, 2, 17–22.

Aldcroft, D. H. 1964. The entrepreneur and the British economy, 1870–1914. *The Economic History Review*, 17, 113–134.

Andreoli, T. 1996. Message to retail industry: Teens should be seen and heard. *Discount Store News*, 35, 30–32.

Arksey, H. & Knight, P. T. 1999. *Interviewing for social scientists: An introductory resource with examples*, London, Sage.

Auslander, G. K. & Gold, N. 1999. Disability terminology in the media: A comparison of newspaper reports in Canada and Israel. *Social Science & Medicine*, 48, 1395–1405.

Baker, S. M. 2006. Consumer normalcy: Understanding the value of shopping through narratives of consumers with visual impairments. *Journal of Retailing*, 82, 37–50.

Baker, S. M., Holland, J. & Kaufman-Scarborough, C. 2007. How consumers with disabilities perceive 'Welcome' in retail sercicescapes: A critical incident study. *Journal of Services Marketing*, 21, 160–173.

Barnes, C. 1992. Qualitative research: Valuable or irrelevant? *Disability, Handicap & Society*, 7, 115–124.

Barnes, C. & Mercer, G. 1997. Breaking the mould? An introduction to doing disability research. *Doing disability research*, 1, 1–4.

Barnes, C. & Mercer, G. 2003. *Disability*, Cambridge, Polity Press.

Barnes, C., Mercer, G. & Shakespeare, T. 1999. *Exploring disability. A sociological introduction*, Cambridge, Polity Press.

Barton, L. 1995. The politics of education for all. *Support for Learning*, 10, 156–160.

Barton, L. 1997. Inclusive education: Romantic, subversive or realistic? *International Journal of Inclusive Education*, 1, 231–242.

Barton, L. 2004. The politics of special education: A necessary or irrelevant approach? *In:* Ware, L. (ed.) *Ideology and the politics of (in) exclusion*, New York, Peter Lang Publishing.

Bauman, Z. 1988. *Freedom*, Milton Keynes, Open University Press.

Bauman, Z. 2007. *Consuming life*, Cambridge; Malde, Polity Press.

Bertelsmann Stiftung BTI. 2010. Lithuania country report. Gütersloh, Bertelsmann Stiftung.

Bettman, J. R., Johnson, E. J. & Payne, J. W. 1991. Consumer decision making. *In:* Robertson, T. S., & Kassarjian, H. H. (eds.) *Handbook of Consumer Behavior*, Englewood Cliffs, NJ, Prentice-Hall.

Bhaskar, R. 1975. *A realist theory of science*, London, Verso.

Bickenback, J. 1993. *Physical disability and social policy*, Toronto, University of Toronto Press.

Blaikie, N. 1993. *Approaches to social enquiry*, Cambridge, Polity Press.

Blaikie, N. 2010. *Designing social research. The logic of anticipation. 2nd edition*, Cambridge, Polity Press.

Blaska, J. 1993. The power of language: Speak and write using 'person first'. *Perspectives on Disability*, 25–32.

Bouloff, J. 1991. *From the old marketplace. A memoir of laughter, survival and coming of age in Eastern Europe*, USA, Harvard University Press.

Boyatzis, R. E. 1998. *Transforming qualitative information: Thematic analysis and code development*, Thousand Oaks, Sage.

Branfield, F. 1998. What are you doing here? 'Non-disabled' people and the disability movement: A response to Robert F. Drake. *Disability & Society*, 13, 143–144.

Bringing Neighbours Closer. 2012. *Neigaliųjų įdarbinimo galimybių plėtra*, Klaipėda. Available: www.nsis.lt/userfiles/Neigaliuju%20idarbinimo%20galimybiu%20 pletra%20%28lietuvių%20k_%29.pdf [Accessed 21/04/2013].

Brisenden, S. 1986. Independent living and the medical model of disability. *Disability, Handicap & Society*, 1, 173–178.

Bryman, A. 2012. *Social research methods*, Oxford, Oxford University Press.

Burckley, E., Tincani, M. & Guld fisher, A. 2015. An iPad™-based picture and video activity schedule increases community shopping skills of a young adult with autism spectrum disorder and intellectual disability. *Developmental Neurorehabilitation*, 18, 131–136.

Burnett, J. J. & Baker, H. B. 2001. Assessing the travel-related behaviors of the mobility-disabled consumer. *Journal of Travel Research*, 40, 4–11.

Burnett, J. J. & Paul, P. 1996. Assessing the media habits and needs of the mobility-disabled consumer. *Journal of Advertising*, 25, 47–59.

Byron, M., Cockshott, Z., Brownett, H. & Ramkalawan, T. 2005. What does 'disability' mean for medical students? An exploration of the words medical students associate with the term 'disability'. *Medical Education*, 39, 176–183.

Campbell, J. & Oliver, M. 1996. *Disability politics. Understanding our past, changing our future*, London, Routledge.

Cheng, K. 2002. *What marketers should know about people with disabilities*, Diversity Inc.

Clapham, D. & Smith, S. J. 1990. Housing policy and 'Special Needs'. *Policy & Politics*, 18, 193–206.

Cohen, L. & Manion, L. 2000. *Research methods in education. 5th edition*, London, Routledge.

Collins, M. 1988. *Money and banking in the UK. A history. Vol. 6*, Oxon, Routledge.

Cook, T., Swain, J. & French, S. 2001. Voices from segregated schooling: Towards an inclusive education system. *Disability & Society*, 16, 293–310.

Crafts, N. 2002. *Britain's relative economic performance, 1870–1999*, London, The Institute of Economic Affairs.

Crow, L. 1996. Including all of our lives: Renewing the social model of disability. *Exploring the divide*, 55, 206–226.

Denzin, N. K. 1970. *The research act: A theoretical introduction to sociological methods*, Chicago, Aldine.

Department for Work and Pensions. 2014. *Family resources survey 2012–2013, annual report*. Department for Work and Pensions.

Dholakia, R. R., Pedersen, B. & Hikmet, N. 1995. Married males and shopping: Are they sleeping partners. *International Journal of Retail & Distribution Management*, 23, 27–33.

European Union. 1992. *Treaty of Maastricht on European Union*, Brussels, European Parliament.

Faulkner, A. & Thomas, P. 2002. User-led research and evidence-based medicine. *The British Journal of Psychiatry*, 180, 1–3.

Fereday, J. & Muir-cochrane, E. 2008. Demonstrating rigor using thematic analysis: A hybrid approach of inductive and deductive coding and theme development. *International Journal of Qualitative Methods*, 5, 80–92.

Finkelstein, V. 1991. Disability: And administrative challenge? (The health and welfare heritage). *In:* Oliver, M. (ed.) *Social work – disabling people and disabling environments*, London, Jessica Kingsley Publishers.

Finlay, W. M. L. & Lyons, E. 2001. Methodological issues in interviewing and using self-report questionnaires with people with mental retardation. *Psychological Assessment*, 13, 319–335.

Foreman, P. 2005. Language and disability. *Journal of Intellectual and Developmental Disability*, 30, 57–59.

Foster, R. L. 1997. Addressing epistemologic and practical issues in multimethod research: A procedure for conceptual triangulation. *Advances in Nursing Science*, 20, 1–12.

French, S. 1993. Disability, impairment or something in between? *In:* Swain, J., Finkelstein, V., French, S. & Oliver, M. (eds.) *Disabling barriers—Enabling environments*, England, Open University Press.

Gabriel, Y. & Lang, T. 1995. *The unmanagable consumer. Contemporary consumption and its fragmentation*, London, Sage Publications.

Gillinson, S., Green, H. & Miller, P. 2005. *Independent living: The right to be equal citizen*, London, Demos.

Gleeson, B. 1999. *Geographies of Disability*, London, Routledge.

Graham, D. F., Graham, I. & Maclean, M. J. 1991. Going to the mall: A leisure activity of urban elderly people. *Canadian Journal on Aging/La Revue canadienne du vieillissement*, 10, 345–358.

Gray, D. E. 2009. *Doing research in the real world*, London, Sage.

Habermas, J. 1970. Knowledge and interest. *In:* Emmet, D. & Macintyre, A. (eds.) *Sociological theory and philosophical analysis*, London, Macmillan.

Habermas, J. 1976. *Communication and the evolution of society*, Boston, Beacon Press.

Habermas, J. 1994. *The past as future*, Cambridge, Polity.

Habermas, J. 1999. The European nation-state and the pressures of globalization. *New Left Review*, 235, 46–59.

Habermas, J. 2001. *The postnational constellation: Political essays*, Cambridge, MIT Press.

Häubl, G. & Trifts, V. 2000. Consumer decision making in online shopping environments: The effects of interactive decision aids. *Marketing Science*, 19, 4–21.

Henn, M., Weinstein, M. & Foard, N. 2006. *A short introduction to social research*, London, Sage Publications.

Herrera, C. D. 1999. Two arguments for 'covert methods' in social research. *The British Journal of Sociology*, 50, 331–343.

Hohnen, P. 2003. *A market out of place? Remaking economic, social, and symbolic boundaries in post-communist Lithuania*, Oxford, Oxford University Press.

Homan, R. 1980. The ethics of covert methods. *The British Journal of Sociology*, 31, 46–59.

Hudson, S., Snaith, T., Miller, G. A. & Hudson, P. 2001. Distribution channels in the travel industry: Using mystery shoppers to understand the influence of travel agency recommendations. *Journal of Travel Research*, 40, 148–154.

Huffcutt, A. I. & Arthur, W. 1994. Hunter and Hunter (1984) revisited: Interview validity for entry-level jobs. *Journal of Applied psychology*, 79, 184–190.

Imrie, R. 2004. The role of the building regulations in achieving housing quality. *Environment and Planning B*, 31, 419–438.
Kaufman-Scarborough, C. 1998. Retailers' perceptions of the Americans with disabilities act: Suggestions for low-cost, high-impact accommodations for disabled shoppers. *The Journal of Consumer Marketing*, 15, 94–110.
Kaufman-Scarborough, C. 1999. Reasonable access for mobility-disabled persons is more than widening the door. *Journal of Retailing*, 75, 479–508.
Kaufman-Scarborough, C. 2001. Sharing the experience of mobility-disabled consumers: Building understanding through the use of ethnographic research methods. *Journal of Contemporary Ethnography*, 30, 430–464.
Kaufman-Scarborough, C. & Menzel baker, S. 2005. Do people with disabilities believe the ADA has served their consumer interests? *Journal of Consumer Affairs*, 39, 1–26.
Kimchi, J., Polivka, B. & Stevenson, J. S. 1991. Triangulation: Operational definitions. *Nursing Research*, 40, 364–366.
Kitchin, R. 2000. The researched opinions on research: Disabled people and disability research. *Disability & Society*, 15, 25–47.
La forge, J. 1991. Preferred language practice in professional rehabilitation journals. *Journal of Rehabilitation*, 57, 49–51.
Lewis, J. 1998. Is the 'Hard Bargaining' image of the council misleading? The committee of permanent representatives and the local elections directive. *Journal of Common Market Studies*, 36, 479–504.
Lietuvos Statistikos Departamentas. 2014. Teritorija ir gyventojų skaičius. Požymiai: administracinė teritorija, statistiniai rodikliai ir metai. Available: http://db1.stat.gov.lt/statbank/selectvarval/saveselections.asp?MainTable=M3010211&PLanguage=0&TableStyle=&Buttons=&PXSId=3767&IQY=&TC=&ST=ST&rvar0=&rvar1=&rvar2=&rvar3=&rvar4=&rvar5=&rvar6=&rvar7=&rvar8=&rvar9=&rvar10=&rvar11=&rvar12=&rvar13=&rvar14= [Accessed 01/07/2015].
Limayem, M., Khalifa, M. & Frini, A. 2000. What makes consumers buy from Internet? A longitudinal study of online shopping. *IEEE Transactions on systems, man, and cybernetics - Part A: systems and humans*, 30, 421–432.
MacDonald, N. M., Majumder, R. K. & Bua-iam, P. 1994. Apparel acquisition for consumers with disabilities: Purchasing practices and barriers to shopping. *Clothing and Textiles Research Journal*, 12, 38–45.
Mallett, R. & Slater, J. 2014. Language. *In:* Cameron, C. (ed.) *Disability studies: Student's guide*, London, Sage.
Mason, J. 2002. *Qualitative researching. 2nd edition*, London, Sage Publications.
Miller, N. J., Kim, S. & Schofield-tomschin, S. 1998. The effects of activity and aging on rural community living and consuming. *Journal of Consumer Affairs*, 32, 343–368.
Miller, R. 1998. Undercover shoppers. *Marketing*, 28, 1–4.
Mollan, S. & Michie, R. 2012. The city of London as an international commercial and financial center since 1900. *Enterprise and Society*, 13, 538–587.
Morris, J. 1993. *Independent lives: Community care and disabled people*, Basingstoke, Palgrave Macmillan.
Niemann, A. 2004. Between communicative action and strategic action: The article 113 committee 1 and the negotiations on the WTO Basic Telecommunications Services Agreement. *Journal of European Public Policy*, 11, 379–407.
Office for National Statistics. 2014. *Population and migration*, London, ONS.
Oliver, M. 1983. *Social work with disabled people*, London, Macmillan, for the British Association of Social Workers.

Oliver, M. 1990. *The politics of disablement*, New York, Palgrave Macmillan.
Oliver, M. 1992. Changing the social relations of research production? *Disability, Handicap & Society*, 7, 101–114.
Oliver, M. 1996. Defining impairment and disability: Issues at stake. *In:* Barnes, C. & Mercer, G. (eds.) *Exploring the divide*, Leeds, The Disability Press.
Oliver, M. & Barnes, C. 1998. *Disabled people and social policy: From exclusion to inclusion*, London, Longman.
Oliver, M. & Barnes, C. 2010. Disability studies, disabled people and the struggle for inclusion. *British Journal of Sociology of Education*, 31, 547–560.
Pahl, J. 1995. His money, her money: Recent research on financial organisation in marriage. *Journal of Economic Psychology*, 16, 361–376.
Partington, D. 2000. Building grounded theories of management action. *British Journal of Management*, 11, 91–102.
Patton, M. Q. 1990. *Qualitative evaluation and research methods. 2nd edition*, London, Sage Publications.
Penn, D. L. & Nowlin-Drummond, A. 2001. Politically correct labels and schizophrenia. *Schizophrenia Bulletin*, 27, 197–203.
Petticrew, M., Semple, S., Hilton, S., Creely, K., Eadie, D., Ritchie, D., Ferrell, C., Christopher, Y. & Hurley, F. 2007. Covert observation in practice: Lessons from the evaluation of the prohibition of smoking in public places in Scotland. *BMC Public Health*, 7, 204–212.
Pierce, J. T. 1998. Linguistic factors as they relate to attitudes towards persons with disabilities. *Journal of Applied Rehabilitation Counseling*, 29, 31–36.
Proctor, S. 1998. Linking philosophy and method in the research process: The case for realism. *Nurse Researcher*, 5, 73–90.
Ray, N. M. & Ryder, M. E. 2003. 'Ebilities' tourism: An exploratory discussion of the travel needs and motivations of the mobility disabled. *Tourism Management*, 24, 57–72.
Rice, P. L. & Ezzy, D. 1999. *Qualitative research methods: A health focus*, Oxford, Oxford University Press Melbourne.
Risse, T. 2000. 'Let's argue!': Communicative action in world politics. *International organization*, 54, 1–39.
Rota, M. & Schettino, F. 2011. The long-run determinants of British capital exports, 1870–1913. *Financial History Review*, 18, 47–69.
Shakespeare, T. 1996. Rules of engagement: Doing disability research. *Disability & Society*, 11, 115–121.
Shakespeare, T. 2000. *Help*, Birmingham, Birmingham Venture Press.
Stewart, J., Harris, J. & Sapey, B. O. B. 1999. Disability and dependency: Origins and futures of 'special needs' housing for disabled people. *Disability & Society*, 14, 5–20.
Stone, D. A. 1984. *The disabled state*, Philadelphia, Temple University Press.
Stone, E. & Priestley, M. 1996. Parasites, pawns and partners: Disability research and the role of non-disabled researchers. *The British Journal of Sociology*, 47, 699–716.
Terzi, L. 2004. The social model of disability: A philosophical critique. *Journal of Applied Philosophy*, 21, 141–157.
Thornton, P. & Lunt, N. 2006. *Employment policies for disabled people in eighteen countries: A review*, New York, Cornell University ILR School.

Thurmond, V. A. 2001. The point of triangulation. *Journal of Nursing Scholarship*, 33, 253–258.

Titchkosky, T. 2001. Disability: A rose by any other name? 'People-first' language in Canadian society. *Canadian Review of Sociology/Revue canadienne de sociologie*, 38, 125–140.

Tsoukas, H. 1989. The validity of idiographic research explanations. *The Academy of Management Review*, 14, 551–561.

Turner, D. W. 2010. Qualitative interview design: A practical guide for novice investigators. *The Qualitative Report*, 15, 754–760.

United Nations. 2006. *Convention on the rights of persons with disabilities*, New York, United Nations.

UPIAS. 1976. *Fundamental principles of disability*, London, The Union of the Physically Impaired Against Segregation.

Vebra, R. 1994. Political rebirth in Lithuania, 1990–1991: Events and problems. *Journal of Baltic Studies*, 25, 183–188.

Verovšek, P. J. 2012. Meeting principles and lifeworlds halfway: Jürgen Habermas on the future of Europe. *Political Studies*, 60, 363–380.

Walker, E. S. 1993. Interpersonal caring in the 'good' segregated schooling of African-American children: Evidence from the case of caswell county training school. *The Urban Review*, 25, 63–77.

Wilton, R., Fudge Schormans, A. & Marquis, N. 2018. Shopping, social inclusion and the urban geographies of people with intellectual disability. *Social & Cultural Geography*, 19, 230–252.

Wolfinbarger, M. & Gilly, M. C. 2001. Shopping online for freedom, control, and fun. *California Management Review*, 43, 34–55.

Zola, I. K. 1972. Medicine as an instrument of social control. *Sociological Review*, 20, 487–504.

Zola, I. K. 1975. In the name of health and illness: On some socio-political consequences of medical influence. *Social Science and Medicine*, 9, 83–87.

Zola, I. K. 1977. Healthism and disabling medicalization. *In:* Illich, I., Zolla, I. K., Mcknight, J., Caplan, J. & Shaiken, H. (eds.) *Disabling professions*, New York, Marion Boyars.

Zola, I. K. 1993. Self, identity and the naming question: Reflections on the language of disability. *Social Science & Medicine*, 36, 167–173.

1 Disabled people in the market

Disabled people's exclusion and marginalisation in society is well documented. Alongside restricted participation in mainstream education (Barton, 1995, 1997, 2004, Buchner et al., 2014, Connor and Bejoian, 2014, Cook et al., 2001, Polat, 2011), limited access to health care (Iezzoni, 2011, Osborn et al., 2012, Ubido et al., 2002), family life (Anderson and Kitchin, 2000, Goodley and Tregaskis, 2006) and leisure (Devine and Dattilo, 2000, Tregaskis, 2003), people with impairments are not free and independent agents when choosing their position and activities in the market either as employers (Barnes, 1999, Barnes and Mercer, 2005, Ravaud et al., 1992) or as consumers (Baker, 2006, Baker et al., 2007, Chan and Puech, 2014, Department of Trade and Industry, 2000, Kaufman-Scarborough, 2001, Nemeth and Del Rogers, 1981). Historic marginalisation of older and disabled customers was partly premised on their limited spending power and market autonomy. Poor recognition as equal market participants manifests in the creation of special markets (Office for Disability Issues, 2010), their legal position as 'vulnerable' customers (Mansfield and Pinto, 2008) and is evidenced through an inaccessible shopping. In addition, tensions in professionals' ontologies regarding accessibility (Pirie, 1979), insufficient user involvement in developing accessible environments and products (Heylighen, 2008, Imrie and Hall, 2001, Till, 2005) as well as business' focus on non-disabled customers further the exclusion.

After ratification of the United Nations (UN) Convention on the Rights of Persons with Disabilities (CRPD) (2006), it has been argued that in order to achieve independent life and full participation in society, disabled people have to have equal access to the private market and exercise equal consumer rights as non-disabled individuals. Even though the overall situation is improving, equality of practice is still more rhetorical than actual. Aiming to understand the nature and the roots of the phenomenon, the present chapter sheds light on three key dimensions: disabled people's position in markets as consumers; shopping as an accessible shopping chain; and concepts of accessibility, reasonable accommodation and universal design (UD) in the context of consumer participation.

The discussion starts by addressing some changes in disabled people's position in markets, related with consumption and consumer participation. Provided insights aim to grasp the rationale behind the current construction of people with impairments as 'vulnerable' consumers. It then proceeds to discuss shopping process as an accessible chain. It first sheds light on customer information, discusses the journey to the shop and then turns to navigation and interaction in retail premises. It suggests that society and industry's orientation towards non-disabled citizens and customers is founded on ableism and is an important factor in shaping disabled consumers' exclusion. This is followed by a discussion on how more accessibility could be introduced to retail markets. The chapter explores the notion of accessibility, provides a critique of user-centred design (UCD), addresses ontological tensions in developers' professional realities and explores why principles of UD should be applied to retail markets.

Disabled people and markets: historical insights and current practice

This section provides an overview of disabled people's transition from passive consumers to active customers. It sheds light on the way people with impairments were perceived as 'useless eaters', passive users of social care services, valuable clientele of special markets for disability products and 'vulnerable' customers in the mainstream private market. Understanding the changes over time and in different market types provides a better understanding of underlying structures that have been preventing disabled people from equal customer participation. The discussion starts by looking at the world wars and the interwar period that positioned people with impairments as wasters of national resources and measured their value by the ratio between consumption and production. It then addresses socially constructed role of passive recipients of rehabilitation goods and services before providing an overview of how personal budgets created new markets and market relationships that previously were inaccessible for disabled people. It then proceeds to discuss how special markets for disability products challenge dominant understanding of people with impairments as market participants who lack autonomy and positions them as valued customers. The section ends by a discussion on practices in current markets for mainstream goods and services. It suggests that private providers perceive people with impairments as 'vulnerable' customers and premise their vulnerability on individuals' impairments.

Useless eaters

Disabled people's exclusion due to their 'deviance' from established norms, standards and expectations in different history stages and social institutions

28 *Disabled people in the market*

and developments is well documented (Barnes, 1991, Priestley, 1997, Robert, 1995) dating back its origins in ancient Greece and Rome (Oliver and Sapey, 2006, Stiker, 2009, Vlahogiannis, 2003), and feudalism (Beier, 1974, Gillin, 1929, Priestley, 1997). Later, in industrialisation and liberal utilitarianism times, the philosophies and practices introduced by Social Darwinism and Eugenics movement continued positioning people with impairments as unworthy living or as a threat to a common welfare (Barnes, 1991, Gleeson, 1999). Economic instability brought by the world wars and political doctrines that emerged in the 20th century portrayed them as consumers of national resources, and the ratio between production and consumption was key measure for participation in society. As a result, disabled individuals were seen as not rendering back consumers of national resources, and this impacted governments' actions. Since it was assumed that 'the right to life did not exist intrinsically but rather must be continually earned and justified by a measure of personal productivity' (Parent and Shevell, 1998:80), people with physical and cognitive impairments were seen as a 'national burden', 'empty husks', 'ballast lives' or 'useless eaters' (Burleigh, 1994, Mostert, 2002, Parent and Shevell, 1998, Thomas et al., 2006). Burleigh (1994) notes that human value was directly linked to contribution to the country and calculated by the amount of consumed food, water, drugs, clothing, beddings and salaries for staff in asylums. As a result, expenditure cuts on institutionalised disabled people's needs were introduced in the second quarter of the 20th century – the most drastic saving measures being applied by the German government. Such policy agenda led to significant decrease in the number of institutions, beds and caring personnel (Proctor, 1988). As an example, Klee (1985) notes that since people with cognitive impairments occupied the lowest strata among those doomed as unworthy to live, the expenditures for meeting their needs dropped to 40–38 pfennig for one person per day, which often was insufficient for survival. Although the German Psychiatric Association questioned such measures (Burleigh, 1994), the position that spending for the disabled people from the national budget is irrational as they are unproductive (Hoche, 1920 in Burleigh, 1994) was deeply entrenched in national policies and dictated related decisions.

The association of human value with consumption and economic productivity and portrayal of disabled people as unproductive individuals (Proctor, 1988) led to the introduction of policies such as 'mercy death' or 'alleviation of suffering' (Mostert, 2002) that aimed to release the country from the 'burden' brought by people with impairments (Burleigh, 1994, Proctor, 1988). Likewise, sterilisation, castration, euthanasia, gas chambers and shooting (Burleigh, 1994, Mostert, 2002, Proctor, 1988) were common and justified as countries', especially Germany's, liberation from 'useless eaters' and their wasteful consumption. As a result, while the damnation of institutionalised disabled children and adults to cold or starvation with the hope for a natural death saved money that would had been spent on injections and gas (Thomas et al., 2006), sterilisation and euthanasia had the greatest effect on 'rescuing' the economy. For instance, sterilisation of 390,000 in 1936–1943

(Lifton, 2000) and the killing of 80,000 disabled individuals (Tamura, 2004) allowed Germany to save 10 million Reichsmark (RM) for medical insurance, expenditures for 22,800 nurses' salaries and money for maintenance of 786 medical care institutions (Proctor, 1988). Altogether, the euthanasia operation had saved the German economy an average of 245,955.50 RM per day and 88,543,980.00 RM per year (Proctor, 1988:184). While the apogee of disabled people's association with waste of resource and their killings aimed at de-burdening the economy was in Germany, some European countries (Thomas et al., 2006) and states of the United States also applied euthanasia as a means of preventing economic challenges (Silver, 2004). For Straight (1935 in Proctor, 1988), the logic of such policies is simply the combination of pure nation ideology and the ratio between consumption and production: 'they could no longer manufacture guns in return for the food they consumed; because their death was the ultimate logic of the national socialist doctrine of promoting racial superiority and the survival of the physically fit'. While individuals who acquired impairments during the wars were treated as more valuable, a number of rehabilitation programmes were introduced aiming to return disabled war veterans into the labour market (Greasley and Oxley, 1996, Jongbloed and Crichton, 1990, Linker, 2011). The programmes aimed to get individuals off the compensation system (Jongbloed and Crichton, 1990), but since they were founded on the individual model, they positioned veterans with impairments as passive service users instead of active actors in physical and social rehabilitation process. The following section, therefore, discusses how such practice (service provision shaped around the individual model) eliminates disabled people's agency and independency, and converts them into a passive service user.

Passive service users

In the rehabilitation market, disabled people are usually perceived as passive users and have limited choice and control over acquired goods and services. According to Zola (1977:59), the 'expansion of what in medicine is deemed relevant to a good practice of life' is one of the factors in positioning people with impairments as passive receivers, who have limited possibilities to actively participate in the decision-making process about which goods and services they receive. The decision on what should be purchased usually depends on an individual and the professional. However, having historically and legally established control over technical procedures and medication prescriptions (Zola, 1977), professionals seem to dominate in the process. Due to the use of legitimate power, language and culture to label disabled people as 'special', 'needed to be fixed' or 'vulnerable' (Albrecht, 1992), professionals entrench individuals' low status and promote a dependency culture. This leads to de-powerment and exclusion from choosing needed and purchased goods and services (Eskytė, 2013, Finkelstein, 1999, 1999a). While Finkelstein (1999, 1999a) identifies professionals who practice such professional behaviour as professionals allied to medicine (PAMs), Broom and Woodward (1996:375) refer to them either as to overtly authoritarian professionals or to professionals who are 'inadvertently paternalistic in their efforts to avoid what they felt to be disabling medicalisation'. Either way, they control the amount of provided information about an individual's condition and the manner in which it is presented. The communication between this type of professionals and service users is insufficient, and this leads to uncertainty, lack of cooperation and misperceptions of service receivers' needs and experiences (Skipper and Leonard, 1965). In such a context, the potential for disabling conditions to be identified and cooperative relationships regarding the creation of more enabling practice to emerge is not exploited.

On the other end of the spectrum is interaction between service users and professionals allied to community (PACs; Finkelstein, 1999, 1999a), or the third group of health-care service providers, as described by Broom and Woodward (1996). This type of professionals acknowledge that medical knowledge and expertise may not provide comprehensive understanding. They prioritise collaborative relationships, recognise the impact of social environment and people's position within the society (Broom and Woodward, 1996) as well as involve individuals in the service planning and provision process. Such practice enables service providers to better understand users' needs and preferences (Brown and Eisenhardt, 1995), position them as experts of needed care (Tait and Lester, 2005) and reduce stigma that often accompanies impairments and especially mental health conditions (Rutter et al., 2004).

Evidence from Lithuania and the United Kingdom suggests that despite changing political and professional discourse in health care and the rehabilitation service market (Juškevičius and Rudzinskas, 2014, Shakespeare et al., 2009), the interaction between professionals and service users is often founded on unequal power relations and positions a person as a passive receiver. As an example, Butkevičienė et al. (2006) demonstrate that disabled children and their parents in Lithuania often do not receive sufficient or relevant information, and feel devalued and excluded from service planning and provision. Likewise, Petrauskienė and Zabėlienė (2014) note that despite Lithuanians with mental health conditions positively evaluate social workers' informal communication and provided services, they often lack information about services and do not feel like being a part of the process. Meanwhile, Crawford et al. (2002) and Mockford et al. (2012) suggest that even though disabled UK citizens have recently become more involved in planning and developing health-care services, the impact of involvement remains unknown. Several reports suggest that individuals often are seen as receivers and not as partners, with this trend being most common regarding people with cognitive impairments (Department of Health, 2001, Mencap, 2007).

Drawing on Habermas' (1984, 1985) and Ritzer's (2004) works, it can be argued that professionals' dominance in deciding rehabilitation goods and services on behalf of disabled people (Albrecht, 1992) is shaped by society's modernisation, dominant focus on a person's functional insufficiency (Golbe, 2004) and governments' failure to encourage professionals' motivation (Eskytė, 2012, Habermas, 1984). Modernisation replaces the implicit meaning patterns with explicit ones (Habermas, 1984), though does not provide more different forms of communication between disabled people and professionals (Finkelstein, 1999, 1999a). Legal standards for achieving professional and procedural effectiveness increase segregation of communicative patterns. Broom and Woodward (1996) argue that settled power, monetary gain and legal requirements entrap professionals and transform them from being a resource to support individuals in overcoming the disabling barriers into being 'modernised' care workers, who follow technical duties and rules rather than disabled people's life peculiarities and expertise (Eskytė, 2012, Finkelstein, 1981, 1999, 1999a). In addition, due to a full rationalisation of a system (Habermas, 1984), professionals become workers who automatically follow the requirements of the system that they operate in. In such a context, their personal and professional decisions and actions are maximally reduced (Ritzer, 2004) and dislodge people with impairments into touchline of choice and active decision-making.

From consumers to producers: example of direct payments

Demographic changes, failure of a welfare state to meet disadvantaged citizens' needs, growth of the public sector, rising consumerism and intensifying discourse of the social model of disability increased public awareness of the importance of social care services and shifted the state's monopolistic market to privatisation. However, emerged social care quasi-markets (Ajzenstadt and Rosenhek, 2000, LeGrand, 1991), competition among conditionally independent private agencies (Priestley et al., 2007) and higher independence in controlling budgets had no significant impact either on greater quality and efficiency of services (LeGrand, 1998) or on disabled people's choice and control over them (Common and Flynn, 1992). Indeed, the actual 'customers' for services and assistive technology were public service professionals, who purchased on behalf of disabled people and so eliminated them from customer choice and control (Glendinning et al., 2000, Hoyes and Harrison, 1993).

The introduction of direct payments or personal budgets as a part of social service system privatisation gradually reshaped the position of people with impairments in the market. Generally,

> personal budgets mean that people in need of services receive a certain amount of money which they can spend on services and support to meet their expressed needs. Usually those needs are assessed by health and social care professionals in consultation with the service user.
> (European Platform for Rehabilitation, 2013:3)

Despite some structural and systematic differences, cultural contexts and public policy frameworks, in countries such as Canada, Sweden, the Netherlands, the United Kingdom, France, and Austria, personal budgets provided disabled individuals with more opportunities for independent life (Carr and Robbins, 2009, Kodner, 2003, Priestley et al., 2007, Riddell et al., 2005, Stainton and Boyce, 2004). In addition, they created new markets and new market relations, both markets for the employment of personal assistants and markets for the sale of assistive technologies. With regard to newly emerged labour market and employment relationships, the received allowances enabled individuals to choose personal assistants who best meet their personal needs and preferences, to train, hire and fire them (Glendinning et al., 2000, Stainton and Boyce, 2004).

Being direct employers rather than objects for professionals' employment (Glendinning et al., 2000), people with impairments seem to exercise greater agency in selecting carers (Kodner, 2003) and have more control over provided services (Carr and Robbins, 2009, Dickinson and Glasby, 2010). Prior to the introduction of direct payments, it was public professionals who purchased assistive technologies on behalf of disabled people. In other words, disabled people were mediated as customers, with occupational therapists being proxy customers for them. Yet, the possibility to manage funds independently transformed disabled people from recipients into purchasers (Glendinning et al., 2000, Scourfield, 2005), who choose assistive technologies (Clark et al., 2010) or home modifications (Kodner, 2003). In addition, several studies suggest that personal budgets have a positive impact on individuals' shopping and customer participation, as people who independently manage funds are more likely to participate in community life and leisure activities, including visits to shops (Carmichael and Brown, 2002, Carmichael et al., 2001, Stainton and Boyce, 2004).

Despite challenges such as insufficient provision of the right support when managing personal budgets (Carmichael and Brown, 2002, Carr and Robbins, 2009), managerial and monitoring difficulties (Clark et al., 2004, Littlechild, 2009) and emergence of 'black markets' (Leichsenring, 2003), personal budgets transformed disabled people into more active market participants and deconstructed the existing power relations between professionals and service users (Carr and Robbins, 2009, Dickinson and Glasby, 2010). The possibility to choose and decide on services and assistive technologies provides an actual and not an illusionary choice and control, and deconstructs the prevailing position about people with impairments as passive and dependant actors.

Having established the link between a state and a customer, it is worth shedding light on how private providers perceive people with impairments as customers. The following discussion provides some insights into the way special markets for disability products position disabled people as a customer group.

A target for new business

Historic marginalisation of older and disabled people as customers was premised on their otherness from what was perceived as a 'normal' market participant, lack of spending power and limited market autonomy. An increasing number of disabled and ageing population in Europe (Coleman and Lebbon, 2010, European Commission, 2011), including Lithuania (Mažionienė et al., 2011) and the United Kingdom (Rutherford T., 2012), gradually increasing disabled people's employment (Grever, 2009) and growing spending power (Eurostat, 2009, Kingman, 2012, Office for Disability Issues, 2010, Ray and Ryder, 2003), has reframed the practice. Some businesses that are aware of older people's financial advantages and a link between ageing and disability (Age Concern and Help the Aged, 2010, Statistics, 2010) position disabled and older people as the target client group (Office for Disability Issues, 2010). Yet, while such practice is rare in the mainstream market, it is alive in 'special' markets for disability products.

Aiming to attract potential profit bringers, 'special' markets employ various marketing (Ludke and Levitz, 1983), management (MacStravic, 1989) and advertising (Adeoye and Bozic, 2007) strategies that contribute to changing the portrayal of a disabled customer. To begin with, while usually marketing and advertising of rehabilitation products shed light on medical features and ability to 'fix' individuals (Adeoye and Bozic, 2007, Bonaccorso, 2002, Ulinchy, 1994), more progressive players of the 'special' market shift this position towards product personalisation and social dimensions of usage. As an example, the Dynamic Controls, producing electronic control systems for power wheelchairs and scooters, aims to understand mobility device users' physical, emotional and social needs, and combines this knowledge with technical product features. Such an approach is premised on an intention to meet clients' physical needs and personal preferences (Dynamic™, n.d.). Customised Mobility offers an opportunity to personalise wheelchairs and to adjust them to individual lifestyles, or to create a unique design theme (Mobility, n.d.). In a similar vein, 'Sports'N Spokes', a magazine for wheelchair sports and recreation, challenges the dominant preconception of who can access the sporting arena (DePauw, 1997, French and Hainsworth, 2001) and provides information about products for doing different kinds of sport.

Fost (1998) indicates that more proactive mainstream retailers include 'special' items in their supply and mix them with products for non-disabled shoppers. Such practice increases shopping convenience, creates a mainstream atmosphere (Fost, 1998), increases disabled and non-disabled shoppers' loyalty (Cheng, 2002) and decreases stigma attached to the products that are usually associated with disability. This results in boost of customer volume (Office for Disability Issues, 2010) and gained profits (Heskett and Schlesinger, 1994, Kim et al., 2013).

34 *Disabled people in the market*

In addition, Kaufman-Scarborough (1999, 2001) notes that private entities that invest in physical accessibility of retail premises (even if the provisions are minimal) are prioritised by disabled customers and receive their grace.

On the one hand, the outlined practices suggest that some business players are becoming aware of the changing customer segment and position disabled people not as passive users, but as active choosers and profitable clients, and aim to meet their needs and preferences. On the other hand, the manifestation of such practices in 'special' markets and their insufficient adoption in mainstream providers' practices suggest segregation of people with impairments in certain market niches. In other words, the focus on people with impairments as active customers within markets for disability products and insufficient attention within the mainstream market may 'lock' disabled individuals in 'special' markets and prevent equal customer participation with non-disabled shoppers. This is likely to frame mainstream providers' understanding of a customer as a non-disabled individual and so to prevent the ontological shift from understanding of customers with impairments in light of social and not individual model of disability. The following discussion sheds light on disabled people's position in the mainstream market and the way current practices position them as 'vulnerable' customers.

Vulnerable consumers

Mainstream private market positions disabled people as vulnerable consumers. While a generic term of vulnerability is usually used to refer to minority groups or individuals, who face one or another form of ignorance, exclusion and are considered as objects for protection (Sime, 1991), one's vulnerability in the market is typically linked to either situational or enduring conditions (Brenkert, 1998, Gentry et al., 1995). With regard to situational causes, factors such as grief (Gentry et al., 1995), temporary unemployment (Macchiette and Roy, 1994), divorce (Jones and Middleton, 2007) or changes in social status (Braunsberger et al., 2004) are often positioned as factors behind this customer state. Mansfield and Pinto (2008:426) suggest that individuals, who are 'unable to navigate in the general marketplace; having diminished access to goods; being physically vulnerable; unable to adequately understand fraudulent claims or advertising messages', are at the opposite end of the spectrum and experience permanent customer vulnerability. In addition to these individual model-founded characteristics, race and ethnicity (Bristor et al., 1995), gender (Hill and Dhanda, 1999) and impairment type (Baker et al., 2001) are seen as factors contributing to the latter type of customer vulnerability.

While the following chapter demonstrates how policy instruments construct disabled people as 'vulnerable consumers', in everyday market practice, they are often seen as opposite to 'other normal adults' (Brenkert, 1998:302), with physical and cognitive features being the ground for this categorisation. Ableism plays an important role in shaping the practice. Goodley (2014:21) notes that

> ableism's psychological, social, economic, cultural character normatively privileges able-bodiedness; promotes smooth forms of personhood and smooth health; creates space fit for normative citizens; encourages an institutional bias towards autonomous, independent bodies; and lends support to economic and material dependence on neoliberal and hyper-capitalist forms of production.

Respectively, in the context of the private market, evaluation of disabled customers' vulnerability refers to what is deemed as normality standards and functions (Amundson and Taira, 2005) and is measured in the presumed competencies of an 'average' customer, who usually has no impairments (Edward et al., 2000). For example, according to Mansfield and Pinto, the main reason why people with cognitive impairments experience challenges using credit cards is 'their disability or low literacy skills' (Mansfield and Pinto, 2008:434). Similarly, Braunsberger et al. (2004) show that college students also experience similar challenges that often lead to financial loss. However, the latter authors do not ascribe customer vulnerability to young individuals. They note that one of the reasons for unwise choice and customer practice is limited knowledge that impacts the ability to evaluate complex and competing product offers. Mansfield and Pinto (2008:434) suggest an advocate working on behalf of individuals with cognitive impairments as a means to overcome credit card–related challenges. Whereas for college students, education and information provision are perceived as the master means for enabling them to act more securely in the marketplace (Braunsberger et al., 2004). Hence, although the experiences of the two groups are similar, their interpretation and applied measures differ. While students' customer vulnerability is seen as a result of commercial practice, analogous challenges experienced by people with cognitive impairments are perceived as a result of their impairments. It is not surprising that college students–oriented 'solution' means are premised on the concept of empowerment, and the means oriented towards people with cognitive impairments are shaped around protection and substitutive decision-making (Dunn et al., 2008, 2010).

Linking customer vulnerability to *who* experiences vulnerability (Baker et al., 2005) leads to perceived rather than actual vulnerability (Smith and Cooper-Martin, 1997) and suggests the individual model approach. Although gender, race, ethnicity and belonging to the category of disability are usually perceived as factors causing permanent customer vulnerability, Baker et al. (2005:130) note that 'there is no empirical proof that biophysical characteristics of individuals (age, ethnicity, disability) should be the sole basis on which to define customer vulnerability'. Similarly, Ringold (1995) suggests that belonging to a certain gender, ethnic or racial group does not determine vulnerability in the market, as representatives of these groups are equally competent customers. On the contrary, stigmatisation and categorisation of those who do not meet predefined market standards and a picture of an 'average' or 'ideal' consumer, contribute to customer vulnerability (Peñaloza, 1995) and create certain groups' exclusion (Baker et al., 2005).

Alongside structural and societal factors, 'physical and logistical elements' (Baker et al., 2005:131) play a role in causing customer vulnerability. As an example, disabled shoppers have to overcome barriers such as lack of information provided in alternative formats (Waddington, 2009), inaccessible parking and pathways (Kaufman-Scarborough, 1999) or inaccessible shop premises (Kaufman-Scarborough, 2001). As a result, the private market and especially shops, which are designed by non-disabled architects for non-disabled customers (Imrie, 1996, Weisman, 1994), discriminate and patronise people with impairments (Kaufman-Scarborough, 2001), create dependency practice (Baker et al., 2001), restrict customer choice (MacDonald et al., 1994) and eliminate them from active and equal customer experience and participation (Baker, 2007). In addition, factors such as inaccessible public transport (Department for Transport, 2013, Kung and Taylor, 2014, Soltani et al., 2012), lack of accessible information about public and private transport facilities (Baker et al., 2001) and inaccessible public environment (Hanson, 2004, Imrie, 1996, 1998, Kitchin, 1998, Marcos, 2011, Matthews and Vujakovic, 1995) eliminate disabled people from free and unrestricted customer choice and play a part in shaping their vulnerability and exclusion.

It seems that disabled people's portrayal as market participants acquires new forms and shades, and the map of their customer participation is expanding. Nevertheless, as mainstream market participants, they are seen as 'vulnerable' customers, and impairment and the dependency to the category of disability are the factors used for classification and measures applied to overcome barriers. The following section aims to challenge such perspective. It identifies key stages of an accessible shopping chain, and addresses key elements within each stage, that may cause customer vulnerability and exclude people with impairments from equal customer participation.

Shopping chain and disabled customers

Although the 'hot spot of shopping' is a shop, shopping itself is not a static practice that happens exclusively in retail premises. Instead, it is a fluid and continuous process, consisting of different stages, and is experienced by each customer in a unique way. With this in mind, this book adapts the 'travel chain' concept that originated in the Scandinavian disability and transport studies. The original concept aims to address every link of the travel chain from start to finish, focuses on the person–environment relationship and aims to assist the legislative process in order to provide disabled and older people with more accessible travel experiences and

Disabled people in the market 37

Figure 1.1 Accessible shopping chain.

rights that non-disabled individuals take for granted (Carlsson, 2004, Iwarsson et al., 2000, Stahl, 1996, 1999). With regard to disabled people's shopping, some attempts to look more broadly than only at individuals' experience in retail premises are present (Baker et al., 2007, Bromley et al., 2007a, Burnett, 1996, Kaufman-Scarborough, 1999, Schmöcker et al., 2008). However, the studies often focus either on specific elements and shopping stages, or on experiences of people with a particular type of impairment. Either way, they do not provide a wide-ranging picture. This chapter, therefore, expands the discussion and addresses how individuals with different impairments acquire customer information, travel to the shop, operate in retail premises and interact with informal shopping assistants and salespeople (see Figure 1.1).

It was decided to focus on the identified elements as they seem to play a key role in shaping customer experience. For instance, different marketing and advertising strategies on TV, radio, newspapers and public spaces (Adeoye and Bozic, 2007, Arens et al., 2009, Buclin, 1965, Jeffords, 2004, Steiner, 2001) are well recognised as important means to communicate with and inform a customer before reaching a shop. Likewise, a number of studies demonstrate the way the pubic environment and transport mould shopping patterns and customer experience (Bromley et al., 2007b, Butler and Bowlby, 1997, Carlsson, 2004, Eskytė, 2014, Imrie, 1996). Of the most significance is the shop, its exterior and interior design, product marketing strategies and interaction with shop assistants. However, identified environments, practices and market relationships seem to be premised on ableism that marginalise, exclude and prevent people with impairments from an accessible and equal shopping process. The following sections, therefore, look at how the focus of business and governments on non-disabled customers and citizens shapes disabled people's customer experiences in the identified shopping chain stages.

Customer information

Information is essential for making customer decisions (Bettman et al., 1991, Hoffmann and Inderst, 2009, Kivetz and Simonson, 2000, Nelson, 1970).

Its gathering starts before leaving home or entering a shop (Barthes, 1973, Gabriel and Lang, 1995). Browsing product catalogues and magazines (Vijayasarathy and Jones, 2000), online websites (Häubl and Trifts, 2000, Peterson and Merino, 2003) or forums (Bickart and Schindler, 2001) is a common experience in the pre-shopping stage. Later on, it continues in public spaces (Ben-Rafael et al., 2006, Rosewarne, 2005) and retail premises, where individuals need to acquire information not only for choosing a shop and finding how to enter it (d'Astous, 2000, Hackett et al., 1993, Otterbring et al., 2014, Passini, 1996) but also familiarising with and evaluating the product, its features, price and other attributes (Chang and Wildt, 1994, Peck and Childers, 2003). The importance of customer information is also recognised by policymakers and is discussed in more depth in the following chapter. However, even though the European Commission (EC) accepts the need to provide customers with information (Maastricht Treaty, 1992, art. 153.1), in actual shopping choices, people are rarely fully informed (Dick et al., 1990, Johnson and Levin, 1985, Simmons and Lynch Jr, 1991).

One of the most marginalised groups in terms of access to customer information is disabled people. Since this group of market participants is not recognised as an important segment in the marketplace (Freeman and Selmi, 2010), and while business players have control over provided information (Kivetz and Simonson, 2000), people with impairments experience additional barriers when accessing information that is taken for granted for non-disabled people. Lack of information provided in alternative formats such as Braille, large print, audio, sign language, text-based information, and easy-to-read texts and symbols (Waddington, 2009) excludes individuals from autonomous and informed decisions. As an example, Baker et al. (2001) note that while people with vision impairments are capable of making sovereign purchase decisions, due to a lack of accessible information, they need assistance in retrieving the information.

Limited access to customer information deprives disabled people from selecting goods and lessens the possibility to participate in the economy (Howells, 2005). Biehal and Chakravarti (1986) suggest that insufficient provision of information limits access to information in customer's memory. Consequently, this has a negative impact on their autonomy, judgements and decisions (Lingle and Ostrom, 1979, Walsh and Mitchell, 2010). This suggests that the way market perceives a customer and uses strategies to inform them limits the availability of accessible information and consequently impedes disabled customer's freedom and autonomy.

After a purchase, retail place or spontaneous consumption decision has been made, individuals step into a public space aiming to reach a shop. With respect to this, the following discussion sheds light on individuals' journey to the shop either as pedestrians or as transport users. This is followed by a brief discussion on potential factors behind particular disabled customers' experiences.

Navigation in retail premises

'Shopping mall as customer habitat' (Bloch et al., 1994), 'the world in the shopping mall' (Crawford, 1992), 'the magic of the mall' (Goss, 1993) and 'the mall as entertainment' (Baker and Haytko, 2000) are the phrases commonly used to describe an ideal customer experience provided by retail outlets. Since environment shapes human behaviour (Mehrabian and Russell, 1974), designers, decorators, managers, sales experts and other professionals adopt various design and branding strategies (Turley and Chebat, 2002), invest time, energy and effort to create the atmosphere which would provide customers with the emotions and affiliations associated with an ideal and positive shopping (Andersson et al., 2012). 'Right' environment of a shop enables market players to control individuals' emotional states (Babin and Attaway, 2000), encourage impulsive and unplanned purchases (Tendai and Crispen, 2009, Turley and Chebat, 2002), pursue hedonic consumption (Ryu and Jang, 2007) and so to increase profit (Babin and Attaway, 2000, Tendai and Crispen, 2009, Turley and Chebat, 2002).

Retailers perceive and exploit retail premises as 'environmental stimuli' (Mehrabian and Russell, 1974) and use various strategies to shape customer in-store behaviour and purchase decisions. To begin with, aiming to stimulate shoppers' senses of pleasure and arousal (Garlin and Owen, 2006, Turley and Milliman, 2000), retailers often choose positive and unobtrusive music (Andersson et al., 2012) fitting with the retail place image (Vida et al., 2007). This stimulates affirmative emotions and has a positive effect on longer shopping time and willingness to wait for the service or to queue. Different lighting effects are used to communicate product price, attract clients (Ryu and Jang, 2007) and build their loyalty (Walsh et al., 2011). As an example, while Summers and Hebert (2001) demonstrate that under the bright light, shoppers tend to examine, touch and pick up more items than under soft lighting, Mangum (1998) notes that lighting directly correlates with product attractiveness perceived by customers and impacts the turnover. Either way, retailers use lighting to attract customers, shape their purchase decisions and achieve own capitalistic goals.

Alongside music and lighting, customer seduction means such as scent (Guéguen and Petr, 2006, Teller and Dennis, 2011), in-store signage (Drèze et al., 1994, Otterbring et al., 2014), atmospheric colours and decor (Ballantine et al., 2010, Ryu and Jang, 2007) are used to sculpt shoppers' positive emotions and affiliations (Turley and Chebat, 2002). Nevertheless, shelves and product display receive special attention as they often play the most important role in attracting customers' attention (Castro et al., 2013, Chandon et al., 2009), which directly correlates with sales and profit (Desmet and Renaudin, 1998, Drèze et al., 1994, Yang and Chen, 1999). As a result, different product location strategies are adopted (Nelson and Ellison, 2005). For instance, since large shelf space significantly increases brand sales (Bemmaor and Mouchoux, 1991) and general sales frequency (Desmet and Renaudin, 1998), retailers tend to double the number of facings. This increases customers' choice of a particular item by 67% (Chandon et al., 2009). The reduction of shelf space has an opposite effect (Eisend, 2014) as this increases the possibility of running out of stock and portrays items as less attractive (Castro et al., 2013, Parker and Lehmann, 2011). The most popular articles and brands are located in the centre (Chandon et al., 2009, Valenzuela and Raghubir, 2009) and are surrounded with store brands, which are less popular but have a direct impact on shops' turnovers (Valenzuela et al., 2013). Edges of the layout are dedicated to promotional items (Valenzuela et al., 2013) and are often accompanied by large-size and intrusive signage. Aiming to boost habitual and frequent consumption, checkout line displays are filled with products such as cigarettes (Drèze et al., 1994), and more expensive or higher-quality products are placed on the top shelves and the cheapest on the bottom (Valenzuela et al., 2013). According to Drèze et al. (1994:312), retailers perceive the eye level of a standing individual as ideal for product location, and lower-middle and bottom shelves as a good place for children's products.

Dominant shop design and product location are oriented towards non-disabled customers' gratification and profit increase, and often have an opposite effect on disabled shoppers' experience. To begin with, Kaufman-Scarborough (1999) notes that before entering a shop, people with mobility impairments and wheelchair users in the United States often have to deal with an accessible but unsatisfactory parking lot surface and an unpleasant to manoeuvre route from a car to the shop. Bromley and Matthews (2007) echo the observation and highlight that although private retailers in the European Union (EU) are required to ensure accessibility of retail premises, apart from large and new shopping malls, access to the majority of shops is littered with obstacles such as steps, narrow doorways and lack of ramps. In addition, the leverage, dexterity and strength that is often needed to open and operate shop doors for customers with certain impairments is likely to cause feelings of fear (Kaufman-Scarborough, 2001). While such business practices and customer experience prevent some people with impairments from visiting specific shops (Kaufman-Scarborough, 1999), they also have a negative impact on individuals' participation in the community life (Bromley and Matthews, 2007).

Disabled customers' exclusion reaches the peak in retail premises. Here, provisions oriented to non-disabled individuals act as barriers for shoppers with impairments. While promotional displays and products waiting to be stocked impede people with mobility impairments and wheelchair users' barrier-free movement (Bromley and Matthews, 2007, Kaufman-Scarborough, 1999, 2001), narrow aisles, multiple-level stairs and balconies intended to create pleasure atmospheres for non-disabled shoppers spatially segregate people with impairments in certain parts of retail premises (Kaufman-Scarborough, 1999) and prevent them from exploring the whole shop.

In addition to manoeuvring and movement, product layout oriented to non-disabled shoppers restricts the choice and independency of customers with impairments. As an example, while because of a horizontal product shelving, wheelchair users are often unable to reach products, coin slots, change machines and ATMs are often inaccessible as they are located higher in order to provide maximum convenience for a 'traditional' shopper (Kaufman-Scarborough, 2001). Being founded on ableism, such practices cause worry and hazard feelings (Kaufman-Scarborough, 1999), prevent an independent reaching and handling of goods (Bromley and Matthews, 2007) and shape dependency practices. A focus on non-disabled customers and limited recognition of disabled shoppers can be further illustrated through fitting rooms. Specifically, limited number, remote location or use as a storage (Kaufman-Scarborough, 1999) as well as insufficient space, highly located clothes hooks and mirrors and challenges in calling shop assistants (Kaufman-Scarborough, 2001, MacDonald et al., 1994) are more a rule rather than an exception, and signalise that people with impairments are neither expected nor desired shoppers.

While the above experiences are more typical to customers with mobility impairments, lack of information about retail premises and products in alternative formats (Baker et al., 2001) has a negative impact on choice and overall shopping experience of customers with vision impairments. Although technological inventions such as body micro- and nano-sensors (Domingo, 2012) and similar devices (López-de-Ipiña et al., 2011) are present and could provide this customer group with more independency, because of the high price, retailers are resistant to make the investments. Trained shop assistants are another potential source of independence that is currently insufficiently available and present (Baker et al., 2001). Instead, individual coping strategies and informal shop assistants are often used as a means to overcome barriers, and this is discussed in more detail in forthcoming chapters.

A lack of communication-related reasonable accommodation means prevents people with hearing impairments from having a constraint-free shopper experience. This customer group is less 'visible' compared to people with mobility or vision impairments (Kaufman-Scarborough, 1998), and business is neither aware of the approximate number of potential clients nor is ready to provide accessible experiences. As an example, Chininthorn et al. (2012) demonstrate that pharmacy personnel in South Africa is often unprepared to communicate with clients with hearing impairments. This causes misleading understanding of provided instructions, and incorrect or ineffective consumption of medication, that may result in health threats and financial loss. While technologies (Chininthorn et al., 2012) or information leaflets (Van Mil, 2005) may assist in overcoming such challenges, the findings of a small-scale master's thesis by Metz (2013) demonstrate that staff awareness and training play a crucial role in creating a more equal and accessible customer experience. Specifically, the author notes that although often real estate staff are unfamiliar with reasonable accommodation of people with hearing impairments, those who are aware of or have experience in interacting with this customer group are more flexible in using alternative communication formats or are able to communicate in American Sign Language. Consequently, such companies have higher customer loyalty, better ensure customer confidentiality and independent decision-making.

Similar to the case of shoppers with hearing impairments, the literature on customers with cognitive impairments and mental health conditions' experience is limited. Goldblum (2006) is one of the few authors addressing the topic. She argues that traumatic brain injury and accompanying communication difficulties are an important source of experienced challenges in retail premises. Such an individual model position makes individuals responsible for difficulties in reading and understanding labels and prices, reaching products, communicating with shop assistants, and manoeuvring in noisy and crowded shops. Instead of addressing disabling shop environment, the emphasis is on individual's performance in a shop and the results of this performance. A similar position is adopted by Cromby et al. (1996), who instead of shedding light on business players' training and awareness raising, positioned training of young people with severe cognitive impairments in a virtual environment as a means for 'successful' shopping. Attribution of experienced barriers to disabled individuals prevents the deconstruction of a historically and socially shaped portrayal of what is deemed to be a customer. It locates private providers in a convenient position, where neither broader group of customers is considered, nor accessibility and reasonable accommodation is provided. In such a context, even though individuals with impairments 'happen to be' in a shop, their bodily integrity is undermined as well as the status of equal customer is denied.

While the retail premises is a key space where customer experience manifests, interaction with shop assistants is equally important (Menon and Dubé, 2000, Rutherford B., 2012). The following section, therefore, sheds light on characteristics that are usually associated with professional and quality customer service, and how this complies with the interaction with disabled shoppers. It also touches upon some of the factors shaping shop assistants' responses to customers with impairments and the role played by training on disability and accessibility.

Interaction in the shop

Interaction with salespeople is an important factor in shaping customer experience and satisfaction (Goff et al., 1997, Menon and Dubé, 2000, Rutherford B., 2012, Wirtz and Bateson, 1999, Wislon, 1998). Aiming to provide an effective and quality service, shop assistants are expected to possess features such as friendliness, attentiveness, respectfulness, expertise and competence (Yuksel, 2004). Prompt reactions, honest answers, hospitality, kind treatment (Reisinger and Waryszak, 1994), awareness of and knowledge about customer emotions and interpersonal processes

(Menon and Dubé, 2000) are vital in meeting individual's desires for a product and shopping process (Szymanski, 1988). Price et al. (1995) note that mutual understanding, extra attention, authenticity and competence are important dimensions of shop assistants' performance and have a direct impact on customers' experience.

Despite businesses looking for employees who would possess such features, professionals often lack knowledge and skills for exercising the aforementioned behaviours, and providing quality service and positive customer emotions. Menon and Dubé (2000) demonstrate that limited knowledge on and ineffective responses to customer emotions manifest through shop assistants' rudeness, unhelpfulness, ignorance and use of sales pressure that generate customer anger. While Rutherford B. (2012) argues that economic satisfaction is the main factor influencing a customer's commitment to a seller, Wirtz and Bateson (1999) note that dissatisfaction with a service provider's behaviour is more likely to have a negative effect on customer experience and purchase decisions than wrongly chosen music, scent or any other design and decor choice. Martin (1987, in Reisinger and Waryszak, 1994:3) supports such position and argues that interaction between a shopper and service provider is more important for and valued by a customer than 'the mechanistic skills of selling and delivering a product'.

These shop assistants' characteristics are equally important and expected in serving disabled customers. However, shoppers with impairments often are at the other end of the spectrum as some shop assistants avoid serving disabled people, 'over-help' them or react in fear (Kaufman-Scarborough, 1999). Others position individuals' impairment in front of the customer–provider interface (Baker, 2007). To illustrate, MacDonald et al. (1994) demonstrate that customers, who need assistance when trying clothes, often find salespeople patronising and identify such an attitude as a barrier that prevents them from a pleasurable and accessible shopping process. Overall, shop assistants' behaviour often receives negative evaluation and is associated with disempowerment, discrimination,[1] negative stereotypes, unequal treatment and disrespect, among others (Ryan et al., 2006, MacDonald et al., 1994).

Discriminatory treatment and disabling service provision is not an intentionally chosen shop assistants' behaviour. It originates from limited procedural and social service delivery knowledge. Specifically, limited information from memory about client groups, inability to ascribe them to particular categories and insufficient information about selling scripts lead to unsuccessful selling practices (Szymanski, 1988). Respectively, limited knowledge about and awareness of disabled people as customers (Freeman and Selmi, 2010) prevent shop assistants from developing respectful and informed selling scripts and service provision. In addition, a team manager's empowering leadership is an important factor, and its insufficiency is an important reason why retail personnel is incapable of acquiring and using customer knowledge (Menguc et al., 2013). Likewise, limited information and skills in service quality management (Yuksel, 2004), tendency to adopt a selling-oriented rather than customer-oriented approach (Goff et al., 1997, Roman et al., 2002), insufficient salespeople's involvement in planning and implementing training (Lassk et al., 2012) and absence of manufacturers' participation in shaping product-related information provision for a customer (Goff et al., 1997) prevent shop assistants from gaining full and detailed information about different customer groups and product features. These, indeed, are important factors that shape shop assistants' disabling attitudes and discriminatory practices when serving shoppers with impairments.

Salespeople's training on disability and accessibility may be one of the ways to overcome disabling seller–customer interaction. While studies addressing this kind of shop assistants' training across the EU are scarce, literature from the United States suggests that sales personnel, who have been provided with the training, tend to respond to disabled customers in a more simple and appropriate way, and treat them with respect, dignity and confidence (Kaufman-Scarborough, 2001, Baker et al., 2007). MacDonald et al. (1994) position shop assistants' training as a means to overcome limited product-related knowledge and tackle attitudinal barriers. In this respect, Baker (2006) demonstrates that shop assistants, who are familiar with reasonable accommodation and allow disabled customers to define the assistance that is needed and, respectively, provide it, enable people to remain active, maintain control and achieve customer independence.

Hence, shop assistants may either exclude or empower disabled customers. However, they are not free and independent agents choosing the occupied role. Although their personality, disability awareness and social sensitivity may play a part when serving shoppers with impairments, a great part of the professional behaviour is shaped by ableism and business' focus on non-disabled customers and achievement of capitalistic goals. Nonetheless, expedient training on disability, accessibility and customer equality may reshape the existing disabling and marginalising practices, introduce more accessible shopping experience and lead towards equal customer participation.

Accessibility and the private market

In addition to the limited disabled people's recognition as equal customers and the historically and socially constructed exclusion, insufficient discourse and tensions in professionals' practice regarding accessibility, reasonable accommodation and UD contribute to exclusion of customers with impairments. This book, therefore, proposes that UD should be the key concept in developing an accessible shopping chain. Instead of treating disabled people as the main users of universally designed products and environments, they should be seen as *one of* the user groups. Nevertheless, since in some instances, it might be impossible to create spaces and items that are usable by all people under all circumstances (Imrie, 2000b, 2013, Imrie and Hall, 2001, Nussbaumer, 2012, Steinfeld and Maisel, 2012), reasonable accommodations and assistive technologies should be provided at any stage of shopping. While UD is often associated with the process rather than the final product (Vanderheiden, 1996) and is applied to *all* people, all products and environments that are provided to the public should be accessible to people with impairments. Accessibility is perceived not only as a technically usable product, environment or service, but it also incorporates contextual and individual dimensions and aims to overcome disabling decisions rather than to 'fix' individuals.

Positioning accessible shopping as a chain suggests that professionals who operate in different stages of the chain have different ontological and epistemological positions on the issue (Pirie, 1979) and operate in different policy contexts, which, respectively, shape their professional realities. With this in mind, after providing an overview of how the involved parties may understand accessibility, the discussion addresses various dimensions that may either lead to or prevent from more accessible shopping. It then suggests that design of retail premises should be founded on UD principles that would lead to unification of the customer segment and elimination of labelling and stigmatisation of shoppers with impairments.

Accessibility and user involvement

A concept of accessibility in the context of disability was provided by Iwarsson and Stahl, who addressed it as 'the encounter between the person's or group's functional capacity and the design and demands of the physical environment. Accessibility refers to compliance with official norms and standards, thus being mainly objective in nature' (2003:61). However, accessibility as an objective character tightly linked with standards, norms and requirements does not necessarily provide accessible experience to a disabled individual. Indeed, Imrie's (2013:289) concern regarding standardisation of design process may be applied to production of standardised accessible items. He argues that standards often result in 'the (re)production of design environments that are not necessarily sensitised to body variations, or to the almost constant changes over the life course'. Having to meet 'prescribed code requirements for people with disabilities' (Centre for Accessible Housing, 1991), accessibility standards introduce similar risks for accessible product development. As an example, Petrie and Kheir (2007) demonstrate that despite website accessibility requirements, experiences of users with vision impairments differ, as well as provisions that should make websites more accessible for one user group may be a barrier for another. Similarly, Imrie (2000a) notes that wheelchair users' barrier-free movement is often restricted by accessibility provisions for people with vision impairments that were installed following legal guidance.

Accessibility should be understood more broadly than in an architectural and standard-based way, as compliance with technical requirements neither ensure quality (Power et al., 2012) nor provide space for considering user diversity and experience (Horton and Sloan, 2014). Furthermore, while common practice is to address accessibility as a physical person–environment interaction (Evcil, 2010, Iwarsson and Stahl, 2003), Kaufman-Scarborough (2001:460) invites considering the psychological dimension and links it with 'feeling of accessibility, dignity, and respect'. In a similar vein, Imrie (2013:289) sheds light on individual's expertise and knowledge about what is accessible, usable and designed in quality. Hence, while accessibility requirements play an important role in widening and increasing accessibility and usability of the public environment, products or websites (Imrie, 1996), the concept should be released from technical standards and requirements. Indeed, as suggested by Kaufman-Scarborough (1999), disabled users should be involved in the development of accessibility standards, and their opinions, expertise and contextual experiences (Sloan and Kelly, 2011) should be considered.

Professionals' knowledge, skills and awareness play a part in shaping the way people with impairments experience accessibility. However, usually, the practice is disabling rather than enabling. To begin with, despite a great volume of information and guidance on how to design in an accessible way (Persad et al., 2007), designers and developers often lack knowledge on how to actually design (Coleman and Lebbon, 2010, Heylighen, 2008, Keates et al., 2000, Imrie and Hall, 2001) and evaluate (Persad et al., 2007) accessible environments and products. They also often lack understanding and knowledge about inclusive design (Imrie and Hall, 2001) and awareness of physiological and bodily diversity (Evcil, 2010, Imrie, 2003, Keates et al., 2000). One of the underlying reasons behind the practice is insufficient presence and availability of resources that address how the requirements should be implemented in design (Goodman et al., 2006). As an example, although the Department of Mechanical Engineering (United Kingdom) is aware that inclusive design and accessibility of products such as plastic and glass containers are important, it lacks knowledge and information about how to improve openability of these products (Langley et al., 2005). Such practices suggest that limited knowledge on how to transform theoretical knowledge into successful and efficient solutions prevents professionals from providing more accessible products and environments.

One way of overcoming the outlined challenges is the adoption of certain principles of user-centred design (UCD). The term that originated in the 1980s emphasises the user's needs and interests as well as usability of the design (Norman and Draper, 1986). Locating this position at the heart of the development and design process (Newell and Gregor, 2000, Norman and Draper, 1986) enables professionals to develop more efficient and safer products (Sharp et al., 2002) that are usable by a larger group of people (Gheerawo and Donahue, 2004). User involvement and their expertise were recognised and formalised in the publication of International Organisation for Standardization (1999, ISO 13407) Human-Centred Design Processes for Interactive Systems. The standard notes that key principles of the UCD are active involvement of users, allocation of function to system and to user, iteration of design solutions and multidisciplinary design. However, although UCD supposes user involvement (Gheerawo and Donahue, 2004, Keates and Clarkson, 2004, Newell and Gregor, 2000), it also suggests that

> in product research and development, the role of potential users who are disabled should not include setting research agendas, developing research questions, and the choice of evaluation methodologies, all of which need trained researchers. Users should be 'involved in' the process, but not have a dominant role in it. (Newell and Gregor, 2000:40)

Such rationale suggests that although disabled people's needs and expertise are perceived as a fulcrum of the design process, their knowledge is valued only to a certain degree, leaving the decision-making power to the professionals (Heylighen, 2008, Till, 2005). Although UCD opens up the space for gaining knowledge about usability and accessible design decisions, it neither encourages broader changes in social, institutional and technical relations and procedures nor does it completely redraw historically entrenched unequal power relations between professionals and disabled people.

The adoption of participatory (Muller and Kuhn, 1993, Sanders, 2002) design doctrine may assist in overcoming the weaknesses of UCD. Specifically, the involvement of users as co-designers (Abras et al., 2004) enables identifying design decisions, usable by non-disabled users, but excluding people with impairments (Heylighen, 2008) and increasing environmental injustice (Gleeson, 1999). Experience-based knowledge and evaluations intensively shared during the whole design process (Abras et al., 2004, Sanders, 2002) and not only in the initial product development and usability evaluation stages (Newell and Gregor, 2000), continuously direct and shape product design. Horton and Sloan (2014) note that while user involvement in the product evaluation stage assists in validating accessibility-related decisions, their participation from the early stages of design process may provide unexpected insights and innovative ways of overcoming inaccessibility. Furthermore, according to Imrie and Hall (2001), the adoption of a participatory approach assists in conceptualising forthcoming changes that could maintain product or environment accessibility despite the changing individuals' needs. Most importantly, participatory design enables users and designers to engage in communication as equal actors (Sanders, 2002), who negotiate their knowledge and enter into compromises (Bucciarelli, 1994, Horgen, 1999). According to Newell and Gregor (2000), methods and techniques of the method have more potential to reveal user needs and knowledge, compared to UCD practices. Finally, direct and proactive participation in the design process (Sanders, 2002) reshifts power relations between professionals and disabled users (Imrie and Hall, 2001), providing people with impairments with more control over the environment they live in and products they use. It also challenges the entrenched and socially constructed understanding of the user (Imrie and Hall, 2001) and introduces a possibility to design sensitised products, reflecting the context of use and enabling users to exercise accessibility, dignity and respect while using the product.

Accessibility and a common language

For shopping to be accessible, professionals who are involved in or responsible for different parts of the shopping chain have to be commitment to (Horton and Sloan, 2014) and share similar ontological positions regarding accessibility. Representing different professional backgrounds, they have internalised definitions and understandings that are clear, known and legitimate in their professional practice. However, these often cause tensions and misunderstandings when working with professionals from other disciplines. For instance, transport planners perceive motor vehicle travel conditions, quality of other modes, transport network connectivity and land-use proximity as key factors for accessible transport infrastructure (Litman, 2008). For land planners, accessibility is determined by the 'spatial distribution of potential destinations, and the magnitude, quality, and character of the activities found there', with travel cost being the central factor (Handy and Niemeier, 1997:1175). Iwarsson and Stahl (2003:58) note that while environmental and planning architects in Sweden treat accessibility as 'the simplicity with which activities in the society can be reached, including needs of citizens, trade, industries and public services', the main emphasis is on distances and time, rather than on human capacity and interaction. Similarly, Pirie (1979:308) in his extensive review of accessibility concepts emphasises the dominant focus on the time–space accessibility measure and acknowledges the multiplicity of the notion and challenges brought by it. Hence, while an accessible shopping process is possible only when its separate stages are accessible and interconnected, professionals who operate in different parts of the chain have different understandings of accessibility. This ontological diversity shapes differences in professionals' everyday practices that are likely to prevent a fluid and consistent transition from one stage to another, as well as their overall compatibility.

Since professionals' ontologies are not static but change over time (Haase et al., 2005), changes in education and training curriculum may be used as a tool to evolve the understanding of the concept across disciplines as well as to introduce more consistency regarding the understanding of accessibility from disability perspective. Currently, this is insufficiently addressed across disciplines (Evcil, 2010, Imrie and Hall, 2001). As an example, although the need for better web accessibility for disabled people is recognised and legally addressed in policy instruments, training and information provision for the developers is either insufficient or absent (Foley and Regan, 2002,

Velasco and Verelst, 2001). A lack of relevant training shapes differences in professionals' knowledge and estranges the way they and disabled users understand and experience environments (Heylighen, 2013). Ontological differences in professionals' mindset continue preventing a systematic shift towards greater transition from specification to design and actual practice (Masuwa-Morgan and Burrell, 2004), which manifests in rhetorically accessible but empirically segregating environments and products.

Since legal instruments emphasise accessibility more than education curriculums do (see the following chapter), they may serve as a tool in encouraging interdisciplinary knowledge exchange and providing accessible practices. In this regard, it is worth shedding light on the American Disability Act (ADA; 1990) and on the Disability Discrimination Act (DDA; 1995) in the United Kingdom. Both documents are well-known punitive legislations that establish the framework within which stakeholders should provide accessibility. On the one hand, as suggested by Keates and Clarkson (2003), the instruments have increased awareness across industry and expanded their knowledge. This led to more accessibility and opened up the possibility for civil society to intervene in the process. On the other hand, both documents address minimal standards and guidelines and in such a way neither create a framework for knowledge exchange nor encourage stakeholders to further the progress and provide more accessibility than is required (Imrie and Hall, 2001). To illustrate, the ADA section 4.3.2 states,

> At least one accessible route within the boundary of the site shall be provided from public transportation stops, accessible parking, and accessible passenger loading zones, and public streets or sidewalks to the accessible building entrance they serve. The accessible route shall, to the maximum extent feasible, coincide with the route for the general public.

Similarly, in the United Kingdom, part M of the Building Regulations (2010) requires providing access where 'reasonable and practical'. Operating in the framework of minimal requirements, developers remain within a particular niche of expertise and rarely cross the boundaries of professional knowledge. This, in turn, prevents bringing in multiple perspectives related to a problem and narrows down the context within which the phenomena manifest (Lay and Mol, 2002). It also isolates knowledge across different disciplines (Klein, 1996) and prevents identifying the ways how to negotiate different professional ontologies and to address the issue (Haythornthwaite, 2006) of inaccessibility. In other words, operating within a legal framework, requiring minimal accessibility provisions and having limited or absent training on accessibility from disability perspective, professionals are neither aware of the issue nor are able to provide accessible solutions in different parts of the shopping chain.

UD and retail premises

Current legal requirements and retail practice lack a consistent and 'chain' approach to accessibility. Focus on assistive devices and instalments, and fragmented provision of accessible solutions within and outside retail premises shed light on individual's impairment (Imrie, 2013) and opens up the space for stigmatisation (Parette and Scherer, 2004). Ramps, accessible entrances in rare or back of buildings (Imrie, 1996), mobile communication tools (Chininthorn et al., 2012) or navigation systems (López-de-Ipiña et al., 2011) signalise that individuals using these devices are not ordinary customers and require different behaviours (Brookes, 1998). Even though accessibility or reasonable accommodation instalments provide people with the final 'product', the experience of the process is often excluding and promotes ableism and non-disabled society's values and norms (Oliver, 1990). In order to introduce accessibility to retail markets that equalise and not exclude customers, all stages of the shopping chain, including retail premises, should be universally designed, 'sensitising design to the capabilities of the human body, in ways whereby anyone, irrespective of how their body performs, is able to gain access to, and make use of, the artefacts' (Imrie, 2013:289).

To its broadest extent, UD can be equalised to a social movement, whose activities are oriented towards 'making products, environments and communication systems usable to the greatest extent possible by the broadest spectrum of people' (Imrie and Hall, 2001:14). In a similar vein, Mace (1988:2) defines UD as 'an approach to design that incorporates products as well as building features and elements which, to the greatest extent possible, can be used by everyone'. Hence, UD 'targets *all* people of *all* ages, sizes, and abilities and is applied to *all* buildings' (Mace, 1988:2). It is important to note that UD acknowledges the importance of assistive devices (Imrie and Hall, 2001). Vanderheiden (1998), for instance, argues that while UD should be prioritised in the development process, its combination with assistive technologies may provide individuals with the best outcome and advantage. In this respect, Mace (1998) notes that while universally designed homes eliminate the need for the majority of assistive devices and additional spending, if needed, special instalments should be provided aiming to ensure an individual's freedom, independency and dignity. Hence, aiming to provide disabled customers with equality and a pleasant shopping experience, public places, transport infrastructure, shops and provided services should prioritise UD but not negate assistive devices and instalments.

Application of UD principles to the shop environment is important not only because of disabled shoppers but also because of the current changes in customer segment. Specifically, with the emergence of shopping malls in the 1880s, middle-aged middle-class females were perceived as the main group of shoppers (Gardner and Sheppard, 1989, Weisman, 1994, Witkowski, 1999). This led to the dominance of beauty, pleasure and aesthetics in external and internal shop environments (Gardner and Sheppard, 1989); diminished designers' social responsibility (Tisdale, 1996); and entrenched the focus on forms and shapes instead of functions (Imrie, 2013). However, such design tendencies are alive in the modern shopping places and have to be reconsidered as the customer profile is becoming more diverse. As an example, the number of males shopping is rapidly increasing (Dholakia et al., 1995, Otnes and McGrath, 2001); shopping is becoming an element of their self-identity creation (Reekie, 1992, Torres et al., 2001). Indeed, traditionally being founded on achievement orientation (Otnes and McGrath, 2001) and satisfaction of clearly defined needs (Anselmsson, 2006), males' shopping behaviour does not fit in the retail environment oriented to meet what is perceived as female's shopping habits and expectations (Anselmsson, 2006, Dholakia et al., 1995, Gardner and Sheppard, 1989, Otnes and McGrath, 2001). Consequently, this shapes males' unpleasant customer feelings and negative attitudes such as 'dislike' or 'hate' (Campbell, 1997). In addition, while in the past, children and teenagers used to be associated with inconvenience in shopping malls (Andreoli, 1996: in Mangleburg et al., 2004), recently, their spending power and customer role is getting to be recognised by the industry (Mangleburg et al., 2004, Quart, 2008), which positions them as desired customers.

Growth of the ageing and disabled population and their spending power, and slowly increasing disabled adults' participation in society (WHO, 2011), suggest that their partaking in the private market and presence in shops may increase. Hence, founded on femininity stereotypes and oriented towards aesthetics and female customers' seduction (Weisman, 1994), shops threaten to exclude or not completely include various groups of potential shoppers, including people with impairments. The employment of UD principles[2] (Connell et al., 1997), sensitisation of the retail environment and integration of impairment accommodations, as suggested by Imrie (2013), may 'unlock' shops and provide a more pleasant shopping experience for more diverse customer groups. Focusing on usefulness and simplicity of places and artefacts in a way they are used to ease individuals' capabilities and functioning in a chosen manner and way (Nussbaum, 2003) simplifies everyone's life and allows different individuals to use the same spaces and artefacts without major differences (Nussbaumer, 2012) and without labelling and stigmatising them (Brookes, 1998, Parette and Scherer, 2004). Most importantly, such practice introduces the discourse of human rights (Nussbaum, 2003) and reflects the philosophy of market accessibility and customer participation as entrenched in the CRPD article 9.2b.

Concluding comments

This chapter has explored three key dimensions regarding disabled people's participation in the mainstream private market as customers. It first explored the position of people with impairments in markets related with consumption and customer participation; it then shed light on the shopping process as an accessible chain and concluded the discussion by examination of the discourse on accessibility, reasonable accommodation and UD in the context of the shopping chain.

In drawing attention to disabled people's position in markets related with consumption and customer participation, this chapter has suggested that people with impairments neither were nor are free agents when choosing and deciding the role and position as market participants. Indeed, state policies and market practice seem to play the dominant role. Not fitting the requirements for a 'standard' or 'beneficial' market participant, people with impairments were either isolated from participation in society and markets or off-sided. The introduction of personal budgets reshaped historic marginalisation that was also partly premised on older and disabled people's lack of spending power and market autonomy. This created new markets as well as new market relations and positioned disabled people as Employers as well as independent purchasers for assistive technologies. Increasing older and disabled people numbers and their spending power encouraged the emergence of special markets for disability products. While this kind of private providers position disabled people as a valuable client group, providers of mainstream goods and services perceive them as 'vulnerable' customers. Such ontological tensions impact service provision practice and may isolate customers with impairments within 'special' markets and prevent engagement with mainstream providers.

There have been significant contributions towards demonstrating different barriers faced by people with impairments (Baker, 2006, Bromley et al., 2007b, Carlsson, 2004, Chouinard, 1997, Fänge et al., 2002, Goldsmith, 2011, Kaufman-Scarborough, 1999, 2001, Nemeth and Del Rogers, 1981). While the studies confirm that facing obstacles is a constant part of disabled people's lives, there is a knowledge lacuna in linking them with customer experience and addressing in the context of the private market. This chapter, therefore, has identified four shopping stages: customer information, the journey to the shop, navigation in retail premises and interaction in the shop. It suggested that barriers in one of the stages may prevent people from experiencing a smooth and independent shopping process, construct customer vulnerability or exclude from participation in the market. In light of the social model of disability, it argues that faced obstacles are shaped not by individuals' impairments but by ableism and state and business' focus on non-disabled citizens and customers.

The present chapter has also shown that focusing on UCD and insufficient disabled people's involvement in the whole design process prevents developers from knowing how to implement accessibility requirements into practice, and to actually design and evaluate accessible products and environments. Accordingly, it argued for the adoption of a participatory design doctrine (Muller and Kuhn, 1993, Sanders, 2002) that alongside assisting the conceptualisation and foreseeing forthcoming changes in individuals' needs and accessibility provisions also acts as a platform for users and developers to communicate and negotiate as equals and to enter into compromises aiming to provide more accessibility. It was also suggested that tensions in ontologies of the professionals, who operate in different stages of the shopping chain, may prevent and in some cases corrupt accessibility provisions and intrude into equal customer experience. While it is unrealistic and disadvantageous to aim to unify professionals' knowledge and perspectives, it is suggested that awareness raising, education about accessibility from disability perspectives and a stronger focus on the issue in legal instruments may encourage interdisciplinary knowledge exchange and reshape current practice. The chapter concludes by suggesting that aiming to lessen disabled customers' exclusion and stigmatisation and to ensure equal participation in the mainstream private market, it is not enough to focus only on accessibility. Indeed, philosophy and principles of UD should be applied aiming to create a shopping process that is equally accessible and pleasant to all market participants.

The following chapter continues the discussion and demonstrates how disabled customers and their accessibility of the mainstream private market are addressed in global, regional and national policies. It focuses on how the emerged discourse on rights and accessibility rhetorically reshaped disabled people as customers and created some tensions across the multi-scalar governance.

Notes

1 In particular, direct discrimination ('treating people less favourably than others because of their dependency to a certain category or group' (Neufeldt, 1995)), indirect discrimination ('imposing a requirement or condition for a job, facility or service which makes it harder for disabled people to gain access to it' (Neufeldt, 1995:177)), positive discrimination ('aims to achieve equality of outcome or results. It discriminates in favour of certain individuals on the basis of characteristics seen as common to their group' (Norris, 2001:3)) and institutional discrimination ('Is evident when policies and activities of all types of modern organisation result in inequality between disabled people and non-disabled people. It is embedded in the excessive paternalism of contemporary welfare systems and is apparent when they are systematically ignoring or meeting inadequately the needs of disabled people. It incorporates extreme forms of prejudice and intolerance usually associated with individual or direct discrimination' (Barnes, 1991:7)).
2 1 – equitable in use; 2 – flexibility in use; 3 – simple and intuitive use; 4 – perceptible information; 5 – tolerance for error; 6 – low physical effort; 7 – size and space for approach and use.

Bibliography

Abras, C., Maloney-Krichmar, D. & Preece, J. 2004. *User-centered design. Bainbridge, W. Encyclopedia of Human-Computer Interaction*, Thousand Oaks, Sage Publications, 37, 445–456.

Adeoye, S. & Bozic, K. J. 2007. Direct consumer advertising in healthcare. *Clinical Orthopaedics and Related Research*, 457, 96–104.

Age Concern and Help the Aged. 2010. The 'grey pound' set to hit £100bn mark. Available: www.easier.com/65065-grey-pound-to-hit-100bn-mark.html [Accessed 20/01/2012] [Press release].

Ajzenstadt, M. & Rosenhek, Z. 2000. Privatisation and new modes of state intervention: The long-term care programme in Israel. *Journal of Social Policy*, 29, 247–262.

Albrecht, G. L. 1992. *The disability business. Rehabilitation in America*, London, Sage Publications.

Amundson, R. & Taira, G. 2005. Our lives and ideologies: The effect of life experience on the perceived morality of the policy of physician-assisted suicide. *Journal of Disability Policy Studies*, 16, 53–57.

Anderson, P. & Kitchin, R. 2000. Disability, space and sexuality: Access to family planning services. *Social Science & Medicine*, 51, 1163–1173.

Andersson, P. K., Kristensson, P., Wästlund, E. & Gustafsson, A. 2012. Let the music play or not: The influence of background music on consumer behavior. *Journal of Retailing and Consumer Services*, 19, 553–560.

Andreoli, T. 1996. Message to retail industry: Teens should be seen and heard. *Discount Store News*, 35, 30–32.

Anselmsson, J. 2006. Sources of customer satisfaction with shopping malls: A comparative study of different customer segments. *The International Review of Retail, Distribution and Consumer Research*, 16, 115–138.

Arens, W. F., Weigold, M. F. & Arens, C. 2009. *Contemporary advertising*, Boston, McGraw-Hill.

Arksey, H. & Baxter, K. 2011. Exploring the temporal aspects of direct payments. *British Journal of Social Work*, 1–18.

Babin, B. J. & Attaway, J. S. 2000. Atmospheric affect as a tool for creating value and gaining share of customer. *Journal of Business Research*, 49, 91–99.

Baker, J. & Haytko, D. 2000. The mall as entertainment: Exploring teen girls' total shopping experiences. *Journal of Shopping Center Research*, 7, 29–58.

Baker, S. M. 2006. Consumer normalcy: Understanding the value of shopping through narratives of consumers with visual impairments. *Journal of Retailing*, 82, 37–50.

Baker, S. M. 2007. How consumers with disabilities perceive welcome in retail servicescapes: A critical incident study. *Journal of Services Marketing*, 21, 160–173.

Baker, S. M., Gentry, J. W. & Rittenburg, T. L. 2005. Building understanding of the domain of consumer vulnerability. *Journal of Macromarketing*, 25, 128–139.

Baker, S. M., Holland, J. & Kaufman-Scarborourgh, C. 2007. How consumers with disabilities perceive 'Welcome' in retail servicescapes: A critical incident study. *Journal of Services Marketing*, 21, 160–173.

Baker, S. M., Stephens, D. L. & Hill, R. P. 2001. Marketplace experiences of consumers with visual impairments: Beyond the Americans with disabilities act. *Journal of Public Policy & Marketing*, 20, 215–224.

Ballantine, P. W., Jack, R. & Parsons, A. G. 2010. Atmospheric cues and their effect on the hedonic retail experience. *International Journal of Retail & Distribution Management*, 38, 641–653.

Barnes, C. 1991. A brief history of discrimination and disabled people. *In:* Barnes, C. (ed.) *Disabled people in Britain and discrimination: A case for anti-discrimination*

legislation, London, Hurst in association with the British Council of Organizations of Disabled People.
Barnes, C. 1999. Disability and paid employment. *Work, Employment and Society*, 13, 147–149.
Barnes, C. & Mercer, G. 2005. Disability, work, and welfare: Challenging the social exclusion of disabled people. *Work, Employment & Society*, 19, 527–545.
Barthes, R. 1973. *Mythologies*, London, Paladin Books.
Barton, L. 1995. The politics of education for all. *Support for Learning*, 10, 156–160.
Barton, L. 1997. Inclusive education: Romantic, subversive or realistic? *International Journal of Inclusive Education*, 1, 231–242.
Barton, L. 2004. The politics of special education: A necessary or irrelevant approach? *In:* Ware, L. (ed.) *Ideology and the politics of (in) exclusion*, New York, Peter Lang Publishing.
Beier, A. L. 1974. Vagrants and the social order in Elizabethan England. *Past & Present*, 64, 3–29.
Bemmaor, A. C. & Mouchoux, D. 1991. Measuring the short-term effect of in-store promotion and retail advertising on brand sales: A factorial experiment. *Journal of Marketing Research*, 28, 202–214.
Ben-Rafael, E., Shohamy, E., Hasan Amara, M. & Trumper-Hecht, N. 2006. Linguistic landscape as symbolic construction of the public space: The case of Israel. *International Journal of Multilingualism*, 3, 7–30.
Bettman, J. R., Johnson, E. J. & Payne, J. W. 1991. Consumer decision making. *In:* Handbook of Consumer Behavior, 50–84.
Bickart, B. & Schindler, R. M. 2001. Internet forums as influential sources of consumer information. *Journal of Interactive Marketing*, 15, 31–40.
Biehal, G. & Chakravarti, D. 1986. Consumers' use of memory and external information in choice: Macro and micro perspectives. *Journal of Consumer Research*, 382–405.
Bloch, P. H., Ridgway, N. M. & Dawson, S. A. 1994. The shopping mall as consumer habitat. *Journal of Retailing*, 70, 23–42.
Bonaccorso, S. N. 2002. Direct to consumer advertising is medicalizing normal human experience. Against. *Education and Debate*, 324, 910–911.
Braunsberger, K., Lucas, L. A. & Roach, D. 2004. The effectiveness of credit-card regulation for vulnerable customers. *The Journal of Services Marketing*, 18, 358–370.
Brenkert, G. G. 1998. Marketing and the vulnerable. *Business Ethics Quarterly: The Ruffin Series*, 1, 7–20.
Bristor, J. M., Lee, R. G. & Hunt, M. R. 1995. Race and ideology: African-American images in television advertising. *Journal of Public Policy & Marketing*, 14, 48–59.
Bromley, R. D. F. & Matthews, D. L. 2007. Reducing consumer disadvantage: Reassessing access in the retail environment. *The International Review of Retail, Distribution and Consumer Research*, 17, 483–501.
Bromley, R. D. F., Matthews, D. L. & Thomas, C. J. 2007. City centre accessibility for wheelchair users: The consumer perspective and the planning implications. *Cities*, 24, 229–241.
Brookes, N. A. 1998. Models for understanding rehabilitation and assistive technology. *In:* Gray, D. B., Quatrano, I. A. & Lieberman, M. L. (eds.) *Designing and using assistive technology. The human perspective*. Baltimore: Brooks.
Broom, D. H. & Woodward, R. V. 1996. Medicalization considered: Toward a collaborative approach to care. *Sociology of Health & Illness*, 18, 357–378.

Brown, S. L. & Eisenhardt, K. M. 1995. Product development: Past research, present findings, and future directions. *Academy of Management Review*, 20, 343–378.

Bucciarelli, L. L. 1994. *Designing engineers*, Cambridge, Massachusetts Institute of Technology.

Buchner, T., Smyth, F., Biewer, G., Shevlin, M., Ferreira, M. A. V., Toboso Martín, M., Rodríguez Díaz, S., Šiška, J., Latimier, C. & Káňová, Š. 2014. Paving the way through mainstream education: The interplay of families, schools and disabled students. *Research Papers in Education*, 30(4), 1–16.

Buclin, L. P. 1965. The informative roles of advertising. *Journal of Advertising Research*, January, 35–53.

Burleigh, M. 1994. *Death and deliverance. 'Euthanasia' in Germany 1900–1945*, Cambridge, Cambridge University Press.

Burnett, J. J. 1996. What services marketers need to know about the mobility-disabled consumer. *The Journal of Services Marketing*, 10, 3–20.

Butkevičienė, R., Majerienė, N. & Harrison, D. 2006. Šeimos, auginančios vaikus, turinčius regos negalią: Santykių su specialistais patirtis ir socialinio darbuotojo veiklos galimybės. *Socialinis Darbas*, 5, 123–131.

Butler, R. & Bowlby, S. 1997. Bodies and spaces: An exploration of disabled people's experiences of public space. *Environment and Planning D*, 15, 411–434.

Campbell, C. 1997. Shopping, pleasure and the sex war. *The Shopping Experience*, 1, 166–176.

Carlsson, G. 2004. Travelling by urban public transport: Exploration of usability problems in a travel chain perspective. *Scandinavian Journal of Occupational Therapy*, 11, 78–89.

Carmichael, A. & Brown, L. 2002. The future challenge for direct payments. *Disability & Society*, 17, 797–808.

Carmichael, A., Evans, C. & Brown, L. 2001. *A user led best value review of direct payments*, Wiltshire, Wiltshire County Council.

Carr, S. & Robbins, D. 2009. *The implementation of individual budget schemes in adult social care*, London, Social Care Institute for Excellence.

Castro, I. A., Morales, A. C. & Nowlis, S. M. 2013. The influence of disorganized shelf displays and limited product quantity on consumer purchase. *Journal of Marketing*, 77, 118–133.

Centre for Accessible Housing. 1991. Definitions: Accessible, adaptable, and universal design (Fact sheet). Releigh, North Carolina State University.

Chan, W. & Puech, B. 2014. *Accessible retail. Every customer counts. A good practice guide to making reasonable adjustments*, Belfast, Equality Commission for Northern Ireland.

Chandon, P., Hutchinson, J. W., Bradlow, E. T. & Young, S. H. 2009. Does in-store marketing work? Effects of the number and position of shelf facings on brand attention and evaluation at the point of purchase. *Journal of Marketing*, 73, 1–17.

Chang, T.-Z. & Wildt, A. 1994. Price, product information, and purchase intention: An empirical study. *Journal of the Academy of Marketing Science*, 22, 16–27.

Cheng, K. 2002. *What marketers should know about people with disabilities*, Diversity Inc. Available: http://www.nod.org/index.cfm?fuseaction=page.viewPage&pageID=1430&nodeID=1&FeatureID=723&redirected=1&CFID=5012936&CFTOKEN=67432879 [Accessed 21/10/2012].

Chininthorn, P., Glaser, M., Freudenthal, A. & Tucker, W. D. 2012. Mobile communication tools for a South African Deaf patient in a pharmacy context. *In:*

Cunningham, P. & Cunningham (eds.) *Information Society Technologies - Africa*. Tanzania: IIMC International Information Management Corporation.

Chouinard, V. 1997. Making space for disabling differences: Challenging ableist geographies. *Environment and Planning D: Society and Space*, 15, 379–387.

Clark, H., Gough, H. & Macfarlane, A. 2004. *It pays dividends: Direct payments and older people*, Bristol, Policy Press.

Clark, M., Goodwin, N. & Network, W. A. 2010. *Sustaining innovation in telehealth and telecare*, WSD Action Network, King's Fund.

Coleman, R. & Lebbon, C. 2010. *Inclusive design*, London, Helen Hamlyn Research Centre, Royal College of Art.

Common, R. & Flynn, N. 1992. *Contracting for care*, York, Joseph Rowntree Foundation.

Connell, B. R., Jones, M. L., Mace, R. L., Mueller, J. L., Mullick, A., Ostroff, E. & Sanford, J. 1997. *The principles of Universal Design, Version 2.0*, Raleigh, Center for Universal Design, North Carolina State University.

Connor, D. J. & Bejoian, L. 2014. Cripping school curricula: 20 ways to re-teach disability. *Review of Disability Studies: An International Journal*, 3(3) 3–12.

Cook, T., Swain, J. & French, S. 2001. Voices from segregated schooling: Towards an inclusive education system. *Disability & Society*, 16, 293–310.

Crawford, M. 1992. The world in a shopping mall. *In:* Sorkin, M. (ed.) *Variations on a theme park: The new American city and the end of public space*. New York, Hill and Wang.

Crawford, M. J., Rutter, D., Manley, C., Weaver, T., Bhui, K., Fulop, N. & Tyrer, P. 2002. Systematic review of involving patients in the planning and development of health care. *British Medical Journal*, 325, 1263–1268.

Cromby, J., Standen, P., Newman, J. & Tasker, H. 1996. Successful transfer to the real world of skills practised in a virtual environment by students with severe learning difficulties. 1st European Conference on Disability, Virtual Reality, and Associated Technologies, 8–10.

D'astous, A. 2000. Irritating aspects of the shopping environment. *Journal of Business Research*, 49, 149–156.

Department for Transport. 2013. *Annual bus statistics: England 2012/2013*, London, Home Office.

Department of Health. 2001. *Valuing people: A new strategy for learning disability for the 21st century: A white paper*, London, Department of Health.

Department of Trade and Industry. 2000. A study of the difficulties disabled people have when using everyday consumer products. London, Department of Trade and Industry.

DePauw, K. P. 1997. The (In) visibility of DisAbility: Cultural contexts and 'Sporting bodies'. *Quest*, 49, 416–430.

Desmet, P. & Renaudin, V. 1998. Estimation of product category sales responsiveness to allocated shelf space. *International Journal of Research in Marketing*, 15, 443–457.

Devine, M. A. & Dattilo, J. 2000. Social acceptance and leisure lifestyles of people with disabilities. *Therapeutic Recreation Journal*, 34, 306–322.

Dholakia, R. R., Pedersen, B. & Hikmet, N. 1995. Married males and shopping: Are they sleeping partners. *International Journal of Retail & Distribution Management*, 23, 27–33.

Dick, A., Chakravarti, D. & Biehal, G. 1990. Memory-based inferences during consumer choice. *Journal of Consumer Research*, 17, 82–93.

Dickinson, H. & Glasby, J. 2010. *The personalisation agenda: Implications for the third sector*, Birmingham, The Third Sector Research Centre.

Domingo, M. C. 2012. An overview of the Internet of things for people with disabilities. *Journal of Network and Computer Applications*, 35, 584–596.

Drèze, X., Hoch, S. J. & Purk, M. E. 1994. Shelf management and space elasticity. *Journal of Retailing*, 70, 301–326.

Dunn, M., Clare, I. H. & Holland, A. 2008. Substitute decision-making for adults with intellectual disabilities living in residential care: Learning through experience. *Health Care Analysis*, 16, 52–64.

Dunn, M. C., Clare, I. C. H. & Holland, A. J. 2010. Living 'a life like ours': Support workers' accounts of substitute decision-making in residential care homes for adults with intellectual disabilities. *Journal of Intellectual Disability Research*, 54, 144–160.

Dynamic™. n.d. *Designers and Manufacturers* [Online]. Available: www.dynamiccontrols.com/designers-and-manufacturers [Accessed 15/04/2012].

Edward, P. C., Almeida, M. D., Gulmann, P. & Jj, J. 2000. Case C220/98, Estee Lauder Cosmetics GmbH & Co. OHG v. Lancaster Group GmbH Available: http://curia.europa.eu/juris/liste.jsf?language=en&num=c-220/98 [Accessed 29/08/2014].

Eisend, M. 2014. Shelf space elasticity: A meta-analysis. *Journal of Retailing*, 90, 168–181.

Eskytė, I. 2012. Disability and social work: Between life-world colonisation and the support to overcome barriers. *In:* Ruskus, J. (ed.) *Social Work for Sustainable Social Development*, Kaunas, Vytautas Magnus University.

Eskytė, I. 2013. Disability and social work. One feature and three positions. *Social Work. Experience and Methods*, 11, 69–83.

Eskytė, I. 2014. The 'Blind Area' of the city: Drawing shopping boundaries for people with vision impairments. *Conference proceedings: Universal Design 2014: Three Days of Creativity and Diversity*, Lund, Sweden.

European Commission. 2011. *The 2012 ageing report. Underlying assumptions and projection methodologies*, Brussels, DG ECFIN, AWG, Economic Policy Committee.

European Platform for Rehabilitation. 2013. Personal budgets: A new way to finance disability services Available: www.epr.eu/images/EPR/documents/policy_documents/Paper%20on%20Personal%20Budgets.pdf [Accessed 03/06/2014].

European Union. 1992. *Treaty of Maastricht on European Union*, Brussels, European Parliament.

Eurostat. 2009. Consumers in Europe. Available: http://ec.europa.eu/consumers/archive/strategy/consumers_europe_edition2_en.pdf [Accessed 26/09/2013].

Evcil, N. 2010. Designers' attitudes towards disabled people and the compliance of public open places: The case of Istanbul. *European Planning Studies*, 18, 1863–1880.

Fänge, A., Iwarsson, S. & Persson, Å. 2002. Accessibility to the public environment as perceived by teenagers with functional limitations in a south Swedish town centre. *Disability and Rehabilitation*, 24, 318–326.

Finkelstein, V. 1981. Disability and professional Attitudes. *NAIDEX'81*. RADAR.

Finkelstein, V. 1999. A profession allied to the community: The disabled people's trade union. *In:* Stone, E. (ed.) *Disability and development: Learning from action and research on disability in the majority world*, Leeds, The Disability Press.

Finkelstein, V. 1999a. Professions Allied to the Community (PACs). Available: www.leeds.ac.uk/disability-studies/archiveuk/finkelstein/finkelstein1.pdf [Accessed 30/03/2012].

Foley, A. & Regan, B. 2002. Web design for accessibility: Policies and practice. *AACE Journal*, 10, 62–80.

Fost, D. 1998. The fun factor: Marketing recreation to the disabled. *American Demographics*, 20, 54–58.

Freeman, I. & Selmi, N. 2010. French versus Canadian tourism: Response to the disabled. *Journal of Travel Research*, 49, 471–485.

French, D. & Hainsworth, J. 2001. 'There aren't any buses and the swimming pool is always cold!': Obstacles and opportunities in the provision of sport for disabled people. *Managing Leisure*, 6, 35–49.

Gabriel, Y. & Lang, T. 1995. *The unmanagable consumer. Contemporary consumption and its fragmentation*, London, Sage Publications.

Gardner, C. & Sheppard, J. 1989. *Consuming passion. The rise of retail culture*, London, Unwin Hyman.

Garlin, F. V. & Owen, K. 2006. Setting the tone with the tune: A meta-analytic review of the effects of background music in retail settings. *Journal of Business Research*, 59, 755–764.

Gentry, J. W., Kennedy, P. F., Paul, K. & Hill, R. P. 1995. The vulnerability of those grieving the death of a loved one: Implications for public policy. *Journal of Public Policy & Marketing*, 14, 128–142.

Gheerawo, R. R. & Donahue, S. J. 2004. Introducing user-centred design methods into design education. *In:* Keates, S., Clarkson, J., Langdon, P. & Robinson, P. (eds.) *Designing a more inclusive world*. London: Springer-Verlag.

Gillin, J. L. 1929. Vagrancy and begging. *American Journal of Sociology*, 35, 424–432.

Gleeson, B. 1999. *Geographies of Disability*, London, Routledge.

Glendinning, C., Halliwell, S., Jacobs, S., Rummery, K. & Tyrer, J. 2000. *Buying independence. Using direct payments to integrate health and social services*, Bristol, The Polity Press.

Goff, B. G., Boles, J. S., Bellenger, D. N. & Stojack, C. 1997. The influence of salesperson selling behaviors on customer satisfaction with products. *Journal of Retailing*, 73, 171–183.

Golbe, C. 2004. Dependence, independence and normality. *In:* Swain, J., French, S., Barnes, C. & Thomas, C. (eds.) *Disabling Barriers - Enabling Environments. 2nd edition*, London, Sage Publications.

Goldblum, G. 2006. *Sales assistants serving customers with Traumatic Brain Injury.* PhD Thesis, University of Pretoria.

Goldsmith, S. 2011. *Designing for the disabled. The new paradigm*, London, Routledge; Taylor & Francis Group.

Goodley, D. 2014. *Dis/ability studies – theorising disablism and ableism*, London, Routledge.

Goodley, D. & Tregaskis, C. 2006. Storying disability and impairment: Retrospective accounts of disabled family life. *Qualitative Health Research*, 16, 630–646.

Goodman, J., Langdon, P. M. & Clarkson, P. J. 2006. Providing strategic user information for designers: Methods and initial findings. *In:* Clarkson, J., Langdon, P. & Robinson, P. (eds.) *Designing accessible technology*, London, Springer.

Goss, J. 1993. The 'magic of the mall': An analysis of form, function, and meaning in the contemporary retail built environment. *Annals of the Association of American Geographers*, 83, 18–47.

Greasley, D. & Oxley, L. 1996. Discontinuities in competitiveness: The impact of the first World War on British industry. *The Economic History Review*, 49, 82–100.

Grever, B. 2009. *The labour market situation of disabled people in European countries and implementation of employment policies: A summary of evidence from country reports and research studies*, Academic Network for European Disability Experts. Available: http://www.disabilityeurope.net [Accessed 29/07/2012].

Guéguen, N. & Petr, C. 2006. Odors and consumer behavior in a restaurant. *International Journal of Hospitality Management*, 25, 335–339.

Haase, P., Van Harmelen, F., Huang, Z., Stuckenschmidt, H. & Sure, Y. 2005. A framework for handling inconsistency in changing ontologies. *In:* Gil, Y., Motta, E., Benjamins, V. R. & Musen, M. (eds.) *The Semantic Web – ISWC 2005*. Berlin: Springer.

Habermas, J. 1984. *The theory of communicative action: Volume 1. Reason and the rationalisation of society*, Boston, Beacon Press.

Habermas, J. 1985. *The theory of communicative action: Volume 2. Lifeworld and system: A critique of functionalist reason*, Cambridge, Polity Press.

Hackett, P. M. W., Foxall, G. R. & VAN Raaij, W. F. 1993. Consumers in retail environments. *Advances in Psychology*, 96, 378–399.

Handy, S. L. & Niemeier, D. A. 1997. Measuring accessibility: An exploration of issues and alternatives. *Environment and Planning A*, 29, 1175–1194.

Hanson, J. 2004. The inclusive city: Delivering a more accessible urban environment through inclusive design. Available: http://eprints.ucl.ac.uk/3351/1/3351.pdf [Accessed 25/04/2013].

Häubl, G. & Trifts, V. 2000. Consumer decision making in online shopping environments: The effects of interactive decision aids. *Marketing Science*, 19, 4–21.

Haythornthwaite, C. 2006. Learning and knowledge networks in interdisciplinary collaborations. *Journal of the American Society for Information Science and Technology*, 57, 1079–1092.

Heskett, J. L. & Schlesinger, L. 1994. Putting the service-profit chain to work. *Harvard Business Review*, 72, 164–174.

Heylighen, A. 2008. Sustainable and inclusive design: A matter of knowledge? *Local Environment*, 13, 531–540.

Heylighen, A. 2013. Transferring disability experience to design practice. Proceedings in: Knowing inside out-experiential knowledge, expertise and connoisseurship, Loughborough, Loughborough University, 47–58.

Hill, R. P. & Dhanda, K. K. 1999. Gender inequity and quality of life: A macromarketing perspective. *Journal of Macromarketing*, 19, 140–152.

Hoffmann, F. & Inderst, R. 2009. Price discrimination and the provision of information. Available: www.wiwi.uni-frankfurt.de/profs/inderst/Theory/info_price_discrimination_oct09.pdf [Accessed 08/10/2012].

Horgen, T. 1999. *Excellence by design: Transforming workplace and work practice*, New York, John Wiley & Sons.

Horton, S. & Sloan, D. 2014. Accessibility in practice: A process-driven approach to accessibility. *In:* Langdon, P. M., Lazar, J., Heylighen, A. & Dong, H. (eds.) *Inclusive designing*, Cham, Springer International Publishing.

Howells, G. 2005. The potential and limits of consumer empowerment by information. *Journal of Law and Society*, 32, 349–370.

Hoyes, L. & Harrison, R. 1993. Quasi-markets and the reform of community care. *In:* Legrand, J. & Bartlett, W. (eds.) *Quasi-markets and social policy*, Basingstoke, The Macmillan Press.

Iezzoni, L. I. 2011. Eliminating health and health care disparities among the growing population of people with disabilities. *Health Affairs*, 30, 1947–1954.

Imrie, R. 1996. *Disability and the city: International perspectives*, London, Sage.
Imrie, R. 1998. Oppression, disability and access in the built environment. In: Shakespeare, T. (ed.) *Disability reader: Social science perspectives*, London, Continuum.
Imrie, R. 2000a. Disability and discourses of mobility and movement. *Environment and Planning A*, 32, 1641–1656.
Imrie, R. 2000b. Disabling environments and the geography of access policies and practices. *Disability & Society*, 15, 5–24.
Imrie, R. 2003. Architects' conceptions of the human body. *Environment and Planning D*, 21, 47–66.
Imrie, R. 2013. Designing inclusive environments and the significance of universal design. In: Swain, J., French, S., Barnes, C. & Thomas, C. (eds.) *Disabling barriers-enabling environments*. 2nd edition, London, Sage Publications.
Imrie, R. & Hall, P. 2001. *Inclusive design: Designing and developing accessible environments*, London, Spon Press.
International Organisation for Standardization 1999, ISO 13407. *Human-centred design processes for interactive systems*, Geneva, ISO.
Iwarsson, S., Jensen, G. & Ståhl, A. 2000. Travel chain enabler: Development of a pilot instrument for assessment of urban public bus transport accessibility. *Technology and Disability*, 12, 3–12.
Iwarsson, S. & Stahl, A. 2003. Accessibility, usability and universal design – positioning and definition of concepts describing person-environment relationships. *Disability and Rehabilitation*, 25, 57–66.
Jeffords, J. M. 2004. Direct-to-consumer drug advertising: You get what you pay. *Health Affairs* [Online]. Available: www.bvsde.paho.org/bvsacd/cd57/jeffords.pdf [Accessed 21/03/2011].
Johnson, R. D. & Levin, I. P. 1985. More than meets the eye: The effect of missing information on purchase evaluations. *Journal of Consumer Research*, 12, 169–177.
Jones, J. L. & Middleton, K. L. 2007. Ethical decision-making by consumers: The roles of product harm and consumer vulnerability. *Journal of Business Ethics*, 70, 247.
Jongbloed, L. & Crichton, A. 1990. A new definition of disability: Implications for rehabilitation practice and social policy. *Canadian Journal of Occupational Therapy*, 57, 32–38.
Juškevičius, J. & Rudzinskas, A. 2014. Civilinės atsakomybės už netinkamą asmens sveikatos priežiūros paslaugų teikimą taikymo Lietuvoje ir Italijoje ypatumai. *Jurisprudencija*, 12, 73–81.
Kaufman-Scarborough, C. 1998. Retailers' perceptions of the Americans with Disabilities Act: Suggestions for low-cost, high-impact accommodations for disabled shoppers. *The Journal of Consumer Marketing*, 15, 94–110.
Kaufman-Scarborough, C. 1999. Reasonable access for mobility-disabled persons is more than widening the door. *Journal of Retailing*, 75, 479–508.
Kaufman-Scarborough, C. 2001. Sharing the experience of mobility-disabled consumers: Building understanding through the use of ethnographic research methods. *Journal of Contemporary Ethnography*, 30, 430–464.
Keates, S. & Clarkson, J. 2004. *Countering design exclusion. An introduction to inclusive design*, London, Springer-Verlag.
Keates, S. & Clarkson, P. J. 2003. Countering design exclusion: Bridging the gap between usability and accessibility. *Universal Access in the Information Society*, 2, 215–225.

Keates, S., Clarkson, P. J., Harrison, L.-A. & Robinson, P. 2000. Towards a practical inclusive design approach. *The 2000 Conference on Universal Usability*, Arlington, ACM.

Kim, M., Vogt, C. A. & Knutson, B. J. 2013. Relationships among customer satisfaction, delight, and loyalty in the hospitality industry. *Journal of Hospitality & Tourism Research*, 39, 170–197.

Kingdom, P. O. T. U. 1995. *Disability Discrimination Act*, London, Parliament of the United Kingdom.

Kingman, D. 2012. *Spending power across the generations*, London, Intergenerational Foundation.

Kitchin, R. O. B. 1998. 'Out of place', 'Knowing one's place': Space, power and the exclusion of disabled people. *Disability & Society*, 13, 343–356.

Kivetz, R. & Simonson, I. 2000. The effects of incomplete information on consumer choice. *Journal of Marketing Research*, 37, 427–448.

Klee, E. 1985. *Euthanasie im NS-Staat: Die Vernichtung lebensunwerten Lebens*, Frankfurt am Main, Fischer Taschenbuch Verlag.

Klein, J. T. 1996. *Crossing boundaries: Knowledge, disciplinarities, and interdisciplinarities*, Charlottesville, University of Virginia Press.

Kodner, L. D. 2003. Consumer-directed services: Lessons and implications for integrated systems of care. *International Journal of Integrated Care*, 3, 1–7.

Kung, S. P. & Taylor, P. 2014. The use of public sports facilities by the disabled in England. *Sport Management Review*, 17, 8–22.

Langley, J., Janson, R., Wearn, J. & Yoxall, A. 2005. 'Inclusive' design for containers: Improving openability. *Packaging Technology and Science*, 18, 285–293.

Lassk, F. G., Ingram, T. N., Kraus, F. & DI Mascio, R. 2012. The future of sales training: Challenges and related research questions. *Journal of Personal Selling & Sales Management*, 32, 141–154.

Lay, J. & Mol, A. 2002. *Complexities: Social studies of knowledge practices*, Durham, Duke University Press.

Legrand, J. 1991. Quasi-markets and social policy. *The Economic Journal*, 101, 1256–1267.

Legrand, J. 1998. *Learning from the NHS internal market: A review of the evidence*, London, King's Fund.

Leichsenring, K. 2003. *Providing integrated health and social care for older persons - a European overview*, Wien, European Centre for Social Welfare Policy and Research.

Lifton, R. J. 2000. *The nazi doctors: Medical killing and the psychology of genocide*, New York, Basic Books.

Lingle, J. H. & Ostrom, T. M. 1979. Retrieval selectivity in memory-based impression judgments. *Journal of Personality and Social Psychology*, 37, 180–194.

Linker, B. 2011. *War's waste: Rehabilitation in world war in America*, Chicago, The University of Chicago Press.

Litman, T. 2008. *Evaluating accessibility for transportation planning*, Victoria, Victoria Transport Policy Institute.

Littlechild, R. 2009. *Direct payments and personal budgets: putting personalisation into practice*, Bristol, The Polity Press.

López-De-Ipiña, D., Lorido, T. & López, U. 2011. Blindshopping: Enabling accessible shopping for visually impaired people through mobile technologies. *In:* Abdulrazak, B., Giroux, S., Bouchard, B., Pigot, H. & Mokhtari, M. (eds.) *Toward useful services for elderly and people with disabilities*, Berlin, Springer.

Ludke, R. L. & Levitz, G. S. 1983. Referring physicians: The forgotten market. *Health Management Review*, 8, 13–22.
Macchiette, B. & Roy, A. 1994. Sensitive groups and social issues: Are you marketing correct? *Journal of Consumer Marketing*, 11, 55–64.
MacDonald, N. M., Majumder, R. K. & Bua-Iam, P. 1994. Apparel acquisition for consumers with disabilities: Purchasing practices and barriers to shopping. *Clothing and Textiles Research Journal*, 12, 38–45.
Mace, R. 1988. *Universal design: Housing for the lifespan of all people*, Rockville, US Department of Housing and Urban Development.
Mace, R. L. 1998. Universal design in housing. *Assistive Technology*, 10, 21–28.
Macstravic, S. 1989. Market and market segment portfolio assessment for hospitals. *Health Management Review*, 14, 25–32.
Mangleburg, T. F., Doney, P. M. & Bristol, T. 2004. Shopping with friends and teens' susceptibility to peer influence. *Journal of Retailing*, 80, 101–116.
Mangum, S. R. 1998. Effective constrained illumination of three-dimensional, light-sensitive objects. *Journal of the Illuminating Engineering Society*, 27, 115–131.
Mansfield, P. M. & Pinto, M. B. 2008. Consumer vulnerability and credit card knowledge among developmentally disabled citizens. *Journal of Consumer Affairs*, 42, 425–438.
Marcos, T. 2011. *Accessibility in the built environment*, Brussels, European Committee for Standardization.
Martin, W. B. 1987. A new approach to the understanding and teaching of service behaviour. *Hospitality Education and Research Journal*, 2, 255–262.
Masuwa-Morgan, K. R. & Burrell, P. 2004. Justification of the need for an ontology for accessibility requirements (Theoretic framework). *Interacting with Computers*, 16, 523–555.
Matthews, M. H. & Vujakovic, P. 1995. Private worlds and public places: Mapping the environmental values of wheelchair users. *Environment and Planning A*, 27, 1069–1083.
Mažionienė, A., Valeckienė, D., Mažionytė, I., Beržinytė, D., Aleksandravičiūtė, T., Bliudžiutė, D., Razmutė, R. & Zakarauskaitė, K. 2011. *Ageing in Lithuania*, Klaipėda, Klaipėdos Valstybinė Kolegija.
Mehrabian, A. & Russell, J. A. 1974. *An approach to environmental psychology*, Cambridge, The MIT Press.
Mencap. 2007. *Death by indifference report*, London, Mencap.
Menguc, B., Auh, S. & Uslu, A. 2013. Customer knowledge creation capability and performance in sales teams. *Journal of the Academy of Marketing Science*, 41, 19–39.
Menon, K. & Dubé, L. 2000. Ensuring greater satisfaction by engineering salesperson response to customer emotions. *Journal of Retailing*, 76, 285–307.
Metz, K. 2013. *How deaf and hard of hearing adults are affected by the current state of real estate*. MA thesis, Rochester Institute of Technology.
Mobility, C. n.d. *Customized Wheelchairs* [Online]. Muskegon. Available: www.customizedmobility.com/Custom_Made_Wheelchairs.html [Accessed 15/04/2012].
Mockford, C., Staniszewska, S., Griffiths, F. & Herron-Marx, S. 2012. The impact of patient and public involvement on UK NHS health care: A systematic review. *International Journal for Quality in Health Care*, 24, 28–38.
Mostert, M. P. 2002. Useless eaters: Disability as genocidal marker in Nazi Germany. *The Journal of Special Education*, 36, 157–170.

Muller, M. J. & Kuhn, S. 1993. Participatory design. *Communication of the ACM*, 36, 24–28.

Nelson, E. & Ellison, S. 2005. *In a shift, marketers beef up ad spending inside stores* [Online]. [Accessed 05/09/2014].

Nelson, P. 1970. Information and consumer behavior. *Journal of Political Economy*, 78, 311–329.

Nemeth, C. & Del Rogers, J. 1981. *Analysis of the consumer needs of disabled persons*, California, San Diego County Department of Education.

Neufeldt, A. H. 1995. Empirical dimensions of discrimination against disabled people. *Health and Human Rights*, 1(2), 174–189.

Newell, A. F. & Gregor, P. 2000. 'User sensitive inclusive design': In search of a new paradigm. *Proceedings on the 2000 conference on Universal Usability*, Arlington, Virginia, USA, 39–44.

Norman, D. A. & Draper, S. W. 1986. *User centered system design. Design: New perspectives on human-computer interaction*, New Jersey, Lawrence Erlbaum Associates.

Norris, P. 2001. Breaking the barriers: Positive discrimination policies for women. In: *Has Liberalism Failed Women?* Palgrave Macmillan, New York, 89–110.

Nussbaum, M. 2003. Capabilities as fundamental entitlements: SEN and social justice. *Feminist Economics*, 9, 33–59.

Nussbaumer, L. L. 2012. *Inclusive design: A universal need*, New York, Fairchild Books.

Office for Disability Issues 2010. *2012 legacy for disabled people: Inclusive and accessible business. Improving messages to SMEs: The case for the disabled customer*, London, BISS.

Oliver, M. 1990. *The politics of disablement*, New York, Palgrave Macmillan.

Oliver, M. & Sapey, B. 2006. *Social work with disabled people*, London, Palgrave Macmillan.

Osborn, D. P., Horsfall, L., Hassiotis, A., Petersen, I., Walters, K. & Nazareth, I. 2012. Access to cancer screening in people with learning disabilities in the UK: Cohort study in the health improvement network, a primary care research database. *Plos One*, 7, 1–10.

Otnes, C. & Mcgrath, M. A. 2001. Perceptions and realities of male shopping behavior. *Journal of Retailing*, 77, 111–137.

Otterbring, T., Wästlund, E., Gustafsson, A. & Shams, P. 2014. Vision (im)possible? The effects of in-store signage on customers' visual attention. *Journal of Retailing and Consumer Services*, 21, 676–684.

Parent, S. & Shevell, M. 1998. The 'First to perish': Child euthanasia in the Third Reich. *Archives of Pediatrics & Adolescent Medicine*, 152, 79–86.

Parette, P. & Scherer, M. 2004. Assistive technology use and stigma. *Education and Training in Developmental Disabilities*, 39, 217–226.

Parker, J. R. & Lehmann, D. R. 2011. When shelf-based scarcity impacts consumer preferences. *Journal of Retailing*, 87, 142–155.

Passini, R. 1996. Wayfinding design: Logic, application and some thoughts on universality. *Design Studies*, 17, 319–331.

Peck, J. & Childers, T. L. 2003. To have and to hold: The influence of haptic information on product judgments. *Journal of Marketing*, 67, 35–48.

Peñaloza, L. 1995. Immigrant consumers: Marketing and public policy considerations in the global economy. *Journal of Public Policy & Marketing*, 14, 83–94.

Persad, U., Langdon, P. & Clarkson, J. 2007. Characterising user capabilities to support inclusive design evaluation. *Universal Access in the Information Society*, 6, 119–135.

Peterson, R. A. & Merino, M. C. 2003. Consumer information search behavior and the internet. *Psychology and Marketing*, 20, 99–121.

Petrauskienė, A. & Zabėlienė, V. 2014. Socialinis darbas pirminėje psichikos sveikatos priežiūros institucijoje: Paslaugų kokybės aspektas. *Socialinis Darbas/ Social Work*, 10, 279–288.

Petrie, H. & Kheir, O. 2007. The relationship between accessibility and usability of websites. *Proceedings of the SIGCHI Conference on Human Factors in Computing Systems,* San Jose, California, USA, ACM, 397–406.

Pirie, G. H. 1979. Measuring accessibility: A review and proposal. *Environment and Planning A*, 11, 299–312.

Polat, F. 2011. Inclusion in education: A step towards social justice. *International Journal of Educational Development*, 31, 50–58.

Power, C., Freire, A., Petrie, H. & Swallow, D. 2012. Guidelines are only half of the story: Accessibility problems encountered by blind users on the web. *Proceedings of the SIGCHI Conference on Human Factors in Computing Systems,* Austin, Texas, USA, 433–442.

Price, L. L., Arnould, E. J. & Deibler, S. L. 1995. Consumers' emotional responses to service encounters: The influence of the service provider. *International Journal of Service Industry Management*, 6, 34–63.

Priestley, M. 1997. The origins of a legislative disability category in England: A speculative history. *Disability studies quarterly*, 17, 87–94.

Priestley, M., Jolly, D., Pearson, C., Riddell, S., Barnes, C. & Mercer, G. 2007. Direct payments and disabled people in the UK: Supply, demand and devolution. *British Journal of Social Work*, 37, 1189–1204.

Proctor, R. N. 1988. *Racial hygiene. Medicine under the nazis,* London, Harvard University Press.

Propper, C. 1996. Market structure and prices: The responses of hospitals in the UK National Health Service to competition. *Journal of Public Economics*, 61, 307–335.

Propper, C., Burgess, S. & Green, K. 2004. Does competition between hospitals improve the quality of care? Hospital death rates and the NHS internal market. *Journal of Public Economics*, 88, 1247–1272.

Quart, A. 2008. *Branded: The buying and selling of teenagers,* New York, Basic Books.

Ravaud, J.-F., Madiot, B. & Ville, I. 1992. Discrimination towards disabled people seeking employment. *Social Science & Medicine*, 35, 951–958.

Ray, N. M. & Ryder, M. E. 2003. 'Ebilities' tourism: An exploratory discussion of the travel needs and motivations of the mobility disabled. *Tourism Management*, 24, 57–72.

Reekie, G. 1992. Changes in the adamless Eden: The spatial and sexual transformation of a Brisbane department store. *In:* Shields, R. (ed.) *Lifestyle shopping: The subject of consumption,* London, Routledge.

Reisinger, Y. & Waryszak, R. Z. 1994. Tourists' perceptions of service in shops: Japanese tourists in Australia. *International Journal of Retail & Distribution Management*, 22, 20–28.

Riddell, S., Pearson, C., Jolly, D., Barnes, C., Priestley, M. & Mercer, G. 2005. The development of direct payments in the UK: Implications for social justice. *Social Policy and Society*, 4, 75–85.

Ringold, D. J. 1995. Social criticisms of target marketing: Process or product? *American Behavioral Scientist*, 38, 578–592.

Ritzer, G. 2004. *The McDonaldization of society* London, Pine Forge.

Robert, G. 1995. *The Eye of the Beholder. Deformity and Disability in the Graeco-Roman World*, London, Duckworth.

Roman, S., Ruiz, S. & Munuera, J. L. 2002. The effects of sales training on sales force activity. *European Journal of Marketing*, 36, 1344–1366.

Rosewarne, L. 2005. The men's gallery: Outdoor advertising and public space: Gender, fear, and feminism. *Women's Studies International Forum*, 28, 67–78.

Rutherford, B. 2012. Building buyer commitment to the salesperson. *Journal of Business Research*, 65, 960–967.

Rutherford, T. 2012. Population ageing: Statistics. *In:* HC (ed.). SN/SG/3228. Social and General Statistics.

Rutter, D., Manley, C., Weaver, T., Crawford, M. J. & Fulop, N. 2004. Patients or partners? Case studies of user involvement in the planning and delivery of adult mental health services in London. *Social Science & Medicine*, 58, 1973–1984.

Ryan, E. B., Anas, A. P. & Gruneir, A. J. S. 2006. Evaluations of overhelping and underhelping communication: Do old age and physical disability matter? *Journal of Language and Social Psychology*, 25, 97–107.

Ryu, K. & Jang, S. S. 2007. The effect of environmental perceptions on behavioral intentions through emotions: The case of upscale restaurants. *Journal of Hospitality & Tourism Research*, 31, 56–72.

Sanders, E. B.-N. 2002. From user-centered to participatory design approaches. *In:* Frascara, J. (ed.) *Design and the social sciences: Making connections,* London, Taylor and Francis.

Schmöcker, J.-D., Quddus, M. A., Noland, R. B. & Bell, M. G. H. 2008. Mode choice of older and disabled people: A case study of shopping trips in London. *Journal of Transport Geography*, 16, 257–267.

Scourfield, P. 2005. Implementing the Community Care (Direct Payments) Act: Will the supply of personal assistants meet the demand and at what price? *Journal of Social Policy*, 34, 469–488.

Shakespeare, T., Iezzoni, L. I. & Groce, N. E. 2009. Disability and the training of health professionals. *The Lancet*, 374, 1815–1816.

Sharp, H., Rogers, Y. & Preece, J. 2002. *Interaction design: Beyond human-computer interaction*, New York, John Wiley & Sons.

Silver, M. G. 2004. Eugenics and compulsory sterilization laws: Providing redress for the victims of a shamefully era in United States history. *George Washington Law Review*, 72, 862–893.

Sime, J. D. 1991. Accidents and disasters: Vulnerability in the built environment. *Safety Science*, 14, 109–124.

Simmons, C. J. & Lynch Jr, J. G. 1991. Inference effects without inference making? Effects of missing information on discounting and use of presented information. *Journal of Consumer Research*, 17, 477–491.

Skipper, J. K. & Leonard, R. C. 1965. *Social interaction and patient care*, Philadelphia, Lippincott.

Sloan, D. & Kelly, B. 2011. Web accessibility metrics for a post digital world. *RDWG Symposium on Website Accessibility Metrics.* Online.

Smith, N. C. & Cooper-Martin, E. 1997. Ethics and target marketing: The role of product harm and consumer vulnerability. *Journal of Marketing*, 61, 1–20.

Soltani, S. H. K., Sham, M., Awang, M. & Yaman, R. 2012. Accessibility for disabled in public transportation terminal. *Procedia - Social and Behavioral Sciences*, 35, 89–96.

Stahl, A. 1996. Adaptation of the whole travel chain: Benefits and attitudes. *The Association for European Transport Conference.*

Ståhl, S. & Iwarsson, A. 1999. Traffic engineering and occupational therapy: A collaborative approach for future directions. *Scandinavian Journal of Occupational Therapy*, 6, 21–28.

Stainton, T. & Boyce, S. 2004. 'Have got my life back': Users' experience of direct payments. *Disability & Society*, 19, 443–454.

Statistics, O. F. N. 2010. *Older people's day 2010*, London. Available: http://webarchive.nationalarchives.gov.uk/20160107141117/http://www.ons.gov.uk/ons/rel/mortality-ageing/focus-on-older-people/older-people-s-day-2011/stb-opd-2011.html [Accessed 21/07/2013].

Steiner, R. L. 2001. Manufacturers' brand advertising and how it influences manufacturers' and retailers' margins. *Journal of Marketing Communications*, 7, 35–46.

Steinfeld, E. & Maisel, J. 2012. *Universal design: Creating inclusive environments*, New Jersey, John Wiley & Sons.

Stiker, H.-J. 2009. *A history of disability*, Michigan, The University of Michigan Press.

Summers, T. A. & Hebert, P. R. 2001. Shedding some light on store atmospherics: Influence of illumination on consumer behavior. *Journal of Business Research*, 54, 145–150.

Szymanski, D. M. 1988. Determinants of selling effectiveness: The importance of declarative knowledge to the personal selling concept. *Journal of Marketing*, 52, 64–77.

Tait, L. & Lester, H. 2005. Encouraging user involvement in mental health services. *Advances in Psychiatric Treatment*, 11, 168–175.

Tamura, K. 2004. The handicapped in Germany: Changing attitudes, changing times. *Verandi* [Online], Fall 2002- Spring 2004. Available: www.sunywcc.edu/cms/wp-content/uploads/2012/04/verdandi_X.pdf#page=57 [Accessed 02/02/2013].

Teller, C. & Dennis, C. 2011. The effect of ambient scent on consumers' perception, emotions and behaviour: A critical review. *Journal of Marketing Management*, 28, 14–36.

Tendai, M. & Crispen, C. 2009. In-store shopping environment and impulsive buying. *African Journal of Marketing Management*, 1, 102–108.

Thomas, F. P., Beres, A. & Shevell, M. I. 2006. 'A cold wind coming': Heinrich gross and child euthanasia in Vienna. *Journal of Child Neurology*, 21, 342–348.

Till, J. 2005. Lost judgment. *In:* Harder, E. (ed.) *Writings on architectural education*, Leuven, EAAE, 164–181.

Tisdale, S. 1996. Is there such a thing as irresponsible art. *Cardozo Studies in Law and Literature*, 8, 253–257.

Torres, I. M., Summers, T. A. & Belleau, B. D. 2001. Men's shopping satisfaction and store preferences. *Journal of Retailing and Consumer Services*, 8, 205–212.

Tregaskis, C. 2003. Towards inclusive practice: An insider perspective on leisure provision for disabled people. *Managing Leisure*, 8, 28–40.

Turley, L. W. & Chebat, J.-C. 2002. Linking retail strategy, atmospheric design and shopping behaviour. *Journal of Marketing Management*, 18, 125–144.

Turley, L. W. & Milliman, R. E. 2000. Atmospheric effects on shopping behavior: A review of the experimental evidence. *Journal of Business Research*, 49, 193–211.

Ubido, J., Huntington, J. & Warburton, D. 2002. Inequalities in access to healthcare faced by women who are deaf. *Health & Social Care in the Community*, 10, 247–253.

Ulinchy, G. R. 1994. Marketing brain injury rehabilitation services: Toward a more ethical approach. *Journal of Head Trauma Rehabilitation*, 9, 73–76.

United States Congress. 1990. *American Disability Act*, Washington, United States Congress.

Valenzuela, A. & Raghubir, P. 2009. Position-based beliefs: The center-stage effect. *Journal of Consumer Psychology*, 19, 185–196.

Valenzuela, A., Raghubir, P. & Mitakakis, C. 2013. Shelf space schemas: Myth or reality? *Journal of Business Research*, 66, 881–888.

Van Mil, J. F. 2005. Pharmaceutical care in community pharmacy: Practice and research in the Netherlands. *Annals of Pharmacotherapy*, 39, 1720–1725.

Vanderheiden, G. 1996. *Universal design... What it is and what it isn't*, Madison, Trace Research and Development Centre.

Vanderheiden, G. C. 1998. Universal design and assistive technology in communication and information technologies: Alternatives or complements? *Assistive Technology*, 10, 29–36.

Velasco, C. A. & Verelst, T. 2001. Raising awareness among designers accessibility issues. *ACM SIGCAPH Computers and the Physically Handicapped*, 69, 8–13.

Vida, I., Obadia, C. & Kunz, M. 2007. The effects of background music on consumer responses in a high-end supermarket. *The International Review of Retail, Distribution and Consumer Research*, 17, 469–482.

Vijayasarathy, L. R. & Jones, J. M. 2000. Print and Internet catalog shopping: Assessing attitudes and intentions. *Internet Research*, 10, 191–202.

Vlahogiannis, N. 2003. Disabling bodies. *In:* Montserrat, D. (ed.) *Changing bodies, changing meanings. Studies on the human body in antiquity*, London, Routledge.

Waddington, L. 2009. A disabled market: Free movement of goods and services in the EU and disability accessibility. *European Law Journal*, 15, 575–598.

Walsh, G. & Mitchell, V.-W. 2010. The effect of consumer confusion proneness on word of mouth, trust, and customer satisfaction. *European Journal of Marketing*, 44, 838–859.

Walsh, G., Shiu, E., Hassan, L. M., Michaelidou, N. & Beatty, S. E. 2011. Emotions, store-environmental cues, store-choice criteria, and marketing outcomes. *Journal of Business Research*, 64, 737–744.

Weisman, L. 1994. *Discrimination by design: A feminist critique of the man-made environment*, Urbana, University of Illinois Press.

WHO. 2011. *World report on disability*, Geneva, World Health Organisation, The World Bank.

Wirtz, J. & Bateson, J. E. G. 1999. Consumer satisfaction with services: Integrating the environment perspective in services marketing into the traditional disconfirmation paradigm. *Journal of Business Research*, 44, 55–66.

Wislon, A. M. 1998. The use of mystery shopping in the measurement of service delivery. *The Service Industries Journal*, 18, 148–163.

Witkowski, T. H. 1999. The early development of purchasing roles in the American household, 1750 to 1840. *Journal of Macromarketing*, 19, 104–114.

Yang, M.-H. & Chen, W.-C. 1999. A study on shelf space allocation and management. *International Journal of Production Economics*, 60–61, 309–317.

Yuksel, A. 2004. Shopping experience evaluation: A case of domestic and international visitors. *Tourism Management*, 25, 751–759.

Zola, I. K. 1977. Healthism and disabling medicalization. *In:* Illich, I., Zolla, I. K., Mcknight, J., Caplan, J. & Shaiken, H. (eds.) *Disabling Professions,* New York, Marion Boyars.

2 Accessibility in the EU markets

The emergence of the discourse on accessibility and rights calls for customer equality and an accessible mainstream private market. Via social claims of public movements and the development of public policy in the area of accessibility and rights, the new discourse brings the private market into the public sphere. While traditionally governments are perceived as key players shaping public debate (Devetak and Higgott, 1999), they are often incapable to independently deal with challenges brought by globalisation, global economic integration and the necessity to develop public policy outside an economic and financial vacuum. Indeed, being able to offer different skills and knowledge, broader perspectives and capital, business is a welcome actor in shaping the public domain (Hodes, 2001). However, as suggested by Hodes (2001) and Drache (2001), business' role in public discourse and in becoming a part of the solution depends on its relation with the state. Nevertheless, the capitalistic nature of the market and its common prioritisation of profit over equal rights (Marx, 1893) should not be ignored and should be considered when developing policies and foreseeing potential scenarios for its implementation.

This chapter, therefore, demonstrates how law and public policy frames public discourse on private market as they relate to disabled customers in the European Union (EU) and so provides a platform for private entities to make the shopping process accessible. It is suggested that the new public discourse aims to reconstruct disabled people from 'vulnerable' consumers to customers. However, the position towards the issue and markets accessibility differs at global, regional and national levels, and certain tensions between these policy discourses are present.

The discussion starts by looking at the global level and exploring concepts entrenched in the Convention on the Rights of Persons with Disabilities (CRPD). They are treated as a 'moral compass' (Kayess and French, 2008, Quinn, 2009b), guiding the discussion. This is followed by an exploration of how the European single market policy system regionally constructs the position regarding accessibility and customer participation. The attention is drawn on legal construction of disabled people as vulnerable EU market customers. This is followed by a discussion on accessibility of customer information and retail premises. This chapter concludes by providing a short overview of how global and regional concepts and positions are integrated into national policies in Lithuania and the United Kingdom. It is suggested that since the adoption of the CRPD, the EU and its Member States (MSs) have been experiencing a transmutation that introduces challenges and potentials in shaping business' positions and disabled customers' participation.

While academic disability literature usually focuses on social policies and so spotlights the 'social dimension' of the EU, the following discussion directly addresses the single market dimension. It aims to untangle some of the processes that may play a part in creating a more accessible and equal EU single market but yet have not received academic attention.

Accessibility in the global context

The CRPD is the first human rights Treaty adopted in the 21st century. Agreed and adopted by the UN General Assembly in 2006, the Convention and the Optional Protocol were open for signature on 30 March 2007. As of July 2018, the number of signatories amounts to 187 for the Convention and 119 for the Optional Protocol. The EU and the majority of the European states have signed the Convention, and 28 EU MSs have ratified it. Article 1 of the Convention notes that the purpose of the Treaty is 'to promote, protect and ensure the full and equal enjoyment of all human rights and fundamental freedoms by all persons with disabilities, and to promote respect for their inherent dignity'. Consequently, in its 50 articles, the Convention covers a broad range of rights. Quinn (2009a) clustered them into dignity, autonomy, equality, solidarity and access and participation rights. The Convention does not introduce new or special rights. It elaborates and clarifies existing human rights and translates them in a manner that addresses situations and needs of people with impairments (Ferri, 2010, Kayess and French, 2008). The Convention combines and blends civil and political rights with economic, social and cultural rights within the whole document and its individual articles (Kayess and French, 2008, Quinn, 2009a). In the light of article 4.2, the MSs are obliged to progressively achieve the same.

The Treaty is often seen as the embodiment of 'paradigm shift' from a social welfare, charity and individual model of disability to a human rights–based approach (Kayess and French, 2008). According to Dyson (2007), the 'paradigm shift' emphasises the partnership between governments and civil society, relegates the central role to disabled people's organisations (DPOs) in the CRPD negotiation and implementation processes and entrenches the principle of 'nothing about us without us'. Kayess and French (2008:4) represent a commonly used view that 'the CRPD is regarded as having finally empowered the "world's largest minority" to claim their rights, and to participate in international and national affairs on an equal basis with others who have achieved specific treaty recognition and protection'. The Committee on the Rights of Persons with Disabilities (Committee) in its General Comment No. 2 on Accessibility (General Comment; 2014) entrenches that the main precondition for exercising the rights, and fully and equally participating in society, is accessibility. With this in mind, the following section addresses the way accessibility is conceptualised in the CRPD. For the purpose of this book, light is shed on disabled people's participation in the mainstream private market.

Accessibility and the CRPD

Accessibility is one of the CRPD principles (art.3f) and is closely linked with other global human rights instruments. For instance, in the General Comment, the Committee (2014) notes that article 13 of the Universal Declaration of Human Rights (1948) and article 12 of the International Covenant on Civil and Political Rights (1966) can be linked with the CRPD's reference to accessible physical environment and public transport. Likewise, access to information and communication can be linked to article 19 and article 19 (par.2) of the same instruments, respectively. The two documents emphasise every citizen's right to have *access to* and link it to equality and non-discrimination. While CRPD also positions *access to* as a right, it takes it further and introduces the concept *accessibility of*, which in 1993 was addressed in the Standard Rules on Equalization of Opportunities for Persons with Disabilities (1993). In other words, the Convention recognises accessibility as 'a vital precondition for persons with disabilities to participate fully and equally in society and enjoy effectively all their human rights and fundamental freedoms' (Committee, 2014:4).

The CRPD does not define accessibility either in the definition article (art.2) or in article 9, outlining State Parties' (SPs') responsibilities regarding the issue. The same practice is observed in the General Comment of the Committee (2014). Identified as a precondition for independent life (art.19), the principle is intertwined throughout the Treaty. To begin with, article 3 characterises accessibility as a general or normative principle which, according to Lord (2010:6), serves as a filter 'through which discrete pieces of existing law should be run to assess conformity with the object and purpose of the CRPD' and guides the implementation of substantive rights. Accessibility as a general principle appears in a preamble paragraph, in two general application articles (3 and 9), articles dealing with substantive rights (21) and implementation measures (31, 32 and 49). Together with respect for inherent dignity and individual autonomy, non-discrimination, full and effective participation in society, equality and respect for disabled children rights, the principle contributes to the provision of what is commonly called as a 'moral principle' of the CRPD (Kayess and French, 2008, Quinn, 2009b). Hence, while Lord (2010) uniforms *access to* and *accessibility of* and positions these as a substantive right and a general principle, respectively, this book echoes the position established by the Committee (2014). It perceives *access to* as a right and *accessibility of* as a precondition for exercising substantive rights.

Article 9.1 outlines SPs' obligations regarding accessibility. It requires taking

> appropriate measures to ensure to persons with disabilities access on an equal basis with others, to physical environment, to transportation, to information and communications, including information and communications technologies and systems, and to other facilities and services open or provided to the public.

Aiming to ensure these rights to disabled citizens, SPs are required to remove barriers and provide appropriate measures both in rural and urban areas, which encompass a principle of geographic equity (Kayess and French, 2008). While the initial report of the United Kingdom on CRPD article 9 (2013) demonstrates that provisions for accessibility are heavily regulated by the Equality Act (EA) and are founded on the principle of exercising human rights, the Lithuanian initial report (2014) suggests the dominance of the individual model approach. Here, accessibility is premised on accommodating 'the specific needs of the disabled' and is often linked to the 'acceptable' rather than equal provisions (Committee, 2014).

With regard to barriers removal, article 9 demonstrates awareness of different forms of obstacles impinging on equality (Ferri, 2010) and autonomy (Mégret, 2008) and interrupting human rights (Lord, 2010). While these obstructions are not specified (Lord, 2010), the article distinguishes the rationale of physical, institutional and attitudinal barriers and calls for cross-disability implication of rights. The Committee (2014) notes that contrary to access to newly designed artefacts, the removal of barriers is a gradual process. National governments are asked to set definite time frames, allocate adequate resources for barriers removal, prescribe responsibilities for different stakeholders, establish effective monitoring mechanisms and monitor sanctions against parties that do not follow the obligation. While the first chapter makes it clear that different barriers shape exclusion, civil society's participation in identifying these obstacles (art.4.3) is positioned as an important factor for achieving the duty (Lawson, 2010).

The CRPD goes further than barriers elimination and lays out specific measures and positive obligations that should be taken in order to ensure accessibility. With regard to accessibility of retail markets and equal customer participation, it is worth shedding light on article 9.2b that requires 'private entities that offer facilities and services that are open or provided to the public take into account all aspects of accessibility for people with disabilities'. These include developing and monitoring the implementation of minimum standards and guidelines; stakeholders' training on accessibility; providing signage in various alternative formats; providing assistance means (human and non-human); promoting access to new information and communication technologies and systems, including the Internet; and promoting design, development, production and distribution of accessible information and communication technologies and systems at an early stage and at minimum cost. While the strength of the language vary among the measures (Lord, 2010), the clear requirement to 'ensure' accessibility refers to accessibility as a justiciable right (UN Commission on Human Rights (39th sess.), 1983 in Hendricks, 2007) that can be decided by a court. The roots of the position can be traced in the requirement to 'take appropriate measures' to ensure access to 'on an equal basis with others' (art.9.1). While Lord (2010) notes that the CRPD does not outline precise conditions under which a failure to provide accessibility may produce discrimination, Lawson (2010:14) states that 'a failure to fulfil this [accessibility] obligation would result in inequality of access which might, at least in some situations, be expected to constitute discrimination on the basis of disability which States are required by Article 5 to prohibit'.

In a similar vein, Quinn (2010) notes that

> there is some elusive line beyond which the non-discrimination principle will not generate the more robust obligations contained in Article 9. Put another way, failure to have an accessible environment is clearly a form of discrimination. Using the non-discrimination tool it is possible to craft some limited positive obligations on States to undo this discrimination. But failure to achieve all the positive obligations outlined in Article 9 is probably not in itself a form of discrimination. By definition, many of these obligations will require resources and extensive systematic change – all subject to the overall obligation of progressive achievement contained in Article 4.2 with respect to socioeconomic rights. Where this line falls is very hard to say – but it does exist.

One of the stipulated measures for ensuring accessibility is to 'develop, promulgate and monitor the implementation of minimum standards and guidelines' (art.9.2a). Recalling the concerns regarding accessibility standards raised in the first chapter, it is worth focusing on the Committee's call to mainstream different accessibility standards and guidelines. According to the Committee, such practice may potentially lead to the generalisation of universal design (UD) (Committee, 2014), which means matching user profile and different utilisation of the product (Burzgali and Emiliani, 2013). The CRPD notes that the standards have to be in accordance with other SPs' standards and developed in close consultation with disabled people, DPOs and international bodies. In addition, article 9.2e addresses provision of different forms of 'live assistance and intermediaries' in order to facilitate access. Hence, it requires to go further than technical and established design standards (Lawson, 2010). In other words, the CRPD recognises that technical features do not ensure accessibility and even if a shop meets technical requirements and minimum standards, personal assistance, for example, in gauging information about product or changes in product layout might be essential for providing access for customer participation and service quality.

Accessibility in the EU markets 75

Accessibility is also related with availability (Halvorsen, 2010, Lord, 2010), which throughout the Convention is addressed in the context of an obligation to provide universally designed goods and services (art.4f), information and communication technologies (art.4g), community services for independent living (art.19c) and assistive devices (art.20b), among others. Halvorsen (2010) links availability with actual product presence in the market and its affordability. In addition to technical product specification, light is shed on distribution of economic resources (Lord, 2010) and suggests that disabled people may be prevented from using accessible products not only because of technical inaccessibility but because of high cost. While this reflects one of the CRPD's goals to blend civil and political rights with economic, social and cultural rights (Charitakis, 2013, Kayess and French, 2008), it also mirrors the economic principle of accessibility established in the General Comment 14 of the Committee on Economic, Social and Cultural Rights (2000) that requires equity to be the fundamental factor determining payment for health-care services.

The Convention goes further and identifies UD as a next step of accessibility. Although the concept is not explicitly articulated in article 9, it can be traced in 'implementation of minimum standards and guidelines' (9.2) and must be read in junction with general obligations outlined in article 4.1.f 'to undertake or promote research and development of universally designed goods, services, equipment and facilities' and 'to promote universal design in the development of standards and guidelines'. Article 2 defines UD as 'design of products, environments, programmes and services to be usable by all people, to the greatest extent possible, without the need for adaptation or specialised design'. In a similar vein, the General Comment notes that

> strict application of universal design to all new goods, products, facilities, technologies and services should ensure full, equal and unrestricted access for all potential consumers, including persons with disabilities, in a way that takes full account of their inherent dignity and diversity.
> (Committee, 2014:5)

In addition, echoing the position hold by UD proponents (Chapter 1), article 2 of the Convention and the Committee notes that UD 'shall not exclude assistive devices, technical aids or live assistance where this is needed', and the application of UD 'makes society accessible for all human beings' (Committee, 2014:5).

When goods and services are inaccessible or cannot be reached via UD, reasonable accommodation should be provided. Article 2 defines this as

> necessary and appropriate modification and adjustments not imposing a disproportionate or undue burden, where needed in a particular case, to ensure to persons with disabilities the enjoyment or exercise on an equal basis with others of all human rights and fundamental freedoms.

76 Accessibility in the EU markets

The Committee (2014) notes that reasonable accommodation provision is an *ex nunc* duty and should be provided from the moment an individual needs and requires it. Although the obligation raises some tensions and discussions, for the purpose of this book, it is important to shed light on three of them. First, the essence of reasonable accommodation demands that the 'consideration be given to identifying the most effective means of removing the relevant disadvantage for the particular person in question' (Lawson, 2010:13). In the context of shops, alternative formats of information about products should be considered as reasonable accommodation means that are identified through dialogue rather than decided in advance and based on retailers' assumptions (Lawson, 2010). Second, while reasonable accommodation is framed within the principle of 'disproportionate or undue burden' (art.2), it should not be associated explicitly with financial cost, as it may include factors varying from situation to situation, and it often brings benefits instead of encumbrances to burden-bearers (Kayess and French, 2008). Third, the level of the 'burden' should be sensitive to each stakeholder (Lawson, 2010), and if needed and agreed, sensible interventions in the market could be undertaken (Lord, 2010) by the state. In the last-mentioned case,

> reasonable accommodation can be used as a means of ensuring accessibility [...] in a particular situation. [And should] seek to achieve individual justice in the sense that non-discrimination or equality is ensured, taking the dignity, autonomy and choices of the individual into account.
> (Committee, 2014:8)

The Convention and the Committee acknowledge that accessibility is often viewed only as an accessible built environment. Aiming to ensure accessibility, availability and affordability of accessible environments and artefacts, SP 'should strive systematically and continuously to raise awareness about accessibility among all relevant stakeholders' (Committee, 2014:10). Article 9.2c requires providing training on 'accessibility issues facing persons with disabilities'. While the General Comment notes that 'training should be provided not only to those designing goods, services and products, but also to those who actually produce them', relevant training should also be provided to actors directly or indirectly participating in any stage of the production process and customer service. This is important because, as the discussion in forthcoming chapters suggests, limited professionals', who operate in any of the shopping stages, knowledge or awareness may prevent disabled customers from acquiring accessible products.

The obligation of accessibility is applied not only to public but also to 'private entities that offer facilities and services open or provided to the public' (art.9.2b). As identified by the Committee (2014:4), 'the focus is no longer on legal personality and the public or private nature of those, who own buildings, transport infrastructure, vehicles, information and communication services. Indeed, their provision to the public is the key factor for being accessible'. The private sector is not seen as the only responsible party in implementing the duty. Indeed, national governments are obliged to 'take appropriate measures' and to shape a framework, within which accessibility of the private sector is ensured. In addition, while discussed concepts are applicable to private entities, the underlying principle of equality across the CRPD and especially article 9 (Ferri, 2010, Kayess and French, 2008, Lawson, 2010) suggests that the diversity of disabled customers should be expected and respected, and they should be treated on an equal basis with non-disabled market participants (Kayess and French, 2008).

With the elimination of social exclusion (Ferri, 2010) and promotion of personal autonomy (Mégret, 2008) being enshrined between the lines of the Convention, accessibility of the private market and equality of the disabled people as active market participants is established. Their portrayal as 'wasting', 'special', 'passive' or 'vulnerable' is redrawn by the Treaty into active and exercising equal rights. Furthermore, SPs are obliged to provide a legal and policy framework, within which private actors engage in the public discourse. With this in mind, the following section sheds light on the regional level. It considers the way the EU, which has signed the Convention and locates the internal market at its heart (COM (2011) 206, final), reacts to and integrates concepts of equal participation in the market and accessibility into its instruments and policies.

Accessibility in the European single market

The EU has signed the Convention on the 26 November 2009, with the concepts of equality and non-discrimination being already rooted in the Union's and MSs' laws and constitutions (Bell, 2003). Many obligations introduced by the Convention reflect and share a common core with EU competences and values (Reiss, 2012) that are linked with the four single market freedoms, which establish free movement of capital, labour, services and goods across the Union (Bellamy, 2012). Similar to the Convention that requires SPs to remove barriers preventing from equal participation in the private market, the EU

> single market is all about bringing down barriers and simplifying existing rules to enable everyone in the EU – individuals, consumers and businesses – to take the most of the opportunities offered to them by having direct access to 28 countries and 203 million people.
> (European Commission, 2014b)

In addition, in 2012, the European Commission (EC) published an initiative to publish the European Accessibility Act (EAA), aiming to improve accessibility of goods and services for the disabled EU citizens (European Commission, 2012a). However, while the initiative is premised on the equality principle and removal of economic and social barriers, it is not yet adopted and so slows down the promotion of equality and accessibility of customer participation. Meanwhile, even though the recently adopted 'Vision for the internal market for industrial products' (COM (2014) 25, final) aims to set recommendations for the legislation on the internal market for the next decade, it does not directly mention disability or accessibility.

It seems that the combination of CRPD duties and obligations and the EU's goal to create a barrier-free single market may supplement each other and shape tradition and praxis that enable EU citizens to equally exercise customer rights. However, the EU seems to be confused between barrier removal for non-disabled citizens' participation aiming to boost the economy and the removal of barriers in order to ensure accessibility of the internal markets to all citizens. These tensions are well reflected in additional laws and directives, ensuring the presence of the single market and demolishing further barriers in specific areas (European Commission, 2014a). The present section, therefore, addresses some of the contradictions in the public discourse surrounding disability, accessibility and retail customers. The discussion starts with an exploration of legal construction of disabled people as customers within the EU single market. This is followed by a discussion on customer information provision and either discriminatory or enabling practices introduced by EU instruments. Finally, requirements for accessible retail premises are discussed.

Disabled customers

The notion of a 'consumer' is separately specified in several EU instruments. The definition has been established in procedural law[1] and contract[2] and non-contractual[3] obligations law. Although the conception within the instruments does not entirely coincide, it shares a common core and identifies a consumer as (1) a natural person, (2) 'acting for purposes which are outside his trade, business, craft or profession' (Council Directive 2011/83/EC, art.1 on Consumer Rights). The EU does not have competence to act solely in the interest of protecting customers. The impact is indirect and the competence on consumer protection is linked to the single market objectives (Miller, 2011).

Seeking to promote customers' interests and to ensure a high level of their protection (Treaty on the Functioning of the European Union (TFEU), 2012, art.169), the EU has established fundamental principles of customer protection, acknowledged existing distortive practices within the private market and defined two groups of customers: 'average' and 'vulnerable'. When particular measures are applied for an 'average' customer protection, the emphasis is on market practice, which 'materially distorts or is likely to materially distort the economic behaviour with regard to the product of the average consumer whom it reaches or to whom it is addressed' (Council Directive 2005/29/EC, art.5.2b on Unfair Business Practices). In contrast, when measures established in the same instrument are applied to 'vulnerable' customers, including people with impairments, one of the identified reasons for the protection is a particular vulnerability 'to the practice or the underlying product because of their mental or physical infirmity, age or credulity' (Council Directive 2005/29/EC, art.5.3 on Unfair Business Practices). While the CRPD does not use terms such as 'customers' or 'vulnerable' and calls for accessibility of the private market in its broadest extent, the EU positions people with impairments as 'vulnerable' customers. This contradicts the equality principle enshrined in the Convention as current EU documents separate non-disabled and disabled market participants and treat impairment as one of the sources of experienced challenges in the market. Such an individual model perspective is often used in court cases as it is easier and more convenient to attribute experienced troubles to customers rather than to marketing strategies or products (Morgan et al., 1995).

Legal evaluation of customer vulnerability may include social, linguistic and cultural factors (Edward et al., 2000). However, since the interpretation of similar connotation in different MSs varies (Abbamonte, 2006, Edward et al., 2000), what is protective in one country may be misleading in another and introduce legal and practical tensions. The interlink between individual's dependency to the category of disability and customer vulnerability may lead to perceived rather than actual vulnerability (Smith and Cooper-Martin, 1997) and maintains unequal power relations between non-disabled and disabled customers. In addition, customer vulnerability assessment is founded on non-disabled customers' competencies (Edward et al., 2000) and refers to normality standards and functions (Amundson, 2005). In such a context, non-disabled individuals are provided with legal superiority in the market. In this respect, those who deviate from the 'normality' standards are devalued as equals. Hence, by introducing categories of an 'average' and 'vulnerable' consumer, the EU communicates to the public what is a 'normal' and expected, and what is an 'abnormal' and less expected participant of the EU single market, and in such a way redeploys unequal power relations and oppression to the retail domain.

Disabled people's categorisation as vulnerable customers introduces misbalance between customer protection and customer rights. While the TFEU (art.153) and especially the Council Directive 2005/29/EC on Unfair Commercial Practices require the EU to ensure a high level of customer protection and rights, disabled people's identification as 'vulnerable' put the emphasis on protection and not so much on rights. As an example, the Council Directive 2010/13/EU par.104 on Audiovisual Media Services equates disabled customers' rights assurance to the protection of minority groups and treats as equally important when seeking of the creation of an open audio-visual media service market. This suggests that while the CRPD shapes disabled people's participation in the private market around concepts of rights, equality and non-discrimination, the EU links it with protection that, if achieved, leads towards a better functioning of the single market economy.

Some changes are occurring in the policy discourse arena, the most significant being documented in the EU staff working document on Knowledge-Enhancing Aspects of Consumer Empowerment 2012–2014 (European Commission, 2012b). The instrument acknowledges that specific circumstances within the market may lead to customer vulnerability. However, a person's impairment is treated as an equally important factor. Hence, while a mild shift from customer vulnerability as an internally predefined feature towards vulnerability as a constructed state is occurring, customers with impairments are still seen as responsible agents for the difficulties they experience. In other words, despite some attempts to shift the responsibility away from an individual to sociopolitical and market causes, the document is premised on an individual model and ascribes responsibility for the performance and the results of the performance in the market to a disabled individual.

The discussed EU policies position disabled people as having low self-esteem, poor decision-making abilities and less personal control (Sanders, 2006); lead to marginalisation and exclusion; and negate their customer strengths, abilities and rights. They legally entrench the status of being 'vulnerable' and position impairment as an important factor, determining customers' position in the market. The marriage of the capitalist economy and the nature of the private market with the existing EU policy discourse separate disabled people's skills, competences and knowledge that they could use to negotiate their position and actions in the market. Positioning disabled people as important and sensitive social concern that needs protection (Baker et al., 2005) supresses their experiences, emotions, expectations and abilities (Edgar, 2006). A legally established portrayal as needing protection intrudes into everyday life, destroying and lessening individuals' meanings of life and weakening their fundamental freedoms and rights.

Information provision

The EU acknowledges the need to provide customers with information (TFEU, art.169.1). However, information provision in alternative formats is overlooked or permeated with discriminatory features. To begin with, the Council Directive 2011/83/EU art.5 on Consumer Rights states that before signing an official contract, the trader should provide the customer with information such as 'the main characteristics of the goods and services […], the identity of the trader […], the total price […] the arrangements for payment […]'. Although the instrument targets technical features of information presentation and invites national governments to introduce 'language requirements regarding the contractual information, so as to ensure that such information is easily understood by consumer', it does not address accessibility of the provided information. Likewise, the Council Directive 2001/95/EC art.16 on General Product Safety states that information about 'risks to consumer health and safety posed by products', which is available to legal authorities, should be available to the general public. While disabled people are more likely to experience risks caused by mainstream products (Department of Trade and Industry, 2000), the directive does not address presentation of the information in accessible formats.

One of the reasons that causes tensions in product and service labelling is a lack of specific agreement on how to balance information presentation needs of 'average' and 'vulnerable' customers (Waddington, 2009). Limited consensus and unestablished practice shape exclusive and discriminatory practices that, in some instances, lead the European Court to acknowledge that some customers will be misled by particular marketing practices, including provided information (Waddington, 2009). As an example, while 'small print' in contracts is usually accessible for people without vision impairments but often causes confusion, risks and financial disadvantage to customers with vision impairments (Eardley et al., 2009), the court may not treat it as a discriminatory practice. This recalls Weatherill's (2011) point about the imbalance and inequality between 'average' and 'vulnerable' customers, suggesting that the second group is 'sacrificed to the interests of self-reliant customers in deregulation, market integration, and wider choice' (Weatherill, 2011:842). Charitakis (2013) concludes that legal instruments that aim to oblige private entities to provide customers with information are not relevant for disabled people, as they do not target information provision in alternative formats. In other words, while current EU provisions address customer information, they shed light on non-disabled market players, so depriving disabled customers' right to an informed choice and decision (Hoffmann and Inderst, 2009, Prahalad and Ramaswamy, 2004).

Only the Council Directive 2004/27/EC on the Community Code Relating to Medical Products clearly requires the provision of information about publically available products in accessible formats. However, its focus is on medical products and information provision in Braille. Thus,

> The name of the medicinal product [...] must also be expressed in Braille format on the packaging. The marketing authorisation holder shall ensure that the package information leaflet is made available on request from patients' organisations in formats appropriate for the blind and partially-sighted.
>
> (art.56a)

On the one hand, the directive challenges current EU customer information concept and provision practice, as it goes further than the requirement to label products in a national language. In such a way, the instrument acknowledges that the customer segment is broader than just non-disabled people. On the other hand, it illustrates the prevailing attitude to people with impairments and associated needs. The obligation to alternatively label only medical products and the lack of similar requirements to label mainstream articles maintains a stereotypical stance that the most important goods and services for disabled people are those related with health or impairment. Furthermore, the directive focuses on information provision in Braille and so discriminates against customers who need other formats. With this in mind, it is worth focusing on Abberley's (1987:7) point that 'at an empirical level, it is to argue that on significant dimensions disabled people can be regarded as a group whose members are in an inferior position to other members of society because they are disabled'. Although the author addresses the relation between disabled and non-disabled individuals, this can be adapted to customers with different impairments in the context of information provision. Specifically, the directive creates a framework within which customers without vision impairments are in an inferior position to people with vision impairments. This includes people who need audio information, easy-to-read texts and symbols and so on. In other words, legal requirements that prioritise particular accessible formats and negate others create division among and segregation of customers with different impairments.

Not all practices are discriminating. As an example, Commission Regulation 1107/2006/EC on the Rights When Travelling by Air requires that 'all essential information provided for air passengers should be provided in alternative formats accessible to disabled persons' (preamble). The Council Directive 2009/136/EU on e-Privacy establishes several requirements regarding information provision for disabled people. The instrument obliges providers to 'regularly inform disabled subscribers of details of products and services designed for them' (art.21f). It adjudicates the power to national regulatory authorities to

> specify, *inter alia*, the quality of service parameters to be measured and the content, form and manner of the information to be published, including possible quality certification mechanisms, in order to ensure that end-users, including disabled users, have access to comprehensive, comparable, reliable and user-friendly information.
>
> (art.22.2)

The two instruments blend the measures for disabled and non-disabled customers and provide both an information provision framework about existing accessible goods and services and a quality and equity framework regulating access to information.

Accessibility of retail premises

The EU law does not directly address either accessibility of the built environment or access to retail premises. Due of potential differences and policy incompatibilities across MS (Prideaux, 2006), the Union locates related instruments within the soft and hard law context and covers accessibility of the built environment in a separate set of legislations. With regard to instruments that may shape accessibility of retail premises, Council Directive 89/645/EEC on Minimum Health and Safety is important. It addresses 'doors, passageways, staircases, showers, washbasins, lavatories and workstations used or occupied by handicapped persons' (Annex I, para.20). While the instrument does not require elements to be accessible, it demands considering disabled workers' needs and usability of the workplace and could benefit disabled and non-disabled customers, who interact in environments used by disabled employees. Council Directive 95/16/EC on Lifts requires designing and constructing lifts in a way that they 'do not obstruct or impede access and use by disabled persons and so allow any appropriate adjustments intended to facilitate its use by them' (M2.1.2). The instrument calls for barrier-free access as a means for assuring disabled people's health and safety rather than equal participation and rights and so implies the individual model perspective.

Similarly, the Council Regulation 305/2011/EU on Construction Products alongside general requirements determines safety and accessibility in use. Thus,

> the construction works must be designed and built in such a way that they do not present unacceptable risks of accidents or damage in service or in operation such as slipping, falling, collision, burns, electrocution, injury from explosion and burglaries. In particular, construction works must be designed and built taking into consideration accessibility and use for disabled persons.
>
> (Requirement No. 4)

Even though the regulation is applicable to private retail premises and addresses accessibility for disabled people, as in the previous instruments, the requirements are underpinned by the assurance of health and safety, instead of equality and non-discrimination.

EU procurement law[4] notes that the award of contracts should be based on principles of free movement of goods and services, equal treatment, non-discrimination, mutual recognition, proportionality and transparency. Contracting authorities and entities are invited (but not required) to address accessibility and UD in technical specifications of tender documents. However, they are free to choose whether to implement the measures advancing equal opportunities in awarding contracts or not:

> Contracting authorities should, whenever possible, lay down technical specifications so as to take into account accessibility criteria for people with disabilities or design for all users. The technical specifications should be clearly indicated, so that all tenderers know what the requirements established by the contracting authority cover.
>
> (Council Directive 2004/18/EC, preamble 29 on Public Works Contracts)

In addition, technical provisions on the built environment and goods and services that are covered by Council Directives 2004/17/EC on Utilities and 2004/18/EC on Public Works Contracts

> shall be set out in the contract documentation, such as contract notices, contract documents or additional documents. Whenever possible these technical specifications should be defined so as to take into account accessibility criteria for people with disabilities or design for all users.
> (Directive 2004/18/EC, art.23)

While the directives provide MSs with freedom to choose the form and method of how to adopt the requirements (Craig and de Burca, 1998) in a way that best meets national peculiarities (Toshkov, 2008), the process usually is slow (Craig and de Burca, 1998) and introduces differences in accessibility practices that shape diversity in customer experience. Most importantly, accessibility requirements are not binding and should be defined 'whenever possible'. This suggests that despite the instruments acknowledge the need to provide more accessibility, they prioritise the interests of contracting entities and provide them with power to decide when it is possible to deliver accessibility.

Aiming to facilitate accessibility of the built environment via public procurement, the EC (2007) issued a mandate to the European Standardisation Organisations (ESO) to draft European accessibility standards (M/420). Contrary to outlined instruments, the mandate shares some similarities with the CRPD and positions accessibility as a right and a precondition for exercising rights. As the Convention, the instrument shifts away the focus from legal personality and the nature of the owner. In long-term-oriented strategic actions, it requires the ensuring of equal and accessible access to built and newly designed environments. It also seeks to develop an online toolkit, available for public procurers that would assist them in making sure that functional accessibility and minimum technical functionality requirements are met. However, Marcos (2011:44) warns that it is not enough to just support procurers. In seeking to achieve outlined goals, it is necessary to treat accessibility standards as a 'fundamental and absolute requirement of the procurement process' and to develop 'a set of accessibility related criteria for awarding the contract and later for carrying out conformity assessment'. Most importantly, the goal of the accessibility standards cannot be seen only as a support resource for procurers. It has to be positioned as one of the means leading towards equality, non-discrimination, independent living and exercising human rights.

In addition to technical requirements, the EU promotes accessibility via provision of financial incentives. Council Regulation 1303/2013/EC on Structural Funds defines accessibility and disability as factors that have to be taken into account during the preparation and implementation of different programmes (art.7). Since the financial instruments may be applied to the private sector (preamble, 36) and can be used to fund infrastructure projects (preamble, 47), the instrument acts as an incentive for the private market to consider and provide accessibility.

Currently, the EU is undergoing conceptual and empirical tensions and transmutations regarding accessibility of retail markets and disabled customers' participation. Aiming to better understand the factors that should be considered in creating a more accessible single market, the revelation of how national governments react to global and regional policies and the way they deal with the outlined contradictions becomes important. With this in mind, the following section sheds light on the positions of and practices in Lithuania and the United Kingdom.

Accessibility in national markets: Lithuania and the United Kingdom

Multi-scalar governance is nuanced, and the ratification and conversion of global (Buergenthal et al., 2009) and regional instruments (Cuthbert, 2012) into domestic is not a hierarchical but a complex and bipartite process (Haas, 1998). While the adoption of global human rights instruments and signing international treaties may be highly symbolic (Koo and Ramirez, 2009), countries' perspectives and practice depend on whether they follow a monist or dualist approach towards international law (Maniruzzaman, 2001). With regard to compliance with the EU instruments, it is mainly a matter of MSs' choice, political calculation (Gourevitch, 1996) and technical factors (Haas, 1998). The adoption of regional instruments have to go through various stages of domestic absorption (Lord and Stein, 2008), with the processes of identification, translation, consultation and adaptation varying from country to country (Toshkov, 2008). The EU has no competence to act solely in the interest of protecting consumers and ensuring accessibility of national markets, except to support and monitor governments' efforts. In this regard, interpretation and innovation at the national level is a key driver and the competence to act in the interest of consumers, and market accessibility lies with the MSs. With this in mind, the present section draws the attention to Lithuania and the United Kingdom. The countries have different economic structures and welfare regimes but operate within the same global and regional policy frameworks. They have ratified the CRPD and are members of the EU, although joined the Union at different times and under different circumstances. With this in mind, the following discussion looks at how the two countries legally construct disabled people as customers and what the foundation is for accessible shopping.

'Socially vulnerable' consumers in Lithuania

The definition of a 'consumer' established in Lithuanian legal instruments is consistent with the notion provided in related EU instruments.[5] There a consumer is defined as a 'natural person, who expresses his intention to buy, buys and uses goods or services to meet his own personal, family or household needs and that are outside his business or profession' (Law on Consumer Protection, art.2, par.15, 2009). Provisions regarding customers with impairments are established in both equality and general framework instruments. With regard to equality legislations, the Law on Equal Treatment (2008) establishes sellers and producers' responsibility to 'provide consumers with equal access to the same goods and services, including housing, as well as apply equal conditions of payment and guarantees for the same products, goods and services or for products, goods and services of equal value' (art.8, para.1). Paragraph 2 of article 8 notes that information provided about products shall not be humiliating, contemptuous or discriminate against people with impairments. Hence, while the instrument does not distinguish disabled people as a separate customer group, some practices should be avoided in order to ensure non-discriminatory participation in the market.

With regard to general framework legislations, although non-disabled customers' protection is established in at least 12 statutes and 5 sub-statutory acts, none of them refer either to disabled customers' rights or to 'vulnerable consumers" protection. Disabled people are categorised as 'socially vulnerable consumers', and some actions oriented towards their protection are established in several instruments. The category of a 'socially vulnerable consumer' is not officially established and may change according to the government or its authorised institution (Law on Electricity, 2012). It usually includes disabled people, single mothers, under-retirement age or unskilled young people, ethnic minorities and people who cannot find a job (VPVI, 2011). Hence, disabled customers are located within the social welfare framework. This means that their participation in the mainstream private market is recognised as a social problem, and their functioning as customers is hardly possible without social interventions and organised activities of governmental and voluntary organisations (Dolgoff et al., 1997).

Similar to the EU level, some changes in conceptualising disabled people as customers are emerging in the Lithuanian policy instruments. To begin with, the National Strategy for Consumer Protection (NSCP) 2007–2010 defines disabled people as 'consumers, who experience social exclusion' and ascribes an individual with the responsibility for facing and fighting the exclusion. The NSCP 2011–2014 replaces the notion 'consumers, who experience social exclusion' with 'socially vulnerable consumers' and introduces a mild shift from premising customer vulnerability on individual characteristics towards the role played by external factors. However, as the following chapters suggest, the changes remain mainly conceptual as customer equality and private providers' ontological position and attitudes change slowly, and there are a number of factors preventing the positive change.

Second, NSCP 2007–2010 acknowledges insufficient education of 'consumers, who experience social exclusion' (para.35), and accordingly aims to provide special needs-based relevant knowledge for informed decision-making (action 3.1). The 2011–2014 Strategy goes further and highlights the necessity to develop 'socially vulnerable consumers'' skills that would allow for more effective practices in the marketplace (para.18.2.2). Although the latter instrument refers mainly to e-commerce, finances, insurance, transport and tourism, the shift from having knowledge to having knowledge and skills is present. On one hand, this suggests government's awareness that challenges experienced by disabled customers cannot be overcome using only knowledge. In order to convert knowledge into effective customer participation, particular skills are necessary. On the other hand, despite this conceptual fracture, the ideological position remains the same as the shift from knowledge to knowledge and skills strengthens disabled people's individual responsibility for their performance in the market. Instead of emphasising the responsibility of the state and business, the government seeks to convert people with impairments into knowledgeable and confident actors, who are responsible for their customer performance and exercised customer rights. In such a way, the Lithuanian government establishes what Bauman (2000) calls as customer's de jure autonomy. In other words, the responsibility for overcoming the barriers that are common to and experienced by masses is ascribed to separate individuals, with this duty being entrenched in legal instruments.

With regard to provisions focusing on disabled customers specifically, service affordability measures are the most common. As an example, the Law on Electricity (2012) anticipates additional guarantees for electricity supply and affordability measures (art.43). 'Socially vulnerable' users are obliged to pay 20% of the inputs of the electricity network operator or other prices based on this proportion (art.67, para.6). Similarly, the Law on Natural Gas (2001) establishes availability and sufficiency of natural gas for a reasonable price as one of the means to protect this customer group. Article 58 notes that in the context of customers' rights protection, one of the functions of the National Control Commission for Prices and Energy is to ensure that adequate remedies are applied to ensure 'socially vulnerable consumers'' rights (art.58). This suggests that at the everyday level protection of 'socially vulnerable customers' is founded on financial measures and provisions that aim to ensure them remaining solvent clients.

In some instances, measures on non-disabled customer rights' protection may prevent disabled people from exercising and demanding customer rights. As an example, the Law on Consumer Protection (2009) protects customers' rights only when service or supply relations between a customer and a provider exist. This means that if, for example, a person using a wheelchair cannot enter a shop because the entrance is inaccessible, customer rights protection law is not applicable, since there is no provider–customer relationship. Such practice can only be addressed as an impediment into barrier-free movement in the built environment. This suggests that the customer rights protection approach is relatively narrow and customer rights assurance is directly linked with and depends on individuals' participation in activities that generate profit.

Rights of customers with impairments are not addressed by current customer rights protection bodies. As an example, while the State Consumer Rights Protection Authority is the main agency responsible for the assurance of customer equality and rights, it does not specialise in disabled customers' rights nor does the European Consumer Centre in Lithuania. Similarly, other consumer protection agencies, private lawyers or DPOs do not specialise in disabled customers' rights and protection against unfair commercial practice. This maintains the position that individuals, belonging to the category of 'socially vulnerable consumers' are customers de jure and are individually responsible for participation in the market.

'Vulnerable consumers' in the United Kingdom

The notion of a customer established in the UK legal instruments is in line with the EU instruments and shares a common core with the definition provided in Lithuanian documents. The Consumer Protection from Unfair Trading Regulations (2008) defines a customer as 'any individual who in relation to a commercial practice is acting for purposes which are outside his business' (part 1, para.2). A similar position is established in the Consumer Protection Act (1987; part 3), the Unfair Terms in Consumer Contracts Regulations (1999; part 3) as well as in other related acts and regulations.

In terms of disabled customers, similar to the EU and Lithuania, the United Kingdom categorises people with impairments as 'vulnerable consumers'. As in Lithuania's case, the primary UK legislation in the customer area lacks focus on and reference to disabled people. The only exception is established in the Consumer Protection from Unfair Trading Regulations (2008), which refers to 'mental or physical infirmity, age or credulity' (part 1.2(5)):

> (5) In determining the effect of a commercial practice on the average consumer
> (a) where a clearly identifiable group of consumers is particularly vulnerable to the practice or the underlying product because of their mental or physical infirmity, age and credulity in a way which the trader could reasonably be expected to foresee.

Guidance on the UK Regulations (May 2008) implementing the Unfair Commercial Practice Directive (Office of Fair Trading, 2008) consolidates this position. It states that 'consumers are only treated as vulnerable, to a practice or to the underlying product, if they are vulnerable because of infirmity, age or credulity' (14.37). Thus, as in the case of EU instruments, the United Kingdom positions impairment as one of the reasons for and a cause of disabled customers' vulnerability.

Over the last two decades, disabled customers' position in the United Kingdom's general customer rights and protection system has been constantly changing. In 1999, the White paper 'Modern Markets: Confident Consumers' (Department Trade & Industry, 1999) introduced a term 'consumer empowerment', which remains an important concept in current policy discourse. At that time, much like the presently undergoing changes in Lithuania, it was acknowledged that having only knowledge is insufficient, and the development of particular skills is necessary for enabling customers to become more confident and demanding market actors (Department Trade & Industry, 1999). In a disability context, the document referred only to information provision in alternative formats (para.3.2) without specifying the actual formats. Later, despite the significance of customers' empowerment being emphasised in the 2005 report A Fair Deal for All (Department of Trade and Industry, 2005), it did not refer to disability. Furthermore, while the Consumer Empowerment Strategy (2011) positions access to information and skills as one of the means to empower customers, it does not refer to information provision in accessible formats. Although the instrument aims to empower non-disabled customers, it excludes individuals who need alternative formats, such as Braille, large print, easy-to-read or audio formats. This discriminates against customers with impairments and prevents them from making informed customer decisions.

Similar to the Lithuania's case, five UK regulatory bodies address special measures for general services and utilities that aim to protect the interests of 'vulnerable consumers' including disabled people. These include postal services, water services, gas and electricity, communications and railway services (House of Lords, 2006–2007). However, these are only five out of ten main regulatory bodies that have statutory power and seek to protect non-disabled consumers' interests. Thus, despite the duty to protect customers' interests, rights and protection of customers with impairments do not receive equal attention. This fragmentation in the system is likely to create a separation between disabled and non-disabled market participants.

In terms of the provisions for disabled people, the identified documents require considering disabled people or chronically sick customers' interests. Hence, there is a necessity to operate within a Disabled People's Protection Policy. Nevertheless, separate documents have different practices for addressing disability-related issues. As an example, similar to Lithuania's case, the United Kingdom's regulations on postal and railway services do not refer to a particular type of impairment and group all disabled people into the category of 'vulnerable consumers'. Contrary, the Communications Act (2003) determines some requirements for the provision of 'Television services for deaf and visually impaired' (part.3.303) and links these with reasonable accommodation. In other words, in terms of regulatory bodies who have established the duty to protect 'vulnerable consumers', there are both general disability and specific impairment protection frameworks.

Disabled customers' protection is also addressed under the equality or non-discrimination framework. The EA (2010) is the main instrument and covers the provision of and access to different goods, services and facilities. While Priestley (2012) notes that under the Act, provision of accessible information may be treated as reasonable adjustment, part 10 of the Act determines that the contract may be treated as unenforceable if it constitutes, provides or promotes unfair treatment of a person because of his/her impairment (142.2). In such a case, a county court or the sheriff can remove or modify the contract (143.1).

Similar to Lithuania, the number of bodies promoting and representing disabled customers' rights in the United Kingdom is limited. Specifically, although the Office of Fair Trading is the main organisation that seeks to 'make markets work well for consumers [...] by promoting and protecting consumer interests throughout the UK' (2012a), neither in its general agenda, nor in the Annual Plan 2012–2013 (2012b) does it refer to customers with impairments. Disability Rights UK (2012), the largest national disability organisation led by disabled people, also does not emphasise disabled customers' rights protection, this being a common practice in other DPOs.

Accessibility in Lithuania

The Law on the Social Integration of the Disabled People (2004) is the key instrument regarding accessibility requirements for people with impairments. It positions accessibility as one of the principles for social integration that allows participation in all spheres of life and the use of available sources (art.3 (par.6)). The Law on Equal Treatment (2008) is the main instrument on equal opportunities and addresses the prohibition of discrimination on the basis of disability. However, it neither links accessibility with non-discrimination, nor positions it as a precondition for exercising human rights.

Recalling the concept of an accessible shopping chain, it is worth looking at how national instruments address accessibility with regard to customer information, built environment and retail premises. In terms of customer information, there is a lack of mechanisms addressing its accessibility. The most comprehensive is the recent National Programme of the Disabled Integration (2012). As one of its goals, it aims to ensure access to information that is available to the general public. The document acknowledges limited information accessibility, including product packaging and customer information. It calls to consider UD and disabled users' involvement when developing and providing accessible information. Concurring with the challenges outlined in the programme, Ruškus and Motiečienė (2012) demonstrate that the practice is insufficient, fragmented and is usually initiated by the non-governmental organisations (NGOs).

With regard to accessibility of the built environment, the Law on Social Integration of Disabled People (2004, art.11) requires its implementation through (1) the planning of territories and construction design and

(2) through the adaptation of public buildings, dwellings and their environments, public transport objects and the infrastructure and the information environment in a way they meet special needs of disabled people. Similar to the CRPD, the instrument establishes a relatively broad understanding of accessibility and incorporates the requirement to consider it from the early stages of the development. It covers accessibility of urban infrastructure and the built environment and in such a way lays a path for barrier-free movement and connectivity between places. However, the instrument is premised on an individual model of disability. It positions the provision of accessibility as a means to meet disabled people's 'special needs' and so interconnects accessibility with impairment rather than with provisions that are beneficial for all society members.

While the Law on the Social Integration of the Disabled People (2004) deals with the accessibility concept, the Law on Construction (2011a) and the Technical Regulations for Construction (TRC; 2001) address specific requirements to make the built environment accessible. While the Law on Construction (2011a) briefly establishes that 'design, construction, reconstruction or overhaul of buildings (with the exception of renovation (modernization) of apartment houses) and civil engineering works must be carried out in such a way that they will accommodate the specific needs of disabled people' (art.6, para.3), the TRC is more comprehensive. The document provides a systematic approach to technical requirements for accessibility in/of cities, towns and villages; footpaths; parking lots and garages; and public and commercial buildings; among others. The measures are treated as a means through which disabled people's social integration and free usage of different elements in the built environment should be ensured.

Although public and private bodies have to follow the requirements when preparing construction projects, the reality is different. As an example, physical and social environments, including cultural heritage objects (Vilnius Tourism, 2012), public institutions (Ruškus and Motiečienė, 2012), public and renovated public buildings (Merkevicius, 2012) remain inaccessible, as they are designed for non-disabled individuals. For instance, the Lithuanian Association of People with Disabilities (2011) describes the journey to the shop as requiring 'para-Olympian's courage and persistence'. Shortcomings in national legislations, insufficient financial support by the state (Merkevicius, 2012), ableist practices, disablist attitudes and limited awareness (Mačiulevičiūtė, 2012) play a part in shaping inaccessibility. Likewise, limited interpretation and innovation of regional requirements by the Lithuanian government contribute to creating exclusion. Specifically, mirroring EU practice to focus on accessibility provisions for people with mobility and vision impairments, requirements regarding provisions for individuals with hearing or cognitive impairments and mental health conditions are left aside. This is well reflected in projects and academic studies evaluating accessibility that are usually funded by the government (Ruškus and Motiečienė, 2012). This suggests that Lithuanian instruments are insufficiently innovative with regard to regional policies and that current academic studies do not efficiently challenge national policy discourse.

Regarding accessibility of retail premises, section 7 of the TRC (2001) addresses the entrance into the building, free movement and usage of all accommodations for visitors, exits, evacuation routes, sanitary facilities and special means designated to make an internal and external environment accessible for people with impairments. The instrument acknowledges that different elements of the built environment have to be accessible in order to provide a barrier-free environment. However, similar to the discussed EU instruments, it positions accessibility as a health and safety issue (par.73) and consolidates the stereotype that disabled people are vulnerable market participants and need protection. Hence, while the instrument acknowledges the need for more accessible buildings, it positions the concept as 'protecting' certain groups rather than ensuring their equality. In terms of the internal shop environment, paragraph 79 notes that all items and instalments that are provided to customers in shops have to be easy to reach for disabled people. Although currently, there is no available evidence on disabled customers' experiences in shops in Lithuania, the following chapters suggest a mismatch between this policy rhetoric and empirical reality.

Accessibility in the United Kingdom

The emphasis on accessibility in the UK equality and general framework legislation is more explicit than it is in Lithuanian policy documents. With regard to equality instruments, the EA (2010) outlines a number of requirements relevant to accessibility; anticipatory reasonable accommodation and indirect discrimination being of particular importance for customer participation.

Anticipatory reasonable accommodation duty requires to anticipate

> ways in which disabled people (or broad groups of disabled people with particular types of impairment) might be placed at a substantial disadvantage in accessing services and to take reasonable steps to ensure that this does not happen by 1) altering provisions, criteria and practices, 2) altering or removing physical features and 3) providing auxiliary aids or services.
>
> (Lawson and Woodin, 2012:1)

The duty to ensure accessibility via the anticipatory reasonable accommodation is broad in its nature and is 'subject to the qualifier of "reasonableness", which may be enforced by disabled individuals through actions of discrimination' (Lawson and Woodin, 2012:1). While Fraser Butlin (2011) notes that the requirement to provide reasonable accommodation when a person experiences substantial disadvantage contradicts the rights-based approach, in reality, it manifests in experienced difficulties in accessing goods and services (Office for Disability Issues, 2011).

Accessibility in the EU markets 93

Another important concept of the EA (2010) is indirect discrimination (section 19). It is group oriented, tackles systematic barriers and institutional discrimination and can be applied in addressing accessibility barriers faced by individuals with particular types of impairment. Nevertheless, its significance regarding the provision of reasonable accommodation in the area of goods and services is questionable (Lawson and Woodin, 2012). It is a novel concept in the disability realm, and there is no established legal practice of how it should be used in demanding and ensuring accessibility.

With regard to general framework instruments, the Approved Document M (Document M; 2010) and standards produced by the British Standard Institution (BSI) play a role in indirectly shaping accessibility of retail markets. To begin with, Document M outlines accessibility requirements for new buildings, extended or altered existing non-domestic buildings and for existing buildings or their parts, which are altered into public or commercial use buildings such as shops. Alongside accessibility of indoor facilities, the document addresses elements, ensuring access to (section 1) and into (section 2) the buildings and so facilitates the connectivity between some of the shopping chain elements. The instrument does not set strict methods but is advisory in nature regarding certain building situations, and the parties are free to decide how to meet the requirements.

The increasing number of disabled and older people and their rising spending power shaped the demand for more accessible facilities in different life spheres (British Standard Institution, 2012). The changes led the BSI in collaboration with the Disabled Experts' Reference Group to develop a set of British, European and international standards that are often considered by manufacturing and service industries, national governments and customers. One of such standards is 8300:2009. It is a detailed advisory code of practice, which targets designing convenient, accessible and usable public and residential buildings, with the exception of dwellings. The Standard emphasises that the environment of commercial buildings, including retail places, must be fully accessible for disabled people, including disabled children. As a result, a shop environment shall ensure disabled individuals' independent functioning, regardless of whether they are customers or staff members. In planning and projecting retail premises, signing should be considered, seeking to reduce the level of experienced barriers when finding different places, goods and services within a shop (section 13.3.3). The code also covers accessibility of approach routes to shops, as well as setting-down points for different types of transport and parking spaces. Furthermore, section 13.3.3.3 determines that

> all counters, checkouts and service points should be accessible to disabled people. A clear space should be provided in front of them, and writing surfaces for seated and standing customers should be provided. Where feasible, hearing enhancement systems should be fitted.

94 *Accessibility in the EU markets*

The standards also cover accessibility of external (car parking, routes around and to the building, etc.) and internal (steps, stairs, ramps, lifts, etc.) environments of commercial buildings and different internal facilities (changing rooms, shelves, telephones, ATMs, etc.).

However, despite the policy developments and increasingly positive service providers' attitude towards disabled people (Simm et al., 2007), disabled customers in the United Kingdom continue experiencing barriers and exclusion. As an example, over the four years (2005–2009), the number of customers with impairments 'experiencing difficulties related to their impairment or disability in accessing goods and services' decreased only by 5% (from 37% in 2005 to 32% in 2009). Furthermore, a study conducted by Gore and Parckar (2010) demonstrates that while 40% of disabled customers experienced difficulties in accessing goods and services in the last 12 months (2009–2010), 23% felt to be discriminated against because of their impairment in the same time period. The reported difficulties behind the experienced customer exclusion are reflected in the majority of shopping chain stages. The main severe impediments are related to public transport (16%), lack of facilities for disabled people (15%) and entering or getting around premises (13%).

Concluding comments

This chapter has demonstrated that there have been some legislative attempts to make the private market more accessible for disabled customers. However, there are some tensions between global, regional and national instruments in the way they address market accessibility and disabled customers' participation.

At the global level, the CRPD positions accessibility as a general principle, which should be applied to all substantive human rights. The Convention does not use the term 'customer' and links accessibility with disabled customers' participation in the mainstream private market on an equal basis with others. Contrary to this, the EU does not recognise people with impairments as equal customers and legally construct them as 'vulnerable' consumers. The entrenched division between non-disabled and disabled market participants is premised on individuals' dependency to the category of disability, and impairment is an important factor for the classification. By positioning disabled people as 'vulnerable' customers, the EU violates its obligations, adopted after signing the CRPD, and promotes an individual model approach within the EU single market. The same tendencies are alive in the United Kingdom and Lithuania. Here, people with impairments are defined as 'vulnerable' and 'socially vulnerable' customers, respectively, with physical or cognitive features being the foundation for the distinction.

With regard to accessibility, the Convention intertwines the concept with the removal of different kinds of barrier, implementation of specific measures and positive obligations, non-discrimination, progressive realisation, UD, reasonable accommodation, availability and affordability, among others. These measures and the underlying principle of equality require an expectation and respect of disabled people and to treat them on an equal basis with others. Meanwhile, despite a number of instruments defining and addressing accessibility, the EU lacks a unified position and often links the concept with the assurance of health and safety rather than equality and non-discrimination. Only the Standards M/420 position accessibility as an issue of equality. It can be argued that such contradiction within the regional instruments is shaped by the need to balance complying with the Convention, the obligation to ensure citizens' fundamental rights and the aim to assure stable and efficient functioning of the single market. National policy discourse introduces more tensions. Specifically, even though Lithuania and the United Kingdom have ratified the Convention and operate under the same regional instruments, Lithuania links accessibility with social integration and the United Kingdom with non-discrimination and provision of reasonable accommodation. In terms of technical implementation, the practices also differ and require further research addressing the reasons, shortcomings and potentials behind the practices.

In terms of accessibility of the mainstream private market, the Convention requires SPs to shape a framework within which private entities could and would engage into accessibility discourse and practice and provide disabled and non-disabled customers with an equal and quality service. However, similar to the position towards disabled customers, EU provisions regarding market accessibility share some features typical to an individual model. As an example, provision of accessible customer information is mainly addressed in the context of medical products and services and so reflects a dominant attitude towards disabled people as needing to be 'fixed' or 'cured'. However, requirements on accessibility of retail premises are broader. Even though they are addressed indirectly, a great number of separate legislations set the framework, within which accessibility of shops should be ensured.

With regard to national instruments, the United Kingdom's requirements for retail premise accessibility are more comprehensive than Lithuania's. The United Kingdom's position shares more similarities with the position entrenched in the CRPD and has stronger links with the social model. It can be argued that a stronger disability movement, longer experience in the EU and better familiarity with the promoted values, philosophy and rights provided the United Kingdom with better opportunities to position disability and accessibility within a social model and human rights context. Meanwhile, being independent only for 25 years, Lithuania has still imbibed some of the practices, perspectives and values that were typical for the Union of Soviet Socialist Republics. Experiencing the period of transition from socialist to human rights' values, the country is shaping the understanding practices.

96 *Accessibility in the EU markets*

There are some significant contradictions in the public policy discourse surrounding disability, accessibility and retail customers, and some form of cooperative action is needed to address the issue. The following chapter, therefore, suggests how adaptation of some concepts of Habermas' theory of communicative action may be employed to approach the outlined tensions and to introduce more equal customer experience.

Notes

1 Council Regulation 44/2001/EC on Jurisdiction in Civil and Commercial Matters; Council Regulation 593/2008/EC on Contractual Relations.
2 Council Directive 2008/48/EC on Credit Agreements for Consumers.
3 Directive 85/374/EC on EU procedural liability.
4 Directive 2004/17/EC and Directive 2004/18/EC.
5 Directive 2008/48 on credit agreements for consumers, Directive 85/374/EC on EU procedural liability and Directive 2011/83 on consumer rights.

Bibliography

Abbamonte, G. B. 2006. Unfair commercial practices directive: An example of the new European consumer protection approach. *The Columbia Journal of European Law*, 12, 695–712.

Abberley, P. 1987. The concept of oppression and the development of a social theory of disability. *Disability, Handicap & Society*, 2, 5–19.

Amundson, R. (ed.) 2005. *Disability, ideology and quality of life: A bias in biomedical ethics*, Cambridge, Cambridge University Press.

Baker, S. M., Gentry, J. W. & Rittenburg, T. L. 2005. Building understanding of the domain of consumer vulnerability. *Journal of Macromarketing*, 25, 128–139.

Bauman, Z. 2000. *Liquid Modernity*, Cambridge, Polity.

Bell, M. 2003. The right to equality and non-discrimination. *In:* Hervey, T. & Kenner, J. (eds.) *Economic and social rights under the EU chatter of fundamental rights: A legal perspective*. Portland, Hart Publishing.

Bellamy, R. 2012. The liberty of the moderns: Market freedom and democracy within the EU. *Global Constitutionalism*, 1, 141–172.

British Standard Institution 2012. *Guidance on accessibility of large hotel premises and hotel chains*, London, BSI.

Buergenthal, T., Shelton, D. L. & Stewart, D. P. 2009. *International human rights in a nutshell. 4th edition*, St. Paul, Minnesota, West Academic Publishing.

Burzgali, L. & Emiliani, P. L. 2013. Universal access: A concept to be adapted to technological development and societal change. *In:* Stephanidis, C. & Antona, M. (eds.) *7th International Conference, UAHCI 2013*, Las Vegas, Springer.

Charitakis, S. 2013. An introduction to the disability strategy 2010–2020, with a focus on accessibility. *Ars Aequi*. Available: www.nuigalway.ie/dream/downloads/an_introduction_to_the_disability_strategy_20102020_with_a_focus_on_accessibility.pdf [Accessed 15/04/2015]

Committee on the Rights of Persons with Disabilities 2014. *General comment No. 2. Article 9: Accessibility*, New York, United Nations Human Rights. Office of the Hight Commissioner for Human Rights.

Craig, P. & de Burca, G. 1998. *Eu law: Text, cases, and materials. 2nd edition*, Oxford, Oxford University Press.

Cuthbert, M. 2012. *Nutshells. European Union Law. 7th edition*, London, Thomson Reuters.
Department for Business Innovation and Skills 2011. *Better choices: Better deals. Consumers powering growth*, London, Business Innovation and Skills.
Department Trade and Industry 1999. Modern markets: Confident consumers – the government's consumer white paper (Command paper), London, Stationery Office Books.
Department of Trade and Industry 2000. *A study of the difficulties disabled people have when using everyday consumer products*, London, Department of Trade and Industry.
Department of Trade and Industry 2005. *A fair deal for all. Extending competitive markets: Empowered consumers, successful business*, London, Department of Trade and Industry.
Devetak, R. & Higgott, R. 1999. Justice unbound? Globalization, states and the transformation of the social bond. *International Affairs*, 75, 493–598.
Disability Rights UK 2012. *Disability rights UK factsheets* [Online], Disability Rights UK. Available: www.disabilityrightsuk.org/factsheets.htm [Accessed 07/09/2013].
Dolgoff, R., Feldstein, D. & Stolnik, L. 1997. *Understanding social welfare. 4th edition*, Michigan, Longman.
Drache, D. 2001. The turn of the public domain after the triumph of markets: Revisiting the most basics of fundamentals. *In:* Drache, D. (ed.) *The market or the public domain*. London, Routledge.
Dyson, R. 2007. *Statement for formal ceremony at the signing of the convention on the rights of persons with disabilities*. Available: www.un.org/esa/socdev/enable/documents/Stat_Conv/nzam.doc [Accessed 08/04/2013].
Eardley, T., Bruce, J. & Goggin, G. 2009. *Telecommunications and community wellbeing: A review of the literature on access and affordability for low-income and disadvantaged groups*. Sydney, University of New South Wales Consortium.
Edgar, A. 2006. *Habermas. The key concepts*, Oxon, Routledge.
Edward, D.A.O., Moitinho de Almeida, J.C., Gulmann, C., Puissochet, J.-R. & Jann, P. 2000. Case C220/98, Estee Lauder Cosmetics GmbH & Co. OHG v. Lancaster Group GmbH. Available: http://curia.europa.eu/juris/liste.jsf?language=en&num=c-220/98 [Accessed 29/08/2014].
European Commission 2007. *No. M/420 Standardisation mandate to CEN CENELEC and ETSI in support of European accessibility requirements for public procurement in the built environment*, Brussels, European Commission.
European Commission 2011. *Single Market Act. Twelve levers to boost growth and strengthen confidence. 'Working together to create new growth'*, COM 206, final.
European Commission 2012a. *Roadmap. European Accessibility Act: Legislative initiative to improve accessibility of goods and services in the internal market*, Brussels, European Commission.
European Commission 2012b. *No. SWD (2012) 235 Commission staff working document on knowledge-enhancing aspects of consumer empowerment 2012–2014*, Brussels, European Commission.
European Commission 2014a. *A vision for the internal market for industrial products*, COM 25, final, Brussels, European Commission.
European Commission 2014b. *The EU single market: General framework*. Available: http://ec.europa.eu/internal_market/top_layer/index_en.htm [Accessed 02/05/2015].
European Council *No. 89/654/EEC Directive concerning the minimum safety and health requirements for the workplace*, Brussels, European Council.

European Council *No. 95/16/EC Directive on the approximation of the laws of the Member States relating to lifts*, Brussels, European Council.
European Council *No. 305/2011 Regulation laying down harmonised conditions for the marketing of construction products and repealing Council Directive 89/106/EEC*, Brussels, European Council.
European Council *No. 2001/95/EC Directive on general product safety*, Brussels, European Council.
European Council *No. 2004/17/EC Directive coordinating the procurement procedures of entities operating in the water, energy, transport and postal services sectors*, Brussels, European Council.
European Council *No. 2004/18/EC Directive on the coordination of procedures for the award of public works contracts, public supply contracts and public service contracts*, Brussels, European Council.
European Council *No. 2004/27/EC Directive on the community code relating to medicinal products for human use*, Brussels, European Council.
European Council *No. 2005/29/EC Directive concerning unfair business-to-consumer commercial practices in the internal market*, Brussels, European Council.
European Council *No. 2010/13/EU Directive on the provision of audiovisual media services*, Brussels, European Council.
European Council *No. 2011/83/EU Directive on consumer rights*, Brussels, European Council.
European Council *No. No 1107/2006 Regulation regarding the rights of disabled persons and persons with reduced mobility when travelling by air*, Brussels, European Council.
European Council *No. No 1303/2013 Regulation laying down common provisions on the European Regional Development Fund, the European Social Fund, the Cohesion Fund, the European Agricultural Fund for Rural Development and the European Maritime and Fisheries Fund and laying down general provisions on the European Regional Development Fund, the European Social Fund, the Cohesion Fund and the European Maritime and Fisheries Fund and repealing Council Regulation (EC) No 1083/2006*, Brussels, European Council.
European Council 2012. *The treaty on the functioning of the European Union*, Brussels, European Council.
Ferri, D. 2010. *The conclusion of the UN convention on the rights of persons with disabilities by the EC/EU: Some reflections from a 'constitutional' perspective*, Verona, Università di Catania.
Fraser Butlin, S. 2011. The UN convention on the rights of persons with disabilities: Does the Equality Act 2010 measure up to UK international commitments? *Industrial Law Journal*, 40, 428–438.
Gore, E. & Parckar, G. 2010. *Rights and reality. Disabled people's experiences of accessing goods and services.* London, Leonard Cheshire Disability.
Gourevitch, P. A. 1996. Squaring the circle: The domestic sources of international cooperation. *International Organization*, 50, 349–373.
Haas, P. M. 1998. Compliance with EU directives: Insights from international relations and comparative politics. *Journal of European Public Policy*, 5, 17–37.
Halvorsen, R. 2010. Digital freedom for persons with disabilities: Are policies to enhance e-Accessibility and e-Inclusion becoming more similar in the Nordic countries and the US. *In:* Quinn, G. & Waddington, L. (eds.) *European yearbook of disability law. Volume 2*, Antwerp, Intersentia.
HM Government 2010. *Access to and use of buildings: Approved document M*, London, HM Government.

Hodes, R. 2001. The contested competence of NGOs and business in public life. *In:* Drache, D. (ed.) *The market or the public domain,* London, Routledge.
Hoffmann, F. & Inderst, R. 2009. Price discrimination and the provision of information. Available: www.wiwi.uni-frankfurt.de/profs/inderst/Theory/info_price_discrimination_oct09.pdf [Accessed 08/10/2012].
House of Lords 2006–2007. *UK economic regulations: Volume I: Report* HL Paper 189-I. London, House of Lords.
Kayess, R. & French, P. 2008. Out of darkness into light? Introducing the convention on the rights of persons with disabilities. *Human Rights Law Review*, 8, 1–34.
Koo, J.-W. & Ramirez, F. O. 2009. National incorporation of global human rights: Worldwide expansion of national human rights institutions, 1966–2004. *Social Forces*, 87, 1321–1353.
Lawson, A. 2010. Reasonable accommodation and accessibility obligations: Towards a more unified European approach. *European Anti-Discrimination Law Review*, 11, 11–21.
Lawson, A. & Woodin, S. 2012. *National accessibility report. ANED 2012 Task 4. United Kingdom*, Academic Network of European Disability Experts, ANED. Available: www.disability-europe.net/country/united-kingdom [Accessed 25/11/2013].
Lietuvos Respublikos Seimas 2001. *No. STR 2.03.01:2001 Statybos techninių reikalavimų reglamentas. Statiniai ir teritorijos: Reikalavimai žmonių su negalia reikmėms*, Vilnius, Lietuvos Respublikos Seimas.
Lietuvos Respublikos Seimas 2004. *No XI-2228 Neįgaliųjų integracijos įstatymas*, Vilnius, Lietuvos Respublikos Seimas.
Lietuvos Respublikos Seimas 2008. *No. X-1602 Lygių galimybių įstatymas*, Vilnius, Lietuvos Respublikos Seimas.
Lietuvos Respublikos Seimas 2009. *No. I-657 Vartotojų teisių apsaugos įstatymas*, Vilnius, Lietuvos Respublikos Seimas.
Lietuvos Respublikos Seimas 2011a. *No. I-1240 Statybos įstatymas*, Vilnius, Lietuvos Respublikos Seimas.
Lietuvos Respublikos Seimas 2011b. *No. XI-1564 Gamtinių dujų įstatymas*, Vilnius, Lietuvos Respublikos Seimas.
Lietuvos Respublikos Seimas 2012. *No. XI-1919 Elektros įstatymas*, Vilnius, Lietuvos Respublikos Seimas.
Lietuvos Respublikos Vyriausybė 2011. *No. 848 Valstybinė vartotojų teisių apsaugos 2011–2014 metų strategija*, Vilnius, Lietuvos Respublikos Vyriausybė.
Lietuvos Respublikos Vyriausybė 2012. *No. 1408 Nacionalinė neįgaliųjų socialinės integracijos 2013–2019 metų programa*, Vilnius, Lietuvos Respublikos Vyriausybė.
Lord, J. E. 2010. Accessibility and human rights fusion in the CRPD: Assessing the scope and content of the accessibility principle and duty under the CRPD. *The General Day of Discussion on Accessibility, CRPD Committee*, Geneva, United Nations.
Lord, J. E. & Stein, A. M. 2008. The domestic incorporation of human rights law and the United Nations convention on the rights of persons with disabilities. *Washington University Law Review*, 83, 9–37.
LŽNS 2011. *Ar Vilnius išliks Kliūčių Ruožas?* [Online], Vilnius. Available: www.negalia.lt/?p=3 [Accessed 20/10/2012].
Mačiulevičiūtė, O. 2012. *Ar aplinka tebėra kliūtis neigaliesiems?* [Online], Bičiulystė. [Accessed 12/03/2015].
Maniruzzaman, A. F. M. 2001. State contracts in contemporary international law: Monist versus dualist controversies. *European Journal of International Law*, 12, 309–328.

Marcos, T. 2011. *Accessibility in the built environment*, Brussels, European Committee for Standardization.

Marx, K. 1893. *Capital. Volume 2. Book Two: The process of circulation of capital*, Moscow, Progress Publishers.

Mégret, F. 2008. The disabilities convention: Human rights of persons with disabilities or disability rights? *Human Rights Quarterly*, 30, 494–516.

Merkevicius, J. 2012. *Tyrimo 'Pasiūlyme dėl Europos tarybos direktyvos, kuria įgyvendinamas vienodo požiūrio į asmenis, nepaisant jų religijos ar tikėjimo, negalios, amžiaus arba seksualinės orientacijos, principas, nuostatų, reglamentuojančių naujų, renovuojamų ir visų kitų esamų visuomeninės paskirties pastatų pritaikymą neįgaliųjų poreikiams Lietuvoje ekonominių kaštų analizė'. Galutine ataskaita*, Vilnius, Sempera.

Miller, L. 2011. *The emergence of EU contract law*, Oxford, Oxford University Press.

Morgan, F. W., Schuler, D. K. & Stoltman, J. J. 1995. A framework for examining the legal status of vulnerable consumers. *Journal of Public Policy & Marketing*, 14, 267–277.

Office for Disability Issues 2011. *Disability equality indicators. Comparing the life chances of disabled people to non-disabled people*, London, Office for Disability Issues.

Office of Fair Trading 1999. *Unfair contract terms guidance: Guidance for the unfair terms in consumer contracts regulations*, London, Office of Fair Trading.

Office of Fair Trading 2008. *Guidance on the UK regulations (May 2008) implementing the unfair commercial practices directive*. Available www.businessballs.com/freepdfmaterials/consumer_protection_regulations_guide26may08_oft931int.pdf [Accessed 14/16/2012].

Office of Fair Trading 2012a. *Making markets work well for consumers* [Online], Office of Fair Trading. Available: www.oft.gov.uk/ [Accessed 01/11/2012].

Office of Fair Trading 2012b. *Office of fair trading annual plan 2012–2013*, London, Office of Fair Trading.

Parliament of the United Kingdom 1987. *Consumer Protection Act*, London, Home Office.

Parliament of the United Kingdom 2003. *Communications Act*, London, Home Office.

Parliament of the United Kingdom 2010. *Equality Act*, London, Home Office.

Prahalad, C. K. & Ramaswamy, V. 2004. Co-creating unique value with consumers. *Strategy & Leadership*, 32, 4–9.

Prideaux, S. 2006. *Good practice for providing reasonable access to the physical built environment for disabled people*, Leeds, Centre for Disability Studies.

Priestley, M. 2012. *Consumer protection. ANED 2012 Task 3*, Academic Network for European Disability Experts. Available: www.disability-europe.net/country/united-kingdom [Accessed 17/02/2013].

Quinn, G. 2009a. Bringing the UN convention on rights for persons with disabilities to life in Ireland. *British Journal of Learning Disabilities*, 37, 245–249.

Quinn, G. 2009b. United Nations convention on the rights of persons with disabilities: Toward a new international politics of disability. *Texas Journal on Civil Liberties and Civil Rights*, 15, 33–53.

Quinn, G. 2010. *The interaction of non-discrimination with article 9: Added reasonment*, Unpublished paper.

Reiss, J. W. 2012. The convention on the rights of persons with disabilities in the post-Lisbon European Union. *Human Rights Brief*, 19, 4–10.

Ruškus, J. & Motiečienė, R. 2012. *National accessibility report, Lithuania. ANED 2012 Task 4*, Academic Network of European Disability Experts. Available: www.disability-europe.net/country/lithuania [Accessed 10/10/2013].

Sanders, K. Y. 2006. Overprotection and lowered expectations of persons with disabilities: The unforeseen consequences. *Work*, 27, 181–188.

Simm, C., Aston, J., Williams, C., Hill, D., Bellis, A. & Meager, N. 2007. *Organisations' responses to the Disability Discrimination Act*, London, Department for Work and Pensions.

Smith, N. C. & Cooper-Martin, E. 1997. Ethics and target marketing: The role of product harm and consumer vulnerability. *Journal of Marketing*, 61, 1–20.

The Secretary OF State 2008. *No. 1277 The Consumer protection from unfair trading regulations*, London, The Secretary of State.

Toshkov, D. 2008. Embracing European law: Compliance with EU directives in Central and Eastern Europe. *European Union Politics*, 9, 379–402.

UN Commission ON Human Rights (39th Sess.) 1983. *No. E/CN.4/Sub.2/1987/23 The new international economic order and the promotion of human rights*, Geneva, UN Commission on Human Rights.

United Nations 1948. *Universal declaration of human rights*, Paris, United Nations.

United Nations 1966. *International covenant on civil and political rights*, New York, United Nations.

United Nations 1993. *Standard rules on equalization of opportunities for persons with disabilities*, New York, United Nations.

United Nations Committee on the Rights of Persons with Disabilities 2013. *Consideration of reports submitted by States parties under article 35 of the Convention: Initial reports of States parties: United Kingdom of Great Britain and Northern Ireland*, New York, United Nations.

United Nations Committee on the Rights of Persons with Disabilities 2014. *Consideration of reports submitted by States parties under article 35 of the Convention: Initial reports of States parties: Lithuania*, New York, United Nations.

UN Committee on Economic, Social and Cultural Rights (CESCR) 11 August 2000. *General Comment No. 14: The Right to the Highest Attainable Standard of Health (Art. 12 of the Covenant)*, E/C.12/2000/4. Available: www.refworld.org/docid/4538838d0.html [Accessed 23/08/2014].

Vilnius Tourism 2012. *Maršrutas po Senamiestį* [Online], Vilnius. Available: www.vilnius-tourism.lt/turizmas/vilnius-jums/neigaliesiems/marsrutas-po-senamiesti/ [Accessed 20/12/2012].

VPVI 2011. *Socialinės integracijos paslaugų socialiai pažeidžiamų ir socialinės rizikos asmenų grupėms situacijos, poreikių ir rezultatų vertinimas, siekiant efektyviai panaudoti 2007–2013m. ES struktūrinę paramą*, Vilnius, Viešosios Politikos ir Vadybos Institutas.

Waddington, L. 2009. A disabled market: Free movement of goods and services in the EU and disability accessibility. *European Law Journal*, 15, 575–598.

Weatherill, S. 2011. Consumer Policy. *In:* Craig, P. & de Burca, G. (eds.) *The evolution of EU law*, Oxford, Oxford University Press.

3 Communicative action and the EU markets

Discussion in the previous chapters revealed tensions in market practice and public discourse surrounding disability, accessibility and retail customers. Illustration of disabled people's exclusion from participation in the mainstream private market as equal customers was provided. This was followed by evidence of how public discourse on rights and accessibility has rhetorically reconstructed people with impairments from consumers to 'vulnerable' customers and introduced some tensions between different policy discourses. Despite the occurring changes, disabled customers remain excluded from equal participation, and a cooperative action is needed to tackle the issue. For this purpose, elements of Habermas' theory of communicative action (CA) are adapted, as this can provide useful insight and understanding to inform the way customer rights and market accessibility can be ensured. Being aware of the width of the theory and recalling the essence of the social model of disability, three elements of CA are adapted: lifeworld, access to the discourse and power relations. The concepts are employed to explore the roots of the tensions that lay in global, regional and national policy instruments and customer service.

Since democracy, emancipation (Godin et al., 2007) and human rights (Habermas, 1998, 2012) are central concerns in Habermas' work and premise the chosen concepts, the use of the Habermasian theory is appropriate, as it reflects ontological and epistemological positions of this book. In addition, employment of the three concepts in other authors' studies on disability has been verified at the theoretical level as well as provided valuable empirical insights, leading towards more inclusion, emancipation and equality (Bates and Davis, 2004, Godin et al., 2007, Silver and Francis, 2000). Habermas is also concerned with Europeanisation and democratisation of the discourse. He emphasises opportunity for all citizens to access the discourse, develop capacity for democratic debate (Godin et al., 2007) and so to achieve enlightenment and emancipation (Habermas, 1974). This, indeed, enables strengthening the adaption of the emancipatory research approach, expanding the general obligation of the CRPD to involve civil society in the policy decision-making process (art.4) and calling for all relevant stakeholders' involvement in shaping ontological and epistemological premises for an accessible European Union (EU) single market.

Habermas' theory of CA is linked with ethics of discourse, where he is primarily concerned with the public sphere and contrasts it with the private sphere. This dichotomy has been criticised, especially by feminist scholars (Fraser, 1990, Godin et al., 2007, Goodman, 1992, Kellner, 2000, Young, 1985), who identify it as too idealistic, prioritising white property-owning men and neglecting excluded groups, among others. However, since this book deals with the private market and not with the private sphere, this criticism does not devalue the chosen theoretical framework. Specifically, as it was demonstrated in the previous chapter, recent establishments of social claims and policies for disability rights and accessibility impinge upon the discourse and relations between the market stakeholders that were previously 'private'. The private market is brought into the public space as a legitimate focus for policy discourse. Furthermore, in Habermas' ethical frame, access to the discourse is about democratisation of access to the formation of public discourse through free communication and debate. Private ownership and private opinion are excluded from the ethics of the public sphere.

Habermas is mainly concerned with discussing common public affairs and shaping public opinion, opposing state power and elite's interests that may potentially mould citizens' everyday life realms (Kellner, 2000). This is particularly relevant when addressing disabled people's participation in the mainstream private market. While their involvement in shaping policies on the accessible market is rhetorically established at the global policy instruments and especially the CRPD, in reality, it is insufficient and citizens are prevented from accessing the formation of the discourse. Indeed, people with impairments should be recognised as equally capable to shape the rhetoric and practice of the EU single market as well as have equal access to the discourse on the issue.

This chapter, therefore, explores existing preconditions for CA on the EU single market to emerge. The discussion starts by an overview of the relationship between the lifeworld, EU policies, and the private market. Then, a closer look is given to the concept of CA, access to the discourse and equal power relations with a focus on bargaining and arguing practices in international relations. Finally, the potential of the open method of coordination (OMC) to provide relevant stakeholders with an access to the formation of the discourse on the accessible private market is explored.

Insights have been gained through the use of Habermas' work and literature on the EU, international relations and the private market. The chosen theoretical framework has provided useful insights and understanding that current EU policies and private market practice may either lessen or sharpen the contradictions and tensions outlined in the previous chapters. Specifically, the EU may serve either as a framework for a common lifeworld to emerge, or act as a system, colonising national lifeworlds. In a similar vein, although the private market is more likely to colonise EU customers' lifeworlds, under specific circumstances, they may share similar values and contribute to the maintenance of the lifeworld. The balance between strategic and CA is also dual. Although the first dominates over the second, communicative rationality and CA may also be present and emerge in particular contexts.

This knowledge set is important and will serve in the following chapters when analysing stakeholders' norms, values, notions and positions towards market accessibility and the underlying reasons behind them.

Market accessibility and a lifeworld

Lifeworld is one of the key factors for CA to emerge (Habermas, 1984, 1985, 1991, 1996b). This section examines the patterns of the lifeworld shared and created by the EU and the private market. Such an approach assists in understanding the possibilities and preconditions for CA regarding an accessible EU single market to emerge. The discussion starts by exploring the concepts of lifeworld and system as introduced by Habermas but positions the lifeworld as a collective rather than an individual domain. This is followed by a discussion on whether EU policy development processes create a framework for a common lifeworld among EU members to emerge or act as a system colonising national realms. The focus is on large and small and medium enterprises (SMEs) operating within the EU, and the way two types of business contribute to maintaining a common lifeworld across the Union. This section ends in a discussion on how retail practice and new movements in consumer culture may intervene into shoppers' realities and reshape their values, norms and customer behaviour.

'System' and 'lifeworld'

Habermas borrowed the concept of the 'lifeworld' from Edmund Husserl and Alfred Schutz and after significant developments used it as an opposition to Adorno's point that individual's acts and thoughts are administratively controlled by modern capitalism. Although Habermas is concerned with how capitalism and bureaucracies restrict people's freedom, he uses the lifeworld as an evidence that to a certain degree, society is created and sustained by human actions (Edgar, 2006). He integrates Durkheim's 'conscience collective' (Habermas, 1984:113–152) as the lifeworld of a social group, and its internal and external interactions are the preconditions for social interrelation. Sayer (2001:689) adds that lifeworld is 'a product of the relation between embodied actors and the cultures into which they are socialised, though it can, of course, become an object of reflection by actors'. In such a context, lifeworld does not serve as background knowledge for understanding the world or communicating about it. Its function is to 'ensure that interpersonal relations are ordered in a way which makes society function effectively' (Fairthlough, 1991:550). In the ongoing discussions on CA, Habermas emphasises an inbuilt role of the lifeworld in the process:

> Subjects acting communicatively always come to an understanding in the horizon of a lifeworld. Their lifeworld is formed from more or less diffuse, always unproblematic, background convictions. This lifeworld background serves as a source of situation definitions that are presupposed by participants as unproblematic. The lifeworld also stores the interpretative work of preceding generations. It is the conservative counterweight to the risk of disagreement that arises with every actual process of reaching understanding.
> (Habermas, 1984:70)

In addition to using phrases such as 'pre-reflective' and 'naively mastered skills', Habermas also addresses a variety of competences and knowledge used by individuals to negotiate their position in the world, relate to and interact with others, and maintain social relationships. Such acts are located within the intersubjective realm of people's everyday life and are shaped by 'taken-for-granted background assumptions' (Habermas, 1984:335). These usually include created and shared knowledge, values and language actions and the justification of such actions (Fields, 1991).

Individuals' everyday beliefs and skills that are taken for granted have to be critically reviewed, questioned and justified (Habermas, 1984, 1985). While this strengthens and reproduces the shared lifeworld, it also provides a framework for the rationalisation of the lifeworld. Rationality, in Habermas' (1984) understanding, is necessary for the lifeworld and is an inextricable part of social evolution of modern and emancipated societies. As long as rationalisation is guided by commonly achieved understanding and happens in small-scale homogeneous cultures, the lifeworld does not lose its power for individuals and societal processes, as 'cultural reproduction, social integration, and socialisation' (Habermas, 1985:374) are secured. However, due to the growth of and increasing diversity within society, and the nature of rationalisation shaped by modern capitalist societies, the lifeworld 'gets cut down more and more to one subsystem among others' (Habermas, 1985:154). Complexity of the society and the market determines that previously legitimate narratives in justifying law and morality become replaced by generalised and abstract ideas and principles (Edgar, 2006). In other words, value generalisation (Habermas, 1985:179) takes place. Habermas borrowed this concept from Talcott Parsons, who proposed that 'the more differentiated the system, the higher level of generality at which the value-pattern must be "couched" if it is so to legitimate the more specified values of all of the differentiated parts of the system' (1971:307). Habermas (1985:179–185) radicalised this approach and noted that value generalisation results in an uncoupling of CA from all behaviour patterns that previously were perceived as normatively binding. Society's traditional norms become

106 *Communicative action and the EU markets*

detached from the basis for social cooperation. In such a context, the need for means to regulate social conflict and maintain social relations and society's functionality emerges. For instance, religiously anchored agreement is replaced by institutionalised rules and procedures, and more rational and technical means, such as judiciary. The increase of social growth and diversity as well as the intensity of value generalisation in modern capitalistic societies lead to the expansion and proliferation of social labour necessary to coordinate and manage societal processes. As a result, socially significant coordination of social processes and actions happens not through the language but through steering media, mostly through money and power, including bureaucratic power and market (Habermas, 1985). Hence,

> the lifeworld contexts in which processes of reaching understanding are always embedded are devalued in favour of media-steered interactions, the lifeworld is no longer needed for the coordination of action.
> (Habermas, 1985:183)

In Habermas' terms, the result of the transfer of action coordination from language over to steering media (Habermas, 1985) is a creation of steering media–regulated institutions, such as the market and the state – or in other words – the system. Social interactions steered by the system lose the connection with society's moral and political ideologies and foundations. Steering media erases a great part of interpersonal human activity and estrange it from the practices alive in pre-modern societies. In other words, 'the more complex social systems become, the more provincial lifeworlds become' (Habermas, 1985:173). Nevertheless, lifeworld is the domain of everyday personal and social life as intersubjective communication:

> Only the limited segments of the lifeworld brought into the horizon of a situation constitute a thematizable context of action oriented to mutual understanding. [...] The lifeworld appears as a reservoir of taken-for-granted, of unshaken convictions that participants in communication draw upon in cooperative processes of interpretation.
> (Habermas, 1985:124)

However, sometimes, the influence of steering media is so strong that people are unable to understand and justify processes happening around them. The structure of the lifeworld is affected in a way that regular lifeworld renewal processes and CA practices no longer exist. In Habermas' terms, this is when 'the mediation of the lifeworld assumes the form of colonisation' (1985:196).

For Habermas, colonisation of the lifeworld is the undermining of individual freedom by more complex societies. Large-scale social processes are routinised, formalised and governed by employing different, especially bureaucratic, rules and procedures. Such practices make social relations, practices and responses static, standardised and fixed. This restricts individuals' actions that are subject to such practices in modern societies. Communicative forms of social interaction are replaced by actions mediated through money and power. While in the lifeworld, actions are coordinated through consensus, here, they are synchronised through 'a functional interlocking of system "inputs" and "outputs" (found, for example, in the capitalist marketplace of supply and demand)' (Edwards, 2008:304). The system intrudes not only into personal lifeworlds but also into society as a lifeworld. Following Habermas (1984, 1985), colonisation erodes society-, personality- and culture-related lifeworld resources, and this affects not only actions per se but also the manifestation of individual lifeworlds in the context of the system.

Having established the notion of the lifeworld and its colonisation, it is worth looking at how EU policies may impact the processes related with either creation or colonisation of MSs' lifeworlds. Can the EU provide a framework for a common lifeworld to emerge? Or perhaps it acts as a system colonising national lifeworlds? Answers to these and other questions are explored in the following discussion and further elaborated in the subsequent chapters.

EU policies and the lifeworld

EU can either provide a framework for a common lifeworld to emerge, or it can act as a system intruding into national lifeworlds. With regard to the Union's role in creating a common lifeworld, a great volume of literature exploring European integration argue that the EU by its nature can be considered as a lifeworld or that it provides conditions for a common lifeworld to emerge (Lewis, 1998, Müller, 2004, Niemann, 2004, Risse, 1996b, 1999, 2000). The premise for this proposition is 'dense interaction patterns within highly regulated international institutions' (Risse, 2000: 15), which although differ from issue area to issue area, are present across the EU policymaking processes (Risse, 1996a). Having high socialisation and institutionalisation of the negotiating settings (Lewis, 1998), the Union provides a scene for creating collective identity and sharing common values and norms. This, according to Niemann (2004), is one of the preconditions for a shared lifeworld among the MSs to emerge.

Since the single market is the foundation of the EU and since the basic freedoms are premised upon it, values and norms that are introduced by the Union and play a part in creating a framework for a common lifeworld to emerge should be critically assessed. Specifically, in 2001, the European Commission (EC) released a White Paper on European Governance, where the reinforcement of 'European identity and the importance of shared values within the Union' (COM (2001) 0428, final:3.3) were highlighted.

The emergence and the content of the document were influenced by the Maastricht Treaty (1992: art.2), where one set of goals is to establish

> a common market and an economic and monetary union and by implementing the common policies or activities [...], to promote throughout the Community a harmonious and balanced development of economic activities, sustainable and non-inflationary growth respecting the environment, a high degree of convergence of economic performance, a high level of employment and of social protection, the raising of the standard of living and quality of life, and economic and social cohesion and solidarity among Member States.

On the one hand, this suggests that a framework for common norms, values, activities and obligations among EU members have been introduced and legally established. On the other hand, potential impact of the EU's position towards the single market and free movement of capital as a value questions the origins and the content of the values and common norms. In other words, do the introduced values contribute to the creation of a lifeworld as suggested by Habermas, or do they act as a tool, reshaping and transforming intersubjective everyday life realms into settings, that are convenient for maintaining and boosting the regional economy? If the latter is the case, then EU surreptitiously colonises national and individual lifeworlds and encapsulates them in a new form or new values. While there is no room for an exhaustive discussion of this duality, some of the instances are outlined below.

To begin with, as it was discussed in the previous chapter global and regional instruments provide MSs with rules, norms and procedures, that either encourage the engagement into interaction with and development of legal norms, values and rights or provide a framework for ignoring them (Risse, 1996b). For example, by signing and ratifying the CRPD, the EU and national governments adopted similar vocabularies, definitions, norms and human rights values in the area of disability (Kayess and French, 2008, Lord, 2010, Quinn, 2009) that should be translated into national policies and everyday practices. While this can be treated as a positive example, legal construction of disabled people as 'vulnerable' customers in the EU instruments, followed by the implementation of the same conventions at national level suggests opposite practice. Specifically, by ascribing and legally establishing the responsibility for participation in the market to an individual, the EU neither reflects upon nor tackles the actual roots of customer vulnerability. Contrarily, it intrudes into and corrupts individual realities. On the one hand, this duality demonstrates the power of global and regional instruments in shaping a normative framework, which structures stakeholders' interaction and serves 'as arenas in which international policy deliberation can take place' (Risse, 2000:15). On the other hand, this questions

MSs' reflexivity, power and willingness to challenge and negotiate EU institutionalised values and norms that shape collective identity and constitute a common lifeworld across the Union.

Unchallenged internalisation of the proposed EU framework for the common lifeworld can be linked with Wessels (1992) discussion. He suggests that due to the growth and complexity of modern states, citizens' needs and prospects cannot anymore be met only by national governments. As a result, welfare states joined into one union aiming to regulate the ongoing processes. On the one hand, this provides cohesive means to tackle increasing challenges; ensures more coordinated economic growth, universalised rules and standards; and introduces the foundation for more equal individuals' treatment across the Union (Schmidt, 1997). On the other hand, it eliminates states' freedom and control in making decisions such as resource distribution or service provision (Schmidt, 1997, 2005, Wessels, 1992).

The shift of policy decision-making from national governments to the European Council and the Parliament (Verovšek, 2012) weakens national parliaments (Schmidt, 1997). Nevertheless, currently, the EU is responsible for over 75% of all legislation passing through national governments, including 90% of consumer protection legislation (Schmidt, 2006: 63–64). This may challenge the realities of MSs that are not actively involved in the process or share atypical features. As a result, national lifeworlds may become diffused and national democracies get in deficit (Schmidt, 2005). Such practices can be interpreted as the EU as a system's intrusion into states' lifeworld. According to Habermas (2001, 2006), this and unequal distribution of power between the EU and its members can be overcome by developing EU democracy at the supranational level. This can be achieved by 'providing political institutions and citizenry that can be mobilised, as well as economic social milieu that can be administered legitimately' (Verovšek, 2012:369).

Literature on international relations identify another challenge caused by the fact that decisions made by the EU are often shaped around the preferences of large states, such as Germany, France and the United Kingdom (Lewis, 1998, Moravcsik, 1991, Schneider, 2011, 2013). This may affect bargaining outcomes, norms, values and vocabularies introduced to the community in a specific issue area. It may also intrude into smaller and less powerful members' lifeworld and realities. Hence, even though the EU has a potential and preconditions for providing a framework for a common lifeworld across Europe to emerge, the introduced norms, values and their content should be critically assessed, as under specific circumstances national realms and lifeworlds may be intruded or corrupted.

Having established the link between EU policies and the lifeworld, it is worth turning the attention to the private market. The following discussion, therefore, provides some insight into the relation between the EU, large enterprises and SMEs. It aims to answer the question of how this interaction contributes to shaping a common lifeworld across the Union.

Large business, SMEs and the lifeworld

Despite the prevailing assumption that large and multinational enterprises dominate in the EU economy, 99% of all European business is comprised of SMEs (European Commission, 2013). Small or medium size of a company provides more freedom, flexibility, personalisation (Man et al., 2002, Nooteboom, 1988) and better opportunities to bring in and reverb specific time- and place-related norms, values and conventions (Hammann et al., 2009, Lagendijk, 2004a). Contrary to large businesses, SMEs are often characterised by socially responsible behaviour and management (Fox, 2005, Hammann et al., 2009) that correlates with a local community's practices, values, norms and trust (Jenkins, 2004). In addition, while governments and corporate businesses are looking for order, formality, accountability, control measures, formal standards, systems and positional authority, small businesses are characterised by features such as trust, more informal relations and interactions, holism and freedom (Gibb, 2000). SMEs are more likely to connect with and reflect local customers' realities that mirror culturally and locally embodied knowledge, regional identity and the lifeworld (Lagendijk, 2004a).

Quantitative advantage of SMEs over large global enterprises is dominated and diminished by the latter's profit precedence. The Annual Report on European SMEs (Gagliardi et al., 2013:7) demonstrates that while the value-added decline of large enterprises in 2012 was €8.6 billion, medium-sized enterprises lost €17 billion, followed by micro-enterprises (€14 billion) and small-sized enterprises (€13.2 billion). In addition, in 2012, the SME sector as a whole (99% of all the EU business) delivered 57.6% of the gross value, with 42.4% delivered by large enterprises (less than 1% of all the EU business; Gagliardi et al., 2013). On the one hand, this may be linked with the economic crisis in 2008 and treated as an exception and not as a common practice. On the other hand, financial dominance of large enterprises is well documented over time (Chen and Huang, 2004). This suggests that SMEs' strong regional identity may be challenged and dominated by global companies that are more likely to use financial advantage as a steering media and act as a system.

SMEs' vulnerability may also be shaped by trade policy developments, applicable to foreign (Fliess and Busquets, 2006) and domestic (Gagliardi et al., 2013), small and large companies. Under such circumstances, multinational business players and their goal rationality dominate SMEs' value rationality (Nooteboom, 1988) and restrict professionals' competences and informal practices (Man et al., 2002). This suggests that in aiming to create a single market, the EU inadvertently introduce policy instruments and promote market practices that are oriented towards profit origination and circulation. Respectively, being more resistant to financial instabilities and generating more turnovers (Gagliardi et al., 2013), large global enterprises are in a more beneficial position compared to small and local companies. Such actions of governance in juncture with global market mechanisms strengthen SMEs' vulnerability and become disconnected from local norms and values or, in Habermas' terms, are 'delinguistified' (Habermas, 1985:154).

Marketisation and ongoing growth of global enterprises provides large companies with characteristics, typical to a system (Lagendijk, 2004b), which are 'relatively formal and have a logic and momentum of their own that go beyond the subjective experience of actors, both insofar as they impart a formal rationality to action through their interlacing and consequences of action' (Sayer, 2001:691). In such a context, some processes and policy traditions may intensify SMEs' lifeworld colonisation, making it 'more and more subject to the identity-blind mechanisms that rule the "systemworld"' (Lagendijk, 2004b:513). On the other hand, stronger SMEs' position in the single market may maintain and connect personal, regional and national lifeworlds (Hammann et al., 2009), leading to better and more available knowledge about the customers, their needs and preferences (Lagendijk, 2004b). Policy developments and incentives, empowering SMEs and harmonising power relations between large, medium and small enterprises may potentially create a framework enabling customers' voice and diversity to be heard and taken into account.

The following discussion focuses on the micro level and addresses customer experience in the private market. The focus is on marketing strategies and innovations that may intrude into and reshape customers' lifeworld.

Private market, customers and the lifeworld

Back in 1981, Karl Marx made it clear that individuals' choices are rarely made of their own choosing. Similarly, the dominant theme in Bauman's work is the way the market restricts customers' freedom. Such theoretical positions were supported and illustrated in the first chapter demonstrating how retailers control customers' emotions and feelings, shape choice, consumption style, eliminate rational purchase decisions and do this for profit-oriented purposes. Even though customers are becoming aware of the controlling retail environment (Jackson, 1999), their power to reshape existing practices is insufficient (Bauman, 1988). These and other examples suggest that customer purchase decisions do not guarantee customer freedom. Indeed, choice, preferences, wishes, desires and the way they are met are shaped by industry. Hence, retail market restricts customers' lifeworld as they are prevented from freely implementing and expressing values, positions and preferences.

New forms of consumption, such as ethical (Carrigan et al., 2004, Cherrier, 2007) and green or sustainable consumption (Connolly and Prothero, 2008, Gilg et al., 2005, Prothero et al., 2011), introduce and promote new values, penetrating into customer practices and personal realities. On the one hand, the emergence of these forms increases individuals' altruistic (Karp, 1996), ecocentric and biospheric values (Gilg et al., 2005) and environmental concerns (Stern et al., 1995). Likewise, particular practices of recycling, food consumption (Connolly and Prothero, 2008) and respect for animal rights (Cooper-Martin and Holbrook, 1993) become more present. On the other hand, by introducing new consumption patterns the market provides a framework within which individuals pursue and exercise their identity (Cherrier, 2007) and reconstruct current beliefs, norms and values. In other words, even though new consumption modes are usually founded on positive intensions, by positioning them as a form of value, market covertly shapes customers' perspectives. While the purpose of this control does not necessarily lead to destruction of customer freedom, it regulates and constrains human interaction and introduces certain shared elements, through which customer experience intrude into their everyday life realms and reshape knowledge, moral values, positions and understandings.

While business players are proactive in communicating and promoting to customers certain values and consumption practices, this rarely reaches disabled people. Focus on non-disabled customers and limited accessibility provisions prevent people with impairments from gaining the same degree of customer knowledge, shaping norms and values. Being deprived from constrain-free access (whether it is customer information or built environment), people become loyal and tend to come back to accessible shops and producers (Chan and Puech, 2014, Office for Disability Issues, 2010). This, respectively, shapes their customer service experience and knowledge about products. In other words, while non-disabled shoppers are able to gain information and build knowledge sets about a wider spectrum of goods, providers and consumption trends and movements, for disabled people, this kind of knowledge and experience is partial. In such a context, an 'intersubjective coordination of actions' (Habermas, 1985:137) does not take place, as non-disabled and disabled customers do not share the same meanings, and a stock of customer culture knowledge is limited. Thus, since lifeworld as a resource for action per se, disabled individuals' customer lifeworld and participation in the market are constrained more than are the same domains of non-disabled people.

Having established lifeworld patterns at policy, market and customer levels, the following section explores whether current practice of shaping EU policy instruments provides possibilities for democratising access to the formation of public discourse. It aims to explore whether current communication and debate are free and provide a framework for CA to emerge regarding the EU single market.

Access to the discourse and power relations

Access to the discourse and recognition of each other as equal partners in communication are important factors for engaging into CA (Habermas, 1984, 1985, 1991, 1993, 1996b). Being related with 'ethics of discourse' and concerned with the public sphere, CA is about democratisation of access to the formation of public discourse through free communication and debate among all relevant citizens. Positioning CA as the way of addressing and solving the outlined tensions and contradictions in the public discourse surrounding disability, accessibility and retail customers, this section briefly introduces the concept of CA as described by Habermas. Aiming to provide deeper insights and reflecting the idea of lifeworld and system, the focus is on communicative and strategic communication models and arguing and bargaining communication modes. Being associated with reasoning and rational argumentation, arguing is frequent in global and regional international politics and international relationships (Lagendijk, 2004a, Müller, 2004, Niemann, 2004, Risse, 1996a, 1999, 2000). Likewise, bargaining that is premised on lying (Seymour, 2013), efficiency, effectiveness (Johnson, 1991) and logic of consequences (Habermas, 1984) is also present (Risse, 1996a, 1999, 2000).

With this in mind, the following discussion provides some insights into the manifestation of the two communication models and modes in the EU policy development process and private market practice. It explores whether they serve in overcoming or strengthening the tensions in public discourse. The discussion is concluded by an overview of OMC, its limitations and a potential in creating a framework for CA to emerge.

Communicative action

Habermas started the discussion on CA in the essay 'What Is Universal Pragmatics' (Habermas, 1976). In this and later work, he defined it as a meaningful interaction between two or more individuals, who establish and maintain social relationships in oral or written formats of ordinary language or in gestures. However, CA should not be equalised with language or communication acts. In the discussions on reason and the rationalisation, Habermas (1984) makes it clear that language is a mechanism for coordinating the action. Respectively, teleological, dramaturgical, normative and strategic models of action use language as a medium to achieve the goals determined by the nature of each of the models. For instance, teleological action perceives language 'as one of several media through which speakers oriented to their own success can influence one another in order to bring opponents to form or to grasp beliefs and intentions that are in the speakers' own interest' (Habermas, 1984:95). Dramaturgical action employs language for self-presentation, and normative model perceives it as a 'medium that transmits cultural values and carries a consensus that is merely reproduced with each additional act of understanding' (Habermas, 1984:95). Language as a mechanism to coordinate actions is also used in strategic action. Specifically, here, it is used to direct participants' actions 'through egocentric calculations of utility' and to coordinate these 'through interest positions' (Habermas, 1984:94). Only the

> communicative model of action presupposes language as a medium of uncurtailed communication whereby speakers and hearers, out of the context of their reinterpreted lifeworld, refer simultaneously to things in the objective, social, and subjective worlds in order to negotiate common definitions of the situation.
>
> (Habermas, 1984:95)

114 *Communicative action and the EU markets*

In other words, while the first four types of action take language as a one-sided medium, CA positions it as an interactive medium.

Actors involved in CA have to utter 'something understandably', give the hearer 'something to understand', make 'himself thereby understandable' and come 'to an understanding with another person' (Habermas, 1976:2). This shapes the content of three validity claims that can and should be challenged in the communication process. These are the intention to communicate true content in order to share knowledge with the communicating partner; do this truthfully, in order to build trust with a hearer; and 'the speaker must choose an utterance that is right [richtig] so that the hearer can accept the utterance and speaker and hearer can agree with one another in the utterance with respect to a recognised normative background' (Habermas, 1976:3). In other words, actors who engage in CA are guided by the aim of and act towards reaching mutual understanding and not by egocentric intentions for personal success. Their individual positions and intentions have to be constructed in a way that allows coordinating and harmonising these with individual objectives of participating agents and be founded on shared definitions of the situation (Habermas, 1984:385–386). Within such communicative milieu, actors do not treat objectives and preferences as fixed. Indeed, they perceived them as fluid that may change through the whole argumentative process and can be challenged and questioned by the participating actors.

With regard to communication mode, strategic action employs bargaining and CA uses discussion, deliberation, arguing and reasoning as the main modes of communication and speech acts. Aiming to achieve reasoned understanding, participants lay the path for the 'ideal speech situation', where only a better argument counts and the engaged parties aim to convince each other in light of the three validity claims (Habermas, 1993:56–57). If validity claims are questioned, the speaker has to provide explanations and reasoning in a rational discourse. Summarising Habermas' work Niemann (2004:382) notes that 'by arguing in relation to standards of truth, rightness and sincerity, agents have a basis for judging what constitutes reasonable choices of action, through which they can reach agreement'.

Communication mode plays a crucial role when engaging in any model of action. Hence, the following discussion focuses on bargaining and arguing that are associated with strategic and communicative actions, respectively. It is important to know the essence of the concepts, as later on this enables understanding the practice of accessing the discourse on accessibility of the EU single market and to identify possibilities for improving the praxis.

Bargaining and arguing

Bargaining and arguing are two types of speech modes (Holzinger, 2001), linked to strategic and communicative actions, respectively. As discussed, Habermas (1984, 1985, 1991) makes a clear distinction between the use of language as a medium to state facts, and speech acts which use meaningful and truthful language to construct and maintain social relationships. Using Habermas' theory of CA as a framework, Müller (2004:397) summarises Kratochwil's (1991) work and describes speech acts as 'complete structured utterances that use elements (words) which have a certain meaning in a given language community, conduct a specific activity and are intentionally directed to achieve a specific effect in the audience'. While Holzinger (2001) notes that arguing and bargaining are simply two different types of speech act, broader academic debate attribute them to social theories such as CA theory and rationalism or ontological positions such as holism and individualism, respectively. Habermas refers to bargaining in discussions on strategic action and to arguing on CA.

With regard to bargaining, Habermas (1991:117) notes that competing opponents, who are 'determined by the intention of influencing each other's decisions in a purposive-rational way, that is, in a way oriented only to each's own success' are more likely to use different bargaining strategies, than the actors, oriented to reaching common understanding. In bargaining situations, stakeholders are aware that strategic goals can be achieved only if other actors agree and consent (Nash, 1950). Their cooperative relationships often last as long as the processes fit their purposeful and egocentric interests (Habermas, 1991, Niemann, 2004, Powell, 2002). In addition, since the main goals of bargaining are to influence opponents' decisions and to force them to consent with the provided claims (Habermas, 1984, Johnson, 1991), self-interested actors often invoke threats and promises as a means to achieve the goal (Elster, 1991). Operating in different environments, often having unequally distributed resources and decision-making systems (Johnson, 1991), actors vary in their access to and usage of threats as warnings of punishment and promises as offers of reward (Schelling, 1958). Croson et al. (2003) refer to such actions as 'cheap talk', which aim to affect specific beliefs and outcomes typical to particular situations as well as provide an advantage to one of the opponents (Cheney et al., 1972) and power over the another (Cheney et al., 1972, Croson et al., 2003, Elster, 1991).

In discussions on the discourse principle, Habermas (1979, 1993) notes that non-neutralisable bargaining power should be disciplined by its equal distribution among the parties. More specifically, the negotiation of compromises should follow procedures that provide interested actors with equal opportunities for pressure. That is, equal opportunities to influence one another during the actual bargaining, so that 'all the affected interests can come into play and have equal chances of prevailing' (Habermas, 1996b:166). Otherwise, negotiated agreements should not be treated as fair. Strategic convey of information often accompanies promises and threats in the bargaining process (Seymour, 2013), as this enables increasing the size of the 'pie' (Powell, 2002). While such practice makes it difficult to establish trust and credibility (Cheney et al., 1972, Croson et al., 2003, Seymour, 2013), 'the existence of potential gains from acting jointly creates an incentive to cooperate' (Powell, 2002:2). Therefore, strategic action and bargaining have to be bounded or institutionalised (Habermas, 1991). This would found the consensual action on intersubjectively recognised validity claims (Habermas, 1991) and strategic values would become replaced by delegated duties, trust and responsibility that are usually assigned by the authority or more powerful actors (Müller, 2004).

Contrary to this, arguing actors behave in a communicative manner and introduce their positions and arguments. They coordinate or harmonise individual perspectives in the framework of shared notions and circumstances of particular situations (Habermas, 1984:385–386). Each actor who enters the arguing process has an individual position and is aware that the objectives and preferences are not fixed, are flexible and change through the process of argumentation (Niemann, 2004). In some cases, individual views of the world, interests and identities may also change (Risse, 2000). Speakers themselves are aware of potential persuasion and are ready to be persuaded. In this respect, Habermas refers to argumentation as a

> procedure for the exchange and assessment of information, reasons, and terminologies […]. The procedure cannot itself generate these elements; its task is to ensure that the argumentative exchange can proceed on the basis of all relevant information and reasons available at a particular point in time within the most fruitful and appropriate descriptive framework in each distance […]. Arguments are essential components of reflexive learning processes that for their part certainly cannot be explicated solely in terms of argumentation.
>
> (Habermas, 1993:58)

Drawing on Searle's (1969) and Austin's (1975) works, Habermas notes that provided validity claims can be challenged only if they are understandable. The content of the provided information and statements have to be true, the intentions expressed truthfully and the manifested intention is right (Habermas, 1991). Then, the hearer is able to filter and share received information, trust the speaker and be sure that they mean what they say. Actors participating in the argumentative process thematise debatable validity claims and criticise or challenge them through arguments. In this respect, arguments are treated as strong only if they fit within a given context, and provided reasons convince the actors and motivate them to question validity claims (Habermas, 1984). Arguing may be time-consuming as reasoning is often a slow and fractious process (Mercier and Sperber, 2009). However, arguing, reasoning and deliberating are the main modes via which parties can engage in a 'successful' arguing (Niemann, 2004) that manifests as a 'better argument' (Habermas, 1984, Risse, 2000) leading to CA.

Having established the concepts of communicative and strategic action, and arguing and bargaining as communication modes, it is worth focusing on their manifestation in international relations and EU policy settings.

Bargaining, arguing and international relations

Habermas (1984, 1985, 1991) argues that aiming to achieve an ideal speech situation, power relations should be absent and only a 'better argument' should count. Contrarily, the literature on international relations demonstrate that the nature of and power distribution within international politics and business define who is provided with access to the discourse and which argument is defined as a 'better argument' (Elgström and Jönsson, 2000, Lewis, 1998, Risse, 2000, Schneider, 2013). As an example, Risse (2000) uses the UN Security Council to demonstrate how more powerful states, such as the United States and Germany that have a permanent access to the deliberations and economic power, introduce power asymmetry and prevent stakeholders from developing better arguments and achieving an ideal speech situation. Similarly, Schneider (2013) uses an example of the EU budget to demonstrate that although more powerful countries should be aware of the importance of equality and non-hierarchical decision-making processes, they are often informally ascribed with and exercise their advantage during the bargaining process of finance distribution.

The practice of when few states constantly dominate is more a rule than an exception (Elster, 1991, Jacobsson and Vifell, 2003, Lewis, 1998, Moravcsik and Vachudova, 2002, Schneider, 2011, 2013). Such practice is often accompanied by a joint-decision trap (Scharpf, 1988) and leads to bargaining, instead of arguing practice and strategic rather than communicative rationality. As an example, since the 'agreement of constituent governments must be unanimous or nearly unanimous' (Scharpf, 1988:254), powerful EU MSs do not avoid either threatening to delay or vetoing proposed decisions (Schneider, 2011) or stalling the negotiations until they meet their state's strategic interests (Schneider, 2013). In addition, Dür and Mateo's (2010) discussion on the negotiation of the EU's Financial Perspective (2007–2013) suggests that hard bargaining strategies such as coalition formation, public criticism of other countries or the Council and public commitment not to give-in are frequently employed as they are more effective and efficient than soft bargaining strategies. However, they are more accessible and available for dominant and large countries than less powerful EU members. Weaker MSs adopt soft bargaining strategies, such as praise, public positions and concession, which are less likely to ensure the same results as hard bargaining strategies. As a result, large MSs' preferences, positions and needs often dominate smaller and weaker countries' interests and positions.

National governments acknowledge 'a value in reaching agreement, in collectively solving problems, and understanding each other's domestic political constraints' (Lewis, 1998:489). As a result, aiming to achieve strategic interests, they usually employ cooperative strategies based on reciprocity. To illustrate, Lewis (1998:489) quotes a deputy of a large MS, 'there is a higher sense of defending national interests and of leaving aside instructions, which is rooted in preserving the goodwill of my colleagues for the future. Without this, I won't have their respect and their help next time'. Hence, MSs' willingness to cooperate and make political sacrifices may be motivated by the achievement of strategic interests, rather than the creation of a common knowledge and position. Under such circumstances and decision-making culture, actors risk getting involved in political-strategic interests persuasion. Unanimity and unequal power relations aspirate trust and fairness, without which neither common knowledge nor common position can be shaped (Habermas, 1984, 1985). Since the 'bargaining style of decision-making' (Scharpf, 1988:686) is common within the EU, it creates challenges for the Union when mitigating social dilemmas (Risse, 2000) and structural changes (Elgström and Jönsson, 2000), especially in marginalised areas such as disabled customers' rights or market accessibility.

It would be misleading to state that the current EU decision-making process is explicitly premised on bargaining or is disconnected from communicative rationality and is constantly moving towards strategic action (Elgström and Jönsson, 2000, Lewis, 1998). Although equal access to the discourse is hard to achieve in world politics and private market (Dür and Mateo, 2010, Elgström and Jönsson, 2000, Elster, 1991, Howorth, 2010, Moravcsik and Vachudova, 2002, Schneider, 2013), non-hierarchy, argumentative consistency, weaker actors' empowerment and actions justification may lead towards communicative rationality and 'the better argument' (Risse, 2000:18–19). As an example, the study on the World Trade Organisation liberalisation of basic telecommunications (Niemann, 2004) demonstrates that in pre-negotiations stage, the processes typical to CA dominated over strategic action. Actors engaged into communicative rationality and argumentative practices as they shared a strong lifeworld had insufficient knowledge about the subject, dealt with cognitively complex issues, had a possibility to discuss, were persuasive and the level of politicisation was low (Niemann, 2004:385–391). This recalls Risse's (2000) observation that international politicians are more likely to engage in truth-seeking behaviour when the issue area is highly institutionalised, interaction is more informal than formal and is based in network-like settings.

When actors are not certain of national interests, they are more likely to be willing and able to communicate in a meaningful way. Crawford (2009) adds that stakeholders have to share similar linguistic and factual understanding of the issue. As an example, with regard to a common lifeworld, although the process of socialisation of international human rights norms into domestic policies often involves 'cheap talk' and rhetorical action, due to a global human rights regime that provides a 'collectively shared principles and norms and common discourse' (Risse, 1999:537), actors are able to engage in argumentative practice more effectively. Furthermore, while unequal power relations prevent negotiating parties from engaging in arguing and communicative rationality, Niemann (2004) uses negotiations on article 133 of the Amsterdam Treaty as an example, illustrating that by putting aside rank, status and qualification, parties are more likely to open up a scene for achieving a common goal and engaging in CA. These and other examples suggest that even though the EU decision-making process is often characterised by bargaining, non-coerced understanding-oriented and communicative rationality–oriented practices are also possible.

Habermas (1993) notes that arguing and CA should not take place behind closed door. In modern democracies, it should be public. This encourages speakers to be truthful and regularly explain and justify behaviour. However, public spheres in international politics and business relations are dynamic and not static (Risse, 2000). In addition, in public speaking, policy players are likely to use a rhetorical type of argumentation, focus on convincing the audience and avoid being persuaded. The involvement of NGOs (Seymour, 2013) and different social movements (Crossley, 2003) may help to reshape the practice, frame the agenda, improve the introduction of arguments and appeal to existing language, knowledge, norms and discourses. Indeed, international debates that involve NGOs and other non-governmental representatives usually are more open and accessible (Risse, 2000).

Since neither strategic nor CAs may appear in a pure form (Risse, 1996a, 1999), the EU policy decision process is distinguished by a mixture of communicative and strategic arguments (Crawford, 2009, Niemann, 2004, Risse, 2000). Such practice is a direct result of socially constructed processes and interactions (Wendt, 1994) that are typical to the EU as an institution (Lewis, 1998). One of the scenarios that may assist to reshape existing practice and to poke the processes towards arguing and CA is the adoption of the OMC. The following section, therefore, addresses the concept and discusses its potential to provide a scene for CA to emerge regarding the EU single market.

Communicative rationality and OMC

Positions towards the OMC vary, and the method is criticised as well as is supported. The opponents often shed light on hierarchy, different forms of control (Lodge, 2007), insufficient involvement of civil society organisations (Friedrich, 2006) and selective involvement of elite actors (Casey and Gold, 2005, Friedrich, 2006). This results in limited ability to challenge and reshape current power relations and structures (Chalmers and Lodge, 2003). Likewise, a lack of public discussion about the OMC (Friedrich, 2006), focus of the EU on information dissemination and limited attention to the procedure (Casey and Gold, 2005) and insufficient time for discussions (Kröger, 2009) corrupt the intended learning process (Mailand, 2008) that is essential for creating common knowledge (Habermas, 1984, 1985, 1996b, Habermas and Cronin, 1993). It is also argued that the introduction of the OMC has changed policy discourse, shedding light on competitiveness and 'rational (economic) interpretations of public problems and their solutions' (Radulova, 2009:12). This, indeed, may support neoliberal political rationality (Flear, 2009) and, respectively, shape the relations between an individual, the state and the market (Kröger, 2009).

Scholars' position towards the OMC depends on their interpretation of the instrument and attitudes towards soft law (Kröger, 2009). Hence, the outlined points should not be treated as a disproof of the OMC and its potential. On the contrary, recalling the ontological position of this book, it is legitimate to argue that OMC may be a useful instrument, employed for creating a framework for CA between citizens, the state and the market to emerge. Location of the principles of the communicative rationality and the procedures of the OMC within the deliberative democracy framework (Cohen, 1989, Eriksen and Fossum, 2002, Habermas, 1996a) is one of the ways to achieve the goal. Similar to CA, deliberative democracy puts the emphasis on public arguing and reasoning of citizens, who are seen as free and equal (Cohen, 1989, Cohen and Sabel, 1997, Habermas, 1996a). Clifford (2012) notes that deliberative democratic scholars and disability rights activists perceive inclusion as a keystone of legitimacy and political participation. However, alternative modes of communication should be ensured, otherwise the speech may be disabled and some individuals may be excluded from participation in the discourse formation. In this respect, the Lisbon Strategy (2000:para.37) introduced the OMC as a

> fully decentralised approach [...] applied in the line with principle of subsidiarity in which the union, the MS, the regional and local levels, as well as the social partners and civil society, will be actively involved, using variable forms of partnership.

The EU as a system privileges organised lobbies and large states (Eriksen and Fossum, 2002) and is driven by the ideology of free market, economic competitiveness and the interests of big businesses (Andersen and Burns, 1996, Radulova, 2009, Traxler and Schmitter, 1995). The inclusiveness and participation of different agents, and especially of small or weak countries and civil society organisations, may help to reshape power relations and introduce the praxis of public arguing and the provision of justifications and reasons (Cohen, 1989, Seymour, 2013). In other words, OMC premised on common guidelines and objectives (Jacobsson and Vifell, 2003) may 'bridge the gap' (Armstrong, 2002) and enable citizens to express their concerns, interests and ideas and exercise self-governance (Friedrich, 2006). Such processes may enable MSs, industry, civil society and other actors to 'share a commitment to the resolution of problems of collective choice through public reasoning' (Cohen, 1989:72) and change opinions and positions when 'faced with qualitatively better argument' (Eriksen and Fossum, 2002:402).

Some procedures and decisions of the EU bureaucratic mechanism are unavailable or inaccessible to the general public (Eriksen and Fossum, 2002). Hence, by implying a non-hierarchical mode of governance (Lodge, 2007), the OMC reduces the power of the European Council in the agenda-setting process (Chalmers and Lodge, 2003) and transfers more power to national governments. Horizontal and transnational communication within and between MSs through regular benchmarking and peer review of own and of other states' programmes (Casey and Gold, 2005) enables the countries to learn from each other and exchange information and best practices. It provides comparative analysis and advice as well as promotes innovative approaches and evaluates experiences as it is established in the Amsterdam Treaty (1997, art.129). Such practices of creating knowledge, exchanging information and changing preferences enable the participating agents to form a common will (Jacobsson and Vifell, 2003) and step towards communicative rather than strategic rationality. On the one hand, while collective choices made in a deliberative way (Cohen, 1989) dilutes the Commission's role in steering the system and producing a common agreement on particular issues, they also allow individual differences across the MSs (Scott and Trubek, 2002:17) and do not colonise their national lifeworlds. On the other hand, common agreement on broad objectives among the members of the Union introduces a possibility for bottom-up practices not only when shaping policies (Lodge, 2007) but also when altering the EU's common beliefs and moulding its lifeworld.

Concluding comments

Recalling the discussion in the previous chapters on the contradictions in market practice and public discourse surrounding disability, accessibility and retail customers, the present chapter explored how Habermas' theory of CA could be employed aiming to provide insights and understanding, informing the way EU single market could become more accessible. It focused on the lifeworld as a collective domain and explored the conditions under which EU policy and market practices either enhance market accessibility or prevent its achievement. It was suggested that while 'dense interaction patterns within highly regulated international institutions' (Risse, 2000:15) may introduce a framework for a common lifeworld regarding an accessible EU single market to emerge, some practices and decision-making procedures may corrupt and destabilise national and customer realities. It was argued that the CRPD introduced similar vocabularies, definitions, norms and values regarding disability and accessibility and so to some degree unified regional and national positions towards market accessibility and customer equality. Meanwhile, unchallenged internalisation of regional instruments into national policies and insufficient MSs' innovation in the area continue maintaining exclusionary discourse and prevent from creating a more accessible EU single market.

Financial advantage of large enterprises over SMEs prevents the emergence of a common lifeworld. Specifically, large business' nature and practice are often disconnected from local norms and values. Their financial advantage and dominance in the market prevent small businesses to reflect, connect and maintain personal, regional and national lifeworlds. In such a way, available knowledge sets about what would work in creating an accessible market are negated and the potential remains unused. At a customer level, in addition to business' role in controlling customer decisions, market innovation, despite its positive intensions, may intrude and reconstruct customers' everyday realities and values. While these processes are applicable to both non-disabled and disabled customers, their impact on participation of customers with impairments is more severe.

The present chapter has also outlined key elements and differences between strategic action accompanied by bargaining and CA going together with arguing, reasoning and a 'better argument'. This was linked with the EU policies and processes in international relations. The discussion suggested that prioritisation of political interests, unequal power distribution among MSs and strategic rationality behind the processes, decisions and legislations prevent introducing more equality and accessibility for disabled customers. On the contrary, communicative rationality and a 'better argument'-oriented interaction, civil society's participation, shared lifeworld, equality and high institutionalisation of the issue may enable stakeholders to engage in CA and position markets accessibility as a common goal. In this respect, the OMC located within a framework of deliberative democracy can be used as an instrument for reshaping power relations among the EU, its members, market and disabled citizens.

Bibliography

Andersen, S. & Burns, T. 1996. The European Union and the erosion of parliamentary democracy: A study of post-parliamentary governance. *In:* Andersen, S. & Eliassen, K. (eds.) *The European Union: How democratic it is?* London, Sage Publications.

Armstrong, K. A. 2002. Rediscovering civil society: The European Union and the white paper on governance. *European Law Journal*, 8, 102–132.

Austin, J. L. 1975. *How to do things with words*, Oxford, Oxford University Press.

Bates, P. & Davis, F. A. 2004. Social capital, social inclusion and services for people with learning disabilities. *Disability & Society*, 19, 195–207.

Bauman, Z. 1988. *Freedom*, Milton Keynes, Open University Press.

Carrigan, M., Szmigin, I. & Wright, J. 2004. Shopping for a better world? An interpretive study of the potential for ethical consumption within the older market. *Journal of Consumer Marketing*, 21, 401–417.

Casey, B. H. & Gold, M. 2005. Peer review of labour market programmes in the European Union: What can countries really learn from one another? *Journal of European Public Policy*, 12, 23–43.

Chalmers, D. & Lodge, M. 2003. *The open method of co-ordination and the European welfare state*, London, ESRC Centre for Analysis and Risk Regulation.

Chan, W. & Puech, B. 2014. *Accessible retail. Every customer counts. A good practice guide to making reasonable adjustments*, Belfast, Equality Commission for Northern Ireland.

Chen, H.-L. & Huang, Y. 2004. The establishment of global marketing strategic alliances by small and medium enterprises. *Small Business Economics*, 22, 365–377.

Cheney, J., Harford, T. & Solomon, L. 1972. The effects of communicating threats and promises upon the bargaining process. *Journal of Conflict Resolution*, 16, 99–107.

Cherrier, H. 2007. Ethical consumption practices: Co-production of self-expression and social recognition. *Journal of Consumer Behaviour*, 6, 321–335.

Clifford, S. 2012. Making disability public in deliberative democracy. *Contemporary Political Theory*, 11, 211–228.

Cohen, J. 1989. Deliberation and democratic legitimacy. *In:* Matravers, D. & Pike, J. (eds.) *Debates in contemporary political philosophy. An antology*, London, Routledge.

Cohen, J. & Sabel, C. 1997. Directly-Deliberative Polyarchy. *European Law Journal*, 3, 313–342.

Connolly, J. & Prothero, A. 2008. Green consumption: Life-politics, risk and contradictions. *Journal of Consumer Culture*, 8, 117–145.

Cooper-Martin, E. & Holbrook, M. B. 1993. Ethical consumption experiences and ethical space. *Advances in Consumer Research*, 20, 113–118.

Crawford, N. C. 2009. Homo politicus and argument (nearly) all the way down: Persuasion in politics. *Perspectives on Politics*, 7, 103–124.

Croson, R., Boles, T. & Murnighan, J. K. 2003. Cheap talk in bargaining experiments: Lying and threats in ultimatum games. *Journal of Economic Behavior & Organization*, 51, 143–159.

Crossley, N. 2003. Even newer social movements? Anti-corporate protests, capitalist crisis and the remoralization of society. *Organization*, 10, 287–305.

Dür, A. & Mateo, G. 2010. Bargaining power and negotiation tactics: The negotiations on the EU's financial perspective, 2007–13. *Journal of Common Market Studies*, 48, 557–578.

Edgar, A. 2006. *Habermas. The key concepts*, Oxon, Routledge.

Edwards, G. 2008. The 'lifeworld' as a resource for social movement participation and the consequences of its colonization. *Sociology*, 42, 299–316.

Elgström, O. & Jönsson, C. 2000. Negotiation in the European Union: Bargaining or problem-solving? *Journal of European Public Policy*, 7, 684–704.

Elster, J. 1991. *Arguing and bargaining in the Federal Convention and the Assemblée Constituante*, Center for Study of Constitutionalism in Eastern Europe, School of Law, University of Chicago.

Eriksen, E. O. & Fossum, J. E. 2002. Democracy through strong publics in the European Union? *Journal of Common Market Studies*, 40, 401–424.

European Commission 2000. *Lisbon strategy*, Lisbon, EC.

European Commission 2001. European governance - A white paper (2001/C 287/01). *COM/2001/0428*.

European Commission 2013. Fact and figures about the EU's Small and Medium Enterprise (SME). Available: http://ec.europa.eu/enterprise/policies/sme/facts-figures-analysis/index_en.htm [Accessed 16/07/2014].

European Union 1992. *Treaty of Maastricht on European Union*, Brussels, EU.

European Union 1997. *The treaty of Amsterdam amending the treaty of the European Union, the treaties establishing the European Communities and certain related acts*, Amsterdam, EU.

Fairthlough, G. H. 1991. Habermas' concept of 'Lifeworld'. *Systems Practice*, 4, 547–563.

Fields, E. E. 1991. Understanding activist fundamentalism: Capitalist crisis and the 'Colonization of the lifeworld'. *Sociological Analysis*, 52, 175–190.

Flear, M. L. 2009. The open method of coordination on health care after the Lisbon Strategy II: Towards a neoliberal framing? *European Integration online Papers (EIoP)*, 13, 1–16.

Fliess, B. & Busquets, C. 2006. *The role of trade barriers in SME internationalisation,* Paris, OECD Publishing.

Fox, T. Small and medium-sized enterprises (SMEs) and corporate social responsibility: A discussion paper. Proceeding of Collaborative Project Between IIED, AICC, DA, IISD, IUCN and RIDES Addressing the Implications of CSR Standardisation (AICC et al., 2004), and Discussions in an Internal IIED Workshop on SMEs and Sustainable Development, 2005. Ventus Publishing ApS.

Fraser, N. 1990. Rethinking the public sphere: A contribution to the critique of actually existing democracy. *Social Text,* 25/26, 56–80.

Friedrich, D. 2006. Policy process, governance and democracy in the EU: The case of the open method of coordination on social inclusion in Germany. *Policy & Politics,* 34, 367–383.

Gagliardi, D., Muller, P., Lossop, E., Caliandro, C., Fritsch, M., Brtkova, G., Bohn, N. U., Klitou, D., Avigdor, G., Marzocchi, C. & Ramlogan, R. 2013. *A recovery on the horizon? Annual report on European SMEs 2012/2013,* Brussels, European Commission.

Gibb, A. A. 2000. SME policy, academic research and the growth of ignorance, mythical concepts, myths, assumptions, rituals and confusions. *International Small Business Journal,* 18, 13–35.

Gilg, A., Barr, S. & Ford, N. 2005. Green consumption or sustainable lifestyles? Identifying the sustainable consumer. *Futures,* 37, 481–504.

Godin, P., Davies, J., Heyman, B., Reynolds, L., Simpson, A. & Floyd, M. 2007. Opening communicative space: A Habermasian understanding of a user-led participatory research project. *The Journal of Forensic Psychiatry & Psychology,* 18, 452–469.

Goodman, D. 1992. Public sphere and private life: Toward a synthesis of current historiographical approaches to the old regime. *History and Theory,* 31, 1–20.

Habermas, J. 1974. *Theory and practice,* London, Heinemann.

Habermas, J. 1976. *Communication and the evolution of society,* Boston, Beacon Press.

Habermas, J. 1984. *The theory of communicative action: Volume 1. Reason and the rationalisation of society,* Boston, Beacon Press.

Habermas, J. 1985. *The theory of communicative action: Volume 2. Lifeworld and system: A critique of functionalist reason,* Cambridge, Polity Press.

Habermas, J. 1991. *Communication and the evolution of society,* Cambridge, Polity Press.

Habermas, J. 1993. *Justification and application: Remarks on discourse ethics,* Cambridge, MIT Press.

Habermas, J. 1996a. *Between facts and norms,* Cambridge, MIT Press.

Habermas, J. 1996b. *Between facts and norms: Contributions to a discourse theory of law and democracy,* Cambridge, MIT Press.

Habermas, J. 1998. Remarks on legitimation through human rights. *The Modern Schoolman,* 75, 87–100.

Habermas, J. 2012. The concept of human dignity and the realistic utopia of human rights. *In:* Corradetti, C. (ed.) *Philosophical dimensions of human rights,* Netherlands, Springer.

Habermas, J. & Cronin, C. 1993. *Justification and application: Remarks on discourse ethics,* Cambridge, Polity Press.

Hammann, E.-M., Habisch, A. & Pechlaner, H. 2009. Values that create value: Socially responsible business practices in SMEs – empirical evidence from German companies. *Business Ethics: A European Review*, 18, 37–51.

Holzinger, K. 2001. Verhandeln statt Argumentieren oder Verhandeln durch Argumentieren? Eine empirische Analyse auf der Basis der Sprechakttheorie. *Politische Vierteljahresschrift*, 42, 414–446.

Howorth, J. 2010. The EU as a global actor: Grand strategy for a global grand bargain? *Journal of Common Market Studies*, 48, 455–474.

Jackson, P. 1999. Consumption and identity: The cultural politics of shopping. *European Planning Studies*, 7, 25–39.

Jacobsson, K. & Vifell, A. Integration by deliberation? On the role of committees in the open method of coordination. Conference proceedings: Cidel conference on the forging of deliberative supranationalism in the European Union, 2003 Florence.

Jenkins, H. 2004. A critique of conventional CSR theory: An AME perspective. *Journal of General Management*, 29, 37–57.

Johnson, J. 1991. Habermas on strategic and communicative action. *Political Theory*, 19, 181–201.

Karp, D. G. 1996. Values and their effect on pro-environmental behavior. *Environment and Behavior*, 28, 111–133.

Kayess, R. & French, P. 2008. Out of darkness into light? Introducing the convention on the rights of persons with disabilities. *Human Rights Law Review*, 8, 1–34.

Kellner, D. 2000. Habermas, the public sphere, and democracy: A critical intervention. *In:* Hahn, L. E. (ed.) *Perspectives on Habermas*, Illinois, Open Court Publishing Company.

Kratochwil, F. V. 1991. *Rules, norms, and decisions: On the conditions of practical and legal reasoning in international relations and domestic affairs*, Cambridge, Cambridge University Press.

Kröger, S. 2009. The Open Method of Coordination: Underconceptualisation, overdetermination, de-politicisation and beyond. *European Integration online Papers (EIoP)* [Online], 13, 1. Available: http://ssrn.com/abstract=1553795 [Accessed 14/06/2012].

Lagendijk, A. 2004a. Global 'Lifeworlds' versus local 'Systemworlds': How flying winemakers produce global wines in interconnected locales. *Tijdschrift voor economische en sociale geografie*, 95, 511–526.

Lagendijk, A. 2004b. Global 'lifeworlds' versus local 'systemworlds': How flying winemakers produce global wines in interconnected locales. *Tijdschrift voor economische en sociale geografie*, 95, 511–526.

Lewis, J. 1998. Is the 'Hard Bargaining' image of the council misleading? The committee of permanent representatives and the Local Elections Directive. *Journal of Common Market Studies*, 36, 479–504.

Lodge, M. 2007. Comparing non-hierarchical governance in action: The open method of co-ordination in pensions and information society. *Journal of Common Market Studies*, 45, 343–365.

Lord, J. E. 2010. Accessibility and human rights fusion in the CRPD: Assessing the scope and content of the accessibility principle and duty under the CRPD. *Presentation for the General Day of Discussion on Accessibility, CRPD Committee*, Geneva, United Nations.

Mailand, M. 2008. The uneven impact of the European Employment Strategy on member states' employment policies: A comparative analysis. *Journal of European Social Policy*, 18, 353–365.

Man, T. W. Y., Lau, T. & Chan, K. F. 2002. The competitiveness of small and medium enterprises: A conceptualization with focus on entrepreneurial competencies. *Journal of Business Venturing*, 17, 123–142.

Marx, K. 1987. *Capital. A critique of political economy. Vol. 1. Book One: The process of production of capital*, Moscow, USSR, Progress Publishers.

Mercier, H. & Sperber, D. 2009. Intuitive and reflective inferences. *In:* Evans, J. S. B. T. & Frankish, K. (eds.) *In two minds: dual processes and beyond*, Oxford, Oxford University Press.

Moravcsik, A. 1991. Negotiating the Single European Act: National interests and conventional statecraft in the European Community. *International organization*, 45, 19–56.

Moravcsik, A. & Vachudova, M. A. 2002. National interests, state power, and EU enlargement. *Perspectives*, 21–31.

Müller, H. 2004. Arguing, bargaining and all that: Communicative action, rationalist theory and the logic of appropriateness in international relations. *European Journal of International Relations*, 10, 395–435.

Nash, J. F., Jr. 1950. The bargaining problem. *Econometrica: Journal of the Econometric Society*, 18, 155–162.

Niemann, A. 2004. Between communicative action and strategic action: The Article 113 Committee 1 and the negotiations on the WTO Basic Telecommunications Services Agreement. *Journal of European Public Policy*, 11, 379–407.

Nooteboom, B. 1988. The facts about small business and the real values of its 'Life World': A social philosophical interpretation of this sector of the modern economy. *American Journal of Economics and Sociology*, 47, 299–314.

Office for Disability Issues 2010. *2012 legacy for disabled people: Inclusive and accessible business. Improving messages to SMEs: The case for the disabled customer*, London, BISS.

Parsons, T. 1971. Comparative studies and evolutionary change. *In:* Vallier, I. (ed.) *Comparative Methods in Sociology*, Berkeley, University of Chicago Press.

Powell, R. 2002. Bargaining theory and international conflict. *Annual Review of Political Science*, 5, 1–30.

Prothero, A., Dobscha, S., Freund, J., Kilbourne, W. E., Luchs, M. G., Ozanne, L. K. & Thøgersen, J. 2011. Sustainable consumption: Opportunities for consumer research and public policy. *Journal of Public Policy & Marketing*, 30, 31–38.

Quinn, G. 2009. Bringing the UN convention on rights for persons with disabilities to life in Ireland. *British Journal of Learning Disabilities*, 37, 245–249.

Radulova, E. 2009. The construction of EU's childcare policy through the Open Method of Coordination. *European Integration online Papers*, 13, 1–20.

Risse, T. 1996a. Exploring the nature of the beast: International relations theory and comparative policy analysis meet the European Union. *JCMS: Journal of Common Market Studies*, 34, 53–80.

Risse, T. 1996b. Exploring the nature of the beast: International relations theory and comparative policy analysis meet the European Union. *Journal of Common Market Studies*, 34, 53–80.

Risse, T. 1999. International norms and domestic change: Arguing and communicative behavior in the human rights area. *Politics & Society*, 27, 529–559.

Risse, T. 2000. "Let's argue!": Communicative action in world politics. *International Organization*, 54, 1–39.
Sayer, A. 2001. For a critical cultural political economy. *Antipode*, 33, 687–708.
Scharpf, F. W. 1988. The joint-decision trap: Lessons from German federalism and European integration. *Public Administration*, 66, 239–278.
Schelling, T. C. 1958. The strategy of conflict prospectus for a reorientation of game theory. *Journal of Conflict Resolution*, 2, 203–264.
Schmidt, V. A. 1997. European integration and democracy: the differences among member states. *Journal of European Public Policy*, 4, 128–145.
Schmidt, V. A. 2005. Democracy in Europe: The impact of European integration. *Perspectives on Politics*, 3, 761–779.
Schmidt, V. A. 2006. *Democracy in Europe: The EU and national polities*, Cambridge, Cambridge University Press.
Schneider, C. J. 2011. Weak states and institutionalized bargaining power in international organizations. *International Studies Quarterly*, 55, 331–355.
Schneider, C. J. 2013. Globalizing electoral politics: Political competence and distributional bargaining in the European Union. *World Politics*, 65, 452–490.
Scott, J. & Trubek, D. M. 2002. Mind the gap: Law and new approaches to governance in the European Union. *European Law Journal*, 8, 1–18.
Searle, J. R. 1969. *Speech acts: An essay in the philosophy of language*, Cambridge, Cambridge University Press.
Seymour, L. J. M. 2013. Let's bullshit! Arguing, bargaining and dissembling over Darfur. *European Journal of International Relations*, 0, 1–25.
Silver, A. & Francis, L. (eds.) 2000. *Americans with disabilities. Exploring implications of the law for individuals and institutions*, London, Routledge.
Stern, P. C., Dietz, T. & Guagnano, G. A. 1995. The new ecological paradigm in social-psychological context. *Environment and Behavior*, 27, 723–743.
Traxler, F. & Schmitter, P. C. 1995. The emerging euro-polity and organized interests. *European Journal of International Relations*, 1, 191–218.
Verovšek, P. J. 2012. Meeting principles and lifeworlds halfway: Jürgen Habermas on the future of Europe. *Political Studies*, 60, 363–380.
Wendt, A. 1994. Collective identity formation and the international state. *American Political Science Review*, 88, 384–396.
Wessels, W. 1992. *Staat und (westeuropäische) Integration. Die Fusionsthese*, Opladen, Springer.
Young, M. I. 1985. Impartiality and the civil public: Some implications of feminist critiques of moral and political theory. *PRAXIS International*, 4, 381–401.

4 The chain of an accessible shopping

To better understand accessibility of the European Union (EU) single market, examination of disabled customers' everyday shopping experience in the mainstream private market is essential. This chapter, therefore, starts an empirical journey of the book. It adopts a holistic approach and demonstrates how disability/ableism and barriers/accessibility shape the shopping experience and practice of people with impairments. The discussion raises questions for thinking more in-depth about accessibility of the EU single market and the underlying reasons for disabled customers exclusion and vulnerability. This is then explored in the following chapters, using Habermas' communicative action theory as a framework for the analysis.

As suggested in the first chapter, shopping is approached as a chain, consisting of four stages. The discussion focuses on shopping in the retail market for information and communication technologies (ICT) products, although with wider implications for other markets. The sections draw on findings from mystery shopping and customer interviews conducted in the United Kingdom and Lithuania. Aiming to provide deeper insights, salespeople's accounts are used.

Disabled customers' experiences suggest that people with impairments usually go through all stages of the shopping chain, but the order, individual experience and faced obstacles differ. While some of them are more common than others, they impede customer participation and shape exclusion and vulnerability. The discourse of ableism is rooted in the mindset of the state and the private market, with ableist assumptions being the driving force behind the practice and the experiences of customers with impairments. Despite the faced barriers, disabled people are not passive, and evidence of customer resilience is provided, as well as positive and enabling practices are discussed.

This chapter starts by examining disabled shoppers' experiences of acquiring customer information. This is followed by a discussion on customer journey to a shop, focusing on home and public environments and public and private transport. Then, navigation in retail premises is addressed followed by the examination of the interaction with informal shop assistants and salespeople.

Customer information

As shown in the first chapter, customer information is an inextricable part of participation in the market. While customers are rarely fully informed (Dick et al., 1990), due to insufficient provision of customer information in accessible formats, shoppers with impairments experience additional exclusion. It is evident that the focus of legal instruments and business practice on non-disabled citizens and customers create information acquisition and shopping contexts that shape vulnerability, exclusion and inequality. The discussion begins with an overview of how people acquire information about shops and links it with spatial isolation in the market. It then gives an overview of how current product information provision practices exclude disabled people from informed customer choice. Finally, information delusion about product accessibility is addressed.

Disabled people's experiences when acquiring customer information is an under-researched topic in disability, marketing and other disciplines. This section provides a modest contribution to narrowing down this knowledge lacuna. It also challenges disabled customers' vulnerability as a static position and offers some insights into the deconstruction of vulnerability experiences caused by inaccessible information.

Information about shops

Two kinds of barriers regarding information about shops were reported. These include limited information about shops provided in accessible formats and lack of information about accessibility of retail premises.

With regard to accessible information about shops, customers from both countries discussed how business' practice to not provide this kind of information in accessible formats limit the number of shops they visit, cause dependency on others and require employing coping strategies. With an exception of people with mobility impairments, many informants addressed barriers in different media channels and leaflets. People noted that usually the information is provided only in a 'standard format', ignoring Braille, large print, audio information and easy-to-read texts and symbols, among others. In this respect, while shoppers with mobility impairments are usually free to access information about shops via radio, TV, Internet, newspapers, promotional flyers and other channels, people with hearing impairments gain this information mainly via the Internet and, in particular, shop-related reviews and discussion forums. Customers with vision impairments noted that usually they find out about shops via the Internet, radio and TV, with other information sources often being inaccessible. Ramune's (Lithuania, age 18–40) example of inability to access information on promotional flyers distributed by retail networks is a great representation of how non-disabled customer–oriented information provision concept and practice shape the knowledge of customers with vision impairments:

> I find all these promotional flyers in my post-box and I believe they are informative and provide more options in terms of products and price. But they are printed on a glossy paper and letters are small. Although I could use my magnifying glasses, the glossiness of the paper makes it impossible to see and read the information. Even though all these papers come to my house, they do not come to my brain and do not expand my knowledge either about products or about shops.

In contrast, for some shoppers with cognitive impairments, promotional flyers are an important and accessible source of information about shops:

> It is very good that I get brochures. I like pictures and also I like that they draw the name of the shop in the same way as they hang it above the entrance. It is much easier not to get confused.
>
> (Maryte, Lithuania, age 65+)

Hence, while traditional information sources about shops are available to disabled customers, their accessibility for people with certain impairments differs. Nevertheless, despite the differences, the exclusion practice is more common than accessibility and is typical across the board. This suggests that accessibility of customer information should not be linked with one particular format. Indeed, aiming to ensure customer equality, business should consider differences in customer segment and ensure that shoppers can choose from different accessible formats.

Similarly, information means chosen to communicate to customers about shops in high streets and public spaces usually do not take into account accessibility. For the majority of shoppers with vision impairments, this acts as a barrier that prevents free and independent customer experience. To illustrate, Jack (United Kingdom, age 41–64) said,

> It is always difficult finding a specific shop along the street. If I am looking for HMV, then probably I will walk in two or three different shops, before I find HMV.

In a similar vein, Ramune (Lithuania, age 18–40) noted that she visits new coffee houses or pizzerias only when she is accompanied by her daughter. Due to limited information provision in accessible formats, the woman struggles to find a place or gets lost. Other informants with vision impairments echoed Jack and Ramune and noted that their shopping is faster and includes more shops if they are accompanied by people who are able to access information provided in standard formats. These and other experiences suggest that while retailers invest in shop name branding strategies to communicate with non-disabled clientele (Birtwistle and Freathy, 1998, Bridge and Dowling, 2001), accessibility is usually not considered. As a result, the freedom of some disabled people and especially those with vision impairments to choose where to purchase is reduced. Rolandas (Lithuania, age 41–64) illustrates how this affects his shopping place decisions:

> I go only to few shops that I really know and know where they are, because there are lots of other shops that I even cannot think about or imagine.

In addition to assistance provided by other individuals, some participants with vision impairments noted that if they go shopping alone, they often use the senses of smell or hearing, learnt routes or intuition, as a means to find a way to the shop. To illustrate, Jack (United Kingdom, age 41–64) said,

> I find myself using a sense of touch and a sense of smell and sounds. So there's a shop called Lush, and you can smell that from several shops away. And I hardly ever go into that shop, but it serves as a sort of landmark for the shops around it. HMV I would usually find by the sound because they'll usually be playing music. But I guess the difficulty is, it's not the only shop that plays loud music. So there are a couple of clothes shops nearby. If I'm trying to find a shoe shop, I can usually do that by smell. So you step inside the shop, breathe in, and if I can smell leather, then I'm probably in a shoe shop.

On the one hand, the narrative demonstrates that disabled customers are not passive and employ various coping strategies for finding shops and remaining independent. On the other hand, together with other cases of this study, the examples insinuate that while non-disabled customers are overloaded with information (Bettman et al., 1991), due to limited availability of accessible information, disabled people often are not free to choose shops. The manner and format of branding and communicating shops' names often cause dependency practices and prohibit disabled customers' choice and control. This divides non-disabled and disabled people as information-consumers and isolate the latter group in particular niches of the market. In other words, having internalised the ideology of ableism and having a great control over the content and manner of the provided information (Kivetz and Simonson, 2000), business shape the 'composition' of their clientele and create consumption contexts, which contribute to transforming disabled people into vulnerable customers.

Alongside insufficient provision of accessible information about shops, lack of information about accessibility of retail premises isolates some disabled customer groups and causes inconvenience and stress. To begin with, while participants with hearing and cognitive impairments did not find this topic relevant, a great number of people with vision and mobility impairments reflected on their experiences when after a journey to a shop they were either unable to enter retail premises or faced various barriers. As an example, Kristupas, who is using a wheelchair (Lithuania, age 18–40) said,

> After the accident it used to happen very often that I actually come to the shop, but I can't get in, because there are steps and no ramp. Now it doesn't happen, because I know which shops are accessible, but back then I had to turn around and look for another shop.

In this respect, Pranciska (Lithuania, age 41–64) echoed experiences of other informants with vision impairments and noted that the provision of this kind of information would allow choosing accessible shops and avoiding unpleasant experiences:

> They could find a little niche ... A niche where they say whether the shop has stairs, lift, mirrors, day lighting and so on. It would be so much better. Then I could choose if I can go to that shop. Because for me personally to go to the shop with bad lighting, mirrors and steps is a tragedy. I would never go. Yes, it happens that I go to such shops, because there is no way to find out.

In addition to physical impediments, inability to obtain information about accessibility of retail premises may cause emotional and psychological tensions. For instance, Daphne (United Kingdom, age 18–40) and some other participants with mobility impairments addressed 'the feeling of uncertainty accompanying during the whole trip to the shop', especially when travelling to an unknown shopping site.

Being aware of such practices and possible effects, disabled customers look for solutions. Some participants noted that before the trip to an unfamiliar shop they ask for other disabled people's advice, while others browse for information in online forums or shop websites. Karolis (Lithuania, age 41–64) was the only participant who noted that before a trip to new retailers, he calls the shop and enquires about its accessibility for wheelchair users. Although a considerable number of interviewees said that despite the absence of such information, they take a risk and travel to chosen shops, the majority of shoppers and especially those with severe impairments and older people prefer going to familiar and 'checked' shops. As an example, Hilda (Lithuania, age 65+) said,

> Oh no, I don't go to new shops alone. I have my own shops where I usually go. Well, there are few shops that I am familiar with, so I go only there. It's complicated enough.

It is important to mention that while accessibility of retail premises is addressed in the UK and Lithuanian policy instruments, accessibility of information about the shop and its premises is not explicitly addressed either in EU or in national policy instruments. As a result, the synergy between the focus on non-disabled customers and limited provision of accessible information about shops exclude disabled customers from informed choice; increase the risk of barriers; and cause stress, inconvenience, dependency on others and customer segregation.

Information about products

Insufficient emphasis on accessibility of customer information in legal instruments accompanied by business' focus on non-disabled shoppers excludes people with impairments not only from an informed choice where to buy but also which products to purchase. A majority of the participants with hearing impairments revealed their exclusion from information provided via radio. With regard to TV, while the British participants did not refer to barriers related to this information channel, Lithuanians addressed frequent exclusion. For instance, Justas (Lithuania, 18–40), representing experiences of other informants with hearing impairments said,

> I am not a big fan of TV, but sometimes I think it would be nice if they captioned not only news, but also different programmes, including ads. Although they [advertisements] are the 'fish-hook of the devil', sometimes they may provide you with useful information.

Similarly, Herbertas (Lithuania, age 65+) noted that he finds out about advertised products only at home, where he is using his home-made speakers:

> Sometimes there are great advertisements on TV, but if I am not at home and thus I do not have my special speakers, I am excluded from what other people in the room hear. It is annoying. Once I visited my son and saw an advertisement about a special offer for quite rare flowers. I did not hear and my son was not in the room at that moment, so he could not re-say what was on that advertisement. Then I came back home and watched TV for almost two days while finally saw the same advertisement and finally could hear it. This was very tiring, but worth it.

Although the Lithuanian Government legally recognises that captioning, notes, sound recording and sign language are important means for providing more access to participation in cultural life, recreation and different leisure activities (Lietuvos Respublikos Vyriausybė, 2012), legal requirements are applied only to the adjustment of information in the field of education (Lietuvos Respublikos Vyriausybė, 2005). In addition, although the possibility to increase accessibility of TV existed before the switch from analogue terrestrial to digital television in 2012, none of the related legislations were amended. Consequently, since broadcasters are free to choose which programmes and movies should be captioned, only a minority of TV programmes and none of the advertisements are accessible for people with hearing impairments. The situation in the United Kingdom differs. Here, the requirements for subtitling, sign language and audio description that apply to television services are outlined in the Code of Television Access Service (Ofcom, 2010). In this respect, although British research participants noted that captioning '*is not always available*', the majority shared positive experiences and identified services as '*good*'.

People with vision impairments complemented examples of the detachment of personal control when accessing product information. They noted that sources such as promotional leaflets, advertisements in newspapers, public spaces and shop windows often do not fulfil the function, as usually they are shiny and glossy. As an example, Pranciska (Lithuania, age 41–64) noted that advertisements in newspaper back pages often are too colourful and tire her eyes. This was echoed by Christine (United Kingdom, age 18–40), who said that the only way she can find out about this kind of information is through the assistance provided either by the personal assistant or by other individuals without vision impairments. These and other similar narratives echo the discussion on accessible information about shops. They illustrate how information presentation oriented to non-disabled customers makes available customer information unusable, limits disabled customers' choice and excludes them from making informed product decisions.

While the majority of the participants found promotional text messages or emails about available products and offers intrusive and annoying, several informants with cognitive impairments and mental health conditions noted that they prefer this source of information. Indeed, a great part of their shopping decisions are founded on promotional text messages and emails sent by retailers. As an example, Maryte (Lithuania, age 65+) said,

> I leave my telephone number and then I get a text message about discounts and where I should go to get these discounts.

Albinas (Lithuania, age 41–64) echoed,

> They send [information] to my email. Many shops have my email address and then they send me information and I know where and what can be found.

Interviews with shoppers who are labelled as having cognitive impairments or mental health conditions suggested that pictures accompanied by specific and brief information about a product shape this customer groups' preference for this information source. However, incompatibility between customer attraction in the pre-shopping stage and actual customer service in some of the shops in Lithuania was a concern. Specifically, Ignas (Lithuania, age 18–40), Andrius (Lithuania, age 18–40), Salomeja (Lithuania, age 65+) and some other participants with cognitive impairments' choice of which shop to go for mystery shopping was based on the received promotional text messages. Contrary to attractive information in the text messages, shop assistants' behaviour was unwelcoming and excluding. A few salespeople tried to avoid serving two participants and used many technical terms and jargons, and the overall atmosphere was distant and patronising. Thus, while an attractive format of the promotional messages provided the individuals with accessible information, the service provision was excluding and discriminating. Such practice seems to be shaped by the hierarchy of disabled people as customers as well as limited shop assistants' training on disability, accessibility and customer equality that are discussed in more detail in the following chapters.

As a contrast, people with mobility impairments seem to have access to the majority of information sources that are targeting non-disabled customers. Their shared experiences may be illustrated by statements such as *'usually there are no problems'* (Vakare, Lithuania, age 61–64), *'no, I do not face any problems'* (Pranas, Lithuania, age 18–40) or *'I have no problem with this'* (Rachel, United Kingdom, age 41–64).

Despite faced obstacles, disabled customers are not passive receivers of inaccessible information and often employ various coping strategies. Some participants with vision impairments said that they use magnifying glasses and others referred to accessible software. Christine (United Kingdom, age 18–40) noted that her partner reads her promotional emails and describes products. Herbertas (Lithuania, age 65+) showed his special 'home-made' speakers that allow him to listen to the radio and to watch TV, and Justas (Lithuania, age 18–40) and Chris (United Kingdom, age 18–40) noted that they download subtitles for movies or series from the Internet. Overall, past customer experience and informal interpersonal communication are important sources that enable people with impairments to overcome barriers created by inaccessible information and be informed about products and market offers. To illustrate, Juozas (Lithuania, age 41–64) said,

> We get information in the same way as you, non-disabled people, get. The only thing is that not all information is accessible for us. However, what is inaccessible via official channels is accessible via own and informal channels and ways.

These informal channels usually are disabled peers in different disabled people's clubs, disabled people's organisations (DPOs), day care centres, online forums and discussion groups, as well as family members and friends. Juozas' experience implicitly demonstrates that even though the EU and national governments are moving towards more accessible customer information, the actions that have been taken are neither sufficient nor efficient for providing customer equality. As a result, people with different impairments often are excluded from information that is taken for granted by non-disabled customers. Under such circumstances, disabled people do not exercise real customer choice. Their decisions on products and shops are shaped by the list of options provided in information sources that are accessible to them. In other words, dominant information provision practices impede the purchase and draw boundaries within the private market inhabited by shoppers with impairments.

Information about product accessibility

Information about product accessibility is a concerning issue particularly for people with vision and hearing impairments. Experienced challenges can be divided into three areas: pre-shopping information, product description in shops and information provided by shop assistants. Their concordium causes information delusion that limits access to accessible items and causes financial loss and unpleasant customer experience.

As discussed earlier, many customers look for product information before they go to shops. Internet seems to be an important source for information at the pre-shopping stage. Research data demonstrated that while information on ICT producers' websites is the most exhaustive and provide detailed description of general and accessibility features of a product, trade networks are not so pernickety. For example, while Company X on their website identifies around 100 general product characteristics, Lithuanian retailers describe the same products using around 30 features. Although the United Kingdom's ICT sellers are more exhaustive and provide more details, product accessibility features are rarely included, with an identical practice being present in Lithuania. Mystery shopping revealed that usually 12–20 characteristics are used to describe the product in the shop in both countries, with accessibility features being rarely included. As a result, the majority of the participants who are concerned with product accessibility noted that before the visit to a shop, they usually browse for information in different online forums or chat groups. However, technical jargons and overload of general product information often prevent them from accessing relevant information in a time-efficient way. According to customers with vision and hearing impairments, the situation could be improved by a better service quality of shop assistants. As an example, Jack (United Kingdom, age 41–64) identified shop assistants as a potential information filter that may enable selecting the most accessible technology:

> Then it [online sources] would have thrown ten, twenty, fifty responses to say, which one is any good which one is not? Which is useful, having a member of staff in the shop, hopefully they can filter that information better than I can.

However, this expectation is usually unmet, as shop personnel often lack knowledge on product accessibility. Hence, compared with information provided on manufacturers' websites, product accessibility information significantly decreases in the shop. First through product description, and then through salespeople's limited knowledge (see Figure 4.1).

The chain of an accessible shopping   137

Figure 4.1 Delusion of information about accessible products.

Nevertheless, the distinction should be made between practices in brand-specific ICT shops[1] (BSHs) and non-brand-specific ICT shops[2] (NBSHs). With regard to information provided by shop assistants in the BSHs visited by mystery shoppers, salespeople provided technically exhaustive and detailed information. However, some customers noted that provided information reminded them of 'a well learned pocsy' (Nick, United Kingdom, age 41–64), as shop assistants did not know how this knowledge could and should be applied in practice and which product features are accessible or inaccessible for customers. As an example, Nick (United Kingdom, age 41–64) reflected,

> Yeah, although I think she was out of her depth, to be honest. You know, she didn't understand really how well it worked. She did her best. She made a lot of effort, but really didn't understand how all the – how VoiceOver versus Siri worked in combination with one another. So I think it was a training issue. She hadn't been sufficiently made familiar. I also think there were a number of things she could have tried. Like we could have put a headphone splitter in there and both had headphones to actually hear what was happening, because a lot of the problems she was having in showing me was that neither of us could actually hear the thing in that environment.

Other participants with vision impairments echoed Nick's experience and identified two types of product accessibility knowledge hold by the BSH assistants: information for service performance and actual information.

Specifically, while salespeople are usually well familiar with officially provided product accessibility information, their knowledge does not completely concur with disabled users' accessibility expectations.

There are some differences between information provision about product accessibility in small and large BSHs. Specifically, in small-sized shops where the average number of salespeople is 5–7, all shop assistants are usually able to serve customers with impairments. Meanwhile, in large-sized BSHs in the United Kingdom, most shop assistants were not able to provide accessibility-related information. Such shops have one or two employees trained in product accessibility and thus responsible for serving disabled customers. Indeed, these shop assistants were called when mystery shoppers enquired about accessible products. Some informants noted that such practice labels them and creates a sense of being different customers. As an example, Elisabeth (United Kingdom, age 41–64) who has multiple impairments noted,

> In my opinion, it is a strange practice. I cannot choose to which shop assistant I would like to talk with. For me it is important. If I come to a wrong one, he prescribes me with a new one, who knows more than he does. And then I have to wait.

While such practice may provide disabled shoppers with more exhaustive technical information about product features, the prescription with special shop assistants creates alienating practices and unpleasant customer experience, and strengthens disabled people's portrayal as 'different' or 'special' shoppers.

With regard to information about product accessibility provided by shop assistants in NBSHs, research data revealed potential extinction of the information. Mystery shopping and customer interviews suggested that salespeople often lack knowledge on whether products are accessible and what accessibility features they have. As an example, few shop assistants in both countries printed product descriptions out or browsed online; others tried products together with the customers. A shop assistant who served Jack (United Kingdom, age 41–64) spent around 10–15 min looking for information online whether certain laptop has in-built features that make it accessible for people with vision impairments. Later, he thanked Jack for teaching him new things about the product and noted that prior serving him, he had no knowledge about accessibility of this product and now is keen on expanding the knowledge. Even though this was a unique case, it suggests that shop assistants' behaviour is not necessarily biased against people with impairments, and their limited knowledge is not always an outcome of ignorance or discrimination. Indeed, alongside some factors discussed in the next chapter, it is shaped by the received training and information available to them.

Even though NBSH assistants lack relevant knowledge, they are usually helpful and keen to assist. However, three shop assistants in Lithuania demonstrated more excluding professional practice. They advised the customers to check for more specific information about the products and then come back to the shop. In addition, in two small-sized shops, the sellers stated that mobile phones that are accessible for people with vision or hearing impairments do not exist. Interestingly, in both shops, accessible technologies were in stock and in some cases were located next to or in front of the shop assistants. Recalling the paragraph above, such practices demonstrate that limited sales personnel's training and lack of knowledge are important factors moulding disabled peoples' exclusion and vulnerability when obtaining customer information and making an informed choice. Such shop assistants' behaviour can be explained by the cognitive sales paradigm perspective (Leong et al., 1989, Sujan et al., 1988). Specifically, since disabled people are a new group of customers of mainstream goods and services, shop assistants have limited or no knowledge about their needs, preferences or behaviour models. As a result, their selling practices are unsuccessful, discriminating and excluding. Additionally, the requirement and expectation to provide non-disabled customers with basic information about all products that are in stock dominates information about their accessibility. Furthermore, while usually NBSH personnel have to attend professional training, product accessibility is usually not addressed. To illustrate, the manager of the NBSH (Lithuania) noted,

> Twice per year all my shop assistants have to attend special training on products that we sell. Then suppliers come to us and provide my people with information, organise different demonstrations of new products. Accessibility and disability? I can't remember that we have ever discussed such topics. You see, business care about slightly different topics.

The results support the argument made in the literature that disabled customers are not the priority for the private market, and accessibility and customer equality are often dominated by the orientation to profit. Hence, business' actions that are shaped around non-disabled customers (Knights et al., 1994) portrayal people with impairments as undesirable or different shoppers and contribute to information delusion about product accessibility. This leads to restricted customer choice, alienation, vulnerability and inequality.

After people make a decision about a product or retail place, or simply want to engage in shopping as leisure and pleasure, their journey to the shop begins. In respect of this, the following section addresses disabled customers' experiences on the way to the shop. It demonstrates how the focus of the state and private market on non-disabled citizens and customers assist in shaping disabled people's exclusion from and spatial isolation in the market.

The journey to a shop

Public environment and public infrastructure were the key themes when discussing journey to the shop. People with mobility and multiple impairments also addressed home environment and linked its accessibility either to smoothness of the trip or to the complete exclusion from customer experience. While only five informants addressed this dimension of the shopping chain, all participants identified that the public environment and transport infrastructure, designed by and for non-disabled individuals is littered with various barriers and obstacles that prevent them from free and smooth customer choice, control and equal experience.

Home environment

Identification of the home environment as an element of a shopping chain was an anticipated finding. Although it seems to be more an exception than a rule, five wheelchair users addressed its role in shaping customer experience. Three of them referred to single barriers in the home environment such as sills and kerbs. Although these obstacles do not prevent them from shopping, they disturb the smoothness of the journey. As Karolis (Lithuania, age 41–64) said,

> Well, I live in a newly built apartment and it is completely accessible, even the bathroom. But when I need to take my car from the underground garage, I need to jump from one step. And it is fine, I can do that with no problems, but sometimes I think why they could not make it completely accessible? Well, it is ok, but could be better.

Similar experiences were addressed by Vakare (Lithuania, age 41–64) and Kristupas (Lithuania, age 18–40), who noted that although their flats have been adjusted and meet technical requirements, some bits remain inaccessible or are inconvenient.

In contrast, one Lithuanian and one British participant shared more extreme experiences. Barbora (Lithuania, age 41–64), who has two young children and takes care of a severely disabled husband, noted that often her trip to a shop or any other place outside her home ends before it starts:

> We live on the second floor, and the stairs are very steep. So, if there is no one, who could take me down, I just have to stay at home, even though I want or need to go somewhere.

The woman is an independent person who manages family's life and childcare, but due to physical barriers in the home environment as a customer, she becomes dependent on her under-aged children. The participant noted that usually she goes shopping either during the weekend or in the afternoons when children are at home and have finished homework. Mystery shopping and interviews with her were also arranged in the evening, as it is the time when her kids can assist her to leave the house. Similarly, Lisa (United Kingdom, age 18–40) revealed how her shopping time is determined by her mother's schedule:

> I cannot leave home alone, so it [shopping time] depends on my mum. […] I need help with doors and handles, so usually we go to the shopping mall on Sundays.

While the findings are in line with the literature depicting that dwellings are not well suited to people with mobility impairments (Haywood et al., 2001, Imrie, 2004a, 2004b), research data demonstrate that home environment shapes disabled people's experiences not only in spaces where they live but also engagement in market relations. Although experienced not directly in the market realm, accessibility of home environment shapes the level of customer (in-)dependency and opportunities for spontaneous consumption, and locates participation in the private market within a particular time frame, which usually does not depend on disabled people.

After leaving home, individuals enter the second stage of the shopping chain and start their journey to the shop. With this in mind, the following discussion sheds light on their experiences in the public environment.

Public environment

Mystery shopping and interviews with customers in Lithuania and the United Kingdom echo some insights discussed in the first chapter and suggest that accessibility of the public environment is an important factor that shapes the participation of people with impairments in the mainstream private market. To begin with, it impacts individuals' choice of routes and itineraries to retail outlets. While informants with cognitive and hearing impairments did not address this element of the shopping chain, people with vision and mobility impairments shared opposite experiences. They reported that due to different obstacles in the city, they are only partly free to choose the route to a shop. As an example, Lisa (United Kingdom, age 18–40) with multiple impairments said,

> There are some bits of the city that I have never visited. You know … It is just impossible, because of accessibility. So I have never been to the shops that are there.

In a similar vein, Ramune (Lithuania, age 18–40) who has vision impairment noted,

> Wherever I go, I have my itineraries, which are secure and I know that they will not put me in trouble.

While the narratives above mirror the experiences of other participants with vision and mobility impairments, research data suggest that individuals are not passive victims. They look for solutions on how to overcome the obstacles. To illustrate, Karina (Lithuania, age 18–40) shared her memories of moving to another city and noted,

> Few night journeys counting curbs and looking to see which I can overcome. Now I know which way is the most accessible for me.

While non-disabled shoppers' route choice usually depends on directness (Hoogendoorn and Bovy, 2004), noise levels and overall pleasantness (Bovy and Stern, 1990), important criteria for disabled customers' decisions are accessibility and safety. The choice of an inaccessible and 'untested' route may result in stress, injuries and misdemeanours of traffic rules or getting lost. This physical restriction has broader implications than just decision which route, path or street to choose in order to reach a retail outlet. Indeed, it spatially segregates people with impairments and prevents them discovering new shops and inhabiting a broader map of the retail market.

Different impact of the public environment on disabled and non-disabled customers' experience was revealed by Pranas (Lithuania, age 18–40). He compared how he experienced the same elements of the built environment before and after he became a wheelchair user. Obstacles in urban design forced him to renegotiate, change and adapt his customer likes, preferences and choices:

> In this city I used to curse pavements, because of potholes and curbs, but compared to this city ... Streets are cruel here. You need aerobatics here. Frankly speaking, there are some shops that I liked before the accident, but now I do not go there only because of pavements, curbs, pits and other nonsenses.

For somebody like Pranas, the issue here is not simply physical inaccessibility of the city, but the changes in his customer identity, shaped by barriers in the public environment. While as a non-disabled customer he was free to visit chosen shops, the transition into a disabled person deteriorated his customer choice and independency. He is not free anymore to purchase where he wants, as his choices now seem to be partly shaped by an inaccessible public environment. He had to renegotiate not only changes of his position in society but also new customer patterns in the market.

An inaccessible public environment and barriers eliminate some people, especially older and with severe impairments, from shopping. A great number of Lithuanian and British participants noted that crumbled pavements, kerbs and similar colour of streets and sidewalks are some of the factors that cause stress and anxiety when travelling to shops. Some people deal with this using public or private transport and do not engage with the public environment as pedestrians. However, the majority noted that they prefer either being accompanied by non-disabled people or delegate shopping to them. For instance, Pranciska (Lithuania, age 41–64) said that she feels better and safer when her son goes together with her. In a similar vein, Christine (United Kingdom, age 18–40) noted that usually her personal assistant accompanies her:

> I do not do shopping alone. I usually go with my assistant. So, they will drive me to the shops, or we'll just walk to town together with my assistant.

While Pranciska (Lithuania, age 41–64) and Christine (United Kingdom, age 18–40) engage in market relations, Hilda's (Lithuania, age 65+) customer pattern is dim, especially in autumn and wintertime:

> I give her [daughter] a list of products that I need and she buys. It is so great that she lives not far away from my home, so I do not need to struggle in the street.

The discussion challenges legally entrenched position that disabled people are 'vulnerable' consumers because of their impairments. It demonstrates how state's focus on non-disabled citizens, expressed through particular practices in the public environment restricts disabled customers' independency and freedom. Urban design elements that usually do not affect non-disabled citizens may convert some shoppers with impairments into dependent actors, whose shopping time, place and well-being on the way to the shop depend on support sources and social networks. This raises the concern that individuals having less access to aforementioned assistance may be eliminated from shopping and so from passive or active socialising (Graham et al., 1991), embedment into social networks and communities (Miller et al., 1998) and the experience of shopping as a leisure activity (Miller and Kim, 1999). In addition, inaccessibility of the city may convert some disabled people, especially older ones, into indirect and passive choosers, when only the 'list' of products depends on personal choice, with the brand and package choice being decided and experienced by others. According to Kishi (1988), choice made under such circumstances should not be interpreted as choice, since it diminishes personal control and provides an illusion that the purchase is an outcome of a person's own decision.

Improper maintenance of the public environment contributes to the exclusion and segregation of some customers with impairments. While none of the British participants referred to this factor, the topic was common in narratives of the Lithuanian customers. A great number of people with mobility and vision impairments referred to the maintenance of the public environment in winter season. As an example, people with vision impairments noted that a proper maintenance of public spaces provides more control over the situation, as the snow changes *'the scenery of pavement'* (Juozas, Lithuania, age 41–64) and then it is easier to get lost. In addition, informants with mobility impairments, and especially wheelchair users, identified untrimmed or covered with ice sidewalks and snowdrifts separating street and sidewalks, as factors limiting their independency. To illustrate, Katrina (Lithuania, age 18–40) said,

> I cannot complain about the place, where I live. It is fully accessible. Except in winter. If there was a heavy snow during the night and cleaning services had not cleaned it before I leave, I just do not leave. My wheels get tied up in snow and I have to stay at home.

Pranas (Lithuania, age 18–40) echoed,

> It is good that my dad lives here. Otherwise, sometimes it would be impossible for me. They clean streets early in the morning, but sometimes they do not clean sidewalks, or make them as wide as the spade is. And then I am in trouble, well actually not in trouble. I am overreacting, because my dad comes and spades the space between the staircase and my car.

Such practices not only limit physical mobility in the city but also change shopping and consumption practices. All Lithuanian participants using wheelchairs revealed that at some point in their life, due to improper maintenance of the public environment, in winter season, they were temporarily imprisoned at home. A great number of them noted that under such circumstances, they either ask neighbours or friends to buy food and basic supplies or order food online. This questions the role of social networks and community support in overcoming disabling situations. People who have strong social networks and/or access to the Internet are more likely to deal with customer vulnerability more effectively. However, those who have weaker support networks or limited access to online retailers may be less resilient and thus become more vulnerable as customers.

In addition to physical barriers in and improper maintenance of the public environment, the land use of the city actuates disabled customers' vulnerability. To begin with, echoing discussion in the first chapter, the density of public spaces was identified as factor that shapes shopping time and overall pleasantness of the shopping trip. As an example, some participants with mobility impairments said that crowded pavements are a challenge on the way to the shop. Additionally, some people with vision and cognitive impairments noted that high pedestrian density burdens and complicates finding the way to a chosen retailer. As a result, the majority of British and Lithuanian participants noted that they prefer doing grocery or other types of shopping during weekdays, usually in the mornings. This may be linked to and explained by other studies, suggesting that the most popular days of non-disabled people's shopping are Fridays and weekends (Boedeker, 1995,

Kahn and Schmittlein, 1989, Kumar and Levinson, 1996). This is also the time when in order to attract more customers, retailers apply more intense marketing strategies and as well as offer more special promotions (Kuo et al., 2003). The synergy of the two adds on physical obstacles in the build environment and boosts disabled customers' vulnerability and exclusion from equal shopping experience.

Disabled customers travel to shops not only as pedestrians. Many of them use public or private transport. With this in mind, the following discussion sheds light on how the two types of transport means shape their shopping experience.

Public and private transport

Public and private transport further shapes the shopping experience and the overall participation of customers with impairments in the market. With regard to public transport, debates among participants in the United Kingdom and Lithuania vary and cover several areas. To begin with, as people with vision and mobility impairments suggested, public transport may have an enabling as well as disabling effect on their shopping. On the one hand, it assists in overcoming the discussed barriers in the public environment and reaching shops faster. On the other hand, limited information provision about public transport in accessible formats causes challenges, stress, financial loss and other uncomfortable and unpleasant situations. As an example, Alison (United Kingdom, age 18–40) shared her experience, which was common in the narratives of other participants with vision impairments:

> In terms of – well, the buses here, like you're getting a bus from wherever to wherever, there's no – like the buses don't stop unless you flag them down. But if you can't really see the bus coming, you kind of are – you don't know where the bus is going and things like that. And you think you're on the right bus and then you're not and you're somewhere else, so that's another issue. Whereas taxis, in terms of you say you want to go to a shop, they take you to that shop. It's just more of a safety and kind of a thing where you know you're going to get to that place.

Ramune (Lithuania, age 18–40) narrated similar experience and noted that since information about and in public transport is usually provided only in a written format, she has to prepare for the trip in advance and to seek other passengers' assistance during the journey:

> If I need to go to the shop, that I haven't been before, I google and check the itinerary. All information is on the website, so I count stops and then I know where to get off. Sometimes I ask for other passengers or driver's help. People are helpful nowadays and I always find someone, who lets me know that the next stop is mine. Otherwise, I may end up in the opposite side of the city – I could tell you a million stories like that.

The examples echo experiences shared by other participants with vision impairments and suggest that due to inaccessibility of information about and in public transport, shopping trip of this customer group is often accompanied by stress and uncertainty and may require relying and be dependent on others. In some cases, such practices transform people from being public service users into becoming clients of private providers, as they have to use taxis. Although this introduces additional form of participation in the private market, the choice is not freely made and has negative impact on person's budget, as taxi services in both countries are more expensive than public transport. As a result, a great part of the participants with vision and mobility impairments noted that usually they visit new or distant shops together with personal assistants or family members, friends and partners. Although support networks may assist in managing the challenges and barriers better, they may also create customer dependency, as shopping time is usually adapted to other's schedules, and the process itself is not experienced independently.

Contrary to shoppers with vision impairments who do use public transport, all informants with mobility impairments, with an exception of one British participant, avoid using public transport for shopping purposes. The most commonly identified reasons echoed the discussion in the first chapter and addressed limited number of low-ground buses, accessible seats and ramps as well as potholes, kerbs and so on. Consequently, they usually travel to shops either by personal transport or are given a lift by others. However, this type of shopping travelling is not barrier free, and the main obstacles are related to parking. While discussion in the second chapter suggests that Lithuanian and British legislations require designing and projecting public spaces, including car parking areas, in a way they are accessible for and usable by disabled people, the reality is different. In terms of physical accessibility, many participants who are using wheelchairs noted that parking of small shops often is less accessible than parking of big shopping malls. As an example, Kristupas (Lithuania, age 18–40) noted,

> Disabled parking spots ... The whole parking area there [talking about X shop] is designed and laid out in a wrong way. Parking spaces are made in a way that if I squeeze the car in, there is no room for me to take my wheelchair out of the car. So this is one of the reasons, why I do not go to that shop.

While some parking spots are manageable in terms of room, obstacles such as potholes, kerbs and rugged sidewalks, which do not impact non-disabled drivers and purchasers' shopping, may prevent wheelchair users from barrier free and safe access to shops. As Katrina (Lithuania, age 18–40) said,

> I am very good in managing my wheelchair, so usually I don't have major problems, but I know that one of my friends, whose arms are weaker,

got stuck in the pothole in the parking of the Z shop. It may sound funny, but actually it is terrible, because you are able to drive and to come to the shop, you are able to manage your wheelchair and to take it out of the car, and you would be able to enter that shop and to bring profit to them. But because of the damned potholes you can't do that and you have to ask other's for help. It is absurd ….

Hence, accessibility of shop parking impacts customers' independency and changes the shopping choices and experience of people with mobility impairments. As some participants noted, even though they would like to purchase in small local shops, accessibility of parking facilities is one of the reasons why they prioritise big shopping malls.

Insufficient number of accessible parking spots was identified as another factor in causing shopping discomfort. This practice is more common with big shopping malls. For instance, Barbora (Lithuania, age 41–64) said,

Quite often parking spots [accessible] are occupied, so I have to drive in circles while find a free space. This happens very often.

Pranas (Lithuania, age 18–40) echoed,

I do not drive, but if I go to the shopping mall with my friends, it happens quite often that there are no accessible spots left.

Two British research participants were late to the mystery shopping and interviews because they could not find free accessible parking spot. This was addressed by a few other informants, especially in Lithuania, and questions private businesses' compliance with the existing quantitative requirements for accessible parking. Specifically, while Statybos Techninių Reikalavimų Reglamentas (2001) in Lithuania determines the measurement and a number of accessible parking spots, not all retailers follow these requirements. Indeed, some of them provide fewer accessible parking spots than is required. As an example, in the X shopping centre, which was opened after the adoption of the instrument, there are 2,400 parking spots, and only 35 of them are accessible. According to legal requirements, this shopping centre should provide *no less* than 96 accessible parking spots. Alongside calling for businesses' compliance with the present set of requirements, the increasing number of older and disabled people (WHO, 2011) consequently requires mirroring this in policy instruments and to increase the quantitative requirements for the number of accessible parking spots.

By the end of this section, we have seen that the home and public environment and public and private transport compose the second stage of the shopping chain and contribute to shaping disabled customers' experience in the mainstream private market. While accessibility of the home environment affects mainly wheelchair users and impacts their customer

148 *The chain of an accessible shopping*

independency and a possibility to engage in spontaneous shopping, different barriers in the public environment and transportation shape the map of shops visited by people with impairments; limit their choice and freedom; and cause customer dependency, stress, financial loss and isolation.

Navigation in retail premises

This section suggests that the third stage of the shopping chain (navigation in the shop) consists of entering the shop and operating in retail premises. Customers reported a number of physical constraints and some enabling elements in external and internal shop environments. Their accounts suggest that while people with different impairments interact in and engage with these dimensions in different and unique ways, disabling practices share similar patterns and are common across the board. It is evident that behind the excluding experience stands business' orientation to non-disabled customers. While design of retail premises and product-marketing strategies are aimed at attracting this customer group and generating profit, they often act as factors shaping disabled customers' exclusion, segregation and vulnerability.

Entering the shop

Entering the shop is one of the tasks, which has to be performed by a customer. However, physical entrance into the retail premises is often accompanied by barriers that may cause customer exclusion and vulnerability. To begin with, Ramune (Lithuania, age 18–40) discussed how different decorations outside shops impact the way she negotiates and experiences the space:

> You saw all these different flowerpots and signs. For some people they are beauty and they need them, and for some disabled people they are interferences. To some of them I hit with my head, to others with something else. There are such obstacles.

Although she was the only participant with vision impairment who explicitly referred to such practices, mystery shoppings and interviews suggest that elements such as flowerpots and statues are not only elements of aesthetics. Indeed, located in consideration to attract non-disabled customers and to create an aesthetically pleasant environment, the artefacts become barriers that prevent people with certain impairments from barrier-free entrance to the shop and cause challenges and risks for their health and safety. Although people attempt to avoid such elements, they cannot eliminate their possibility and existence. As an example, Ramune (Lithuania, age 18–40) continued,

> You measure, learn the route … It takes time to learn the route and the exact location of all these pots, and after few visits I am fine. Of course, I have to be careful and aware that they can place something new, and

of course I can be more relaxed only until they decide to replace these decorations with something new. And then 'catch the ribbon' and start from the beginning.

Alongside such non-disabled customer attraction elements that are barriers resulting from thoughtless and aesthetics-oriented design, shop doors received significantly more attention. The discussion was broad and detailed, conveying the message that limited business' awareness of accessible decisions and practices is the foundation of disabled customers' dependency and vulnerability when entering retail premises. First, British and Lithuanian participants with mobility impairments identified the sliding door as an accessible solution that may provide a barrier-free entrance. However, people with vision impairments and older participants with different impairments noted that often such doors do not have visual signs and are decorated and covered with advertisements and promotional leaflets. This does not distinguish them from glass walls and in such a way restrict entering the shop or cause physical injuries. However, if properly marked, this type of door seems to be the most accessible.

Second, while many informants with hearing impairments identified revolving doors as accessible, the majority of the participants with mobility and vision impairments shared opposite experiences. As an example, Ramune (Lithuania, age 18–40) noted,

> It is impossible to get through such doors alone. If there are such doors, 'vsio' everything is closed.

This was echoed by Lisa (United Kingdom, age 18–40):

> Revolving doors often are too small ... Even if I go with my mum, we need to look for another entrance, cause my wheelchair is too big.

Evidence provided by other participants echoed the statements above and added fear to be injured. However, being one of the best solutions for regulating customer movement volume and optimising heating containment inside a shop (Sandling, 1985), revolving door was common in visited shops in both countries. As a result, three participants with vision impairments and one wheelchair user said that they try to avoid shops that have to be entered through such a door.

Often the visited shops that use a revolving door had 'traditional door' next to it. However, while such shops in the United Kingdom keep these doors unlocked, two visited Lithuanian shopping malls kept them locked and unlock only when the revolving door jams or breaks down. Hence, although an accessible solution exists, it is not used to provide barrier-free access. This exclude people with certain impairments from entering and exploring shops, that according to Gabriel and Lang (1995) is one of the main roles performed and identities exercised by people in the market. In such a context, an inaccessible door becomes a symbol that signalises limited acceptance of those who do not share characteristics typical to non-disabled customers. In other words, doors become a symbol of shops as non-disabled customers' space, which should not be inhabited by people with impairments. This draws the boundaries, symbolising customer division into 'average' and 'vulnerable', and, respectively, constructs disabled customers' realities.

Implicit and thoughtless elements in shops' external design may further maintain disabled customers' exclusion. To begin with, almost all research participants with mobility impairments shared their experiences of being deprived from entering the shop because of steps and podiums with no ramps. While these experiences confirm Matthews and Vujakovic's (1995) point that the rationale of the built environment is founded on the assumption that all people are non-disabled, few research participants in Lithuania revealed 'parasitic' practices openly communicating to the public that disabled customers are not welcomed. The informants referred to provision of ramps leading to the wall, steep ramps that are hard or impossible to use and sills, among others. Karolis (Lithuania, age 41–64) named such practices as 'inaccessible accessibility' that can be illustrated by Katrina's (Lithuania, age 18–40) experience:

> There is a book-shop in X city where they put a railing next to the entrance. One of them is leaned to the wall and another one to the door, and next to them there are steps. So basically, a person (wheelchair user) can neither straddle them nor climb onto them. It is written that they are, but it is impossible to use them.

Pranas (Lithuania, age 18–40) echoed,

> There is a requirement that everything in shops and coffee-houses has to be adjusted, but these adjustments are meaningless. There is a ramp, but it is impossible to 'climb onto' it.

While one of the dominant arguments explaining the lack of accessibility provisions is a misleading assumption of high cost (Russell, 2002), research data demonstrate that even though in some cases, private retailers have certain means to provide accessibility, their implication in practice may be controversial or excluding. On the one hand, this may be linked to unwillingness and unpreparedness to welcome disabled shoppers. This leads to legal minimum requirements to be met officially but not in practice. On the other hand, lack of accessibility considerations in architecture and design studies curriculum (Evcil, 2010; Imrie, 2003), political repudiation of disabled people as customers (Waddington, 2009) and a lack of disability- and accessibility-related awareness among industry players are some of the deeper reasons shaping customer exclusion.

After entering the shop, customers start their shopping activity in the retail premises. The following discussion focuses on some of these experiences as well as factors that shape them.

Operating in retail premises

As suggested in the first chapter, marketing and consumerism studies often discuss the way shop design and product-marketing strategies shape non-disabled shoppers' emotions, feelings, body comfort and consumer behaviour in general. This section employs this knowledge set and demonstrates how these elements affect disabled customers' choice, control and vulnerability and intrude into their participation in the private market.

To begin with, while finding the way is the first task that has to be performed by customers in a shop (Dogu and Erkip, 2000), a lack of accessible information about the shop layout creates a variety of barriers for people with certain impairments. For instance, a great number of British and Lithuanian participants with mobility impairments noted that often it is difficult and sometimes impossible to see shopping mall maps on vertical displays, especially the information which is on the top of the map. Although some of the informants noticed that a few shopping malls also use horizontal displays, for wheelchair users, these often are too high, and a part of the information becomes inaccessible. To illustrate, during the mystery shopping, Karolis (Lithuania, age 18–40) and Rachel (United Kingdom, age 41–64) could not obtain information provided on horizontally displayed maps, since the surface was smooth and not oblique, and it was installed in the 'box' instead of the stanchion. Similar to the discussion on sliding doors, limited designers' awareness of accessibility and absence of disabled people's inclusion as co-designers led to limited exploitation of the existing means and provision of artefacts that are usable only to some and not all customers. A few wheelchair users said that due to limited possibilities to use the maps, in new or unfamiliar shopping malls they have to 'cruise around' and find shops or service providers individually.

For customers with vision impairments, the font of the information in the maps is often too small, scheme lines are blurry and obscure and the colours in and lighting of the map often decrees the visibility of the provided information. As an example, Gitana (Lithuania, age 65+) said,

> Maps are a waste of money: they pay for all the designers, then for the installation, for electricity … And what is the point of wasting all this money if people can't see what is written there? For me … I don't care, they can remove them, I will not care, because even when they are I have to walk around or ask for security guards' help. So what's the point?

Beyond questioning technical accessibility, the account suggests that for some people, inaccessible shopping mall maps cause stress and anxiety, and make the individuals dependent on others' availability and time. Similar to

Gitana (Lithuania, age 65+), Herbertas (Lithuania, age 65+) questioned the complexity of the maps and the potential way to make them more accessible:

> Maps as maps, but they are impossible to see. Although I do not have vision impairment and wear only regular glasses, they are too tiny for me, plus all the lights. They do not help. They should make a regular map on a regular piece of paper and it would be much better. And now they try to do everything fancy and plummy.

Some informants with mental health conditions and cognitive impairments shared similar accounts of inaccessible practices. For example, Dovile (Lithuania, age 41–64) noted that shopping mall maps often are difficult to understand and are confusing:

> These maps are like schemes – no chance to understand what is where: only lines and numbers.

Similarly, Peter (United Kingdom, age 18–40) said that he does not use mall maps to find a particular shop. If needed, he seeks for his mother's assistance:

> No, I don't understand, it's too complicated. My mum helps me.

While the above accounts reveal that people with mobility, vision and cognitive impairments and mental health conditions partly access the information, blind customers are completely excluded. Research participants representing this group noted that none of their visited shopping malls either during mystery shopping or at any point before provide information about the layout of a shop in an audible format.

Information format was questioned and experiences of exclusion, stress and dependency featured prominently in the interviews but often were opposed by narratives of resilience and coping practices. For example, Albinas (Lithuania, age 41–64), who has a mental health condition, said that before he goes to any shopping mall, he prints out the map of the setting and marks the shops that he wants to visit. Similarly, Agne (Lithuania, age 41–64) with a cognitive impairment noted that when she gets lost in a shopping mall, she finds the nearest exist, leaves the building and 'inspects' it from the outside. Some other participants said that when they get confused, they look around and in the worst-case scenario, ask either for other customers or shop assistants and security guards' help. Others develop memory maps (Allen et al., 2002), enabling them to independently operate in retail premises. To illustrate, Katrina (Lithuania, age 18–40) said,

> You need time to get to know the place, especially if it is a big shopping mall. It took some time to figure out where the lift is, which shops are accessible for me, which places are covered with carpets, in which shops shop assistants are nice. So now I do not have any problems.

Thus, despite inaccessibility of shop maps, disabled customers are not passive. Even though discussed information provision practices may exclude and signalise that this customer group is not always welcomed and desired, individuals find ways to overcome the obstacles and develop strategies that enable them to be more active market participants. In such a context, some people unconsciously accept the role of 'de jure' customers, which through symbolic interaction and processes is ascribed to them by social and market practices. As a result, gradually internalised personal responsibility of customer performance leads to different resilience practices, enabling them to 'survive' in the shopping realm.

Excluding information provision practices outlined so far were accompanied by concerns that certain elements of an internal shop design may foster disabled customers' segregation and vulnerability. To begin with, mirrors and reflective glass, which serve to multiply the supply and extend the space of the setting (Fiske et al., 1987), often cause health- and safety-related worries for people with vision impairments. For instance, Pranciska (Lithuania, age 41–64) said,

> There is that shoe shop. And the entire wall is of mirror. And that mirror reflects the opened space. Once I was walking and thought that there are other premises and almost slammed down. And only then saw that it is a mirror. It may sound funny, but that mirror reflects other premises, I saw people going, so thought there are other premises. I almost banged with my head. I was so frightened.

Although Alison (United Kingdom, age 18–40) did not provide explicit explanation, similar to Pranciska (Lithuania, age 41–64), the woman noted that some shops' decision to use two-sided mirrors in fitting rooms prevent her from clearly seeing the visual.

Older research participants and some informants with vision and cognitive impairments hinted at music. They noted that sometimes music is too loud and distracts them as well as may cause anxiety and stress:

> All this music distracts me. I need to be very focused in order to see where I go. So sometimes, especially when I am tired, it becomes very difficult to find the shop and especially the product in the shop or on the shelf.
> (Pranciska, Lithuania, age 41–64)

Sarunas (Lithuania, age 41–64) echoed,

> I like music. I listen to it on my phone, but in the shop they play it very loud, so I cannot hear myself and this annoys me.

Hence, a settled template of one group of shoppers and limited consideration of their variety prevent retailers from meeting diverse shoppers' needs and wants. Insufficient social sensitivity in marketing strategies lead to practices that exclude and threaten those customers who do not share characteristics typical to non-disabled or 'average' market participants.

Reaching products

The first chapter exhaustively illustrated how ableism and business' focus on a healthy, middle-class male as a target client shapes product layout decisions that may cause disabled customers' vulnerability. The following discussion contributes to the ongoing debate and provides a number of examples of common as well as unique experience, supporting the position. To begin with, the dominant practice of a horizontal product layout on shelves often excludes wheelchair users from possible choice options and predetermines the 'list' of articles that can be purchased:

> Sometimes, if I am alone and there is no one, who could reach the product, I just need to go with what I can reach.
> (Kristupas, Lithuania, age 18–40)

Similarly, Daphne (United Kingdom, age 18–40) who has a mobility impairment and does not use a wheelchair addressed how the horizontal item display eliminates her from buying wanted and needed products and shapes her choice of retail places:

> So I often find things high up or really low down, and because I can't really bend down to look at things low down, that frustrates me. So then I just usually don't look in that shop. I just get really annoyed. I just leave it.

Meanwhile, Katrina (Lithuania, age 18–40) shared an example of indirect wheelchair users' infantilisation and ascription with lower-quality and cheaper products:

> Spices are on the top shelf, the cheapest goods or products for children are placed down. In the middle all average-quality products are. But all spices and expensive products or products that I like, like curd, are placed on the top shelves. And curd cheeses are on the bottom shelves, because they are for children, and sellers want children to see all these curd cheeses. I, for example, can't reach meat or sausage.

In a similar vein, some older informants and those with vision impairments criticised products and product information location under glass. The participants noted that such practices often are misleading, limit their choice and may be embarrassing. As an example, Ramune (Lithuania, age 18–40) shared her experience:

> In the X shop I would like more independency in gastronomy section. I can see that there is a cake or rissoles, but I don't know what is actually

there. I miss a list or something similar and not under the glass, but somewhere where I could use it. Of course, I come and ask whether they have pork or chicken, and then they list me these three things and nothing more. But if I could see what they have, I could choose something else. It is quite unpleasant to point a finger to each of the items and ask 'what's this? What's that?' They will say: 'stupid you, this is a rissole or something else'. Well, of course they will not say so, but it is quite uncomfortable. They disrupt my dignity.

Constant replacement of goods was identified as another disruption. It confuses people, causes stress and anxiety and requires spending more time to find items. In this respect, the majority of the informants noted that they prefer going to the same shops, as this enables developing 'memory maps' (Allen et al., 2002) of the shops and products location. To illustrate, Gitana (Lithuania, age 65+), representing experiences of other participants with vision impairments, said,

In shops where I usually go, I already know where different products are placed. In shops where I don't go so often, it is much more difficult, because I don't know where products are and I can't see properly, so for me this is hard.

Familiarity with products location in a shop shapes customers' loyalty to retailers and higher satisfaction with shopping process. As an example, Daphne (United Kingdom, age 18–40), who has mobility impairment, noted that familiarity with products location in a shop eliminates the 'struggle' and is one of the reasons why she returns to the same providers:

I have my favourite shops, where I usually go. And I don't need to struggle there as everything is so familiar to me.

Although the stability of products location in a shop serves as a means providing more independency, as discussed in the first chapter, due to product-marketing purposes, shops constantly change items location. This means that people have to redevelop and re-create 'memory maps'. As a result, time spent looking for articles gets longer and more complicated. To illustrate, Rolandas (Lithuania, age 41–64) shared his wife's, who also has vision impairment, experience:

When they opened X shop, which is close to our home, my wife went there few times just to look around and to 'spy' where what is. When she became familiar with shop's environment and was already able to do shopping alone and faster, they changed products display, and again she couldn't find products that she wanted and needed.

In a similar vein, Herbertas (Lithuania, age 65+) said,

> Business plays its own game. And this is a part of that game. I am too old to think I can change that practice, but what I can do is to dedicate more time for my trip to a shop when I know that they have replaced the products again.

For some participants, such practice causes intense negative feelings and frustration. As an example, Daphne (United Kingdom, age 18–40) said,

> I hate that ... Why do they think it is a right thing to do?

Fortunately, not all product layout–related experiences are excluding. According to the participants, vertical product layout provides an opportunity to try items, enables independently choosing products, testing their accessibility and avoiding financial loss. For Herbertas (Lithuania, age 65+), such practice allows checking if the device is compatible with his home-made speakers:

> I always go to X shop, because all the products are visible, so I take my speaker and test whether it works with the item.

Similarly, Katrina (United Kingdom, age 18–40) identified vertical product layout as a solution for current excluding experiences of customers who are using wheelchairs:

> Shops should change the way they think and act about product layout. I kind of understand the rationale behind the vertical layout, but in my opinion horizontal product display could serve the same purpose and provide customers with even more benefits. I, for instance, would buy more as I would be able to reach products that I want.

Despite differences in participants' experiences, it seems that retail premise design and product-marketing strategies oriented to non-disabled customers often manifest as obstacles for shoppers with impairments. A focus on non-disabled people as the main customer group and insufficient acknowledgement of changing customer segment create unequal, excluding and discriminatory shopping practice. This creates a symbolic universe that holds disabled customers individually responsible for their experience in retail premises, and symbolises non-disabled people's superiority in the market.

In addition to the physical environment, interaction with shoppers or shop assistants plays a part in shaping disabled customers' shopping experience. The following discussion, therefore, positions these interactions as the fourth stage of an accessible shopping chain and sheds light on disabling and enabling factors.

Interaction in the shop

Shop design oriented to non-disabled customers shapes the interaction of people with impairments in retail premises. In order to overcome ableist barriers, they often have to engage in social interaction with other shoppers, shop assistants, family members, friends and personal assistants. Alongside these sources of assistance, service provided by 'special shop assistants' is also important. While usually others are willing to assist and some disabled people are willing to accept provided assistance, the majority of disabled customers prefer independent shopping, and some may withdraw from customer participation if shopping process is not accessible and other's assistance is needed.

Interaction with informal assistants

Family members, friends and other customers are the main source of informal assistance in overcoming disablist barriers in retail premises. Usually, seeking assistance is not a choice but a necessity. As an example, due to inaccessible product layout, wheelchair users who travel to the shop independently often have to seek other customers' assistance. Povile's (Lithuania, age 41–64) example was common in other wheelchair users' narratives:

> For me everything is ok, except if products are located higher – then I can't reach them. I ask people's help (in such a case).

While people like Polive feel confident and comfortable to ask to and be assisted by strangers, individuals who are shyer may find such practice intrusive and unpleasant. To illustrate, Pranciska (Lithuania, age 41–64), who has vision impairment, noted that she rather leaves the shop than engages in such interaction:

> If I see that I can't see, I better leave than ask for others' help. Once I tried to read the consistency of the bread and one woman noticed that I can't read, so she came and asked whether she could help. But she was older than I am, so I got ashamed, thanked her and left the shop.

While usually disabled customers' experience with other shoppers is positive and they receive needed assistance, the majority prefer assistance provided by close and familiar people. As an example, Katrina (Lithuania, age 18–40) noted that she feels more relaxed when she is shopping together with her boyfriend:

> Other people [informal assistants] come, unhook the sausage, I read and if I don't like, they have to hook it back. And here the person [informal shop assistant] has to wait while I read whether that sausage consists E

elements. Now all my problems disappeared, because I am with my boyfriend. He comes, unhooks the sausage, I read, he waits and 'dreams' if it is not interesting for him. So at this point, my all problems are solved.

Similarly, people with vision impairments are often accompanied by people without vision impairments. As an example, Ramune (Lithuania, age 18–40) usually goes shopping with her young daughter. She enables the participant manoeuvring in retail premises, accessing product information and having faster and more pleasant shopping:

> I usually do [shopping] with my daughter. She sees a little bit better than I do and orients in the environment better than I do. So it is faster. I just say her 'take me to this, take me to that', so it is faster. If I go alone, it takes longer to pass all the obstacles, so she drags me.

Other informants with vision impairments shared similar accounts. They noted that assistance by family members or friends enables them to avoid physical barriers, injuries, to find needed products easier and not to get lost in the shop, among others.

In addition to informal assistants, salespeople also assist customers with impairments in overcoming excluding and segregating retail practices. The following discussion sheds light on this interaction in the shop.

Interaction with shop assistants

Identically to non-disabled people, disabled customers' experiences of interacting with shop assistants vary. Shop personnel may create additional barriers as well as provide needed assistance for a more accessible and pleasant shopping experience. With regard to more challenging practices, while salespeople often assist shoppers with impairments in overcoming barriers, the actual process sometimes might be experienced as devaluing and unpleasant. As an example, Katrina (Lithuania, age 18–40) noted that while shop assistants often assist her in reaching high-located items, occasionally the practice is infantilising or implying her dependency to a lower economic class:

> When I ask to hand me spices, usually they [shop assistants] take the cheapest. So only because I am disabled, I am pressed to the lower level, and it is automatically assumed that I have less money. Even if I have less money, I do not need to buy the cheapest spices or curd ... Although often I do choose cheaper products. But it does not mean that I have to buy the cheapest things only because I am disabled.

While narratives of other participants suggested that being offered cheaper and lower quality products is a common experience, Pranas

(Lithuania, age 18–40) and Alison (United Kingdom, age 18–40) noted that several times shop assistants offered them to go directly to the 'sales' section. Girenas (Lithuania, age 18–40) said that sometimes shop assistants *'are very suspicious and unhappy'* if he asks to show or demonstrate more expensive products. Looking at the evidence from the interviews, it is easy to trace historically entrenched societal and market practices viewing disabled people as poor and unbeneficial market players. The stories suggest that despite changes in the economy, labour market and public policy, at the everyday level, disabled people are not seen as equal customers and remain segregated in the mainstream private market. Current forms of exclusion are subtler and less violent but keep signalling that people with impairments are only 'good' for special markets and not for the mainstream.

Depersonalisation by shop assistants was another topic often addressed by customers. Shared stories suggest that when people, especially with vision and mobility impairments, are accompanied by non-disabled people, salespeople usually approach and prefer communicating with informal assistants, instead of them. For instance, Christine (United Kingdom, age 18–40) said,

> They even talk to my assistant instead of me. This is a very common thing; they talk to my PA and not to me.

Depersonalisation was also evidenced in a few of the mystery shoppings, when instead of approaching the person, shop assistants asked me *'what does he/she [a disabled person] want or need'* or tried to have eye contact with me and not with the customer. Drawing on Brisenden's (1986) discussion on depersonalisation, such attitudes and behaviour contribute to the construction of vulnerability and exclusion of customers with impairments. Refusing to accept disabled people as individual market participants who have unique and personal taste, preferences, needs and desires, shop assistants position them as passive instead of active market actors. They characterise customer life of people with impairments as legitimately open to 'active' non-disabled people's choices, decisions and judgements.

A feeling of being unwelcomed may start immediately after entering retail premises. While a few shoppers said that in some retail outlets, salespeople never say 'hi' to them, the majority shared experiences of feeling unwelcomed throughout the whole time spent in a store. For instance, Girenas (Lithuania, age 18–40) said,

> I notice their (shop assistants') apathy quite often. If they see that there is a blind person with a white stick in the shop, who is looking for a technology, they stay aside. I don't know if they are afraid of disabled people [laughs].

Alison (United Kingdom, age 18–40) echoed identical experiences in the United Kingdom and linked them with shop assistants' attitudes:

> Well it's kind of like they're not sort of willing to help. I think they think that because you're disabled, either physical or whatever impairment it might be, that like it's almost like they have to go out of their way. They have a lazy attitude: 'Oh, I have to do something'. It's almost like something else you've asked them to do rather than them wanting to help the customer. I kind of feel as if I would be a burden on them if I was to ask them for help. That's the kind of attitude that I get from them.

In a similar vein, Christine (United Kingdom, age 18–40) said,

> Some staff members actually can be rude with a challenging attitude towards disability issues. Well, I mean, often in the shop you get real patronising or ignorance of the disability issues.

Hence, alongside physical barriers, shop assistants' attitudes and service provision shape disabled customers' experience, which unfortunately, differs from those of non-disabled people and often is disabling and unpleasant. Although served, people with impairments do not feel equally treated to non-disabled purchasers. The current practices often create a sense of being a different or a 'second-class' customer, treated with less respect and dignity.

While so far discussed experiences are likely to be shaped by insufficient shop assistants' training and awareness of disability and accessibility, a few participants with cognitive and vision impairments referred to unfair financial practices. To begin with, Maryte (Lithuania, age 65+), whose experience was also recalled by a few other informants with cognitive impairments, noted that sometimes shop assistants use her impairment to justify their unfair professional behaviour:

> Very often they over-calculate me. It happens very often that the change is 50 cents or 1 Litas less than it should be. And then it is impossible to prove that they are lying. They say that I either lost my money or made up the story.

Similarly, Rolandas (Lithuania, age 41–64) echoed Maryte (Lithuania, age 65+) and provided an example, representing other blind research participants' experiences:

> There were many different shop assistants. As everywhere. And cheaters, who used to give a wrong change. Some were very cheeky and immodest. I usually do not like to check and I trust people, but then I started noticing that they defraud me. They say the amount then give the change and when I check I realise that I lack money. It is not enough that they dis-weight products, but even defraud in returning the change.

None of the British participants referred to similar practices. It can be argued that limited disabled customers' protection and the absence of organisations representing their rights is one of the reasons behind the experiences in Lithuania. While both countries do not sufficiently recognise disabled people as equal customers, the United Kingdom's general system of customer protection has longer traditions than the Lithuanian system. In addition, having a longer history, United Kingdom's disability movement has fragmentally included separate aspects of customer rights and protection in their positions and activities, which is not the case in Lithuanian DPOs' practices. Furthermore, the accounts suggest that customer financial vulnerability does not directly correlate with and is not determined by individuals' impairment or dependency to the category of disability. Indeed, external factors, including salespeople's unfair commercial practice, and lack of support and rights representation are some of the elements behind customer vulnerability.

It would be misleading to state that shop assistants hold only disabling and discriminatory attitudes and that all their practices cause customer vulnerability and exclusion. On the contrary, there were numerous examples of positive interactions with salespeople. Majority of the customers referred to approachability and complaisance, saying that shop assistants show where products are located, hand items to them that are displayed inaccessibly, provide information about products and prices, and so on. Personalisation of customer service was a broadly appreciated feature. For instance, Pranciska (Lithuania, age 41–64), representing the experiences of other customers with vision impairments, said,

> It is so much better when they ask what I want. These young people are so great. Each time I want to buy something, they describe me the colour, show clothes that I may like. And they also tell me if the clothes look good on me; and if the colour goes well with my face.

Individual attention and service provision without prejudice provides customers with impairments with shopping pleasure, satisfaction and shape loyalty to a particular retailer. As suggested by Alison (United Kingdom, age 18–40), it also introduces more choice and options, and creates positive customer experience:

> But another thing, they were willing to help and wanted to – maybe if I had wanted a different size, they would go get it. I tried different items that I would not have picked myself. So in terms of that, it was a really good experience.

Disabled customers value if shop assistants see them as individual clients and not as people with impairments. As an example, Povile (Lithuania, age 41–63) who is a wheelchair user said that in a few shoe-shops, salespeople used to constantly offer her lower quality shoes, which do not look nice. She assumed that such behaviour was influenced by the fact that she is using a wheelchair and thus does not 'use' shoes. As a result, Povile stopped going to these shops and instead chooses retail outlets where shop assistants inquire about her personal taste and preferences and only then offer possible options. Mystery shopping and customer interviews revealed that individualised services are mainly provided in small shops and in shops where shop assistants are familiar with particular clients. Here, they know that a disabled person is a potential client, are familiar with reasonable accommodation provisions and thus are more likely to provide higher quality service. Most importantly, small size of retail outlets provides the two stakeholder groups with more opportunities to know each other better and to engage in conversations about preferences, needs, likes and dislikes than big shopping malls do. Hence, while shop assistants' training and awareness of disability and accessibility is important for shifting the understanding of people with impairments as 'vulnerable' to equal customers, the capitalist nature of the market may colonise these practices by its orientation to massive consumption and generation of profit.

Interaction with 'special' shop assistants

Alongside shop assistants who normally serve non-disabled customers, some grocery shops in the United Kingdom have salespeople who are responsible for serving shoppers with impairments. While this can be seen as a form of reasonable accommodation provisions, the practice has a number of aspects that lead to opposite experiences to accessibility, independency and equal participation. To begin with, the service is often time restricted and limits spontaneous shopping. Specifically, usually disabled customers are expected to ring the shop in advance before the visit. While small shops seem to be more flexible and able to provide assistance whenever disabled customers turn up, big shops are not that flexible and disability-friendly. For instance, Jack (United Kingdom, age 41–64) said,

> Some bigger stores, they've got a bit shirty, a bit – they've not been very friendly when you've just turned up unannounced more recently. So we've tended to ring the night before and say, 'I want to do some shopping tomorrow. Could I book an assisted shop at half past nine tomorrow morning?' That seems to work well.

Contrarily, if customers only give a short notice before they come to big shops, or pop-in without notice, they risk not to receive assistance. Nick (United Kingdom, age 41–64) said,

> And I have had occasion where I've been told, 'Well there's nobody who can help you at the moment. Can you come back?' or, 'Can't you bring

somebody with you?' And as I say, after having been there for years, and only because I'm stroppy have I said, 'No. It's a reasonable adjustment. It's law. You've got to find somebody. I will wait'. And now they've got the hang of that, we're getting on better.

Hence, although assistance sources exist, service arrangement practice locates disabled customers into shopping time frames that are convenient for the retail outlet and not for the customer. This restricts shoppers' freedom and eliminates them from spontaneous shopping. It is important to note that while people like Nick, who are active in the disability movement and familiar with policy instruments, are aware of and demand customer rights, those individuals who are at the opposite end of the spectrum may be excluded from getting the assistance.

Although shops, offering such services, state that staff members have undertaken disability training (Morrisons, 2015, Sainsbury, 2015), research data suggest that the assistants often lack knowledge about reasonable accommodation and understanding how to accommodate people with impairments. For instance, Christine (United Kingdom, age 18–40) said,

> So she (a trained shop assistant) didn't know what she was supposed to do. She was giving me different products, and I can't see them – she had to be aware of this. You should read labels to me. So, we haven't checked the prices or validity. She walked with me and she was trying to be helpful but she didn't know how to be helpful. So she was pointing me to that shelf and that shelf, but I can't see. I need more description than that. That's the whole reason for her being with me.

While some 'special' shop assistants are willing to assist customers and try their best, limited training is a barrier that prevents them from providing shoppers with impairments with more choice and independency. As an example, Nick (United Kingdom, age 41–64) said,

> So I think now there's a lot of willingness there, but not systems. It very much depends upon who's on. So, some weeks I can get a really efficient person who tries to join in. Yes, tries to understand what it is I'm looking for, what I want to buy, helps me find it, draws the sort of thing to my attention that they think I might be interested in because I'm asking about those sort of things, etc. Other weeks, I can get people who I'm sure perform very variable roles, whatever that is, but whose strength isn't customer service, or, for that matter, reading and writing, which, when you're accessing products for me where I can't read or write them, can't see them myself, is kind of quite important really.

Hence, the presence of special shop assistants does not necessarily ensure informed customer choice or pleasant shopping experience. Indeed, due to insufficient training and awareness, it may become a barrier, causing customer dissatisfaction and is unpleasant.

Barriers outlined so far and salespeople's disablist attitudes encourage some disabled customers to start online shopping. For instance, Alison (United Kingdom, age 18–40) said,

> So that's kind of – I kind of feel as if I would be a burden on them if I was to ask them for help. That's the kind of attitude that I get from them. So in terms of online, you don't have to deal with staff attitudes in that kind of respect.

All British participants, but only five Lithuanians, mentioned online shopping. This quantitative difference between experiences in the two countries might be explained by differences in accessing the Internet and purchasing online. Specifically, 65.1% of Lithuanians compared with 84.1% of Britons had access to the Internet in 2012 (European Travel Commission, 2012). While 66% of Britons used the Internet as a shopping source in 2011, only 14% of Lithuanians participated in e-commerce in the same year (European Travel Commission, 2012). In addition, while Lithuania does not have clear guidance for accessible websites, the Equality Act (2010) in the United Kingdom determines an anticipatory requirement to provide web-based services in a way that they do not discriminate disabled people. Individuals who engage in online customer participation addressed it mainly as a replacement of or substitution for a disabling and excluding customer experience in shops. While online shopping might be interpreted as a customer coping strategy, it should not be seen as equally important or equal to shopping in retail outlets. Disabled customers' transition from physical to online shopping is a conscious but not free decision and choice. It symbolises exclusion from more traditional forms of customer participation and the need to look for ways how to remain active in the mainstream private market.

Concluding comments

This chapter explored a range of issues related to disabled people's shopping and customer experience in the mainstream private market. While the literature mainly focuses on the experiences of people with mobility and vision impairments in retail premises, the chapter shed light on the experiences of individuals with different impairments and positioned shopping as a chain, consisting of four main stages: customer information, journey to the shop, navigation in retail premises and interaction with informal shopping assistants and members of staff. While each stage and its elements are experienced differently by each individual, the practice of exclusion, segregation and inequality is common across the board. With regard to acquisition of customer information, it proved to be important in providing individuals with a possibility to make an informed customer choice, explore more options in terms of shops and products and act more independently and freely. However, usually customer information is provided having non-disabled customers in mind. Such practices are founded on ableism and usually have a disabling effect on customer experience of people with impairments. They may restrict individual's freedom when deciding where and what to purchase, spatially isolate them within particular market niches and estrange them from non-disabled shoppers.

The journey to the shop is the second stage of the shopping chain and usually consists of the home environment, public environment and public and private transport. The role played by an accessible home environment in shaping shopping accessibility was an anticipated finding. While only five participants addressed this, it was evident that single barriers in the home environment may prevent a pleasant and smooth journey to the shop. In some cases, it may eliminate people with certain impairments from shopping or convert them into being dependent on other's assistance, time, activities and social obligations. It was suggested that accessibility of the public environment often shape disabled people's decisions on the shop and the route to it, especially those with mobility and vision impairments. It was evident that obstacles in the public environment might cause stress and injuries, prevent from discovering new shops and facilities and make people with impairments dependent on non-disabled individuals. A few older participants noted that due to certain barriers, sometimes they are either converted into indirect customers or are eliminated from shopping. In addition to such impact on customer experience and identity, one participant ascribed the nature and the roots of differences between his past experience as a non-disabled shopper and present practices as a wheelchair user to barriers in the public environment. He noted that while some of them may cause challenges and inconvenience, others may completely eliminate from the past customer interaction.

With regard to public transport, non-disabled passenger–oriented information provision about and in transport means, routes, timetable and other services as well as physical inaccessibility of vehicles often have a negative impact on a person's budget, safety and comfort and shape various dependency practices. This may restrict shopping time and place, choice and independency. With regard to private transport, it was evident that inaccessibility of parking and insufficient number of accessible parking spots are important factors, causing challenges for customers travelling to the shop by private transport.

The third stage of the shopping chain is navigation in the shop. It consists of two elements: entering the shop and operating in the retail premises. It was suggested that various non-disabled customer–oriented retail premise design and product-marketing strategies shape the dependency and exclusion of customers with certain impairments, minimise choice and control, and cause stress and a fear to be injured. Market practices that shape such experiences are premised on ableism and limited business' awareness of changing customer segment. It was suggested that even though some means that could provide more accessibility are present and available in shops, due to limited business' awareness of the disabled customer group and accessibility, they often are not exploited. In some cases, they are transformed into artefacts, signalising that disabled customers are not desired shoppers.

The final stage of the shopping chain is interaction in the shop. It is tightly linked with the previous stage as often disabled shoppers' interaction with informal and shop assistants is sparked by inaccessible retail premises and products layout. While both assistance types usually provide more customer choice and control and make shopping faster, more pleasant and efficient, the informants prefer assistance provided by family members, friends or personal assistants. In addition to the personal familiarity factor, limited awareness of disability and training on reasonable accommodation are potential factors behind the preference. Research data suggest that often shop assistants neither meet disabled customers' needs and preferences nor provide them with an equal and quality service. Indeed, depersonalisation, special treatment, infantilisation, unfair financial practices and similar behaviour are common during service delivery. This may locate disabled people within particular shopping time frames, cause financial challenges and a feeling of being a 'different' customer, and lead to withdrawal from customer practice in particular sites or lead to looking for substitutions such as e-commerce.

The discussed disabled customers' empirical realities in Lithuania and the United Kingdom suggest that state and private market's focus on non-disabled citizens and customers is complemented by ableism. The synergy of the two creates disabled customers' exclusion and segregation, and converts them into 'vulnerable' customers, who are prevented from equal and barrier-free participation in the EU single market. This book argues that one of the factors shaping the outlined experiences and practices is business and civil society's lifeworld regarding disabled customers and market accessibility as well as their access to the formulation of the public discourse. The following chapter, therefore, starts untangling some of the underlying factors and concerns, and focuses on international and national ICT industry and civil society's norms, values, knowledge and positions towards markets accessibility and disabled customers.

Notes

1 Shops that sell products produced by one manufacturer.
2 Shops that sell products produced by different manufacturers.

Bibliography

Allen, C., Milner, J. & Price, D. 2002. *Home is where the start is: The housing and urban experiences of visually impaired children*, Bristol, The Policy Press.

Bettman, J. R., Johnson, E. J. & Payne, J. W. 1991. Consumer decision making. *In:* Robertson, T. S. & Kassarjian, H. H. (eds.) *Handbook of consumer behavior*, 50–84.

Birtwistle, G. & Freathy, P. 1998. More than just a name above the shop: A comparison of the branding strategies of two UK fashion retailers. *International Journal of Retail & Distribution Management*, 26, 318–323.

Boedeker, M. 1995. New-type and traditional shoppers: A comparison of two major consumer groups. *International Journal of Retail & Distribution Management*, 23, 17–26.

Bovy, P. H. L. & Stern, E. 1990. *Route choice: Wayfinding in transport networks*, London, Kluwer Academic.

Bridge, G. & Dowling, R. 2001. Microgeographies of retailing and gentrification. *Australian Geographer*, 32, 93–107.

Brisenden, S. 1986. Independent living and the medical model of disability. *Disability, Handicap & Society*, 1, 173–178.

Dick, A., Chakravarti, D. & Biehal, G. 1990. Memory-based inferences during consumer choice. *Journal of Consumer Research*, 17, 82–93.

Dogu, U. & Erkip, F. 2000. Spatial factors affecting wayfinding and orientation: A case study in a shopping mall. *Environment and Behavior*, 32, 731–755.

European Travel Commission 2012. NewMedia Trend Watch. Lithuania.

Evcil, N. 2010. Designers' attitudes towards disabled people and the compliance of public open places: The case of Istanbul. *European Planning Studies*, 18, 1863–1880.

Fiske, J., Hodge, B. & Turner, G. 1987. *Myths of oz: Reading Australian popular culture*, Sydney, Allen & Unwin Sydney.

Gabriel, Y. & Lang, T. 1995. *The unmanagable consumer: Contemporary consumption and its fragmentation*, London, Sage Publications.

Graham, D. F., Graham, I. & Maclean, M. J. 1991. Going to the mall: A leisure activity of urban elderly people. *Canadian Journal on Aging/La Revue canadienne du vieillissement*, 10, 345–358.

Haywood, F., Oldman, J. & Means, R. 2001. *Housing and home in later life*, Buckingham, McGraw Hill Education.

Hoogendoorn, S. P. & Bovy, P. H. L. 2004. Pedestrian route-choice and activity scheduling theory and models. *Transportation Research Part B: Methodological*, 38, 169–190.

Imrie, R. 2003. Architects' conceptions of the human body. *Environment and Planning D*, 21, 47–66.

Imrie, R. 2004a. Disability, embodiment and the meaning of the home. *Housing Studies*, 19, 745–763.

Imrie, R. 2004b. Housing quality, disability and domesticity. *Housing Studies*, 19, 685–690.

Kahn, B. & Schmittlein, D. 1989. Shopping trip behavior: An empirical investigation. *Marketing Letters*, 1, 55–69.

Kishi, G. 1988. Daily decision-making in community residences: A social comparison of adults with and without mental retardation. *American Journal of Mental Retardation*, 92, 430–435.

Kivetz, R. & Simonson, I. 2000. The effects of incomplete information on consumer choice. *Journal of Marketing Research*, 37, 427–448.

Knights, D., Sturdy, A. & Morgan, G. 1994. The consumer rules? An examination of the rhetoric and 'reality' of marketing in financial services. *European Journal of Marketing*, 28, 42–54.

Kumar, A. & Levinson, D. M. 1996. Temporal variations on the allocation of time. *Transportation Research Record* [Online]. Available: http://ssrn.com/abstract=1091810 [Accessed 19/04/2013].

Kuo, M., Wechsler, H., Greenberg, P. & Lee, H. 2003. The marketing of alcohol to college students: The role of low prices and special promotions. *American Journal of Preventive Medicine*, 25, 204–211.

Leong, S. M., Busch, P. S. & John, D. R. 1989. Knowledge bases and salesperson effectiveness: A script-theoretic analysis. *Journal of Marketing Research*, 26, 164–178.

Lietuvos Respublikos Seimas 2001. *No. STR 2.03.01:2001 Statybos techninių reikalavimų reglamentas. Statiniai ir teritorijos: Reikalavimai žmonių su negalia reikmėms*, Vilnius, Lietuvos Respublikos Seimas.

Lietuvos Respublikos Vyriausybė 2005. *No. T-5 Informacinės aplinkos pritaikymo žmonių su negalia ugdymui metodika*, Vilnius, Informacinės visuomenės plėtros komiteto prie Lietuvos Respublikos Vyriausybės.

Lietuvos Respublikos Vyriausybė 2012. *No. 1408 Nacionalinė neįgaliųjų socialinės integracijos 2013–2019 metų programa*, Vilnius, Lietuvos Respublikos Vyriausybė.

Matthews, M. H. & Vujakovic, P. 1995. Private worlds and public places: Mapping the environmental values of wheelchair users. *Environment and Planning A*, 27, 1069–1083.

Miller, N. J. & Kim, S. 1999. The importance of older consumers to small business survival: Evidence from rural Iowa. *Journal of Small Business Management*, 37, 1–15.

Miller, N. J., Kim, S. & Schofield-Tomschin, S. 1998. The effects of activity and aging on rural community living and consuming. *Journal of Consumer Affairs*, 32, 343–368.

Morrisons. 2015. *Facilities for shoppers with disabilities* [Online]. Available: http://your.morrisons.com/Help-and-information/store-services/Facilities-for-shoppers-with-disabilities/ [Accessed 02/15/2015].

Ofcom 2010. *Code on television access services*, London, Ofcom.

Parliament of the United Kingdom 2010. *The equality act*, London, Home office.

Russell, M. 2002. What disability civil rights cannot do: Employment and political economy. *Disability & Society*, 17, 117–135.

Sainsbury. 2015. *Do you support your disabled customers?* [Online]. Available: http://help.sainsburys.co.uk/help/company-values/disabled-customer-support [Accessed 15/02/2015].

Sandling, K. H. 1985. *Revolving doors*. 4557073 patent application.

Sujan, H., Sujan, M. & Bettman, J. R. 1988. Knowledge structure differences between more effective and less effective salespeople. *Journal of Marketing Research*, 25, 81–86.

Waddington, L. 2009. A disabled market: Free movement of goods and services in the EU and disability accessibility. *European Law Journal*, 15, 575–598.

WHO 2011. *World report on disability*, Geneva, World Health Organisation, The World Bank.

5 The lifeworld of accessible markets

Having explored disabled customers' experiences and describing how disability/ableism and barriers/accessibility become manifest in and shape the shopping process, the current chapter starts the examination of some of the structures that potentially shape the observed customer realities. It adapts a Habermasian concept of a lifeworld and suggests that industry and civil society's notions, positions, values and other elements, constituting their lifeworld towards disabled customers and accessibility, are shaped by policy instruments and professional practice and impact disabled people's shopping experience. Such an approach assists in providing under-researched insights into empirically unobservable structures that shape accessibility of the European Union (EU) single market.

The provided evidence has been gauged through observations of and qualitative interviews with information and communication technologies (ICT) manufacturers, regional representatives of the ICT industry, international and national disabled people's organisations (DPOs), shop managers and shop assistants working in brand-specific and brand-non-specific ICT shops in Lithuania and the United Kingdom. In aiming to provide thicker descriptions, data from mystery shopping and customer interviews are used.

The focus was on the way the stakeholders discursively construct disabled people as customers and markets accessibility via their use of language and customer service. This enabled identifying that the actors acknowledge the need for more accessibility in the EU mainstream private market. However, their lifeworld regarding disabled customers and accessibility differ, and some tensions are present. While some stakeholders premise ontological positions more on the social model of disability, others' lifeworld is informed by the individual model. Such positions are not consciously chosen. The factors shaping particular understandings include policy framework, within which the actors operate, and practices of business players. The variance in stakeholders' relationship with the two causes create differences in the used language, ascribed meanings and values, produce specific knowledge sets and prevent a more accessible and equal disabled customer experience.

170 *The lifeworld of accessible markets*

This chapter begins with an overview of the stakeholders' discursive construction of disabled customers and accessibility. This is followed by the examination of the role played by global, regional and national policy instruments in shaping these notions and stakeholders' lifeworld. Then, the focus is on business practice and the way different approaches towards and processes in providing accessibility may shape manufacturers, international business representatives (IBR) and national retailers' lifeworld.

Notions of disabled customers and accessibility

This section provides an overview of how the EU ICT retail market and civil society position disabled people as customers of ICT products, and accessibility of the ICT market, although with wider implications for other markets. It draws on differences and similarities across the two stakeholder groups and provides some insights into whether disabled people are perceived as different and vulnerable consumers or bearers of customer rights equal to shoppers without impairments. Since language plays a role in creating disability (Barnes, 1991) and engaging in communicative action (Habermas, 1984), the section examines business and civil society's notions used to describe their positions towards disabled customers and accessibility. It was important to reveal whether terminology is premised on the individual or social model of disability and how this may locate people with impairments in the mainstream private market. Instead of asking the informants to define disabled customers and accessibility, the narratives of the whole interview were tackled and the accounts, illustrating common and unique patterns, were extracted. First, business and civil society's notions of disabled people as customers are addressed. Then, light is shed on how the stakeholders associate accessibility with 'needs' and how this creates the division between non-disabled and disabled customers.

International business and civil society's perspectives on disabled customers

International business and civil society actors share similarities and differences regarding disabled customers and users of ICT. Generally, the two stakeholder groups perceive people with impairments as one customer group, whose members are not identical and differ from each other. For instance, the IBR noted,

> Every user has a different experience and a person with disability is not necessarily, has the same disability. There are some identical, but it's not a very homogeneous group.

While the IBR's definition is generic, with no specific implications for undertaken activities, Company X described disabled people as a '*very fragmented group*' and divided it into several subgroups. The division is based on impairment types and guides the company in the development of accessible products:

> As for now, we have got, maybe four customer groups that could be identified. The first one is people with hearing impairments. Then the second one is people with partial sight that have certain needs in how to read the screen, basically, but having some visual capacities. And then the third one is then, let's say, totally blind people with severe visual impairment that would need different ways of accessing the device. And then the fourth group is the group, who pretty much, all their senses are starting to be drained, and then also having maybe motor challenges.
> (Company X)

Similar to the business, the international representatives of the EU disabled people's civil society (international disabled people's organisation – IDPO) acknowledged the versatility of accessibility provisions for disabled ICT users:

> There are different issues of course, for different groups of persons with disabilities.

A practice to divide customers into different groups is well known and documented (Guilding and McManus, 2002, Mittal and Kamakura, 2001, Wang et al., 2004). Likewise, the tendency to see disabled people broadly as one group of individuals who experience similar challenges is common (Woodhams and Danieli, 2000), with more specific categorisation into separate impairment groups being prevalent in policy and service provision practice. Similarly, the focus on specific impairments in the context of technology development has been documented elsewhere, for example, in research on cognitive impairments and education (Williams et al., 2006) or shopping and hearing (Chininthorn et al., 2012) and vision (López-de-Ipiña et al., 2011) impairments. On the one hand, such division enables professionals to better engage in analysis and development and design process that leads to more accessible products. On the other hand, such practice may divide disabled people as ICT users and customers. This is mainly because accessibility provisions, as discussed in the first chapter, often focus on some impairment types and not on others.

Echoing the dominant practices, the informants tended to focus on some impairments and did not dedicate much attention to others. While the IBR mainly referred to vision and hearing impairments, Company X expanded on this and included mobility impairments. These groups were also dominant in the IDPO's narratives, who only twice referred to people with cognitive impairments and mental health conditions. This suggests that focus on certain impairments and potential hierarchy among them in public discourse is present not only in public attitudes (Thomas, 2000, Tringo, 1970), health-care service provision (Janicki, 1970) or labour market (Stevenage and McKay, 1999) but also manifests regarding product accessibility and customer participation. Technical product development peculiarities seem to be some of the factors behind the practice. To illustrate, asked about the IDPO's position towards technology users with cognitive impairments, the informant noted that one of the reasons behind limited focus on this user group is incomplete knowledge about how to translate product standards and coding into a format accessible for people with cognitive impairments:

> On one hand it is true that there is less access [to people with cognitive impairments]. The challenge is the way and that content is built and the information is provided that makes it difficult.

It seems that current ICT standard requirements and data coding practice act as a barrier that prevents industry from providing products accessible to users who do not share features typical to non-disabled customers. Alongside the technical peculiarities, limited recognition of people with cognitive impairments as customers and insufficient designers' training on accessible communication are additional factors that exclude this customer group. To illustrate, in one of the working group meetings in the European Parliament, I asked producing companies why they predominantly seek to develop products accessible for users with vision and hearing impairments but do not aim for the same regarding people with cognitive impairments. The representative of one of the companies replied that they '*would not know where and how to start communicating with these people*'. Informal chats with the EU ICT industry actors support such a position and suggest that limited knowledge about accessible communication is additional factor that prevents industry from developing products accessible for a variety of users.

While accessibility per se gains more and more attention, international business and civil society actors do not prioritise it in the context of customer participation. The informants unambiguously noted that despite their interest in and work towards a more accessible EU single market, neither customer rights nor product accessibility is at the top of their priority and activity list. For instance, the IDPO dedicates attention to web accessibility, access to education, labour market, public environment and transport. It is not surprising then that when asked about activity areas of the organisation, the informant referred to market accessibility and customer rights in the end of the narrative. Since the EU policies and legal instruments frame the organisation's activities, it is likely that such a position is shaped by limited attention to the issue in the regional policy agenda. Meanwhile, relatively low industry's interest in producing accessible technologies is constructed by its focus on and prioritisation of non-disabled customers:

> So I would be lying if I said that it's easy and we get things very well done, but in many cases, other priorities are more important than this accessibility thing.
>
> (Company X)

Although the informant did not specifically identify the nature of the *'other priorities'*, data gathered during the internship suggest that the primacy is usually given to 'cool' and novel features that are popular among non-disabled customers. As the IBR informant noted, such actions are founded on the orientation to higher profits:

> If you look from a company point of view, it is all about your turnover and loss and profit. If you sell a Smart phone it is all about the margins, i.e. how much you have earned, what's selling it. Is it that it's basic phone or is it a top-end product that costs 700€? A company doesn't continue to produce properly an accessible phone if it doesn't generate enough turnover.

Hence, even though some ICT industry players perceive disabled people as potential product users, the general practice is to focus on non-disabled customers as they are associated with higher profit. In other words, operating in a capitalist market, the ICT industry prioritises financial success brought by non-disabled customers over the assurance of customer equality for and participation of different user groups.

National business' perspectives on disabled customers

This section draws on semi-structured interviews with and observations of shop assistants and managers, who work in brand-specific ICT shop (BSH) and non-brand-specific ICT shop (NBSH) in Lithuania and the United Kingdom. Research data suggest that disabled people do visit and purchase in ICT shops, but they are not a frequent group of customers. While a Lithuanian BSH manager said that people with impairments visit the shop or purchase products *'once or twice in two weeks'*, the NBSH (Lithuania) manager could not provide an exact answer:

> I don't know. I have never talked about this with my people. This topic has never snagged in.

The informant explained limited knowledge by a lack of *'memorable incidents'* with this customer group:

> I don't know how often they visit us, because as I already have said, this topic has never snagged in and we have never had any memorable incidents, so I can't answer this question.
>
> (NBSH, Lithuania)

This is interesting because majority of the disabled customers noted that for ICT acquisition purposes, they visit this particular NBSH because of its central location and accessibility of the premises. Meanwhile, the manager is at the opposite end of the spectrum and has minimal knowledge

174 *The lifeworld of accessible markets*

about this customer group. Uneven division of knowledge about and between customers and retailers prevent the two actor groups from learning about each other, creating common language and sharing similar interpretations and norms. This restricts an opportunity to share and create a common lifeworld (Habermas, 1984, 1985). It is also worrying that retailers who share similar positions and level of knowledge about customers may associate shoppers with impairments with incidents and events that are perceived as negative in retail domain. The discourse of deviance was furthered by juxtaposing disabled shoppers with foreigners, strangers and drunk shoppers:

> Of course, we meet different clients, including more strange customers: those, whose Lithuanian language is not fluent, sometimes it happens to have drunk people, also, disabled. But not very often.
> (NBSH, Lithuania)

Although the manager did not directly identify disabled people as 'strange' customers, a repetitive reference to 'drunk', 'strange' and 'disabled' in the answers to the same questions suggests that some professionals perceive people with impairments as unusual clients, who differ from 'average' and expected shoppers. However, shop assistants working in NBSH in the United Kingdom and in BSH in Lithuania shared opposite positions. As an example, two salespeople in British NBSH noted that despite the impairment, they treat all customers equally. One of them said,

> Well, they all are customers, and the physical condition doesn't matter.
> (X NBSH, United Kingdom)

In a similar vein, the manager of the Lithuanian BSH positioned disabled people as shoppers, whose customer satisfaction and loyalty is important to the shop's financial performance:

> Our aim is a happy person, despite whether he is disabled or not, who would come back, be interested in, buy and use our products.

Similarly, one shop assistant working in a small BSH in the United Kingdom noted that despite the need for accessible product features, there are no major differences between disabled and non-disabled customers. According to the informant, while the serving of disabled people may require additional knowledge, the impairment does not determine customer status. This was echoed by other shop assistants and managers, who, similar to the manufacturers, position impairment type as a factor that may influence service delivery process. As an example, BSH manager (Lithuania) noted that although they treat customers equally and '*do not distinguish the clients*', the actual serving process may differ and depend on

The lifeworld of accessible markets 175

the shopper's impairment. The informant provided an example of serving blind customers:

> When blind people come we usually describe the product and how the it works; usually we spend much more time with the person, because we give him time to try and test everything. Sometimes we recommend to take some time and think and to come back the next day, so that the person could check how he feels the product.
>
> (BSH, Lithuania)

Hence, the type of impairment may shape practical aspects of service delivery. As the informant's further narrative suggests, such an approach assists in identifying reasonable accommodation means that should be provided in aiming to ensure service quality and best product choice. To illustrate, the BSH manager (Lithuania) provided an example of serving deaf shoppers:

> Then we communicate in writing, they write what they want. Basically we take a pen and a piece of paper and write and communicate about what they want. Sometimes they come with a sign-interpreter. They communicate in sign language, say what they want and need and then we solve the problem.

While not ideal, the discussed practices seem to share some elements of the principles of social model of disability and reflect some aspects of personalised service. Whereas the BSH manager (Lithuania) positioned impairment as guidance towards a more quality service delivery process, the NBSH manager (Lithuania) identified impairments as a source of challenges:

> Maybe one of the main challenges would be ... I think it depends on person's impairment and on the level of invalidity. For example, if the person is in a wheelchair, so it is ok, you need only to hand and carry the products; but my people do this either way to all clients, thus this would not be an exceptional practice. I think there would be more problems with deaf and hard of hearing people, as there is no way how to communicate with them.

The individual model founded position was echoed later on in the interview:

> There are no major problems with people in wheelchairs. I think it would be much more difficult with people with severe impairments. I would say that they are those who hardly speak, hardly walk, maybe those, who have cognitive impairments. But you cannot condemn them – they are also people, they also need things – they also need to watch television, to listen to the radio or do something else, like for example, to play with computer.
>
> (NBSH, Lithuania)

While these accounts are important for many reasons, for the purpose of this book, it is worth focusing on two of them. First, the understanding of the NBSH manager of disabled people as customers seems to be founded on an individual model of disability. While this echoes the discussion in the first three chapters, the use of words and expressions such as 'invalidity', 'problems' and 'they are also people' suggests conceptual and empirical alienation and estrangement of people with impairments in the shop and wider retail market. Second, similar to manufacturers, the NBSH locate disabled customers within clearly undefined but still present hierarchy. While wheelchair users are seen as not causing 'major challenges' and being 'ok', customers with hearing impairments are perceived as causing more difficulties. People with cognitive and severe impairments were identified as the most 'complicated' groups and people with vision impairments were not mentioned at all. While not explicitly expressed, the logic behind the categorisation seemed to be founded on the idea of 'fixing' impairment, rather than overcoming inaccessibility of the retail practices, and more in-depth research is necessary.

In addition to the impact of national business' perspectives on shaping disabled customers' experiences as discussed in the previous chapter, the position of national civil society is equally important. With this in mind, the following discussion addresses the way national DPOs perceive disabled people as customers and tackle their rights in the retail market.

National civil society's perspectives on disabled customers

Similar to the international stakeholders and national retailers, national DPOs identified disabled people as one group of customers and ICT users, who are not identical but differ from each other. While expressions such as 'many different conditions', 'different severities' and 'different adaptations to severities' are common in the UK representatives' narrative, Lithuanian participants several times repeated that disabled people are not a homogeneous group and different policies should address the needs of different groups more explicitly.

Informants' accounts seemed to be founded on the social model of disability. However, similar to business players, they mainly referred to people with mobility and vision impairments, leaving aside individuals with hearing and cognitive impairments and mental health conditions. Such practice seems to be in line with current and recent studies, focusing on disabled people's shopping as discussed in the first chapter. Complying with this discourse and framing activities within the context of only few impairment types, civil society, respectively, constructs and defines knowledge that is later exchanged in communication with other stakeholders, including policymakers and business players. On the one hand, by addressing the same impairment types, the actors potentially create a scene for deeper communication that may introduce more accessibility. On the other hand, by leaving aside other impairments, they risk limiting the possibility to introduce and create new sets of knowledge, norms and values, leading towards a broader and wider accessibility practice.

Discussing disabled customers' participation, representatives of the British and Lithuanian DPOs addressed various restrictions. For instance, the UK participant linked being a disabled customer with some barriers addressed in the first chapter and emphasised their interconnectivity throughout the shopping process:

> So do you have the money? So do you go online to buy or do you go to the shops? Or if you go to the shops, can you get to them? If you get to the shops, are they accessible? If you talk to the people who work in those shops, do they understand your needs? Can they give you good advice? Are they responsive to you with your impairment, the severity of your impairment and the adaptation to it that you are able to make?
> (DPO, United Kingdom)

Having similar rationale in mind, the Lithuanian DPO addressed more specific barriers such as inaccessible ATMs, sills, steps, lack of elevators, inaccessible public transport, lack of accessible information and limited shop assistants' awareness, among others. Interestingly, in outlining the barriers, Lithuanian informants referred only to people with mobility and vision impairments. This, indeed, is a narrower position than held by other stakeholders, including business players.

In the eyes of the Lithuanian DPO, alongside physical barriers disabled people often lack self-recognition as customers, and this has an impact on their participation in the market:

> People do not understand yet that they have rights as customers and that they can demand those rights.

This limited self-recognition is most likely to be shaped by exclusion and segregation from equal participation with non-disabled customers. According to the informants, it results in shame and avoidance to complain if service or a product is of low quality or shop personnel are discriminating. To some extent, this was indirectly evident in the mystery shopping interviews with Pranciska (Lithuania, age 41–64), Rolandas (Lithuania, age 41–64) and Jack (United Kingdom, age 41–64) who have vision impairments, as well as with Daphne (United Kingdom, age 18–40) who has mobility impairment and Dovile (Lithuania, age 41–64) who has mental health condition. They all pointed to experiences when instead of requiring reasonable accommodation, they either withdrew from the shopping or employed different coping strategies to independently deal with the barriers.

Similar to international business and civil society, national DPOs noted that customer-related issues are not the priority of their activities:

> But it isn't a current priority for our organisation.
>
> (UK DPO)

This was echoed by the Lithuanian DPO:

> No, we do not pursue activities oriented specifically to customers.

Nevertheless, the two organisations are aware of the importance of customer participation and have established certain conceptions. While the Lithuanian DPO conceptualises customer participation as a matter of non-discrimination, the UK DPO informant linked it with equality and rights:

> We want disabled people to see themselves firstly as citizens but also as consumers, able to purchase and obtain the same services and goods as other people. So we are concerned about consumer rights and consumer protection, and we're concerned about people being able to obtain, as I say, the goods and services they need at a price they can afford.
>
> (UK DPO)

The majority of business and civil society actors link accessibility with disabled customers' impairments. The participants positioned impairment as a factor, for identifying 'accessibility needs' for either product or service provision. The following discussion, therefore, sheds light on how 'accessibility needs' are perceived and constructed by regional and national business and civil society.

International stakeholders' perspectives on accessibility

Positioning disabled people as one, albeit heterogeneous, group may enable the stakeholders to come up with more and better accessibility solutions. However, such practice may transform accessibility provisions from means to overcome ableist barriers into means to 'fix' impairments. Specifically, discussing disabled customer groups and accessibility, the informants often framed the accounts within the discourse of 'need' and ascribed it to an individual. As an example, in Company X's narrative, expressions such as 'people with accessibility needs', 'specific needs', 'certain needs', 'need different ways of accessing the device' and 'for special people with special needs' were common. The following IBR quotation illustrates how such focus divides non-disabled and disabled customers in business practice and public discourse:

> Because again, it's not only having a new feature and seeing if it really takes off, it actually should address the need, it is really the need's

space, it's not like – we all can live without Smart-phones because we don't want any more. But if you have a disability and you have a need to contact someone, if they need to purchase something, if they need to get a service, because it is very important for your life, then you need to find appropriate solutions.

International business' focus on needs raises several concerns. First, in product development, the focus on 'needs' and the elimination of 'wants' may impact the aesthetics of an item. While wanted and desired things usually are aesthetically pleasant, things that are 'needed' do not have the same requirement to be beautiful because their functionality is perceived as the most important (Newell, 2003). Second, the perception of technologies as a solution for impairments recalls controversial discussions on their role in 'improving', 'liberating' and 'empowering' disabled people (Poplin, 1995, Raskid, 1993) instead of providing them with equal opportunities and access. Third, ascription of needs and wants to different customer groups may become a marker conceptually and empirically dividing disabled and non-disabled people as users of mainstream goods and services. In such a context, non-disabled people are those who want and desire products and disabled people who need them because of their impairments.

The IDPO also referred to 'accessibility needs'. However, contrary to business, the organisation interpreted accessibility not only through the lens of the 'need' because of impairments but linked it to equality and participation:

> Different impairments bring along different needs. So the position is in terms of ensuring that there is equal access for persons with disabilities to the different services, for instance in the area of transport or in other areas. It could be banking services, for instance, as well as different goods on one hand.
>
> (IDPO)

The difference in the international stakeholders' positions is not without some foundation. While the following sections provide deeper insights, at this point, it is evident that having to comply with technical requirements and standards, as well as principles of competitiveness, ICT producers and the IBR have internalised particular understanding of impairments and accessibility. For this stakeholder group, an impairment is a factor, going alongside specific 'needs' and acting as a technical guidance for meeting minimum standards and developing accessible products. Contrary to this, the IDPO, that premises its activities on the United Nations Convention on the Rights of Persons with Disabilities (UN CRPD), positions accessibility in the light of equality and participation. It sees it as a general principle of and a prerequisite for exercising substantial human rights and for engagement in civic participation. In addition, addressing a broader range of everyday life dimensions and not only the use of technologies, the IDPO's understanding of accessibility is broader than technical product features and interlinks various service types.

National stakeholders' perspectives on accessibility

Similar to international players, national business and DPOs construct notions of accessibility around needs and occasionally wants. The strongest emphasis on needs was in the NBSH manager's narratives. To describe shop personnel's assistance for non-disabled shoppers, the informant used words such as 'want' and 'prefer'. In contrast, while 'want' was used only once when talking about disabled people's technology purchase, 'need' was the dominant verb for the process description. While the participant often addressed price or quality when speaking about non-disabled customers, these were not present when talking about customers with impairments. To illustrate, the informant described the product offering process for non-disabled customers:

> It depends on several factors. First and the most important are client's requests. The second factor on the list is the price that the person is able to spend on a product. I think these are two main factors that determine shop assistants' suggestions. In terms of wants, it is important to ask about the purposes of using the product, what are client's expectations and so on. It depends very much on the product as well, because what suits to find out about the preferences for the TV set, not always suits to find out about which PC would meet individual's preferences.
> (NBSH, Lithuania)

Contrary to this, talking about disabled customers' choice for articles, the informant referred to 'needs' and ascribed the responsibility of choice to individuals:

> In terms of deciding on technologies, such people should come clearly knowing what they need and what is suitable for them.
> (NBSH, Lithuania)

Similarly, some shop assistants who served mystery shoppers in British NBSHs also focused on their needs and questions such as 'what exactly do you need' often followed the general phrase 'how can I help you today?' Nevertheless, they did not ignore questions about price and general product features. Hence, similar to international business players, who seem to treat non-disabled people as wanting and disabled people as needing users, national sellers adopt similar rationale for grouping the shoppers and constructing the division between them. However, shop assistants' awareness of accessibility, expectation and preparedness to equally communicate with non-disabled and disabled customers about factors such as price, purpose of

The lifeworld of accessible markets 181

use and expectations could introduce a scene for seller–customer interaction and communication that would challenge current prejudice towards shoppers with impairments. In addition, the mystery shopping and customer interviews suggested that such interaction might allow customers finding accessible products of higher quality and value. Meanwhile, while people with impairments are 'locked' in the notion of the 'need', they are not provided with an opportunity to engage in this kind of interaction and customer experience. In shops, where such customer categorisation and service delivery practice is present, they are perceived as the only agents, responsible for the exclusion and exercised choice. Their customer experience and participation and the performance and the results of this performance are seen as their individual responsibility.

Examples of customer division were strengthened by narratives on alienation and estrangement. Expressions such as 'their capabilities' and 'what they need' were not isolated cases and were frequent in the Lithuanian NBSH manager's narrative. Although the informant used the word 'people' when talking about disabled shoppers, it was dominated by expressions such as 'they', 'such people' and 'disabled'. This suggests that for some retailers, especially those holding more disablist attitudes, customers' physical and cognitive features may become a marker, shaping their position and activities in the shop. In such a context, the distinction between disabled and non-disabled customers, accompanied by the focus on 'wants' and 'needs', introduces a discourse of 'we' and 'they' as citizens. This is because as suggested by Gabriel and Lang (1995), links between being a customer and a citizen get more intense.

Fortunately, not all practices are disabling and discriminating. Research data suggested that BSH's positions towards disabled customers share some features typical to the social model rather than the individual model of disability. The Lithuanian BSH manager addressed 'needs' for a product only once. Expressions such as 'wants and expectations for a product' and 'we need to know what the person actually wants' were common in the narrative. Likewise, the BSH assistants who served mystery shoppers in both countries usually used questions such as 'what would you like' or 'what are you interested in'.

Recalling the discussion on manufacturers' limited knowledge on accessible communication, the Lithuanian BSH manager addressed 'communication needs' when serving customers with hearing or speech impairments:

> We meet deaf people, we meet people with speech impairments, and then we have some problems with communication. Then we usually communicate in written format, they write what they want. Well we take a piece of paper, a pen, write and communicate in a way they need to communicate.

While at first sight the account locates 'communication needs' within an individual model perspective and links it to a person's impairment, later on the informant acknowledged staff's unpreparedness to communicate in different formats:

> Simply speaking, we try to find a solution in each situation when we can't communicate in their language.
>
> (BSH, Lithuania)

Although the discourse of 'we' and 'they' was present in the narrative, the shift from the individual towards social model of disability is observed. The informant put emphasis on the staff's unpreparedness to serve a diverse group of customers as well as addressed some reasonable accommodation means for making the process more accessible. This suggests that disabled customers' *'needs'* are associated not only with a product but also with other elements of the shopping chain, such as interaction between shop personnel and a customer. This was confirmed by the UK DPO, who entwined product and service delivery-related 'needs':

> If you get to the shops, are they accessible? If you talk to the people who work in those shops, do they understand your needs? Can they give you good advice? Are they responsive to you with your impairment, the severity of your impairment and the adaptation to it that you are able to make?

Contrary to industry players, the UK DPO addressed 'needs' not as an inextricable feature of an individual but as a litmus to indicate whether the retail sector is able and ready to provide reasonable accommodation and serve disabled people as equal customers.

The discussion has demonstrated how international and national business and civil society actors perceive disabled people as customers and the accessibility of the EU single market. Even though their positions share some differences, the stakeholders identify disabled people as one group of customers, who are not identical but differ. The division is premised on individuals' impairments that leads to uneven development of accessible products and may create hierarchical relationships among people with impairments as customers and users of ICT products. It was also detected that disabled customers and market accessibility are often linked with 'accessibility needs' and are perceived by the stakeholders differently. Their ontological positions are shaped by professional activities and the policy framework within which they operate. Manufacturers, for instance, perceive 'accessibility needs' as guidance that enables them to better meet technical standard requirements, and retailers adopt the same logic for customer service. Such practice divides non-disabled and disabled customers and positions them as wanting and needing users, respectively. The following section, therefore, sheds light on how policy instruments that shape business players' practices influence the discussed perspectives and positions.

The role of policy discourse

As suggested in earlier chapters, policy discourse shapes business and civil society's lifeworld regarding the EU single market and in such a way indirectly influences disabled customers' participation. With this in mind, this section investigates how global, regional and national policy instruments mould international and national stakeholders' lifeworld. It draws on empirical data from the interviews with business and civil society actors and sheds light on the way legal instruments shape their positions, knowledge, values and norms. With regard to the impact of global instruments, alongside the UN CRPD certain US legislations and standards are addressed, as these are key instruments for operating in global markets. The discussion then focuses on regional instruments. The section concludes by focusing on the role of national policies in either increasing or decreasing the potential for the private market to become more accessible.

Global regulations

With regard to global instruments, all informants except national retailers addressed either the CRPD or some of the US legislations. While none of the business players mentioned the Convention, the IDPO identified it as an instrument that frames their activities as well as enabled the organisation to gradually expand the focus on accessibility in regional instruments:

> Things developed over time. So, for instance, at the beginning accessibility was addressed through the area of non-discrimination so the first step there was really to have the possibility to address issues relating to persons with disability so there was inclusion of non-discrimination in the treaties and then legislation and initially IDPO wanted to have legislation on all areas, but we had only on employment and training. Then there was work which was done on transport, which led to having specific, because there were a lot of cases of discrimination for people travelling in air transport, so we managed to have legislation there and then this ended up including persons with disability in all passenger's rights issues in different modes. Then, with the UN Convention also, this became broader, so little by little in ICT and other areas, it was possible to include issues relating to persons with disability and the access. One thing was also to promote legislation on accessibility of goods and services, which was then taken up with the Commission who included it in their work programme and they are now trying to have this legislation proposed.

Alongside providing the framework for professional activities, the Convention enabled the organisation to expand its initial focus on accessibility and shift the understanding from non-discrimination to non-discrimination and rights. Being a globally recognised human rights instrument, the Convention provided the IDPO with a legal argument to influence regional policies and the Commission's agenda and to use the Treaty as a tool to shape national DPOs' understanding of accessibility:

> I think it's a big challenge still that we have because the organisations of persons with disabilities [national] they are more and more evolved with time and also a bit was non-discrimination legislation, now a lot with the convention in looking at the issue from an angle of rights. So, to be able to participate, to whole of society including the access to goods and services. This has taken some times also in the disability movement.

Interestingly, while the previous discussion suggested that the UK DPO links participation in the market with rights and equality, the informant representing the organisation did not refer to the Convention at any point of the interview. Contrary to this, while Lithuanian DPO representatives located accessibility and customer equality in the context of non-discrimination, they several times noted that the Convention has enabled the organisation 'to push things forward at the political level'. Hence, national DPOs do not use the Convention as heavily as the IDPO does. Even though both organisations have internalised some values and positions entrenched in the CRPD, at an empirical level, their perspectives are fragmented and lack ontological consistency and compatibility across the disability community.

Contrary to civil society, for business players and especially manufacturers, the CRPD is not as important as some of the US accessibility regulations are. As an example, the informant from the Company X noted that the US accessibility requirements were the key driver that shaped the manufacturer's interest in producing accessible ICT products:

> It has originally been driven by the legislation. In part of a review, there was this hearing aid compatibility requirement already. And after that, there has been legislation. And now, again, the US is at the moment leading in legislation with this act in communication media, an accessibility act coming into force next October.
>
> (Company X)

The US instruments on accessibility shaped not only manufacturers' but also the IBR's interest. The informant noted that the requirements provided directions for activities of one of the groups of the organisation:

> Then you have [legislations on accessibility] in the US, for a long time – standards are being developed and guidelines and things like this. I think that's why it [accessibility] is in the group because we looked at it more from a standardisation point of view.
>
> (IBR)

It seems that even though Company X and the IBR are based in Europe and operate under the EU law, they equally value and in some cases prioritise US requirements. On the one hand, it can be argued that the United States, offering access to one of the largest markets in the world and a high number of customers, dictates rules which, if infringed, may have a negative impact on accessing the market, selling products and gaining profit. On the other hand, globally recognised and implemented technical requirements may introduce similar vocabularies, positions and practices that are not bounded to a particular geographical location but are recognised by all actors who are engaged in the global ICT market.

US regulations provide manufacturers not only with technical requirements that have a potential to introduce common language but also with some decision-making procedures that may encourage similar practices within different companies. To illustrate, the Company X informant referred to the requirement to take minutes and how this may ensure that disabled customers–related and accessibility-related issues are not ignored in internal company meetings:

> We write the minutes of those [company meetings] so that there's a record of what we discussed. In this US legislation, actually, there is a requirement that we take the needs of disabled people into account and actually keep records. So [this is] a requirement as well. But we don't do that only because of the legislation; we want to know their priorities.

Official encouragement to adopt new models of working and documenting meetings may incentivise internal collaboration (Andreoni ct al., 2003) and create an environment for exchanging knowledge and experience. In such a context, professionals are likely to start questioning their ontologies on accessibility and potentially engage in the creation of a common language and knowledge across the departments.

Incompatibility between the US and EU requirements may prevent the creation and distribution of accessible products as well as the development of common language and norms regarding accessibility and disabled customers. The IBR informant explained,

> I think it all becomes a bit trickier when you have different national requirements or different European from the US. So if you stick to a global level, as a company that makes your life so much easier because you know what you're dealing with, you know exactly what the requirements are and you don't have to re-negotiate things or make changes in the way that you operate or how you decide to develop. The company that I'm involved in, have experience of accessibility in other regions and they'd rather have it harmonised at the global level if possible, i.e. at least have European legislation to some extent, wellbeing at least close to the requirements that we have elsewhere. Because otherwise every

region would require a new, a tailor-made product in relation to accessibility and again, I think we don't believe that impairments are really different in the US and Europe.

(IBR)

The Company X informant echoed the IBR and noted that incompatibility between global and regional legislations may compound business' activities. Referring to longer US experience in accessibility, the informant noted that future EU legislations, and especially the European Accessibility Act (EAA), should take into account current US practices and avoid introducing significantly different regulations:

> It will become interesting in Europe with European accessibility act whenever it comes. We are a global company, so it becomes a nightmare to us if there's a very different legislation in all market areas. So, here, US legislation is in place, so we do want that there's not too much difference to Europe on this type of – it would be good if something is not so variable in the US so that we can comply.

(Company X)

Contrary to international business, for the IDPO, the incompatibility between US and EU regulations is a potential 'tool' to shape lagging manufacturers' understanding of and activities when developing accessible products:

> I would say it's more and more interest because for some of them, accessibility is becoming also sales component of the products. There is also – some of – in the area of ICT also because of the legislation in the US, some companies develop certain things and then other companies found themselves a little bit maybe in a more difficult situation because they had not reacted so promptly to this. Now they are trying to catch up so there is interest on that and we have to take advantage of that in a positive way.

In order to achieve this goal, the organisation actively participates in stakeholder meetings, is a member of several working groups and has employed other strategies for becoming recognised and valued by business and policymakers. Hence, even though the IDPO's activities are premised on human rights instruments, the organisation is aware of market principles, relations and dynamic, and is ready to accept the rules of the game. In other words, being aware that accessibility is becoming a factor in providing access to larger markets, making higher sales and gaining customers' loyalty, the organisation avails the policy gap between global and regional instruments to shape some market players' knowledge, positions and actions.

EU instruments

Alongside global instruments, EU policies and legislations influence business and civil society's knowledge about, and positions and actions towards accessibility and disabled customers. While Company X informant referred only to the EAA, the IBR addressed European standardisation documents. The IDPO referred to the majority of instruments identified by manufacturers and the IBR. The instruments shaping the actors' activities are not identical but overlap and are valued by all actors. For instance, the Company X informant, representing other international stakeholders' accounts, noted that the EU requirements 'made it possible to proceed with these accessibility things'. Similarly, the IDPO identified EU instruments as an important mechanism in providing a framework for activities in the field. When asked about their significance on ICT accessibility, the informant said,

> I think they do impact a lot.
>
> (IDPO)

While the international stakeholders acknowledge the importance of the EU instruments, their application in practice differs and depends on professional activities. Nevertheless, the application is related with the provision of more accessibility and may provide a platform for common language, norms and values to emerge. For example, Company X treats EU legislations as guidance in the process of accessible product development:

> In our company, I also think in other companies, this EU regulation and legislation is a language that is very well understood inside product development. So, we just implement those, and that's a very good thing.

This suggests that manufacturers translate legislations into a language that identifies accessibility features and guides product development and production process. Requirements and standards for product development may be a risky proposition and intrude into some companies' activities (Fomin et al., 2003). Nevertheless, having limited experience and expertise in accessible product development, some manufacturers, and especially those who are more proactive in the field, are positive about the standards and position them as a starting point guiding the process.

For the IBR, EU instruments provide a framework for communication and interaction with the ICT industry, policymakers and other partners such as the IDPO. Working with the instruments that are applicable to other stakeholders' activities allows the organisation to be familiar with others' realities, faced constraints and obligations (see the following chapter), and identify actions needed for complying with policy requirements. In such a context, EU instruments provide the IBR with a framework for interaction with member organisations and may become a unifying element, which summons the partners for collaboration and cooperation:

> Every time we have a legal proposal being talked about, and suggested and drafted, this is where the association obviously, becomes active. Let's say the most usual thing where we certainly will have to look at it because then it becomes concrete and then it's about, again, specific requirements and then it's about often framework within which the companies have to operate and then maybe different from the current situation.
> (IBR)

Similarly, the IDPO employs EU instruments as a premise for initiating communication with national member organisations and as a tool to shape changes of national policies:

> Now we have, for example, this proposal for legislation on accessibility of websites, public bodies' websites. If it is adopted, and hopefully it is, the scope is a bit enlarged, can have a really important impact because now there are on one hand, still a few countries, who do not have any rules on accessibility, some that have, but they do not really apply them and you have also a difference of requirements. So this legislation could uniform requirements and make it much easier to have accessible websites for public authorities and hopefully also at least the providers of services which are used by the majority of people. We hope that there will also be some enforcement mechanisms so I think it can have an impact.
> (IDPO)

Similar to the manufacturers' case, EU instruments may unify MSs and civil society's provisions and practices regarding accessibility. Following the same legal guidance, the two actor groups are likely to share similar language, values and practices that are important for achieving consistent and interconnected accessibility practice.

The regulative power of voluntary and binding EU legislations has different impact on the stakeholders' engagement in accessibility debate and practice. With regard to voluntary EU agreements, the IBR noted that industry usually either partly complies with this type of legislation or ignores it:

> A voluntary agreement is something else in reaction to legislation. It can prevent legislation, can substitute legislation, but it only goes this far because it's based on voluntary engagement and not everyone may want to engage. Not all TV manufacturers engage.

ICT manufacturers' positions towards voluntary agreements differ. Some companies are more proactive and ready to engage with this type of legislation and if needed to sacrifice company's self-interests. Others are less open and shape the actions and agenda so that they do not have a negative impact on their business strategy and profit maximisation. Such fragmentation suggests that business' interests and values regarding accessibility are not strong enough to follow voluntary agreements. Drawing on the discussion in the earlier chapters and Habermasian thought, it can be argued that voluntary instruments do not create interaction patterns within which common language, norms and values among business would emerge and lead towards the lifeworld of accessible EU markets. This is mainly because accessibility is a new area in the retail market practice. Its conceptual and practical implementation does not have strong and long-lasting traditions and experience, and a paradigm shift from profit generation to ensuring equal participation to all customers in business mindset has not yet taken place.

Contrary to this, binding EU instruments seem to have greater potential to provide international stakeholders with a framework, structuring their activities and involvement in accessibility debate and practice. The IBR noted that hard law obliges manufacturers to comply with accessibility requirements and so introduces common language and shapes their lifeworld. Nevertheless, they do not stop companies from overstepping the boundary of law, if it may lead to more or better accessibility provision:

> Again, each company has to make its own decision, unless you have legislation and then there is no choice; you have to do it and they will do it [...]. While, if you have legislation, now we are looking at a suitability act, that's a different sort of animal because then it is binding for everyone and then obviously the attention is there [...]. So I think it's important to just say once, if you are still in the voluntary area, then the approach may be very, very fragmented, while once you move into legislation obviously there's a certain level of harmonisation by default, but it doesn't mean you can't do more than that. Not everyone does it, but it could be a policy.

The importance of binding regulations was acknowledged by Company X. Although the informant did not refer to specific binding EU instruments, previously discussed examples of integrating EU directives and US legislations into the company's activities suggest that binding rules have stronger potential to shape business' commitments and activities.

National policies

While global and regional instruments have a great impact on international business and civil society's positions, national policies do not have a major effect on their activities. However, while national instruments on accessibility do not have a significant impact on DPOs' activities, some policies that are not directly related to accessibility or customer participation hinder DPOs' initiatives to make retail market barrier free and accessible to more and different customers. To illustrate, earlier discussed limited DPOs' interest in issues related to disabled customers and market accessibility is not a strategic or conscious decision. Informants representing DPOs in both countries noted that their plans and actions depend on activity agenda priorities set by and funds received from the government. To illustrate, asked about the factors that shape the Lithuanian DPO's interests and activities, the informant said,

> Everything leans on money [received from the government].

The UK DPO representative referred to similar reasons behind the organisation's limited focus:

> So that's where the focus is because we only have so much limited resources.

The focus mentioned by the participant includes areas such as participation in the labour market and education, accessibility of public transport and websites, and independent living. It does not, however, include customer rights and participation and accessibility of the retail market. Respectively, areas that are on or comply with the government's agenda receive financial support, and these that are not on the list are left aside. This means that DPOs are not able to sufficiently address these issues, raise public awareness and implement the change. In such a context, funds provided by the State becomes a medium, which shapes small and less powerful actors' such as national DPOs' priorities and activities and in such a way colonise their lifeworld. Having to comply with governments' eligibility criteria for financial support, DPOs are not free and independent creators of their visions, missions and the way promoted values and priorities should be translated into practice. By providing strict and pre-established criteria to access funds, the State introduces a framework within which civil society has to operate. Through such restriction, it limits the opportunity and process of creating and sharing common language and knowledge and engaging in wider initiatives. Being locked within the knowledge, positions and values of the system of the State, DPOs are prevented from creating their own lifeworld, and from introducing and sharing values and knowledge that could expand other society members' norms, knowledge and positions towards disabled people's participation as equal customers.

Alongside current practice of funds distribution to DPOs, austerity measures that affect people with impairments shape national DPOs' activities and may erode their focus on customer participation:

> The priority for most disabled people organisations, or organisations of disabled people is to resist those cuts to benefits because that's where the majority of disabled people are and that's the issue that's affecting

them most, and if you haven't got very much money to spend, you're not going to be going to the shops anyway. So the focus is not on disabled people – the focus of our UK society is not on disabled people as consumer, but is on disabled people as participants, and resisting so-called welfare reform changes that affect the level of benefits and their entitlement to benefits.

(UK DPO)

The narratives suggest that national governments' finance-related decisions shape disabled citizens and DPOs' experiences and positions. Having to resist the cuts, individuals and organisations prioritise and focus on the activities that are directly related to their 'survival' and participation in society. In such a context, shopping, customer participation and market accessibility become a secondary issue and are eliminated from a public discourse and public's knowledge and awareness.

Contrary to the DPOs, national policies seem to have no direct impact on international actors' lifeworld and activities. To begin with, the Company X informant could not remember legislation of any MS that would influence their activities. Similarly, the IBR did not address national legislations as a force for positive change or innovation. On the contrary, the informant noted that under certain circumstances national instruments on ICT may cause incompatibility issues and close markets for some products. To illustrate, it is worth referring back to the IBR's account on the incompatibility of the US and EU instruments:

I think it all becomes a bit trickier when you have different national requirements or different European from the US. So if you stick to a global level, as a company that makes your life so much easier because you know what you're dealing with, you know exactly what the requirements are and you don't have to re-negotiate things or make changes in the way that you operate or how you decide to develop. The company that I'm involved in, have experience of accessibility in other regions and they'd rather have it harmonised at the global level if possible, i.e. at least have European legislation to some extent, wellbeing at least close to the requirements that we have elsewhere. Because otherwise every region would require a new, a tailor-made product in relation to accessibility and again, I think we don't believe that impairments are really different in the US and Europe.

(IBR)

It seems that for global and regional businesses, national legislations neither serve as a tool, ensuring accessible ICT provision to national markets, nor contribute to the creation and amplification of their accessibility-related knowledge, actions and lifeworld. On the contrary, if incompatible with international and global standards, national instruments may serve as a barrier in preventing higher supply of accessible products. This highlights the importance of harmonisation of global, international and national instruments and their potential power in unifying the language used in different political and empirical levels.

Similarly, the IDPO did not identify national instruments as an influential source for creating accessibility-related knowledge and practice. On the contrary, the participant positioned national legislation as an object for change by applying international policies:

> As this legislation [EU level] is actually somehow our source of the national legislation, if you don't manage to influence the new level, you do not have an impact at national level. It's much more difficult.
>
> (IDPO)

International actors perceive minimal national product accessibility requirements as an opportunity to either avoid restrictions at national level (business case) or introduce international standards into national initiatives and so avoid potential incompatibility (international civil society case). The approach of national DPOs is opposite. As an example, the UK DPO identified limited national provisions and requirements as one of the factors behind insufficient accessibility of the shopping chain and accessible product availability:

> There is some consumer protection rights under the Equality Act, particularly as I say around reasonable adjustments, but what's missing is a requirement on manufacturers to produce accessible goods. I understand there's going to be a procurement directive from the EU and that there's going to be consultation around a procurement directive. And if I'm correct, then that will mean that manufacturers have to start building-in accessibility in their products. At the moment, they have no obligation to do that, or very little requirements for them to do that. So people, as consumers, have got some protection in visiting shops and the treatment they can expect in those shops, but there's a big problem with what is the goods that are sold in those shops. Are they accessible? And can they get the accessible products in those shops? Most of the time, the answer is no.

Although the informant is aware that regional instruments play a key role in shaping product accessibility requirements, the necessity to address it in national policies is also important. To illustrate, the participant referred to how the Disability Discrimination Act encouraged service providers to consider accessibility provisions for disabled customers:

> In the UK, there are rights that people have got under the Disability Discrimination Act, which then became part of the two thousand and ten Single Equality Act. So there are requirements, for example, for

retailers to provide reasonable adjustments and there are some good examples of reasonable adjustments that have been made. Some of the – I think Weatherspoon's, for example, pubs have made it easier for people in wheelchairs to visit their pubs. [...] Some of the providers in the hospitality and leisure industry, like the Intercontinental Hotel Group have trained their staff in the needs of disabled customers.

(UK DPO)

This suggests that national policy guidelines and requirements and the initiative and willingness of private businesses to provide more accessibility should not be disconnected. Indeed, synchronised legal rhetoric and business practice oriented towards the same outcome may introduce practices in setting grounds for disabled and non-disabled customers' equal participation as users and customers of goods and services that are open or provided to the public.

This discussion suggested that policy discourse shapes accessibility of the EU single market and disabled customers' participation. It was evident that due to the stakeholders' operation in different policy frameworks, their knowledge about, ascribed values to, and positions and lifeworld regarding accessibility and disabled customers differ. Manufacturers' lifeworld is shaped mainly by global and regional accessibility standards that, if met, provide access to larger markets and higher number of customers. This leads to positioning impairments as guidance of how to comply with technical requirements and is a key reason behind perceiving product accessibility as a 'need' rather than a means for more equal participation. IDPOs' lifeworld is shaped mainly by the CRPD. This leads to linking markets accessibility and customer participation with equality and non-discrimination. All international and national business and civil society actors recognise value and use regional instruments that shape the way the stakeholders perceive and understand accessibility as well as implement actions in their areas of expertise. However, national instruments neither shape the stakeholders' lifeworld nor ensure free access to goods and services for the citizens. Contrarily, limited recognition of accessibility and customer rights by MSs leads to implementation of policies that erode the issues from the public discourse and DPOs' activities. Incompatibility between global, regional and national policies may corrupt accessibility. Nevertheless, EU instruments seem to have internal power and potential that enables the stakeholders to share and create common language, knowledge and positions that are essential for creating a common lifeworld and practice of an accessible EU single market.

The role of business practice

This section continues the discussion on the factors that shape stakeholders' lifeworld. The focus is on how business' practices influence industry actors' notions of and ascribed values to disabled customers and accessibility. The discussion starts by looking at the relationship between expenditures for and received profit from producing accessible products. This is followed by brief discussion on manufacturers' corporate social responsibility (CSR) and information about product accessibility available to shop assistants. Finally, the way training provided to shop assistants shape their positions towards disabled shoppers and knowledge about accessible products is addressed.

Accessibility, expenditures and profit

Expenditures for product production and received profit are important factors in shaping ICT industry's lifeworld towards accessibility. With regard to expenditures, as all decisions, the incorporation of accessibility features is well thought-through and calculated. Despite the general tendency to estimate potential costs, positions and practices among the manufacturers differ. To illustrate, the IBR noted that companies' views are fragmented and depend on different factors:

> But it's like every person, you have different preferences, you make your choices accordingly and it will add cost, you will have to dedicate resources, you will have to follow the tune of course, that's if your policy is a medium, long-term process.

Alongside company-related factors, some legal instruments impact funds allocation to accessible features of ICT. To illustrate, Company X provided an example of how US accessibility requirements impact manufacturers' spending:

> The hearing aid requirement in the US means that when you sell a mobile phone, in one third of the products you need to have one component here on the back that connects to the hearing aid device. It costs about $1, this component.

While product quantity-oriented requirements increase product availability, regulation of accessibility provisions via financial measures may become a medium that positions accessibility as a forcible element, instead of as 'one of' the provisions in ensuring barrier-free technology use.

Alongside expenditures, calculation of potential profit received from selling accessible products is important in deciding what accessibility features and for which user group should be installed into forthcoming products. Although the Company X informant did not explicitly refer to profit as the premise for accessibility decisions, references to the 'biggest' user groups, requiring similar instalments, confirm the hypothesis. To illustrate, the informant noted,

> So I guess we have been looking at somehow, the biggest user groups in that sense. If there is a big group of people with very similar needs, than

it's clear that it becomes kind of a company like us who can serve those customers. If it's a very specific need and totally a need that requires something very, let's say, costly or special, then I think it's more of a company with assistive technologies that should provide that.

(Company X)

While *'specific needs'* are associated with a smaller customer group, higher production costs, lower profit and are ascribed to 'disability' markets, the impression that profit is one of the drivers behind decisions of whose 'needs' will be met was confirmed in the discussion on technologies for older consumers:

It's for the elderly people that we have been providing these types of classical devices for a longer time and not moving only to this type of work with touch smartphones. So I think we have a good share of elderly people that rely on us.

(Company X)

The increasing number of older EU citizens (European Commission, 2011) boosts this customer group and shapes product development decisions of the company. Although touchscreen features have become an inextricable part of ICT products, the account suggests that some manufacturers are willing to continue developing products with less fashionable or popular functions in order to meet 'accessibility needs' of certain customer groups and gain higher profit. In other words, the estimate of potentially higher turnover reshapes business' understanding of traditionally most popular 'average' users and position towards product accessibility. This was further elaborated by the IBR:

If you look at it from a company point of view, it is about your turnover and loss and profit. If you sell a Smart phone it is also about the margins, i.e. how much have you earned, what's selling it? Is it that it's a basic phone or is it a top-end product that costs 700€? I think it's all about this. A company doesn't continue to produce properly an accessible phone if it doesn't generate enough turnover.

Potentially higher profit has a positive impact on business players' position towards accessibility and customers who do not meet the criteria applied to 'average' market participants. However, the ratio between expenditures and profit as reasoning for provision of more accessibility is likely to become a steering media that coordinates manufacturers' positions, actions and lifeworld on accessible markets.

Provision of accessible products lead to superiority in competitive business environment and so becomes a factor in shaping industry's positions and actions. The Company X informant traced some changes over time and how they structured their position towards accessibility:

> Although I feel that it hasn't probably been big a competitive advantage so far, especially with the smart devices, it has become very, let's say, competitive than what the situation was ten years ago. Now it's a very simple competitive field. So there's pretty much four different alternatives for people to choose. And when somebody has something in accessibility, it becomes clear that everybody knows that that's the best category. So it has become this type of real kind of business competition. Also, when you know somebody has something, others need to follow. And the consumer groups are not that small and are a more ageing population in the western world. So, although it has been more social corporate responsibility, I feel it's becoming more real business competitiveness. That's maybe one message that I have had that there is a strong business element here.

A limited number of providers of accessible products, increasing customer group and changes in the public discourse redefine industry's position. Initially being an object for complying with policies and standards, accessibility has gradually become a feature, shaping manufacturers' initiatives and actions in the market. This suggests that a competitive nature of a small and emerging market contributes to value creation of a disabled customer and product accessibility.

The IBR echoed the shift from positioning accessibility as a legal compliance issue to a demanded feature and marketing element that attracts customers:

> Then you build in accessibility features because you believe that's why people will maybe buy this product.

In addition, some industry players perceive accessibility as an element to gain and ensure customers' loyalty. According to the Company X, product accessibility features are communicated to the public alongside general product characteristics and often are associated with CSR:

> We want to also make this a kind of visible element in our brand promise that Company X is designing products for all. [...] But other than that, I think it comes indirectly through our brand that our brand is seen as the very best responsible company taking people into account and giving a trusted brand as well.

This suggests that more proactive ICT manufacturers redraw their lifeworld on an accessible market. They overstep the association of accessibility with legal compliance and position it as an important product feature and philosophy inbuilt in company's vision, mission and values.

Corporate social responsibility

Manufacturers' commitment to CSR is another factor that shapes markets accessibility and customer experience discussed in the earlier chapters. The IBR noted that although it may serve as a positive framework for encouraging more accessible practices, business' interest in and commitments to it are fragmented:

> So the company is very market-focused I would say and companies can take decisions on something like corporate social responsibility and you would ask yourself again, 'Why do some companies put such an emphasis on it and develop a programme and a policy and have audits and all these things, and others don't?' In some way it's a company choice unless it's legally binding to have a policy on it, or some aspects of it.

Company X also addressed the role played by CSR in accessible product development. The informant noted that while technical requirements were the major force for the activities, CSR enabled the company to advance and produce products that are more accessible than it is legally required:

> So these are the things [legal] that made it possible to proceed with these things [accessibility], but then as part of this corporate responsibility, we want to do more than just the legal. But we don't do that only because of the legislation; we want to know their [users'] priorities.

The relation between CSR and non-disabled customers' satisfaction has been highlighted elsewhere, for example, in research done on banking (McDonald and Rundle-Thiele, 2008), tourism (Henderson, 2007) and shopping (Mohr et al., 2001). Giving its impact on benefits, such as customer loyalty, profit increase and positive public attitudes towards the company (Brown and Dacin, 1997, Sen and Bhattacharya, 2001), CSR is often considered in various business' activities. However, the Company X informant noted that CSR regarding product accessibility is a relatively new concept in both public discourse and manufacturers' practice:

> In other areas of this corporate responsibility, we have a much longer history in discussing it with the commission in legislation and so on. So this is a rather new area and, in this area, we have mainly been involved in the US legislation that has been somehow showing the way.

On the one hand, the application of CSR on product accessibility may be seen as a strategic action that provides an advantage over the competitors and has a positive impact on customers' loyalty. On the other hand, the account suggests that while legislations act as an initial foundation for accessible product development, manufacturers, who have strong CSR, are more likely to recognise and acknowledge differences in customer segment.

Consequently, this leads to a more constructive assessment of needed changes in product design, redefinition of accessibility concept and implementation of certain accessibility practices.

Product accessibility information

Manufacturers' communication with national retailers and information provision practices contribute to shaping salespeople's lifeworld towards disabled customers and accessibility. To begin with, some differences were observed in how shop assistants working in NBSH and BSH acquire information about product accessibility. Specifically, the interview with the NBSH manager (Lithuania) and observations of NBSH assistants (United Kingdom, Lithuania) indicated that this group of professionals receive the information about products in stock mainly from product catalogues, Internet and training. As discussed in the earlier chapters, asked about accessible product features, NBSH assistants searched for information on instructions leaflets or Google, and others checked e-data bases of the retail network or other online sources. With regard to practices in BSH, research data suggested that here shop assistants are provided with information directly by the manufacturer. As the BSH manager (Lithuania) noted, the information includes product accessibility, is provided in different formats and is the main source used by salespeople:

> There is manufacturer's information that is used. There is Internet training base that has all the descriptions, you can find really big presentations with video material; many things, including accessibility, are addressed there.

The NBSH manager (Lithuania) noted that salespeople use the Internet in 'emergency' cases that also include serving customers with impairments:

> If something very urgent comes up, then the Internet is the main source. They [shop assistants] look for information there.

As discussed in the previous chapters, sources available online usually provide information about generic product features and rarely include details on accessibility. Hence, since NBSH personnel use mainly online sources to find out about products, their knowledge set is likely to be around non-disabled customers and they may lack the same understanding regarding shoppers with impairments. This creates a certain understanding of a customer and their product interests and usage. In other words, product information oriented to non-disabled customers may prevent the 'existence' of disabled people as customers in knowledge domain of shop assistants who mainly use non-disabled customers–oriented information. This may position disabled customers as 'different' shoppers and service delivery as a 'special' event.

Practices at the BSH were different. The BSH manager (Lithuania) hinted to shop assistants' personal initiatives to acquire additional information:

> We read additional information. Then we deepen the knowledge individually, because it is an interesting job and the process itself is interesting.

Having access to comprehensive information that does not position product accessibility as a special dimension, BSH assistants are more likely to perceive accessibility as *one of* the features, get interested into its novelty and be better informed.

In addition to acquisition of factual information about a product, BSH assistants (Lithuania) seek for practical skills:

> When we get a product, we test it, because then we will have what to tell to our customers – and they will definitely ask, so we are keen to know. We try all these functions, like sound, text zoom, voice-over, is it possible to convert colours. We try everything, so we could answer all the questions.

While none of the NBSH representatives identified similar practices, the BSH manager (Lithuania) added that ICT users' expertise and knowledge is important and valued:

> I would say that in terms of accessibility, the main source of practical information is disabled people. We introduce ourselves with technical features pretty well, but together with people we understand how they actually work, how they work in different cases and how they can be used or not used by different people. I would say that we acquire theoretical information from the literature and practical – from people.

The quotation recalls earlier discussion on information for service performance and actual information and highlights the importance of disabled customers' participation in bridging the gap between the two knowledge dimensions.

Trainings

Professional training received by salespeople contributes to shaping their knowledge about and perspectives on disabled customers and product accessibility. Interviews with Lithuanian BSH and NBSH managers and informal chats with shop assistants in the United Kingdom suggested that shop assistants are regularly provided with opportunities to improve their knowledge. However, similar to dominant product information provision practices, the focus is on general product features that are usually associated with non-disabled users. The NBSH manager (Lithuania) said,

> It is very important that once per year, in spring, the suppliers come and organise trainings for my employees. They present new products, demonstrate their features. This is very good, because then my people see 'from close' how the products work. Such information becomes more familiar to them and in such a way they are able to introduce, describe and suggest a product that meets customers' wants and needs at the highest possible level. Such trainings last few days, so that all employees could attend and become familiar with new products.

This was echoed by the BSH manager (Lithuania), who referred to generic customer service techniques:

> General trainings, specifically, selling techniques. So the main attention is paid to the general principles of customer service: what, how, why and so on.

Business is aware that shop assistants' knowledge and service delivery are important for gaining customer loyalty, improving service quality and receiving higher profit. However, service and product accessibility for disabled customers is rarely considered by some market players and is often either absent or limited in their everyday practice and training provided to members of staff. A position shared by the NBSH manager (Lithuania) explains the reasons behind such practice:

> Accessibility and disability? I can't remember that we have ever discussed such topics. You see, business care about slightly different things.

Informal chats with shop assistants in NBSH in the United Kingdom also suggested that accessibility is not a priority and thus is not addressed in staff trainings. However, it was evident that practice in BSH differs. Describing the training content, the Lithuanian BSH manager said,

> One of these things [covered in staff training] is communication and interaction with people with impairments.

Differences in NBSH and BSH staff training are likely to be shaped by different conceptions of and practice in the two shop types. Specifically, the Lithuanian BSH manager noted that being a part of an international network of one manufacturer that is committed to accessibility, the shop is obliged to address accessibility in the organised trainings. Meanwhile, the NBSH sells items produced by different manufacturers that are not necessarily committed to accessibility. Consequently, product accessibility is dominated by product features oriented towards non-disabled customers.

Despite the commitment to accessibility, training techniques used by the Lithuanian BSH should be called into question. Specifically, the BSH manager (Lithuania) described the training process:

> We discuss the situations that we have already had [serving disabled customers], discuss how we solved them and how we can improve the situation in the future. We have prepared situations, introduce ourselves to them, analyse, and share the experience. We are four shops in the country, so we use our common experience to decide how to do things. It is our own initiative. When it comes to training on disabled people, again, there is nothing very strict or written, because everything depends on the type of impairments. Overall, this is only additional dimension of service delivery.

The account suggests that disabled shoppers' experiences are perceived, sensed and interpreted through the lens of non-disabled shop assistants' positions and experiences. Such representation and imitation is very likely to not reflect disabled customers' realities and prevent the identification of barriers and potentials in service delivery process. Salespeople, by deciding what and how is experienced by shoppers with impairments, introduce a space for unequal power relations between the two actor groups to emerge. The ascribed power to decide how some of the shopping chain elements are experienced by disabled customers strengthens their exclusion, segregation and portrayal as vulnerable, as well as eliminates them from common knowledge creation about markets accessibility.

The discussion suggested that business practices contribute to shaping the lifeworld of accessible markets. The ratio between expenditures for accessible product production and received profit is an important factor in shaping manufacturers' positions towards accessibility and user groups on which they decide to focus. It was evident that while legal instruments are an initial impetus for developing accessible items, engagement with CSR with regard to accessibility shapes the way producers move beyond legislation in providing accessibility and valuing disabled people as a customer segment. In other words, competition in the capitalist market and the need to comply with norms that have public acknowledgement and are perceived as a 'good' business practice contribute to reshaping manufacturers' lifeworld and redefining what product accessibility means.

It was also suggested that product information provided by manufacturers to sellers shapes the latter's work environment and professional practice sources that lead either to disabled customers' exclusion and labelling as 'different' clients or to positioning them as equal shoppers. Likewise, non-disabled customer–oriented training provision for shop assistants is likely to erase people with impairments from salespeople's knowledge set about this customer group. It was evident that disabled people are usually not involved in professionals' training development and delivery and this is likely to lead to unequal power relations between the two actor groups. Overall, it was suggested that even though disabled people are present actors in the market, business practices shape different and contradicting perspectives to and knowledge about this customer group. This, respectively, shapes service provision and the lifeworld of accessible markets.

Concluding comments

The present chapter was the first out of the two chapters examining some structures that shape disabled customers' exclusion, marginalisation and vulnerability, discussed in the beginning of this book. It adapted a Habermasian concept of lifeworld and explored manufacturers, IBR, civil society and national retailers of ICT products' views, understandings and positions towards disabled people as customers and accessibility of the EU single market. It suggested that the stakeholders' lifeworld does shape disabled people's shopping experience. It addressed policy discourse and business practice as two potential factors shaping the positions and practices. Previous literature has shown relatively little investigation in the way EU single market actors perceive people with impairments as market participants. The chapter, therefore, aimed to narrow down this knowledge lacuna. Evidently, specific issues emerged.

To begin with, it was suggested that all stakeholders perceive disabled people as one group of ICT users and customers, who share differences within the group because of their impairments. The categorisation seems to be partly shaped by policy instruments and market practices. For instance, ICT manufacturers find the classification useful as it helps to respond to standard requirements and to achieve legal compliance. The IDPO focuses on separate impairment groups as this enables the organisation to better communicate different barriers to the stakeholders and ensure they are addressed in policy instruments. National retailers also tend to classify disabled shoppers. Here, the categorisation is premised on the frequency of serving shoppers with certain impairments. It was evident that all stakeholders tend to focus on or are more familiar and comfortable with some types of impairment, leaving others aside. Such practice mirrors policy rhetoric discussed in the second chapter and may create hierarchical relationships among disabled people as ICT customers.

This chapter has also shown that product accessibility and customer service are often linked with 'accessibility needs' that are usually associated with an individual's impairment. On the one hand, this may enable identifying product or service delivery features that prevent barrier-free experience and lead to more accessible and pleasant experience. On the other hand, such practice may divide disabled and non-disabled customers. For instance, people with impairments are often perceived as 'needing' technologies, and this often leads to poorer product aesthetics, prevents customers from choosing a product of the highest quality and value and ascribes the responsibility of finding the 'needed' item to a disabled shopper. Meanwhile non-disabled people are seen as 'wanting' customers, who are free and independent agents in making shopping choices. The focus on disabled people's needs and the linkage of product features with impairment transforms accessibility solutions from means to overcome disabling product design into means to 'fix' an individual's impairment. It was also evident that national retailers, who sell products produced by different manufacturers, are more likely to emphasise the 'need' than the retailers selling products of one provider who is committed to accessibility. It was also suggested that manufacturers' CSR and provided information to national retailers plays a role in shaping shop assistants' perspectives and responses to disabled customers and service delivery patterns.

This chapter positioned policy discourse and business practices as two potential factors that shape the discussed positions and practices and locating them in the context of the social or individual model of disability. As an example, civil society that develop their activities around human rights instruments seem to have internalised the social model perspective more than the informants, whose professional activities are framed by technical requirements. The IDPO mainly referred to the CRPD, and values established in the Treaty were best articulated by this organisation. While conceptual perspectives of the Convention were detected in national DPOs' lifeworld and activities but were not articulated in the interviews, they were absent in business' perspectives. Indeed, US and EU legal instruments seem to play a key role in shaping their lifeworld and activities. The fact that EU business follows US legislations even though they are not legally obliged to do this suggests that legal instruments, that may provide access to larger customer groups, can be employed as a tool to shape business' lifeworld and practices towards the issue.

With regard to EU policies, international stakeholders identified them as having a positive impact on their activities but addressed the difference between voluntary and binding instruments. While soft legislations are usually considered by stakeholders who are more committed to accessibility and include it into the CSR commitments, they are often ignored by actors prioritising profit-oriented goals. Nevertheless, EU instruments have a potential to provide the actors with a common language and a framework within which common values, positions, norms and lifeworld may be shaped. However, to fully achieve this, compatibility between US and EU instruments, as well as all stakeholders and disabled customers' involvement in the policy development process, is essential.

National instruments seem to be at the other end of the spectrum. While they do not impact international stakeholders' agendas and activities, national DPOs provided some evidence suggesting that national governments' focus on 'disability' issues, social service provision and the current fund allocation system often erase markets accessibility and customer rights from their lifeworld and professional activities. Similarly, the IDPO acknowledged insufficient focus on markets accessibility in national policies and positioned them as an object for change by international and global instruments. It was evident that harmonisation and compatibility across global, regional and national policies concerns international informants as this may either introduce a framework for employing similar language and creating common knowledge and practice or diminish business' activities in some parts of the EU single market.

In addition to policy instruments, certain business practices play a part in shaping industry's understanding of disabled customers, accessibility and related lifeworld. With regard to manufacturers, the ratio between expenditures for and received profit from the production of accessible items is an important factor in making business decisions about which features and for which user groups will be considered. Likewise, superiority in competitiveness and higher customer loyalty may increase producers' interest in accessibility and respectively shape design decisions. Furthermore, the inclusion of accessibility into CSR commitments and cooperation with end-users are important factors that lead towards the overstepping of legal standards and providing greater accessibility than is legally required.

With regard to national sellers, it was evident that actors such as BSH, who receive clear information about product accessibility that is not distinguished as special but is provided alongside general product features, position individuals' customer role before their impairments and treat them as equal shoppers, who may need personalised service delivery. Meanwhile, NBSH assistants, who usually are not provided with information about and training on disability and accessibility, are less aware of disabled customers and accessibility and often have stronger disablist attitudes.

Bibliography

Andreoni, J., Harbaugh, W. & Vesterlund, L. 2003. The carrot or the stick: Rewards, punishments, and cooperation. *The American Economic Review*, 93, 893–902.

Barnes, C. 1991. A brief history of discrimination and disabled people. *In:* Barnes, C. (ed.) *Disabled people in Britain and discrimination: A case for anti-discrimination legislation*. London, Hurst in association with the British Council of Organizations of Disabled People.

Brown, T. J. & Dacin, P. A. 1997. The company and the product: Corporate associations and consumer product responses. *The Journal of Marketing*, 61(1), 68–84.

Chininthorn, P., Glaser, M., Freudenthal, A. & Tucker, W. D. 2012. Mobile communication tools for a South African Deaf patient in a pharmacy context. *In:* Cunningham, P. & Cunningham, M. (eds.) *Information Society Technologies – Africa*, Tanzania, IIMC International Information Management Corporation.

European Commission. 2011. *The 2012 ageing report. Underlying assumptions and projection methodologies*. Brussels, DGECFIN, AWG, Economic Policy Committee.

Fomin, V., Keil, T. & Lyytinen, K. 2003. Theorizing about standardization: Integrating fragments of process theory in light of telecommunication standardization wars. *Sprouts: Working Papers on Information Environments, Systems and Organizations*, 3, 29–60.

Gabriel, Y. & Lang, T. 1995. *The unmanagable consumer. Contemporary consumption and its fragmentation*, London, Sage Publications.

Guilding, C. & Mcmanus, L. 2002. The incidence, perceived merit and antecedents of customer accounting: An exploratory note. *Accounting, Organizations and Society*, 27, 45–59.

Habermas, J. 1984. *The theory of communicative action: Volume 1. Reason and the rationalisation of society*, Boston, Beacon Press.

Habermas, J. 1985. *The theory of communicative action: Volume 2. Lifeworld and system: A critique of functionalist reason*, Cambridge, Polity Press.

Henderson, J. C. 2007. Corporate social responsibility and tourism: Hotel companies in Phuket, Thailand, after the Indian Ocean tsunami. *International Journal of Hospitality Management*, 26, 228–239.

Janicki, M. P. 1970. Attitudes of health professionals toward twelve disabilities. *Perceptual and Motor Skills*, 30, 77–78.

López-de-Ipiña, D., Lorido, T. & López, U. 2011. Blindshopping: Enabling accessible shopping for visually impaired people through mobile technologies. *In:* Abdulrazak, B., Giroux, S., Bouchard, B., Pigot, H. & Mokhtari, M. (eds.) *Toward useful services for elderly and people with disabilities*, Berlin, Springer.

Mcdonald, L. M. & Rundle-Thiele, S. 2008. Corporate social responsibility and bank customer satisfaction: A research agenda. *International Journal of Bank Marketing*, 26, 170–182.

Mittal, V. & Kamakura, W. A. 2001. Satisfaction, repurchase intent, and repurchase behavior: Investigating the moderating effect of customer characteristics. *Journal of Marketing Research*, 38, 131–142.

Mohr, L. A., Webb, D. J. & Harris, K. E. 2001. Do consumers expect companies to be socially responsible? The impact of corporate social responsibility on buying behavior. *Journal of Consumer Affairs*, 35, 45–72.

Newell, A. 2003. Inclusive design or assistive technology. *In:* Clarkson, J., Keates, S., Coleman, R. & Lebbon, C. (eds.) *Inclusive design*, London, Springer.

Poplin, M. S. 1995. The dialectic nature of technology and holism: Use of technology to liberate individuals with learning disabilities. *Learning Disability Quarterly*, 18, 131–140.

Raskind, M. 1993. Assistive technology and adults with learning disabilities: A blueprint for exploration and advancement. *Learning Disability Quarterly*, 185–196.

Sen, S. & Bhattacharya, C. B. 2001. Does doing good always lead to doing better? Consumer reactions to corporate social responsibility. *Journal of Marketing Research*, 38, 225–243.

Stevenage, S. V. & Mckay, Y. 1999. Model applicants: The effect of facial appearance on recruitment decisions. *British Journal of Psychology*, 90, 221–234.

Thomas, A. 2000. Stability of Tringo's hierarchy of preference toward disability groups: 30 years later. *Psychological Reports*, 86, 1155–1156.

Tringo, J. L. 1970. The hierarchy of preference toward disability groups. *The Journal of Special Education*, 4, 295–306.

Wang, Q., Makaroff, D. J. & Edwards, H. K. 2004. Characterizing customer groups for an e-commerce website. *The 5th ACM Conference on Electronic Commerce*, New York, ACM.

Williams, P., Jamali, H. R. & Nicholas, D. 2006. Using ICT with people with special education needs: What the literature tells us. *Aslib Proceedings*, 58, 330–345.

Woodhams, C. & Danieli, A. 2000. Disability and diversity – a difference too far? *Personnel Review*, 29, 402–417.

6 Access to the discourse and power relations

Having established differences and similarities in stakeholders' lifeworld regarding markets accessibility and disabled customers, the current chapter argues that even though sometimes actors do inhabit the same lifeworld, their access to the formulation of the discourse in the public sphere may differ. Misbalanced power and elimination from equal contribution to shape the discourse are the key factors that prevent stakeholders from creating comprehensive and quality knowledge about markets accessibility, and manifests in disabled customers' exclusion and vulnerability discussed in the earlier chapters. Drawing on Habermas' theory of communicative action, the focus is on how international and national information and communication technologies (ICT) business and civil society access the discourse; interact with each other; and what communication strategies, facilitators and barriers are present that prevent from or lead to reconciliation.

Provided evidence has been gauged through semi-structured interviews with and observations of regional and national business and civil society. Two stages of the process were identified. First, stakeholders internally shape a unified position, and second, communicate it to and with other actors. The internally unified positions reflect stakeholders' lifeworld, norms, perspectives, values and the nature of their activities. Policy framework within which they operate, decision-making culture and practice, power relations within a setting and position towards accessibility impact the access to the discourse and the process of shaping a unified stakeholder position.

Having shaped a unified position, actors engage in interaction and communication with each other. Even though the previous chapter suggested that they recognise the need for more accessibility in the European Union (EU) single market, often the interest in the interaction is premised on strategic goals. This chapter addresses some of the underlying strategic reasons and suggests that at an empirical level, stakeholders' actions provide a certain degree of accessibility, but the provisions usually do not meet disabled customers' realities. It is suggested that democratisation of the process by which the discourse is shaped may change the horizons of the lifeworlds and enable national governments and the EU to provide a framework within which the EU mainstream private market becomes more accessible for customers with impairments.

The first part of this chapter deals with internal processes within the settings when shaping stakeholder position on accessibility. The second part examines the way actors communicate internally agreed positions to and with other stakeholders.

Formulating the discourse: internal processes

The process of accessing the formulation of the public discourse begins by shaping a unified position on the issue within a setting. Before engaging in interaction and communication with other stakeholders, actors have to create and use common language, understand the external world and environment in a similar way, share the same social norms and conventions, and understand each other's self-expressions (Habermas, 1979, 1984, 1985). While common understanding in general is difficult to achieve, to do this in the private market is even more complicated. One way to facilitate the process is to have a clearly defined position regarding a specific issue. Research data suggest that the actors are aware of this condition and aim to construct a position that reflects their lifeworld and represents norms, conventions and goals. Nevertheless, even though actors within the same setting often inhabit identical or similar lifeworld, some of them are dominated by others. This leads to diversity of positions within the setting, introduces unequal power relations and limits availability of accessible products. Looking at the stakeholder, position-building process has assisted in better understanding the nature of the position, the balance between strategic and common goal–oriented intensions, differences and similarities as well as strengths and weaknesses of the process.

The discussion starts by looking at the international perspectives. The focus is on how ICT manufacturers, the international ICT business representatives (IBR) and the international disabled people's organisation (IDPO) shape unified positions and what are the similarities and differences of the process among the actors. This is followed by an exploration of experiences of national retailers and civil society in Lithuania and the United Kingdom. Finally, disabled users and customers' role in the position-shaping process is addressed.

Stakeholder position: international perspectives

International stakeholders' lifeworld and position in the public sphere regarding market accessibility is not monolithic; its content depends on who and how is provided with the access to its formation. With regard to manufacturers, the Company X informant noted that product accessibility is first discussed between accessibility designers and disabled users. However, their knowledge of intersubjective realms of everyday life is not treated as fully suitable for business realms. It has to be translated into language of costs and benefits and in discussions of forthcoming technologies is transmitted as a quantitative argument. However, even after this reconstruction of the commonly created knowledge and position, it is rarely accepted as matter of course or as unquestionably valuable. Indeed, it must be presented and communicated within the company as an attractive factor leading to financial success. To illustrate, the Company X informant noted,

> I am representing accessibility in the Company X and they note that down and I start to push that [accessibility] if there's a clear message coming that there is a huge amount of people behind that need. So we try to make the different needs coming from different directions so we may then start a priority list, a top ten. Then my job is to negotiate that internally and try to get that to happen.

The focus on financial reasoning in the decision-making process was echoed by the IBR. The informant noted that although business' position towards accessibility is fragmented (see the previous chapter), profit-oriented aims, power relations and unequal access to shaping the position are typical and dominant across the board:

> There's people deciding at the top and then they have different products, they have different positions in the market, they are in different markets. So the company is very market-focused I would say.

While cost–benefit analysis is an inextricable part of accessible product development (de Assunção et al., 2010, Sey, 2008, Vimarlund and Olve, 2005), the accounts suggest that power relations within a company are an important factor in determining professionals' access to the discourse when shaping company's position on accessibility and the development of accessible products. While the Company X informant did not explicitly identify misbalanced power, their used words such as 'they', 'I start to push' and 'to try that to happen' suggest a particular culture of arguing and reasoning a professional position within the company. On the one hand, such practice and professional tensions may assist in crystallising and sharing knowledge, as well as identifying barriers and potentials (Niemann, 2004) for further development and growth. On the other hand, the IBR informant's reference to 'people deciding at the top' suggests that those who occupy higher positions in company's administrative hierarchy, have better access to the process of shaping company's position, than professionals directly engaged with users and knowing their experiences. This creates a risk that knowledge developed together by users and designers is minimised by more powerful actors and business' focus on the ratio between costs and benefits and the overall financial success.

The assumption that accessibility designers' access to the discourse is often restricted was furthered by the IBR:

> And also, keeping in mind that some of these companies have many people that are involved in accessibility and we're dealing primarily with the engineers, the technical people that do the behind-the-scenes work. So we might see all the work that they're doing, but they don't have a communications type of role to play and promote their own agendas.

Direct interaction with engineers and experts in accessibility provides the IBR with knowledge set that could be used to influence policy agenda, standard requirements or communicated to other stakeholders. However, even though accessibility designers have the best knowledge about user preferences and product features that would make technologies accessible to a greater variety of customers, their role usually does not have a representative power. Consequently, even though the IBR is aware of current practices, needs, barriers and potentials, it is not able to use this knowledge in official or public communication. IBR's reference to the difference between designers' 'own agendas' and company's strong focus on the market was echoed by the IDPO. The informant said,

> People, who are working on accessibility issues want to have their own agendas – to show that they have done as well, to have a bit of work recognised.

While this confirms the presence of unequal power relations, it also suggests that such practice may lead to a diversity of positions on accessibility within a company. Specifically, designers seem to own positions that reflect their professional lifeworld, which is shaped together with disabled users. These do not entirely match with a company's position, which usually is founded on the ratio between expenditures and received profit. In such a context, financial calculations become a medium, via which designers' and users' lifeworlds are colonised not in the sense of destroying them, but through instrumentalising their participation and contribution and measuring a 'better argument' in financial terms.

Unequal opportunities to access the discourse and the mismatch between professionals' positions limit the consideration of disabled users' perspectives in product development process. This and inability to 'communicate own agendas' suggest that knowledge about accessibility and potential accessibility solutions are more developed and thicker than they are available to the public. In other words, being excluded from fully communicating gathered knowledge, accessibility designers are prevented from effectively translating it into practice. If this is the case, then ICT manufacturers that are characterised by such or similar processes are at risk of making product development decisions that limit availability of accessible items.

While manufacturers' position on accessibility is reflected in product features but does not equally reflect all professionals' lifeworld, the IBR aims to involve all member organisations and to construct a position representing a general standpoint of the EU ICT industry:

> Well, many times it's just a group trying to create a unified position. So we might have a subject, a different piece of legislation or an approach to different use of standards, for example, and we'll dialogue together and discuss the issue and see if we can find a common approach that represents industry. So we always try to have more of a consensus-based approach.

One of the factors behind the IBR's aim and effort to involve the members is contractual obligations. Specifically, member organisations pay an annual membership fee, and their obligations to the IBR as well as received benefits from the IBR, including representation in the EU policy debate, are established in the membership contract. The contractual obligation to approach each member organisation and to equally consider their position provides an institutionalised framework for sharing and creating common knowledge and values. Such practice is likely to introduce clarity and commonality among the members and shape similar identity, common values and norms that lead towards the emergence of a common lifeworld on and communicative action regarding accessibility (Niemann, 2004). Involving members who operate in different regions and market sectors, listening to and considering their perspectives enable the IBR to reflect on individual and group positions and actions and to justify them in policy debate (Fields, 1991). Equality of all members' involvement in shaping the unified position introduces common language that enables to establish a common ground among EU ICT business and to communicate it to other actors. In addition, a jointly shaped position serves as a 'bumper', taking away from the companies a part of the responsibility when communicating with customers, policymakers or other stakeholders. To illustrate, the IBR said,

> So we really need to internally mediate positions to reconcile it as much as possible. So internally we really try to then speak on behalf of industry and present the position. If you wouldn't do that, I think how would you talk to industry, ever? You have national members and they all have different markets and they all have different experiences, they have different levels of experience and accessibility, but then again, if they want to talk to us they also need to have a position because it is just simply true that you can't speak to 200 people, you're going to need maybe two or three weeks in a debate and we are one of the key stakeholders to do that. That makes it also easier for our members because they don't feel they're, they only want to be talked to. In some way we provide a platform, which also gives it a certain amount of neutrality and objectivity to the debate.

Access to the discourse and power relations 211

The involvement of all members and consideration of their positions and experiences enables the IBR to synthesise separate ideologies, knowledge and strategic goals. This allows constructing positions that reflect the EU ICT business' dominant perspectives that are not too specific or focused on unique cases. The practice when the EU ICT industry holds a unified position as one stakeholder and 'takes off' responsibility from separate members may open a scene for a dialogue. It provides a medium within which companies are freer to share experiences and positions than they would be as independent actors in public or policy debate. In such a context, industry is more likely to become more open and interested in communication with other stakeholders within and outside the ICT industry. However, there is also a risk that such practice may foster depersonalisation, alienating companies from public matters (Amalric and Banuri, 1994) and disabled customers' realities.

Similar to the IBR, the IDPO aims to shape the content of its positions and activities together with national member organisations, while operating within the EU policy framework. For this purpose, the organisation organises regular meetings and events, constantly consults with the members, has set up various working groups and has ascribed roles for member organisations and specific individuals. These means are employed as a space, within which national representatives share experiences, concerns and expectations. Similar to the IBR, the IDPO synthesises gained knowledge and transforms it into a unified position that reflects different national realities but is not too specific to a particular Member State (MS).

The international stakeholders' experience of shaping a position and its content is often affected by imposed time frames by the European Commission. To illustrate, the IBR and IDPO repeatedly referred to time pressure and a need to react and contribute to ongoing policy discussions quickly and within limited time. As an example, accounts such as 'try to come up with a reasonable answer within a reasonable time frame' or 'sometimes it's very short notice and again, it's very complex' were common in the IBR's narratives. Likewise, the IDPO noted that in seeking to equally participate in meetings with policymakers and ICT business, ability to react fast is important:

> And also you have to react fast and in an efficient way. For business time is money and we are aware of this.

Similarly, ICT manufacturers often face the need to be maximally efficient in a minimal time. For instance, in different meetings held by the European Parliament, representatives of ICT companies often emphasised that policymakers have 'no clue about manufacturers' experiences, because the provided time frame to react to the proposals is too short' or 'do not consider business practice'. Under such circumstances, international stakeholders are at risk to shape a position that incompletely reflects national members' realities and lifeworlds. This echoes the discussion in the third chapter and suggests that by imposing insensible time frames to react to policy instruments, the European Commission and the Parliament may act as a system which, through a technicisation of the process, indirectly intrude in international and national actors' realities, colonise their lifeworlds and prevent from engagement in communicative practice.

Stakeholder position: national perspectives

Stakeholder position building and access to the formulation of the discourse in the public sphere at national level differs from the discussed international practices. Echoing the discussion in the previous chapters, it is worth reiterating that historically, socially and politically formed perspective of 'disability issues' and respective distribution of national funds are some of the potential reasons behind a vaguely established national DPOs' position towards market accessibility and their limited access to the discourse on disabled customers participation. To illustrate, the UK informant said,

> There are eighty thousand charities in the United Kingdom. A lot of those charities are concerned with health and disability issues. Some of them will be concerned with disabled people's ability to participate as consumers in society. Some of them will have even people working on those issues, but not very many.

Lithuanian DPO informants echoed the dominant focus on health-related issues and added areas such as employment, vocational training and access to education. Representatives of both countries noted that activity areas are not independently chosen but are informed by national governments and funds distribution. As discussed earlier, MSs' limited recognition of disabled people as customers and identification of the third sector funding priorities directly impact DPOs' agendas and lead to a weak lifeworld towards the issue. As a result, DPOs have not formed norms, values and positions that could be communicated and represented to the public or foster the engagement with other stakeholders. Hence, using funds allocation as a medium, the state acts as a system colonising civil society's lifeworld and regulating their access to the public discourse on market accessibility.

With regard to national ICT sellers, their experiences of accessing the discourse on market accessibility are similar to those of national DPOs and are shaped by the system within which they operate. To begin with, research data suggested that current product-ordering system and practice impact shop managers and assistants' autonomy and shape their use and communication of accessibility-related and disabled customer service-related knowledge. NBSH and BSH assistants' narratives suggested that they have no say in product ordering. Indeed, products to be ordered and sold in shops are in advance decided by retail network management. Such practice dominates over shop assistants' knowledge accumulated during direct interaction with disabled customers and prevents ordering items based on customers' actual needs and preferences. To illustrate, the NBSH (Lithuania) manager said that only products' quantity and ordering time depend on the shop personnel, and actual product selection decisions are made by the corporation:

> We have catalogues and then we decide what and when to order. Actually, it is important to note that the final word when ordering the products depends not on us but on the central office. We coordinate with them only the supply and demand, what people buy the most, what we have already sold out, what we need. In other words, customer related tendencies depend on us, but the product-line itself on the main office, because all our shops offer identical products. This is how we find out – we coordinate everything with the central office but also adjust to our clients demand and wishes.

The BSH manager (Lithuania) echoed such practice. The informant noted that all orders are made via the online system where they provide a list of products that are or soon will be out of stock. The practice is aimed at introducing consistency among the shop branches and assisting shop personnel in making commerce decisions. However, framing customers' needs and preferences within a pre-decided list of products, retailers are likely to deny certain aspects of users' realities and prevent shop personnel from sharing the knowledge about the demand of accessible technologies gathered via direct interaction with disabled customers. Being restricted from ordering items that are not on the list but may have features enquired about by shoppers with impairments, shop assistants are eliminated from contributing to the discourse and practice on making retail markets accessible. This colonises certain parts of their lifeworld, prevents sharing the gathered knowledge and decreases availability of accessible products.

Shop assistants are also excluded from a discourse on accessible retail premises. Informants' accounts suggested that despite their knowledge gathered from disabled customers about disabling and enabling elements of retail premises, they are neither involved in nor have a say when planning layout of a shop or how service should be provided. As an example, the Lithuanian NBSH manager listed several accessible elements:

> There are no sills in the shop; the lighting is good; the products are located low; the space between shelves is big; some of the products are hanged on the wall, so that customers could see a full picture from far; the entrance is wide; the gates open automatically.

However, the informant noted that none of these decisions depend on shop personnel. Indeed, the participant referred to a conception of the retail network aimed at creating comfortable and pleasant experience for a customer:

> Everything comes back to the conception of the shop: we are located only on one floor; the space between shelves is big, because some of our trolleys are bigger than traditional; the layout of products in all shops is the same, so there is no big difference for the client, so that he can feel everywhere the same.
>
> (NBSH, Lithuania)

The Lithuanian BSH manager and two shop assistants in the United Kingdom addressed similar practices that seem to be founded on the logic of macdonalisation (Ritzer, 2004). They noted that retail premise design and product layout depend on the network and are oriented towards the provision of an identical and recognisable environment and customer service across all branches. Nevertheless, the informants noted that some of the shop furniture and instalments cause disruptions for shoppers with impairments. To illustrate, the Lithuanian NBSH manager noted that sometimes tables and vertical displays are too high for wheelchair users and shiny surfaces prevent some shoppers with vision impairments from learning about and exploring products. However, as mentioned earlier, even though shop personnel are aware of some enabling and disabling design decisions, they have no opportunities to comment on or influence forthcoming furnishing. In other words, having empirically generated knowledge on (in)accessibility, salespeople neither have access to the discourse and practice formation nor opportunity to share gauged information with other stakeholders.

Stakeholder position and disabled customers

Despite different and often contradicting practices and lifeworlds, business and civil society seek to know about disabled customers' experiences and realities and incorporate this knowledge in a unified position. This, via user groups and DPOs, provides people with impairments with an indirect access to the public discourse. Nevertheless, the involvement practices differ, and international stakeholders seem to be more proactive in including disabled customers than national actors are. With regard to international practices, research data suggested that Company X and the IDPO are the most open in acknowledging disabled people's expertise and knowledge regarding accessibility. However, the interests behind the two actors' practices differ. Company X informant noted that usually they approach user organisations because they want to identify accessibility features that should be incorporated in forthcoming technologies. Seeking to achieve this goal, accessibility designers aim to provide a platform where users could share their experience and expertise, and treat the received knowledge as valid:

> I think we try to avoid saying to them what they need, and whatever they need, it's a fairly reasonable.
>
> (Company X)

While such user involvement reminds of inclusive design discussed in the first chapter, the practice questions accessibility of the communication and interaction process. It was evident that while some manufacturers are interested in and willing to include disabled customers' accounts into a unified position, they often lack accessible communication skills and means. This calls into question professionals' training discussed in earlier chapters and suggests that a lack of such skills may leave certain knowledge shared by the customers and users unrevealed or misinterpreted.

Since non-disabled customer–oriented features dominate over product accessibility, the quantitative dimension of disabled users' involvement becomes important in internal discussions and position building. The Company X participant revealed that a high number of potential disabled users are often used as a supporting argument in the internal negotiations on accessibility. Such practice provides designers with better possibilities to succeed in the internal discussions. To illustrate, the informant said,

> They [disabled consumer groups and organisations] give a lot of feedback and we do have a constant dialog with them. Based on those discussions, we have a very clear priority list of what are the things from an accessibility perspective that need to be done. And then when we have that, that's then what we negotiate internally in our company, in our business, and they do the business priorities based on this something that we can do or we can do something more. So I would be lying if I said that it's easy and we get things very well done, but in many cases, other priorities are more important than this accessibility thing.
>
> (Company X)

User involvement enables companies to identify demanded accessibility features and to foresee an approximate number of potential buyers. In other words, while designers and users engage in interaction seeking to construct common language and knowledge about accessibility, the capitalistic nature of the private market exploits the process and its outcomes for the profit-oriented purposes. It intrudes into designers and users' interaction and realities and erases some of the bits. Most importantly, this interferes in accessibility as a precondition for equal participation in society and introduces a financial dimension that plays an important role in product development.

Similar to the manufacturers, the IDPO aims to be aware of different accessibility-related realities (see the previous chapters). Accounts such as 'different groups of persons with disabilities', 'different needs' and 'the approach to accessibility is really widening' suggest that the organisation aims to cover a wide range of experiences. Such an approach is likely to provide people with different types of impairment with a possibility to share their accounts and to indirectly participate in the public discourse.

Manufacturers and the IDPO prioritise collective experiences rather than individual cases. As a result, national DPOs that are interested in accessibility and have relevant expertise become valued partners in the IDPO's position-building process. Meanwhile, Company X prioritises collaboration and knowledge exchange with regional and global organisations, which represent people with impairment types that are targeted by the company:

> So, naturally, we have very close collaboration with organisations in X country, just because the majority of the accessibility people are there, not many in our company, are now located here in X country. So we discuss what we're planning with the A organisation of disabled people and B organisation of disabled people, and so on. Then there's one in the UK that's the RNIB. It is also somehow hosting the World Blind Union. So I feel that through them we get a very global view of the needs of both blind people and partially sighted people. So they are a very good partner. And it's also a big organisation, which means that they do have special people that are assigned to these types of high-end projects. So then the discussion becomes very fruitful and both sides are talking kind of the same language.

A 'global view on needs' is important for the company and the IDPO, because positions based on a combination of quantitative and qualitative data are more valued in policy debates (Head, 2010, Mays et al., 2005, Veltri et al., 2014). On the one hand, such practice provides some potential for communicative action to emerge as a high number of diverse actors are involved. This leads to the revelation of knowledge domains that previously were unknown (Habermas, 1984, 1985, Risse, 1999, 2000). On the other hand, a strategic interest or common goal achievement-oriented premise of such actions should be questioned. Specifically, positions founded on qualitative and quantitative data provide the highest possibility to succeed in debates (Mays et al., 2005) and to achieve strategic interests.

Formulating the discourse: public sphere

Having internally shaped a unified position, stakeholders get involved in public communication and interaction with other actors. In holding multiple, sometimes conflicting and changing lifeworlds and positions, participating agents are aware of the differences but seek to engage in a communication process that would create a platform for (1) achieving a common goal of a more accessible private market, (2) implementing strategic stakeholder's

Access to the discourse and power relations 217

goals and (3) raising awareness of accessibility. The present section, therefore, first focuses on stakeholders' interaction, aimed at providing more accessible practice to disabled customers. It then moves on and suggests that in addition to achieving this common goal, stakeholders engage in interaction aiming to attain certain strategic goals that are usually related with their professional activities and policy framework, within which they operate. The section concludes with a discussion on how the interaction may be employed as a tool to raise actors' awareness of accessibility and own alertness of other stakeholders' realities.

Communication and a common goal

Acknowledging the need for more accessibility in the EU single market, international and national business and civil society position it as a common goal and engage in communication with each other in order to achieve it. Despite this ideological commonality, the reasons why the actors engage in the communication differ. With regard to international perspectives, the IBR defined communication with other stakeholders as an 'exchange of views' that enable identifying overlapping and differing positions and activities that would lead towards more accessibility:

> However, we do lots of exchange of views, not necessarily with regulators but also with consumer groups, user groups, looking at how we can both work together to make sure that our manufactured products are accessible.

The IDPO noted that one of the goals behind the communication with other stakeholders, and especially with the industry, is the possibility to test validity of the internal position as this helps to test 'if what we are proposing is feasible'.

Constant communication with other stakeholders enables gathering insights into the context, within which other parties operate. To illustrate, the IBR noted,

> I think, for organisations like the IDPO, not easy to come up with general recommendations of how. You can take it so far and then you run into the problem that you have to be probably more specific than what you're used to and I think that's where the user for this group is harder to capture than for other groups. So I think they have actually a tough job to provide us with relevant feedback that then actually can be taken into consideration.

Locating this account within a broader context of the study suggests that common goal–oriented communication between the IBR and the IDPO often oversteps the need to gather facts and information on specific issues.

It goes beyond the exchange of facts and the employment of language as a medium to coordinate actions and shares elements typical to deeper communication structures. The interaction between the two stakeholders reminds of the shift from using language as a tool for reaching understanding to language as a medium for engaging in communicative action (Habermas, 1984). According to Habermas (1985), such interaction enables actors to mediate their relations, actions and behaviour and to engage in social relationships that provide more potential for achieving a common goal.

National stakeholders' participation in and input to the public discourse on accessibility differs from the international actors. To begin with, while international stakeholders usually perceive each other as equally important and competent actors, interaction and communication between international and national stakeholders are framed within certain power relations. As suggested in the previous chapter, international retail networks usually do not provide a platform for salespeople to share their knowledge about product and retail premise accessibility. As an example, the Lithuanian BSH manager noted that although the new furniture in the shop is more accessible than the previous one, it still causes barriers for shoppers with impairments. However, even if shop personnel have suggestions on how to change disabling practices, there are neither established practices nor available channels for communicating this knowledge to the actors responsible for retail premise design and furnishing:

> The network decides on the furniture, we have no personal influence upon it. We got all this furniture one year ago, they are lower, more accessible. And I believe, they are more comfortable and convenient for the customer. Well, maybe only a cash-desk is a little bit too high, so then we bring the chip and pin device personally to the person. And the mounts are too high for shorter customers, or those, who sit in a wheelchair.
> (BSH, Lithuania)

It seems that due to the inter-sectorial communication and decision-making practice, the process of achieving a common goal is fragmented and remains unrealised. In other words, even though manufacturers and national sellers seek to provide customers with more accessible experience, absent communication and knowledge sharing practice between the two actors cause a variety of barriers. In addition, two UK shop managers who were invited to take part in the study noted that they are not allowed to participate in any research without granting permission by official representatives of the global retail network. This suggests that salespeople's professional realities and communicative potential is often suppressed by more powerful actors, operating at regional or global level.

Unequal power relations are present not only among international and national actors but also among national stakeholders and impact a common goal–related communication. With regard to civil society, while the UK DPO did not explicitly address interaction and manifestation of power relations with national policy bodies, the Lithuanian DPO shared opposite experience. The organisation is rarely involved in the development of legal instruments, and their participation in the discussions with the government usually starts when the final decisions are drafted. Such practice provides limited space for civil society's participation in the public discourse. It also limits the opportunity to influence the policy framework (discussed in the second chapter) within which the organisation builds the lifeworld and activities regarding markets accessibility. This suggests that even though the role and importance of the third sector has increased during the last few decades (Haque, 2002) and its contribution to shaping the political-economic landscape and business' agendas (Teegen et al., 2004) is recognised at international and global levels, some national governments may regulate how DPOs access the public discourse and do not recognise them as competent and important stakeholders. The discussed Lithuanian practice may prevent civil society from sharing and creating knowledge that would contribute to providing the government with information important for shaping effective policies on accessibility. In addition, it may 'deactivate' civil society and turn it into an object of governance. Such interactions potentially position the two actors in opposition and may eliminate the third sector's right to 'seek to identify their rationality as governmental practices' (Sending and Neumann, 2006:652).

By engaging in communication with each other, stakeholders seek not only to introduce more accessibility to the EU single market but also to achieve strategic goals. The following section, therefore, sheds light on such intensions and practices as well as on some potential reasons behind them.

Communication and strategic goals

Engagement in communication often is strategically planned, aiming to gather information about other stakeholders' activities. For instance, communication with business players enables the IDPO to gather information that would support its positions, presented to other stakeholders. The informant provided an example of how knowing about good experiences in the market may be used to strengthen the position and to back it up by cost–benefit-related arguments:

> I mean, in the sense that it is always good [know about business' activities] – we can use things that are good experiences, for instance, to show that it is possible that there is, for example, a market potential for certain goods, if they are accessible.

Finance-related reasoning shapes manufacturers' interest in communication with user organisations. Recalling discussion in the previous section, it seems that information gathered through this interaction enables private companies to identify accessibility needs and preferences, excluding and accessible practices, users' preferences and foreseeing potential risks of investing into the development of certain features. This assists in managing expenditures and receiving maximum profit. To illustrate, it is worth looking back at the account shared by the Company X in the previous section:

> They [consumer groups and user organisations] give a lot of feedback and we do have a constant dialog with them. Based on those discussions, we have a very clear priority list of what are the things from an accessibility perspective that need to be done.

The IBR maintains constant communication with the IDPO. It treats the organisation as an important source of synthesised information about disabled users and their accessibility experiences. The interaction provides the IBR with information that the association would not be able to gather by itself. To illustrate, it is worth recalling the account shared in the previous section:

> I think, for organisations like the IDPO, not easy to come up with general recommendations of how. You can take it so far and then you run into the problem that you have to be probably more specific than what you're used to and I think that's where the user for this group is harder to capture than for other groups. So I think they have actually a tough job to provide us with relevant feedback that then actually can be taken into consideration.

It seems that international stakeholders engage in communication with each other aiming to gather information that is unavailable in their natural settings but is important for successful operation.

International stakeholders often position communication as a means for shaping a common ground on an issue among the actors. The common ground is a conditionally negotiated and agreed position that is recognised by the involved parties. Usually, it is considered in public or policy discussion, especially at the European Parliament and the European Commission. Due to complexity and diversity in stakeholders' interests and activities, the common ground is not a definite, static or documented agreement. It is fluid and flexible. It depends on stakeholders' interpretations and constantly changes, and the participating agents may enter and exit it at different stages. Research data suggested that the dominant reason behind international stakeholders' interest in shaping a common ground is to identify and negotiate issues and perspectives that in public or EU policy discussions may challenge/contradict/support/back up their positions. To illustrate, the IDPO provided an example of how it has strengthened an internal position in the discussions on web accessibility:

> At the same time, we can use them [industry], because, for example, we had an event we organised with them on the available accessibility to public websites and we actually used them to say that this legislation was positive. So for them, okay, they use us, but we also have a benefit because we can say, 'Okay, industry is in favour.' You see and that helps us and at the

same time they can bring some expertise which is also useful in a debate for us. So, I may be a bit cynical, but you have to use this opportunity.

Such an approach is also present in the IBR and some manufacturers' practices. As an example, for some of the IBR members, it is important to know 'what and where civil society is going to say'. This enables adjusting and strengthening their own position. In a similar vein, the IBR aims to maintain interaction with the IDPO as this allows strengthening a unified position that is presented in EU policy debates. Such and similar practices suggest that international players perceive each other as knowledgeable and competent partners in the EU accessibility debate and recognise strategic opportunities provided by the cooperation. In addition, business actors seem to acknowledge civil society's expertise and role played in broadening and adapting activities so that they would meet actual needs of wider populations (Teegen et al., 2004). Even though the underlying reasons behind the interaction are founded on strategic goals, some business actors acknowledge and are aware that operating in the context of current instrumental policy procedures, and having limited knowledge about accessibility, they cannot be successful alone (Lindenberg, 2001). Operating in a relatively new area, stakeholders are internally not self-sufficient (Aldrich and Pfeffer, 1976) and have to interact with the actors, who access and manage accessibility-related information that is unknown or unreachable without their intervention (Pfeffer and Salancik, 1978). According to Bouwen (2002), such interactions make the actors interdependent from each other and encourage them to develop 'inter-organizational influence' (Bouwen, 2002:368) and to exploit it in EU accessibility policy discussions. Hence, it seems that to some extent, strategic goals–oriented communication reshape power relations between business and civil society and reveal knowledge sets important for more accessible practice in the EU single market.

Common past experience and well-established cooperative relationships lead to stakeholders' interdependence and minimise withdrawal possibility. To illustrate, the IDPO provided an example of how they agreed to support the position of one of the consumer organisations and expected the same in return. However, the exchange process did not work, and short time of professional interaction seemed to be one of the reasons behind the practice:

> But I think it takes time and there are some things that do not work well at the beginning. For instance, we tried, for example, to reform our foreign issue that we are going to have a hearing at the European Parliament, the consumers' organisation and how to support that position. We said that we would take on board their position on certain issues and we ask, 'Can you please also refer to this issue when you speak because we have not the possibility and then, in the end, they didn't do it'.

While no legitimate explanations can be made as more research is needed, it is worth shedding light on the exchange theories and models, analysing interactions between the EU business and public actors (Blau, 1964,

Greenwood et al., 1992, Pappi and Henning, 1999). They suggest that before engaging into any exchange practice, the actors measure and calculate costs and benefits of such interaction and, respectively, shape their decisions. The exchange process among the organisations is robust and reliable only when all participating actors benefit from the interaction. Hence, it can be assumed that since accessibility and disabled customer rights is a relatively new area that is yet undiscovered by non-disabled customer rights protection bodies (see the previous chapters), consumer organisations do not value knowledge exchange with the IDPO, as the nature of benefits remains unrecognised.

Research data suggest that international stakeholders are aware of a possibility that other actors may exploit the communicative interaction for the achievement of strategic goals. As an example, the IDPO is aware that in some instances, businesses perceive the organisation not only as a partner but also as a marketing element:

> I think they see us in many cases as a way to get information, sometimes yeah and we may be asked information about certain things. Not always we are able to provide this information. But mainly as a way of also of improving the image sometimes. So no, I know that there is a certain use that they can make of us, but at the same time, we can also make use of them.

The IBR and some manufacturers are in a similar position and are aware that the engagement in communication is closely linked with the achievement of strategic goals. As an example, some of the IBR members noted that they are willing to share information with the IDPO, if this assists the organisation to succeed in its everyday practice. However, provided information should not contradict with the company's internal policy and should not have a negative impact on its position in the market. In this respect, aiming to keep the balance between provided information that may lead to either more accessibility and knowledge or the invasion in business practice, international business players are not completely open to external actors. To illustrate, although the IBR organises regular meetings for accessibility partners, each meeting is usually divided into two parts: public and private. While information exchange about stakeholders' internal and external experiences, perspectives and positions takes place in the public part and various actors, including the IDPO and EU policymakers, can attend it, the private part of the meeting involves only the IBR members. Then, information gathered in the public part of the meeting is discussed, and the focus is on business' perspectives that may be contradicted or challenged by other stakeholders in public or policy discussions.

Stakeholders' communication and interaction is related not only with the achievement of common and strategic goals but also with awareness raising of accessibility. The following discussion, therefore, focuses on the link between stakeholders' interaction and awareness of markets accessibility and disabled customers across the EU.

Communication and awareness

Some international stakeholders perceive communication as a means to increase other actors' awareness of accessibility and their own knowledge of other's experiences. With regard to increasing others' awareness of accessibility, the IDPO noted that they use communication as a 'reminder' to make sure other actors consider accessibility and disability issues:

> So, the goal for us is to ensure that we did the work and that they also don't forget persons with disabilities.

Such an approach allows the IDPO to make sure that organisations representing non-disabled customers' rights gradually include disability and accessibility issues into their agendas. The interaction with various customer organisations provides a platform for the IDPO to achieve two goals. First, to spread the knowledge that some provisions for non-disabled customers may benefit market participants with impairments. Second, certain adjustments have to be anticipated in order to ensure equal customer service:

> They have a goal which is to define the interest of consumers and which is a goal which we can also share. Of course we have specific issues within that that we want to ensure that also consumers with disabilities are on board. But there are a lot of issues on which they work which can have a very positive impact for persons with disabilities even though they might not be affected directly, the issue that they are disabled or not, but they have a positive impact.
>
> (IDPO)

The IBR acknowledged gaps in manufacturers' knowledge about accessibility and addressed awareness raising of users' needs and preferences:

> But I think it is also a process of awareness raising and I wouldn't always claim that manufacturers are the first ones to know everything that helps in society. They know probably what the customers like in terms of features, but also on issues like accessibility I think there is [a lack of knowledge].

In a similar vein, the IDPO addressed the need to raise retailers' awareness of accessible products and service delivery:

> You also need a good awareness of the sales sector. Not only how products are developed and built, but also how products are sold and how consumer service is developed. This consumer service is open to consider all the different needs and requires a change.

The narrative recalls the discussion in the first chapter on an accessible shopping chain. According to the IDPO, alongside technical product accessibility, accessible service delivery and shop assistants' role is important. The hint to required change suggests that current practice in the retail sector does not comply with the IDPO's position and should be changed to ensure equal customer practice for disabled people.

With regard to increasing own knowledge of other stakeholders' experiences, it was evident that some informants acknowledge the importance of being alert to other's realities, concerns and experiences. Specifically, the IDPO noted that it is important to be aware of difficulties and challenges experienced by business. This may allow identifying potential solutions, leading to more accessibility. It seems that sometimes the IDPO is willing to support the stakeholders and contribute to overcoming the obstacles:

> If there is some difficulty, we can try to understand them. I think it's very difficult for industry to say that they maybe have a difficulty. I mean, if it's – especially if it's a sincere thing, is not to say, 'Okay, but it's not possible'. But if they say, 'Okay, we have made this feature available in a product but we have the difficulty'. This is a very useful thing to know and it's also useful to know, okay, maybe we have to try to see what we can do with the podcasters and see how to overcome this. So this kind of contribution is very useful.

The IBR and its member organisations hold similar position towards the IDPO. Specifically, some of the IBR members shared that they care not only about the IDPO's positions but also about the organisation's experiences of operating in the field. In this regard, questions such as 'how can we help you' or informal meetings focused on practical aspects of everyday professional activities were common between the IDPO and the IBR. While one can argue that such actions are oriented towards the achievement of strategic goals, research data suggested that the two actors are willing to understand each other's realities.

Stakeholders' communication and raised awareness has an enduring value. To illustrate, the IDPO provided an example of a partnership with a consumer organisation working in the standardisation area:

> We had a partnership with an organisation of consumers in the area of standardisation which is now discontinued, but that means, in any case, we have got to know each other and they are more aware of issues regarding persons with disabilities. That was also helpful for us, because in the end it opened up, for us, the possibility to cooperate directly, which is somehow maybe more effective with the organisations of standardisation in general.
> (IDPO)

It seems that sometimes when the official collaborative interaction is finished, shared and created knowledge about and raised awareness of each other's realities and positions continue being considered. Hence, common goal–oriented communication is elastic, and its results are present and employed after the actors' direct interaction is over.

Concluding comments

The present chapter was the second of two chapters examining the structures that potentially shape disabled customers' experience. It has suggested that even though stakeholders may inhabit the same lifeworld on markets accessibility, one may be oppressed by the other and have limited access to the formulation of the discourse in the public sphere, on what needs to be done to make private market more accessible to disabled customers. It seems that the process of shaping the public discourse consists of two stages: first – shaping a unified position within a setting and second – communicating it to and with other stakeholders. With regard to the first stage, international business and civil society form separate unified positions that reflect their professional activities, policy framework within which they operate and internally negotiated lifeworld. Although the process varies from stakeholder to stakeholder, it is often linked with power relations and money. For instance, manufacturers' orientation to profit maximisation often oppresses the designers' lifeworld that is usually shaped together with disabled users. Unequal distribution of power and insufficient opportunities to access and equally participate in shaping a unified position lead to diversity of positions within a company and prevent from sharing knowledge that could potentially lead to more accessible and better available technologies. Likewise, even though shop personnel, through the direct interaction with disabled customers, have acquired knowledge about accessible products and retail premises, due to unequal power relations and insufficient or absent communication between manufacturers, trade networks and shop assistants are often positioned as voiceless service deliverers and are prevented from sharing gathered knowledge on what works and what does not work in the retail sector.

Contrary to the outlined experiences, the IBR and IDPO provide their members with a better platform for creating a unified position on accessible markets. It can be argued that one of the potential reasons shaping equal opportunities to develop a unified position is an official status of being a member of the organisation. While in the context of society's traditional norms, institutionalised norms and procedures detach the basis for cooperation, in an international business and civil society context, in the form of official membership, they may serve as encouragement or a framework to engage in professional relations towards the issue. Furthermore, in the IBR case, membership is tightly linked with financial obligations. In other words, while actions mediated through money often replace communicative forms of social interaction (Habermas, 1984, 1985), business' financial obligations to each other may create a framework within which one actor is committed to create a platform for interaction and equal access to it, and another actor is aware of the gained right to share knowledge and to contribute to creating a unified position. With regard to national civil society, it was suggested that national governments not only shape DPOs' lifeworld but, through introduction of certain institutionalised procedures in the policymaking process, regulate their access to the discourse and may position them as an object of governance instead of a competent partner in shaping the political-economic landscape.

Research data suggested that an internally shaped unified position introduces common language and to a certain degree removes responsibility. While common language enables the actors to express themselves, make sense of the actions and others' utterances and to act meaningfully, the division of responsibility may either enable them to be more open and involved in shaping a unified position or alienate them from public matters and disabled customers' realities.

After shaping a unified position, stakeholders, especially operating at the international level, engage in the second stage of shaping the discourse in the public sphere. They communicate unified position to and with other actors. The interaction is usually founded on the interest to achieve common and strategic goals and is accompanied by the intention to increase other stakeholders' awareness of accessibility and become more alert to others' realities. With regard to stakeholders' interest in achieving common and strategic goals, it seems that while at an ideological level, clear distinction between the ontological reasoning can be made, at an empirical level, the boundary is faded. With regard to underlying reasons for engaging in communication with other stakeholders, it seems that they are usually premised on strategic interests. As an example, while business seeks to gather information that would enable increasing customer volume and profit, civil society seeks to gather knowledge that would lead towards the realisation of the agenda and compliance with duties outlined in the CRPD. Despite these and other differences and strategic intensions behind the actions, at an empirical level, stakeholders provide a certain degree of accessibility. This suggests the tension between actors' inhabitation of the same lifeworld and recognition of the need for a more accessible EU single market and their strategic calculations aimed to achieve strategic goals.

Operating in a relatively new field, stakeholders are not self-sufficient knowledge owners and aim to engage in communication with others in order to gain knowledge, which is unreachable within the setting. Such interaction provides an opportunity to have an inter-organisation influence on the EU policy processes and public discussions on accessibility. However, revealed limited platform for national retailers to share gathered knowledge and to contribute to changing the practice questions the strength of the inter-organisational influence and the content of the ideas promoted by employing that influence. Limited salespeople's involvement and absent communication between national civil society actors, manufacturers and national retailers should be called into question. The current practice of limited interaction prevents from fully exploiting the potential for more accessibility and may have an excluding effect on disabled customers' experience.

Stakeholders' accounts suggest that the process by which the public discourse is moulded is transfused with unequal power relations and should be democratised. This may minimise certain oppression practice and power manifestation that shape ontological differences in actors' understanding of accessibility and its expression in practice. Most importantly, democratisation of the process by which the discourse is shaped may change the horizons of the lifeworld and position it more as a matter of equal rights rather than as a determinant for customer loyalty and higher profit.

Bibliography

Aldrich, H. E. & Pfeffer, J. 1976. Environments of organizations. *Annual Review of Sociology*, 2, 79–105.

Amalric, F. & Banuri, T. 1994. Population: Malady or symptom? *Third World Quarterly*, 15, 691–706.

Blau, P. M. 1964. *Exchange and power in social life*, London, John Wiley & Sons, Inc.

Bouwen, P. 2002. Corporate lobbying in the European Union: The logic of access. *Journal of European Public Policy*, 9, 365–390.

de Assunção, M., di Costanzo, A. & Buyya, R. 2010. A cost-benefit analysis of using cloud computing to extend the capacity of clusters. *Cluster Computing*, 13, 335–347.

Fields, E. E. 1991. Understanding activist fundamentalism: Capitalist crisis and the 'Colonization of the lifeworld'. *Sociological Analysis*, 52, 175–190.

Greenwood, J., Grote, J. G. & Ronit, K. 1992. *Organized interests and the European Community*, London, Sage.

Habermas, J. 1979. *Communication and the evolution of society*, Boston, Beacon Press.

Habermas, J. 1984. *The theory of communicative action: Volume 1. Reason and the rationalisation of society*, Boston, Beacon Press.

Habermas, J. 1985. *The theory of communicative action: Volume 2. Lifeworld and system: A critique of functionalist reason*, Cambridge, Polity Press.

Haque, M. S. 2002. The changing balance of power between the government and NGOs in Bangladesh. *International Political Science Review*, 23, 411–435.

Head, B. W. 2010. Reconsidering evidence-based policy: Key issues and challenges. *Policy and Society*, 29, 77–94.

Lindenberg, M. 2001. Reaching beyond the family: New nongovernmental organization alliances for global poverty alleviation and emergency response. *Nonprofit and Voluntary Sector Quarterly*, 30, 603–615.

Mays, N., Pope, C. & Popay, J. 2005. Systematically reviewing qualitative and quantitative evidence to inform management and policy-making in the health field. *Journal of Health Services Research & Policy*, 10, 6–20.

Niemann, A. 2004. Between communicative action and strategic action: The Article 113 Committee 1 and the negotiations on the WTO Basic Telecommunications Services Agreement. *Journal of European Public Policy*, 11, 379–407.

Pappi, F. U. & Henning, C. H. C. A. 1999. The organization of influence on the EC's common agriculturalpolicy: A network approach. *European Journal of Political Research*, 36, 257–281.

Pfeffer, J. & Salancik, G. A. 1978. *The external control of organisations: A resource dependence perspective*, New York, Harper & Row Publishers.

Risse, T. 1999. International norms and domestic change: Arguing and communicative behavior in the human rights area. *Politics & Society*, 27, 529–559.

Risse, T. 2000. 'Let's argue!': Communicative action in world politics. *International organization*, 54, 1–39.

Ritzer, G. 2004. *The McDonaldization of society*, London, Pine Forge.

Sending, O. J. & Neumann, I. B. 2006. Governance to governmentality: Analyzing NGOs, states, and power. *International Studies Quarterly*, 50, 651–672.

Sey, A. 2008. *Public access to ICTs: A review of the literature*, Washington, DC, University of Washington, Information Group.

Teegen, H., Doh, J. P. & Vachani, S. 2004. The importance of Nongovernmental Organizations (NGOs) in global governance and value creation: An international business research agenda. *Journal of International Business Studies*, 35, 463–483.

Veltri, G. A., Lim, J. & Miller, R. 2014. More than meets the eye: The contribution of qualitative research to evidence-based policy-making. *Innovation: The European Journal of Social Science Research*, 27, 1–4.

Vimarlund, V. & Olve, N.-G. 2005. Economic analyses for ICT in elderly healthcare: Questions and challenges. *Health Informatics Journal*, 11, 309–321.

7 Summary and conclusions

Disabled people have never been recognised as equal market participants, and their agency of making customer choices and decisions have been often deprived by the market and the state that positioned them as vulnerable consumers and citizens. In 2006, the United Nations Convention on the Rights of Persons with Disabilities (UN CRPD) introduced and legally justified a discourse of rights, accessibility and equality that should also be applied to the EU mainstream private market. However, the EU and Member States (MSs) do not provide the needed framework, within which private providers of mainstream goods and services would take into account all aspects of accessibility for disabled people. Indeed, while some instruments legally construct people with impairments as 'vulnerable' customers, others shape provided measures for markets accessibility around the individual model of disability. Yet, it was argued that the EU may provide a framework within which more effective customer policies and practices could be shaped. However, unequal institutional density at regional and national levels, unequal power relations among the EU, MSs, business and disabled customers and limited focus on the open method of coordination (OMC) and the principles of deliberate democracy convert the Union into a system that colonises national and individual lifeworlds and limits the possibility for more accessibility to emerge. Hence, this study inquired on the disabled customers, EU industry and civil society's perspectives and experiences that should be considered in aiming to facilitate disabled people's participation in the mainstream private market as customers. For this purpose, this book was shaped around three questions:

- What are the experiences of disabled people as customers in the mainstream private retail markets and their perspectives towards accessibility?
- How do stakeholders of the European single market for information and communication technology (ICT) products perceive disabled people as customers, and what factors shape their knowledge and positions?
- How do private business and civil society engage into communication and collaborative innovation to create more accessible EU single market?

After providing an overview of this book, the discussion takes each question in turn. In each instance, the discussion addresses empirical findings and provides a brief discussion on the observed processes and perspectives.

Book overview

The first chapter started framing disabled customers' experiences in the mainstream private market and their perspectives towards accessibility. It suggested that in different kinds of market, disabled people's agency, independency and freedom were restricted or suspended either by the state or by the market. They were excluded from equal participation and constructed as 'vulnerable' consumers. The chapter then adapted the concept of a 'travel chain' from Scandinavian disability and transport studies and introduced the notion 'accessible shopping chain'. It demonstrated that ableism and the focus of the state and the market on non-disabled citizens and customers create a variety of obstacles that exclude people with impairments from equal and barrier-free participation and cause their customer vulnerability. It then was suggested that the discussed physical and attitudinal barriers are partly shaped by differences in professionals' ontologies and their insufficient awareness of and knowledge about accessibility, reasonable accommodation and universal design, as well as limited disabled people's involvement as co-designers in all stages of the accessible shopping chain. It was argued that in aiming to create equal customer experience, universal design should be the founding conception that may transform disabled customers from 'special' or 'different' shoppers to *one of* the customer groups.

The second chapter suggested that public movements and the development of public policy in the area of accessibility and rights via social claims brought the private market into the public sphere. It therefore demonstrated how law and public policy frames public discourse on private market as they relate to disabled customers in the EU and so provides a platform for business to introduce an 'accessible shopping chain'. It was suggested that the new public discourse aims to reconstruct disabled people from 'vulnerable' to equal consumers. However, such practice and position towards markets accessibility is not consistent across global, regional and national levels, and this creates tensions between these policy discourses.

Reacting to the discussion in the first two chapters, the third chapter advocated for a need for a cooperative action. It suggested that Habermas' theory of communicative action can provide useful insight and understanding to inform the way customer rights and market accessibility can be ensured. It shed light on three elements of the theory: lifeworld, access to the discourse and power relations. It suggested that the EU may either provide a framework for more accessibility to emerge or may act as a system preventing MSs and business from creating common language and a more accessible and equal customer experience. It concluded that OMC, located within the deliberative democracy framework, may be used as a tool providing relevant stakeholders with access to the formation of the discourse on the accessible private market.

Summary and conclusions 231

The fourth chapter started the empirical journey of this book. It explored the micro level of disabled customers' experience and was premised on mystery shopping and interviews with customers with impairments in Lithuania and the United Kingdom. It was framed within the concept of an 'accessible shopping chain', identified in the first chapter. It suggested that despite differences in individual experiences, customers with impairments usually go through all stages and face different obstacles in each of them. Faced physical and attitudinal barriers impede customer participation and shape their exclusion and vulnerability in the EU single market. It was suggested that ableism, manifested through state and business' practice, is the driving force behind the exclusion and customer inequality. Alongside the discussion of barriers, disabled customers' coping practices were addressed. This suggested that people with impairments are not passive victims of markets inaccessibility and that their customer vulnerability should be detached from impairments and addressed in the context of external factors.

Following the retroductive research strategy, the fifth chapter started the examination of potential structures that shape the discussed disabled customers' realities. It adapted a Habermasian concept of lifeworld and suggested that international and national business and civil society's lifeworld towards disabled customers and accessible markets impact disabled people's shopping experience. It proposed that policy instruments and business practice often shape stakeholders' notions, positions, values, norms and other elements, constituting their lifeworld. Such an approach assisted in providing unique and under-researched insights into empirically unobservable structures shaping accessibility of the EU single market.

The sixth chapter suggested that even though sometimes the actors inhabit the same lifeworld, their access to the formulation of the discourse in the public sphere might differ, as one may be oppressed by the other. Unequal power relations and elimination from equal contribution to shape the discourse forbid stakeholders from creating comprehensive and quality knowledge about markets accessibility and manifests in disabled customers' exclusion and vulnerability. Drawing on Habermas' theory of communicative action, this chapter sheds light on how international and national ICT business and civil society may access the discourse on markets accessibility, what their interactions, communication strategies and barriers that prevent from or lead to reconciliation are.

What are the experiences of disabled people as customers in the mainstream private retail markets and their perspectives towards accessibility?

Disabled people as customers' experience in the EU single market is tightly linked with exclusion, segregation and inequality; is premised on ableism and shaped by commensurate actions of the state and the market. Discussion in Chapters 1 and 4 provided a number of examples proving the statement. For many people, shopping is accessible only if there are no barriers when acquiring customer information, travelling to a shop, navigating in retail premises and interacting with shop assistants and other customers. These stages of an accessible shopping chain consist of different elements and people experience them in a unique way. What for some shoppers is a barrier, for others is a solution for inaccessibility or does not impede customer experience. Nevertheless, the experience of disablement and exclusion is present across the board and in all stages.

Business' focus on communication with non-disabled shoppers and limited information provision in alternative formats about mainstream and accessible products and accessibility of retail premises limits availability of items, especially accessible. This also prevents informed decision-making and customer choice, and bounds shoppers with impairments to the providers who choose, usually accidently, accessible communication means.

Having acquired customer information, disabled shoppers engage in the second stage of the accessible shopping chain and start their journey to the shop. While academic literature does not dedicate enough attention to the link between the journey to the shop and customer experience, this research suggested that accessibility of home and public environment and of public and private transport plays an important role in shaping disabled customers' participation in the market. Specifically, state's focus on non-disabled citizens often factors the emergence of barriers that prevent disabled individuals from customer freedom and choice, and spatially isolate in the market. While people with different impairments experience the three elements of the stage differently, they all are at risk to be prohibited from choosing the shopping time, route to the shop, transport means as well as the shop. Faced inaccessibility and barriers are shaped by ableism and may cause stress, uncertainty, fear, financial loss and dependency on others; reshape customer identity; and convert people into indirect shoppers or fully eliminate them from shopping process. Disabled customers tackle socially and collectively shaped barriers individually. They employ different coping strategies and support provided by social networks. This, however, indirectly converts them into customers de jure (Bauman, 2000), who are individually responsible for overcoming the barriers that are common to and experienced by the masses.

Having reached the shop, disabled customers engage in the third stage of the shopping chain and start the navigation in the retail premises. However, business' key aim to attract non-disabled customers and to generate profit usually leads to design decisions focused on aesthetics, form and customer seduction, rather than on function and universality. Such practices prevent people with impairments from barrier-free interaction in retail premises, may cause injuries, stress, disgrace, dependency on others, financial loss, infantilisation and a sense of being 'different' or 'special' customers. Business' practices prioritising and aimed at non-disabled customers, respectively, inform product and environment development and service delivery that signalise that people with impairments are not wanted and desired shoppers. Additionally, due to limited awareness of accessibility and disabled customers, some shops completely eliminate people with impairments from entering and navigating in retail premises. For instance, while shops that use only revolving doors may be impossible to enter for blind people, small shops often have steps and no ramps and become unreachable to wheelchair users. Disabled individuals are not passive and adopt various coping strategies. They usually visit shops that they know are accessible and avoid unfamiliar retailers. Hence, by focusing on non-disabled customers, insufficiently recognising changes in clientele segment and having limited awareness of accessibility business exclude disabled customers and create their vulnerability and segregation in the EU private market.

Aiming to overcome barriers and to avoid customer exclusion, disabled people often seek others' assistance. While assistance provided by shop personnel and other customers is available, close people are the most desirable source of assistance. They are familiar with reasonable accommodation and provide continuous instead of fragmented assistance. Contrarily, due to limited training on and awareness of disability and accessibility, assistance provided by shop assistants often lead to limited choice, unequal treatment, financial disadvantage, depersonalisation, infantilisation and attribution to a lower social and economic class. Similar experiences are common in shops that have 'special' shop assistants responsible for serving shoppers with impairments. In addition to the outlined exclusion practices, service provided by the 'special' shop assistants limit equal choice and full control over the process, position disabled customers as different shoppers and promote a discourse of 'otherness' in the private market. Incompatibility between customers' accessibility preferences and expectations and shop assistants' knowledge on and awareness of accessibility prevents people from choosing the most accessible items and impedes the creation of common language and knowledge about accessibility.

The discussion on the experiences of disabled people as customers and their perspectives towards accessibility has suggested that accessibility of the private market should not be perceived in a vacuum of a shop. It has to be approached as a holistic process overstepping market exchange practice in retail premises. This allowed identifying stages of an accessible shopping chain, gaps in literature and professional practice as well as challenged socially and legally constructed disabled people's customer vulnerability and untied it from individual's impairment. Indeed, it provided substantial evidence that the driving force behind disabled shoppers' exclusion, segregation and customer vulnerability in the EU single market is the synergy between the state and the market's focus on non-disabled citizens and customers.

How do stakeholders of the European single market for ICT products perceive disabled people as customers, and what factors shape their knowledge and positions?

Regional and national EU ICT industry and civil society stakeholders recognise the need for a more accessible EU single market for disabled customers. The content and the sparks of this recognition differ, and policy frameworks within which the stakeholders operate and business practices play the key role in shaping these understandings.

EU industry and civil society perceive disabled people as one customer group, whose members vary from each other, and impairment type is an important factor for the differentiation. This reflects the position established in the EU policy instruments that positions impairment as one of the reasons for becoming a 'vulnerable' customer. On the one hand, such an individual model perspective is likely to enable the actors to introduce policy and product development decisions more easily and successfully. On the other hand, the categorisation intrudes into actual and real reality domains. It introduces to the public discourse elements that prevent the shift from treating disabled people as 'special' or 'different' consumers towards positioning them as equal market participants. The conceptual and empirical differentiation creates hierarchical relationships among customers with impairments. Particularly, current policy instruments, business and civil society prioritise some types of impairment over others. Positioning impairment as a central factor creates a division among disabled customers and assist in fragmenting the accessible market as some parts of it receive more attention than others.

While business and civil society divide disabled customers into groups, policy framework within which they operate is an important factor for locating their understanding and positions in the context of either the social or individual model of disability. Specifically, international and national civil society actors, who premise professional activities on the CRPD, have internalised approach similar to the social model of disability and share values entrenched in the Convention. However, while the Treaty provides foundation and framework for the IDPO's activities, national DPOs are aware of the Convention but refer to it less and do not shape the narrative about professional activities around it. This intra-sectorial difference is shaped by the stakeholders' different kind of engagement with this human rights instrument. Specifically, the IDPO, being involved in macro-level activities at which the Convention is usually used as an argumentative tool, have better skills in articulating the norms established in the Treaty. Meanwhile, national DPOs focus on the practical implementation of the Convention at the micro level and refer to it less.

Business perceives customers with impairments mainly through the lens of an individual model of disability. This is mainly shaped by policy instruments that regulate their activities. Specifically, treating product development standards as a key reference, manufacturers and the IBR perceive individual's impairment as guidance of how to comply with the requirements. Likewise, lacking awareness of accessibility and disability, national retailers often follow a similar approach and perceive impairment either as a factor marking customers' 'specificity' or as guidance to provide reasonable accommodation. However, sellers who communicate with manufacturers and disabled customers are provided with clear information about product accessibility and receive training on accessibility and disabled customer service, demonstrating more social model–oriented perspectives.

Industry's positions that are premised on the individual model of disability negatively affect accessibility features, product design, availability of accessible items, service delivery and maintain negative perceptions supporting disablist attitudes towards people with impairments. Hence, operation in different policy frameworks shapes differences between and tensions in stakeholders' knowledge and positions. This questions industry and civil society's possibilities to create common language and knowledge on accessibility and to engage in communicative action aiming to create a more accessible EU single market.

The focus on impairments positions disabled people as 'needing' and non-disabled people as 'wanting' users and customers. The synergy between ableism and the need to comply with standards and regulations shape manufacturers' understanding of disabled people as 'needing' users. The focus on non-disabled customers and limited awareness of accessibility mould sellers' perceptions of disabled people as 'needing' shoppers, who require 'special' service. Information provision and training on accessibility as well as a platform for designers and shop assistants who directly interact with customers to share their experiences and observations may assist in deconstructing the concept 'accessibility needs' and disabled people as 'needing' users and customers. In some instances, civil society also refers to 'needs' when talking about accessibility. However, in such instance, the focus usually is on the identification of different needs in aiming to ensure they are addressed in regional and national policy instruments as advocated in the Convention. The focus on 'needs' in the context of market accessibility and customer equality positions a 'need' as a factor, marking conceptual and practical division between disabled and non-disabled customers. This prevents reconceptualisation of disabled people as 'vulnerable' consumers, entrench their otherness in the private market and assist in maintaining unequal power relations between disabled and non-disabled market participants.

In addition to policy instruments, certain business practices assist in moulding industry's perspectives. Specifically, needed expenditures for and received profit from accessible items and the volume of potential user groups form manufacturers' decisions towards development of accessible products. Likewise, customer loyalty and superiority in competitiveness brought by accessible features are additional factors why some producers position disabled people as a potential user group and are ready to sacrifice fashionable product design for its accessibility. Growing disabled and older customer volume and received profit from producing accessible devices encourage manufacturers to perceive them not only as a reason why certain legal requirements should be met but also as a valuable and profitable customer group. Producers, who have strong corporate social responsibility (CSR) commitments that incorporate disability and accessibility and cooperate with disabled users, are more likely to follow such a position. Hence, certain practices and processes, including competition among a small number of providers of accessible devices, contribute to redrawing accessibility practices within the EU single market.

Disabled people's involvement in shaping policies and business practices is important for moulding the stakeholders' lifeworld and positions. However, business and civil society insufficiently involve people with impairments in market accessibility–related processes and so prevent them from accessing the formulation of the public discourse. Actors, who do acknowledge people's knowledge and expertise, play a leading role in the field and contribute to the deconstruction of disabled people's portrayal as 'vulnerable' or 'different' customers and position them as active society members. Cooperation between business, civil society and disabled customers assists in creating common language and knowledge about accessibility and in reshifting power relations towards more equality. In such a context, customers with impairments are perceived as experts and co-producers of accessibility and active agents of society.

How do private business and civil society engage into communication and collaborative innovation to create more accessible EU single market and facilitate disabled customers' participation?

Inhabitation of the same lifeworld does not ensure equal engagement in communication and collaborative innovation to create more accessible markets. Even when the actors inhabit the same lifeworld, one may be oppressed by the other and excluded from the formulation of public discourse. Indeed, aiming to create a more accessible EU single market and facilitate disabled customers' participation, democratisation of the process by which the discourse is shaped is essential.

Usually, the process of stakeholders' engagement in communication and collaborative innovation consists of two stages: formulating an internally unified position and communicating it to/with other stakeholders. The process of shaping an internally unified position differs among the stakeholders and depends on the nature of professional activities and policy frameworks within which they operate. With regard to manufacturers, capitalistic priorities and dynamics of power within the company often intrude into knowledge innovation and its manifestation in practice. Designers and disabled users have the most intense cooperative relations and share the most similar lifeworlds, knowledge and perspectives. They create the densest knowledge sets that may introduce more accessible products. Even though due to hierarchy of impairments created knowledge may not cover all disabled people's experiences, it is likely to identify product accessibility features that are absent or insufficient. However, decisions on accessibility, as other company decisions, are usually made by individuals, occupying high positions but often having limited or no contact with end-users. On the one hand, such decision-making practice 'de-specialises' or 'normalises' disabled users and accessibility and positions it as an equally important issue for consideration. On the other hand, the practice reduces rationally informed knowledge, values and language; limits availability of accessible products; and prevents knowledge created together by designers and users, to be communicated to the public and used in shaping public discourse.

Financial calculations, that are used as a measure in making decisions on product features, dislodge product accessibility to the end of a company's 'to do' list and prevent the translation of created knowledge into accessible products. Even though designers, disabled users and the company as a business setting acknowledge the need for more accessibility in the market and take certain actions, the first two stakeholder groups are often oppressed by business dynamics. Their created knowledge about accessible product features is often silenced and not translated into practice. This divides the company's position into two parts: first – a position shaped by designers and disabled users, and second – a position shaped and presented by the company as one setting. Inconsistency of and tensions between the two positions create a mismatch between actual possibilities to produce accessible items and their availability in the market. In addition, being shaped by and managed through money and power as a medium, the presence of two positions and disablement of the knowledge created together by designers and disabled users prevent the company from communicating full and comprehensive knowledge and information to other parties and from qualitatively engaging in the public discourse.

One way national business and civil society access the formulation of the discourse in the public sphere is through being members of international organisations and associations. Indeed, in aiming to shape a position, the IBR and IDPO seek to involve the greatest possible number of national members. In such a way, the organisations provide members with a platform to express their experiences and positions. Despite uneven national members' interest and participation, broadness and comprehension are prioritised by the two stakeholders when shaping internally unified position. In some cases, the IBR may avoid addressing issues that may discredit or intrude members' activities in the market. Furthermore, if their positions and experiences are too controversial or too different, the IBR is likely to withdraw from shaping a unified position of the EU ICT industry.

Prioritisation of capitalistic interests sometimes results in the EU ICT industry as a unit having no position towards the issue. In this regard, experiences and perspectives remain uncommunicated to other stakeholders. Such practice prevents actors from acquiring information that is unavailable in natural settings but important for introducing more accessibility. In such a context, separate companies usually are unable to form a common ground and common language. This weakens the possibility to reveal actual experiences and actions that should be considered by other stakeholders in order to innovate knowledge. Due to the absence of a unified position, separate industry players become the only responsible agents when communicating with other actors, policymakers or the public. This often prevents them from being open and sharing certain information, knowledge and perspectives and so minimises the knowledge about practice in accessible markets.

In addition to focusing on most common experiences and positions, the IDPO sheds light on unique issues and accessibility cases and usually locates them in the context of reasonable accommodation. However, hierarchy of impairments and unequal involvement of national DPOs representing different impairments impact the IDPO's final position, as experiences of people with certain impairments are addressed more coherently than others. The IDPO's position and national DPOs' opportunities to access the formulation of the public discourse are indirectly formed by national governments' policies. Specifically, states' focus on social welfare and disability-related issues and provisions and insufficient emphasis on customer equality and markets accessibility, respectively, shape national DPOs' activities that later feed into the IDPO's position. In other words, the way national governments perceive disability and portray it via legislations often construct national DPOs' lifeworld and activities as well as their interest level to communicate it to the IDPO and so to contribute to the public discourse.

National private business and civil society's engagement in communication and collaborative innovation is more passive compared to international actors. One of the possible reasons behind the practice is poor density of national legal requirements and institutionalisation. While international stakeholders constantly refer to legal instruments and in some cases identify them as a springboard for working on accessibility, this is not the case for national informants. They have limited experience of working on customers' rights and markets accessibility and operate in a legal context, within which disabled people are perceived as 'vulnerable' customers and markets accessibility is intertwined with the individual model. National stakeholders lack legal guidance that would enable them to fill in knowledge gaps and start actively working on market accessibility and disabled customers participation. In other words, an insufficient national legal basis on disabled customers' rights and market accessibility does not provide the needed framework for the national actors' lifeworld to emerge and to be communicated to the public.

Similar to national business and civil society, disabled customers contribute to shaping the discourse in the public sphere by being involved in business and civil society's activities. Manufacturers and the IDPO have the most intense cooperative relations with customers with impairments. The two stakeholder groups employ different strategies and channels for the communication and translate provided accounts into language recognisable in specific contexts. For instance, designers usually convert expressed needs and expectations into technical language as this enables them to more easily communicate with other professionals and departments in the company. Similarly, the IDPO translates people's accounts into language recognisable in the EU policy-shaping processes. This suggests that knowledge and positions received from disabled customers are interpreted and used differently and are often translated into language recognisable in certain contexts of the public sphere. On the one hand, this suggests division and fragmentation of a unique set of knowledge and potential usage of disabled customers' accounts for strategic stakeholders' purposes. On the other hand, operating in different contexts and employing different language, the stakeholders reconstruct and communicate users' knowledge in a way that it is understandable and recognisable in different contexts and by different actors. Such practice provides a stronger framework for engaging in meaningful communication that enables to address the same issue from different perspectives and highlights the importance of disabled people's involvement in the policy and product development process.

Having shaped an internally unified position, stakeholders communicate it to and with each other and so engage in communication and knowledge innovation outside the setting. The process can be characterised by three main goals: achieving a common goal, achieving strategic goals and awareness raising. Achievement of a common goal of more accessibility in the EU single market is linked with power distribution. Specifically, the IDPO and IBR, occupying similar positions in certain areas at regional level, are the only actors who treat each other as equals and employ language and communication not only as a medium to coordinate actions but also as enablers for exchanging views, positions, experiences and perspectives. This also enables identifying overlapping and differing matters that may either prevent or lead towards more accessibility. The two stakeholders seek to get familiar with each other's realities and experiences, understand them and support each other in overcoming them. Having a dense set of knowledge and understanding about accessibility, being legally obliged to a great number of members and policy actors, operating within a heavily regulated area and having an opportunity to directly communicate with each other, the two stakeholders are able to coordinate common goal–oriented activities and to engage in social relationships. This, according to Habermas, is an important factor for achieving a common goal and engaging in communicative action. Despite this trigger, the actors do not get closer to communicative action, as strategic goals often dominate over the common goal–oriented activities.

Opposite practices and interactions are observed at national level. Stakeholders' interest in and actions aiming to provide more accessibility are often diminished by unequal power relations, introduced either by the market or by the state. With regard to the role played by the market, shop assistants, having the most intense interaction with disabled customers, are neither provided with a possibility to communicate gained knowledge nor are able to make decisions that would provide more customer equality. Limited or absent communication between manufacturers and sellers, mobilisation of power exclusively in the hands of sales managers and shop assistants' elimination from shaping service delivery are important factors in preventing the EU and MSs from innovating knowledge and providing accessibility. In terms of the state's actions, the way civil society is involved in developing legal instruments often prevents governments from shaping policies that respond to disabled customers' realities. Current involvement and decision-making strategies 'deactivate' civil society's voice and prevent the involved parties from engaging in communicative rationality that aims to achieve more accessibility.

Alongside communication aimed at introducing more accessibility to the EU retail markets, stakeholders interact with each other aiming to achieve strategic goals. First, operating within a particular setting and legal context, they often are able to access only certain bits of information. Indeed, engagement in communication with other actors provides information that is unavailable in their initial settings but is important for building a comprehensive and reliable internally unified position and succeeding in professional activities. To illustrate, manufacturers cooperate with user organisations in aiming to gather information about missing product accessibility features and potential customer volume. Alongside common goal achievement–oriented intensions, one of the reasons behind this interaction is the company's financial success and leadership in the market. Similarly, the IDPO is willing to know about business' experiences. One of the ways the organisation uses this knowledge is to strengthen a position that product accessibility is a financially beneficial investment. Second, being aware of limited knowledge about accessibility, dynamics and challenges in policy-shaping processes, international stakeholders aim to cooperate with each other in order to shape a common ground on different issues. Being a conditionally negotiated and agreed position, a common ground provides stakeholders with some assurance that their position in public and policy discussions is not challenged or discredited by other actors but instead is supported or backed up. Even though it is not a definite, static or documented agreement, it allows the actors to more easily implement strategic goals and succeed in professional activities.

While unequal power relations prevent creating and sharing a common lifeworld and accessing the formulation of the discourse in the public sphere, regional stakeholders' interaction aimed at achieving strategic goals introduces more equal power relations between business and civil society. The exchange of knowledge that is unavailable to others converts the stakeholders into partners who value and position each other as important information sources. Although this shift in power distribution is not premised on the achievement of actors' equality and may encourage the employment of cooperative strategies based on reciprocity (Lewis, 1998), it contributes to softening the dynamics of power between the business and the third sector. Likewise, strategic goal–related interaction often creates stakeholders' inter-dependency and unifies them for having an inter-organisational influence that is availed in accessibility discussions in the European Parliament and European Council.

In addition to achieving common and strategic goals, communication is important for raising stakeholders' awareness of accessibility and other actors' realities. Professional interaction and views exchange are important for smooth inclusion of different perspectives of accessibility and disability issues in actors' knowledge sets and agendas. However, previous experience and foreseen benefits of the interaction are important factors shaping some stakeholders' decision to engage into cooperative relations. On the one hand, actors such as manufacturers, the IDPO and IBR, who have more experience in accessibility and have benefited from communication with each other, are more open and willing to engage in cooperative relations. On the other hand, stakeholders, such as consumer organisations, who often lack such experience and knowledge, are more resistant and passive. Indeed, the EU and MSs should incentivise different actors' communication and cooperation and provide means, meeting national and sectorial contexts.

Discussion on business and civil society's engagement in communication and collaborative innovation to create more accessible EU single market and to facilitate disabled customers participation suggested that despite it is unlikely that the capitalistic nature of the private market and neoliberal agenda of current policies can be reshaped easily, certain processes may be exploited for introducing more accessibility. Hence, regional and national policy bodies should employ various incentivising measures, premised on the CRPD and encouraging the engagement in trans-regional and trans-sectorial communicative practices where disabled customers are treated as equally important stakeholders. In other words, even though the ideal speech situation remains utopic, stakeholders, including disabled people, should continue their present communication practice, and the EU and national governments should provide a stronger framework for such interactions to occur.

Way forward

Having identified the barriers that prevent people with different impairments from barrier-free and equal participation in the EU single market as customers as well as describing some of the structures shaping this exclusion and inequality, this section raises questions regarding potential steps for addressing some of these restrictions.

Improving disabled people's customer participation and shopping experience appears to involve two key factors: connectivity of shopping chain stages and elements within them and challenging the retail industry's attitudes and practices. The retail industry is required to comply with a number of regional and national building regulations, so minimal access is (or should be) provided in new buildings as well as some adjustments made (or should be made) to old developments. However, while this creates greater accessibility compared to past practices, often the provisions lack connectivity and so intrude into an otherwise pleasant and barrier-free shopping experience. While this has been addressed and advocated by many scholars, it seems that international and national policy instruments do not sufficiently recognise and address this issue. Indeed, including accessibility professionals in developing policy instruments or urban design plans representing different disciplines and areas would not only ensure connectivity between different accessible elements or environments but would also challenge professional ontologies.

While current policy discourse encourages design and development practices allowing certain access needs to be met, the approach assumes accessibility exclusively for people with impairments and thus fosters customer segmentation, segregation and stigmatisation. The separation of disabled and non-disabled people's needs is not a long-term answer or strategy for how to overcome inequality in retail markets and society in general. While individual differences have to be recognised and assistive technologies or accommodations provided, policy instruments and practical developments have to address and achieve this in a way that does not relegate disabled customers to only certain localities or niches of the retail market. Hence, the trend towards approaching designing environments, buildings and products not as accessible to or usable by certain individuals or groups but as equally used and shared by the whole population or the greatest number possible may provide some needed improvements (Mace, 1988, Vanderheiden, 1998). International and national design and development standards and requirements should be founded on universal design principles as this may 'unlock' shops and society for a more diverse group than just a 'normal' or 'traditional' customers and citizens.

The move towards design and development standards shaped around universal design would need to occur alongside the pursuit of a change in retail industry attitudes so that, rather than perceiving accessibility of retail premises and provision of more accessible services and products as a financial harm and added cost, the industry would recognise and acknowledge the attractiveness and benefits of serving for a larger and more diverse customer group. Unification of disabled and non-disabled people as customers boosts customer volume (Office for Disability Issues, 2010), increases their loyalty (Cheng, 2002) and received profits (Heskett and Schlesinger, 1994, Kim et al., 2013). More proactive product developers are recognising disabled people as an important and profitable customer segment. Hence, as the Company X informant noted in the narrative about producing accessible ICTs:

> Although I feel that it hasn't probably been so big a competitive advantage so far, especially with the smart devices, it has become very, let's say, competitive than what the situation was ten years ago. Now it's a very simple competitive field.

The perception that making retail outlets accessible and providing accessible customer service is costly should also be challenged. As stated in the first chapter, the increasing number of older and disabled people as well as their growing spending power reshapes their customer role and contribution to a capitalist economy. This respectively suggests the need to make retail outlets accessible and to provide information about their accessibility as well as mainstream and accessible products in alternative formats. While the provision of this kind of information has been implemented by some producers and retailers, it should be required to be implemented nationally, ensuring a certain amount of consistency across the EU MSs.

There would appear to be a strong case for informing and training designers and developers of public environments and transport systems as well as providers within the product development and retail industries to ensure that discriminatory prevailing attitudes are changed, and commonly used terminology that may enforce discrimination is altered. Providers who acknowledge the diversity of this customer segment are aware of accessibility, improve the service without major additional cost and place individuals' customer participation before their impairments. Thus, improving the understanding through education and training may not only improve accessibility and equality of customer experience but also address wider social discrimination and prejudice. Incorporating disability and accessibility issues from a social model perspective into the mandatory designer, developer and retail sector actor qualification training and exams might be one of the measures to directly challenge discriminating attitudes and to ensure social change. Promotion of social understanding of disability would reshape professionals' ontological positions and practices that would potentially lead to connectivity of the shopping chain stages and elements within them, highlight the necessity of moving away from individual or medical understanding of disability and disabled people as 'vulnerable' consumers, and provide the actors with knowledge and skills essential for providing equal and quality service and experience. Such mandatory qualifications should also be extended to manufacturers and shop assistants. This would allow ensuring that accessibility is approached in all its complexity as suggested in the UN CRPD. While some design and product development programmes and retail outlets have incorporated accessibility training into their programmes, such actions should be required to be expanded regionally and nationally.

Another potential way to increase awareness of and knowledge about disability and to make shopping more accessible for disabled people is to promote communication within different retail industry sectors as well as between different professionals. While some manufacturers already provide shop assistants with support, training and information on product accessibility and service delivery to shoppers with impairments, such practice is still an exception and not a rule. Indeed, national governments, reacting to global and regional retail market dynamics and reflecting on national cultural and business peculiarities, should find ways to encourage and incentivise closer communication between international providers and national sellers. In addition to this, national governments should provide a framework within which retail networks and DPOs would be interested in and willing to collaborate with each other as equal partners. Such collaboration could include disabled people's involvement in developing training programmes for shop assistants, deciding on the most accessible shop layout and provision of accessible customer information. Considering the example shared by Company X about weaving accessibility into meeting agendas and documenting relevant discussions, it might be useful to encourage such practices between sellers and DPOs.

Altering positions of the stakeholders of the European single market for ICT products involves changes in two key areas: policy rhetoric and professional practice. Positioning disabled people as 'vulnerable' consumers and so contradicting the position established in the CRPD, regional and national policy instruments prevent the actors' ontological shift from perceiving disability in a social rather than individual context. The separation of disabled and non-disabled people as customers is unlikely to be the long-term answer. As suggested in the first two chapters, while reasonable accommodation and assistive devices have to be provided where needed, this should be achieved in a way that does not categorise disabled customers. The development of customer rights assurance and protection instruments which go further than those that are currently in place may create some positive changes. Indeed, the focus of the relevant policy instruments should be on distortive market practices that cause customers' vulnerability, not on individuals' impairments. In addition to this, national and international consumer rights organisations should include disabled customer rights into their agendas as currently their rights are insufficiently recognised and represented by such bodies. Another change in policy rhetoric should tackle policy instruments surrounding design and development of accessible products and environments. Instead of being tightly linked with impairments and the necessity to comply with minimum requirements, accessibility standards should be uncoupled from disability, while aiming to address needs and wants to 'the greatest extent possible by the broadest spectrum of people' (Imrie and Hall, 2001:14).

The move towards accessibility standards shaped around universal design principles rather simply focused on meeting the needs formed by impairment should go hand in hand with all stakeholders and disabled people's involvement in shaping policy instruments and business practice. Technical requirements, customer rights protection legislations and human rights treaties currently seem to be ontologically disconnected. This raises a number of tensions on an empirical level. Tackling the situation directly might involve developing new strategies and practices that would provide an opportunity for all the actors to directly and preferably physically participate in public discussions or policy instruments moulding processes. Such interaction would not only ensure that all perspectives are considered and addressed in forthcoming instruments but would also encourage the shift in the actors' ontologies, realities and used vocabularies as well as introducing the possibility of creating a common language to be used during and after the process.

While the discussion above does not aim to criticise either the retail industry for their profit-oriented practices, or regional or national governments for insufficient focus on social aspect of disability, it does intend to highlight potential ways in which the barriers that are partly created by the industry and policy rhetoric may be reduced. This research provided some evidence, suggesting that addressing the obstacles requires legislation, education and institutional action. Education and training shaped around the principles of the UN CRPD and including disabled people and their organisations as experts or advisory bodies may help to reduce the barriers. While legislation may be required to guarantee enforcement, policy instruments should be also developed by involving all relevant parties and basing the process and content on the Convention.

While changes in policy rhetoric, provision of training and awareness raising are important factors in creating change, it is essential to recognise the role played by the capitalist economy within which businesses operate. Being profit oriented and needing to constantly identify and quantify customers (Vaivio, 1999) to successfully function within the market, retail markets tend to focus on the 'general' population whose customer needs are not only satisfied but also shaped by businesses and capitalism. Having to constantly compete, companies seek growth and security (Harrison, 1979), which may prevent them from shedding light on customer groups who do not fit the 'average' customer characteristics and so may threaten their position in the capitalist or market-led economy. Despite these structural forces being difficult to challenge, current discriminatory processes and practices have to be identified, understood and changed, if the aim is the assurance and provision of equal opportunities to all EU customers and members of society.

Bibliography

Bauman, Z. 2000. *Liquid modernity*, Cambridge, Polity.
Cheng, K. 2002. *What marketers should know about people with disabilities*, Diversity, Inc. Available: http://www.nod.org/index.cfm?fuseaction=page.viewPage&pageID=1430&nodeID=1&FeatureID=723&redirected=1&CFID=5012936&CFTOKEN=67432879 [Accessed 21/09/2012].
Harrison, M. L. 1979. Risk capital, equal opportunity, and urban issues. *Environment and Planning A*, 11, 59–63.
Heskett, J. L. & Schlesinger, L. 1994. Putting the service-profit chain to work. *Harvard Business Review*, 72, 164–174.
Imrie, R. & Hall, P. 2001. *Inclusive design: Designing and developing accessible environments*, London, Spon Press.
Kim, M., Vogt, C. A. & Knutson, B. J. 2013. Relationships among customer satisfaction, delight, and loyalty in the hospitality industry. *Journal of Hospitality & Tourism Research*, 39, 170–197.

Lewis, J. 1998. Is the 'Hard Bargaining' image of the council misleading? The committee of permanent representatives and the local elections directive. *Journal of Common Market Studies*, 36, 479–504.

Mace, R. 1988. *Universal design: Housing for the lifespan of all people*, Rockville, Department of Housing and Urban Development.

Office for Disability Issues 2010. *2012 legacy for disabled people: Inclusive and accessible business. Improving messages to SMEs: The case for the disabled customer*, London, BISS.

Vaivio, J. 1999. Examining 'The quantified customer'. *Accounting, Organizations and Society*, 24, 689–715.

Vanderheiden, G. C. 1998. Universal design and assistive technology in communication and information technologies: Alternatives or complements? *Assistive Technology*, 10, 29–36.

Index

Note: Italic page numbers refer to figures and page numbers followed by "n" denote endnotes.

ableism: barriers 178; customer information 165; interactions in the shop 44; reaching products 154; shop premises 37; UD and retail premises 50; vulnerable consumers 35
access, discourse and power relations: awareness 223–5; common goals 217–19; communication 217–25; conclusions 225–7; disabled customers 214–16; formulating the discourse 207–25; international perspectives 207–12; national perspectives 212–14; overview 2, 18–19, 206–7, 216–17, 231; public sphere 216–25; stakeholder position 207–16; strategic goals 219–22
accessibility: common language 48–9; conclusions 51–3, 94–6; CRPD principles 72–7; disabled customers 78–80; European single market 77–85; global context 71–7; information provision 80–2; lifeworld of accessible markets 178–9; Lithuania 85–8, 90–2; obligation 76–7; overview 17, 70–1; private market 44–5; reasonable accommodation 41, 75–7; retail premises 50–1, 82–5; United Kingdom markets 85, 88–90, 92–4; Universal Design 50–1; user involvement 45–8; US instruments 184–6
accessibility, expenditures and profit: role of business 194–6
advertisements 133–4
A Fair Deal for All 89
Age Concern 33
'alleviation of suffering' 28

alternative formats, information: barriers to information about shops 129–33; discriminatory features 80; impact on disabled consumers 36–8; provision of 81; reasonable accommodation 76
American Disability Act (ADA) 49
Amsterdam Treaty 118
animal rights 111
Annual Report on European SMEs 110
anonymity 13
Approved Document M 93
arguing: discourse access and power relations 114–16
argumentative exchange 116–19, 122
attitudes 159–60, 180–1
audio format and information 82, 89, 129, 134, 152
Audiovisual Media Services directive 79
autonomy, personal 77
availability 75
awareness, discourse (access) and power relations 223–5

banking 197
bargaining: discourse access and power relations 114–19
barriers: accessibility 94–5; barrier-free movement and connectivity 91; entering the shop 148–51; examining through disabled customers 9; gradual process 73; information about shops 129–33; interaction of people in the shop 157; justification of different levels 2; online shopping solution 164; perspective toward disabled customers 177–8; public environment 142

248 *Index*

Bertelsmann Stiftung (BTI) 11
'better arguments' 117, 122
'black markets' 32
blind customers *see* vision impairments
Braille 38, 81–2, 89, 129
brand-specific ICT shop (BSH) 15, 130–1, 137, 173, 181, 198–201
Bringing Neighbours Closer 10
British Standard Institute (BSI) 93
Building Regulations 49
built environment 76, 82–4, 87, 90–2, 112, 142, 150
buses 145–6
business, role of: accessibility, expenditures and profit 194–6; conclusions 202–4; corporate social responsibility 197–8; overview 193–4; product accessibility information 198–9; training 199–202

capital, free movement 77
captioning 133–4
Centre for Accessible Housing 45
chain of an accessible shopping: conclusions 164–6; customer information 129–39; entering the shop 148–51; home environment 140–1; informal assistants 157–8; interaction in the shop 157–64; journey to a shop 140–8; navigation in retail premises 148–56; operating in retail premises 151–3; overview 8, 18, 128, 231; private transport 145–8; product accessibility information 136–9; products information 133–6; public environment 141–5; public transport 145–8; reaching products 154–6; shop assistants 158–62; shop information 129–33; 'special' shop assistants 162–4
'cheap talk' 115, 118
checkout line displays 40
checkouts, retail premises 93
children, dependency on 140–1
civil society: barrier examination 9; communication and collaborative innovation 236–41; notions of disabled customers and accessibility 170–3; perspectives 14–16
closed doors, arguing and CA 119
Code of Television Access Service 134
cognitive impairments: interaction with shop assistants 160; navigation of retail premises 42; operating in retail premises 152; perspective toward disabled customers 171, 175; product information 134; promotional flyers 130; public spaces 144; seen as receivers 30
colours 39, 142
Commission Regulations 82
Committee on Economic, Social and Cultural Rights (CESCR) 75
Committee on the Rights of Persons with Disabilities (Committee) 72, 75–6
communication: discourse (access) and power relations 217–25; reasonable accommodation 41, 175, 181–2; services 89
communication and collaborative innovation: engagement in 8, 236–41; facilitation, disabled customers' participation 236–41; policy framework 11
Communications Act 89
Communicative Action (CA): data analysis process 16; discourse access and power relations 113–14; overview 2, 17–18; theory 5–6
Communicative Action (CA), EU markets @ chapter 3: arguing 114–16; bargaining 114–19; communicative action 113–14; communicative rationality 119–21; conclusions 121–2; customers 111–12; discourse access and power relations 112–21; EU policies 107–9; international relations 117–19; large business 110–11; 'lifeworld' 104–7; market accessibility and a lifeworld 104–12; OMC 119–21; overview 17, 102–4, 230; private market 111–12; SMEs 110–11; 'system' 104–7
Community Code Relating to Medical Products directive 81
conclusions: role of business 202–4
confidentiality 13
'conscience collective' 104
Construction Products directive 83
'consumer', definition 79
Consumer De-powerment Strategy 89
Consumer Protection Act 88
Consumer Protection from Unfair Trading Regulations 88
Consumer Rights directive 78, 80
consumers to producers: disabled people 31–2

consumption, new forms of 111–12
contracts 81, 83–4
contradictions 96
control, using language to 3
Convention on the Rights of Persons with Disabilities (CRPD): accessibility 71–7, 94; barrier removal 94; CA theory 6; communicative action 102; disabled customers 79; equality 179; full participation in society 2; moral compass 70; overview 1, 17; participation 179; policy framework 11; ratification impact 26; summary 229
cooperative strategies 117–18
coping strategies and solutions: barriers, dealing with 177; online shopping 132, 164; product information 135; public environment 142; shop information 131
corporate social responsibility: role of business 197–8
corporate social responsibility (CSR) 194, 201
cost of investment 39–42, 75, 150, 208, 219, 237
Council Directives: accessibility, retail premises 83–4; disabled customers 78–9; information provision 80–2
Council Regulation 84
counters, retail premises 93
credibility, difficulty establishing 115
credit card-related challenges 35
CRPD see Convention on the Rights of Person with Disabilities (CRPD)
cultural heritage objects 91
'curing' 3 see also 'fixing' individuals
customer information: market accessibility and a lifeworld 111–12; overview 129; product accessibility information 136–9; products information 133–6; shop information 129–33; shopping chain concept 37–8, 37
customers, interviews with 13–14
Customised Mobility 33

data: analysis of 16; coding practice 172; generation strategy 6
deaf see hearing impairments
decision-making process: international relations 117–19; lack of freedom guarantee 111; shift from national governments to the ECP 109

decorations 39, 43, 148–9
defrauding customers 160
de jure autonomy 87, 88, 153
deliberative democracy 120
density, public spaces 144
Department for Work and Pensions 10
Department of Mechanical Engineering (UK) 46
Department of Trade & Industry 26, 81, 89
dependency: on children 140–1; entrenched division 94; individual model of disability 3; promoting by professionals 29; shop practices 129–31
depersonalisation by shop assistants 159–60, 166
de-powerment 29
'difficulty' 3
dignity 155, 160
direct discrimination 53n1
direct payments: disabled people 31–2
disabilities 3–5 see also specific type
disability, models of 3–5
Disability Discrimination Act (DDA) 49, 192
Disability Rights 90
Disabled Experts' Reference Group 93
disabled people: customer experiences 8, 19, 231–6; discourse (access) and power relations 214–16; European single market 78–80; exclusion, vulnerability, and marginalisation as customers 19, 26; facilitating participation 236–41; historical view of 27; legal status of devaluing 80; overview 5; professionals' treatment of 30–1; stakeholder position 214–16; transition, passive to active consumers 27; unworthy of life 27–9; value measurement 27
disabled people, in the market @ chapter 1: accessibility 44–51; common language 48–9; conclusions 51–3; consumers to producers 31–2; customer information 37–8; direct payments 31–2; historical insights/ current practice 27–36; interaction in the shop 42–4; navigation in retail premises 39–42; overview 16–17, 26–7, 230; passive service users 29–31; private market 44–5; retail premises 50–1; shopping chain concept 36–44,

37; target of new business 33–4; Universal Design 50–1; as useless eaters 27–9; user involvement 45–8; vulnerable consumers 34–6
Disabled People's Organisation (DPO): communication and a common goal 217–19; CRPD 74; global context 71; mystery shopping 12; national policies 189–91
discourse access and power relations: awareness 223–5; bargaining and arguing 114–19; common goals 217–19; communication 217–25; communicative action 113–14; communicative rationality 119–21; conclusions 225–7; disabled customers 214–16; formulating the discourse 207–25; international perspectives 207–12; international relations 117–19; national perspectives 212–14; OMC 119–21; overview 2, 18–19, 112–13, 206–7, 216–17, 231; public sphere 216–25; stakeholder position 207–16; strategic goals 219–22
discriminatory practices: accessibility obligation 74; interactions in the shop 42–4; shop assistants 135
distance 48
divorce 34
Document M 93
doors 149–50
dramaturgical model of action 113
duality 108
dwellings *see* home environment
Dynamic Controls 33

easy-to-read texts and symbols 82, 89, 129
economic savings 28–9
education: accessibility and common language 48–9, 53; adjustment of information 133; perspective on disabled customers 171
electricity 87, 89
e-mails, product information 134
emancipation and human rights 102 *see also* Communicative Action (CA)
emancipatory research approach 7, 102
embarrassment: interaction with informal assistants 157–8; reaching products 154–5
emotional tensions 132
entering the shop 148–51

entrance to shop 165–6
e-Privacy directive 82
equality: accessibility 84, 95–6; disabled customers 79, 90
Equality Act (EA) 73, 92–3, 164, 192
ethical consumption 111
EU instruments: policy discourse, role of 187–9
EU policies 107–9
European Accessibility Act (EAA) 77, 186–7
European Commission (EC): accessibility, European single market 77–8, 80; EU policies and the lifeworld 107, 110; intrusion by 211–12; older people 195; time frames imposed by 211
European Consumer Centre 88
European Council (Council) 109
European Governance 107
European single market 77–8, 82–5
European Standardisation Organisation (ESO) 84
European Travel Commission 164
European Union (EU): CA theory 5; navigation of retail premises 40; overview 2; relationship with lifeworld and private market 103
experiences, disabled people 19
exterior accessibility 37, 94, 149–50

facilities accessibility (changing rooms, telephones, ATMs, etc) 94
fairness 118
family/friends, shopping with 157–8, 166
financial decisions *see* cost of investment
fitting rooms 153
'fixing' individuals 29, 33, 176, 178 *see also* 'curing'
flowerpots 148
food consumption 111
formulating the discourse 207–25
forward directions 241–5
fragmentation of system 89
fraudulent shop assistants 160, 166

gas services 87, 89
General Comment, Accessibility 72
General Product Safety directive 80–1
German government 28–9
German Psychiatric Association (GPA) 28
glass containers 46

global context, accessibility 71–7
global policy framework 11
global regulations: policy discourse, role of 183–6
goals, discourse access and power relations 217–19
goods, free movement 77
green consumption 111
grief 34
grocery shops 162–4

Habermas' theory *see* Communicative Action (CA)
hearing impairments: doors 149; enhancement systems 93; hearing aid requirement 194; navigation of retail premises 41; perspective toward disabled customers 171, 175–6; product accessibility information 136; product information 133; shop information 129, 131; 'Television services for deaf and visually impaired' 89
hedonic consumption 39
Help the Aged 33
historical insights/current practice 27–36
home environment 50, 140–1, 165
horizontal product layout 156
hospitality industry 193
Human-Centered Design Processes for Interactive Systems 47
human rights: communicative action 102; global regulation 184; signing/ratifying CRPD 108; Universal Declaration of Human Rights 72; *vs.* individual model approach 71

improper maintenance, public environment 143–4
impulsive purchases 39
inaccessible shop premises 36
Independent Living Movement 4
indirect discrimination 53n1, 93
individual model approach: accessibility 71, 73, 94; overview 3–5, 234; *vs.* human rights-based approach 71; vulnerable consumers 35
infantilisation 154, 166, 232–3
informal assistants 157–8
informal channels, production information 135
information, alternative formats: about shops 129–33; discriminatory features 80; impact on disabled consumers 36–8; provision of 81; public transport 145; reasonable accommodation 76
Information and Communication Technologies (ICT): barrier examination 9; as case study of products 2, 128–68; industry experiences and perspectives 15; perception of disabled people as customers 8; product accessibility information 136
information provision 80–2
institutional discrimination 53n1
in-store signage 39
intensity sampling technique 10
interaction in the shop: informal assistants 157–8; overview 157; shop assistants 158–62; shopping chain concept 42–4; 'special' shop assistants 162–4
Intercontinental Hotel Group 193
interior accessibility 37, 94
international business: notions of disabled customers and accessibility 170–3
International Covenant on Civil and Political Rights 72
International Disabled People's Organisation (IDPO): 'accessibility needs' 179; communication 217, 219–25; EU instruments 187–9; global regulations 183–6; national instruments 192; perspective toward disabled people 171–2
International ICT Business Representatives (IBR): communication 219–25; internal processes 207–11; perspective on disabled customers 170
International Organisation for Standardisation 47–8
international perspectives: discourse access and power relations 117–19, 207–12; stakeholder position 207–12
Internet: access for shopping 164; product accessibility information 198; product information 135; shop information 129
interviews with customers 13–14 *see also specific topic*
intuition 131

jargon 136
joint-decision trap 117

Index

journey to a shop: home environment 140–1; overview 140; private transport 145–8; public environment 141–5; public transport 145–8

kerbs 146–7 *see also* home environment
Knowledge-Enhancing Aspects of Consumer Empowerment 80
knowledge to knowledge-skills 87

labour, free movement 77
land planners 48
land use 144
language: accessibility 48–9; communicative action 113–14; information provision 80; models of disability 3, 4–5; notions of disabled customers 170; signing/ratifying CRPD 108; transfer, action coordination to steering media 106–7
large business 110–11
large enterprises 104, 109, 121
large print 129
large states 109, 120
Law on Construction 91
Law on Consumer Protection 86–7
Law on Electricity 86–7
Law on Equal Treatment 86, 90
Law on Natural Gas 87
Law on Special Integration of Disabled People 90
Law on the Social Integration of the Disabled People 90–1
legal instruments: emphasis 49; ignored 147; non-disabled, legal superiority 79
legal minimum requirements 150
Lietuvos Respublikos Vyriausybė 133
Lietuvos Statistikos Departamentas 10
lifeworld: colonisation of 106–7; manufacturers 193; market accessibility 104–12; market accessibility and a lifeworld 104–7; overview 18; policy framework 11; rationalisation of 105; relationship with EU policies and private market 103
lifeworld of accessible markets @ chapter 5: accessibility 178–9, 194–6; business practice, role of 193–202; civil society 170–3; conclusions 202–4; corporate social responsibility 197–8; disabled customers 173–8; EU instruments 187–9; expenditures and profit 194–6; global regulations 183–6; international business 170–3; national business 173–6; national civil society 176–8; national policies 189–93; notions of disabled customers and accessibility 170–82; overview 2, 18, 169–70, 231; perspectives 173–6, 178–82; policy discourse, role of 183–93; product accessibility information 198–9; stakeholders' 178–82; training 199–202
lifts and elevators 83, 177
lighting 39, 151–2
Lisbon Strategy 120
Lithuania, selected research country 10–11
Lithuanian Association of People with Disabilities 91
lobbies, organised 120
lost 130, 144–5, 152
low self-esteem 80
loyalty of shoppers 33, 155

Maastricht Treaty 108
mall maps 151–3
mall parking 146
manoeuvring 39–42
maps 151–3
maps of shop layout 151–3
marginalisation 26, 33, 80
market accessibility and a lifeworld 104–12; customers 111–12; EU policies 107–9; large business 110–11; 'lifeworld' 104–7; overview 104; private market 111–12; SMEs 110–11; 'system' 104–7
marketing strategies 111
meaningless adjustments 150
medical model of disability 3–5
medical products, alternative labelling 81–2
meeting minutes 185
Member States (MSs): accessibility, retail premises 84; decision process 117–18; EU policies and lifeworld 107–8; ratification of Convention 71
memory maps 152, 155
mental health conditions: navigation of retail premises 42; operating in retail premises 152; perspective toward disabled customers 171, 176–7; product information 134; reduction of stigma 30

'mercy death' 28
Minimum Health and Safety directive 83
mirrors 153
mobile phones 179, 194–5
mobility impairments: doors 149; improper maintenance, public environment 143–4; mall maps 151–2; perspective toward disabled customers 171, 176–7; public and private transport 145; public environment 141–2; reaching products 154
models of disability 3–5
modernisation 31
'Modern Markets: Confident Consumers' 89
monetary theft by shop assistants 160
morality 70, 105–6
movement 39–42
multiperspective approach 2
multiple-level stairs and balconies 40
music 39, 43, 131, 153
mystery shopping: ICT 11–13; insufficient number of parking spots 147; overview 9; product accessibility information 136, 138

'naively mastered skills' 105
narrow aisles 40
national business 173–6
national civil society 176–8
National Control Commission for Prices and Energy 87
national perspectives 212–14
national policies 11, 189–93
National Programme of the Disabled Integration 90
National Strategy for Consumer Protection (NSCP) 86
natural gas services 87, 89
navigation in retail premises: entering the shop 148–51; operating in retail premises 151–3; overview 148; reaching products 154–6; shopping chain concept 39–42
navigation of shop 165–6
'need' 179–82, 195, 235
non-brand-specific ICT shop (NBSH) 15, 137–9, 173–6, 198–200
non-disabled researcher 9–10
non-governmental organisations (NGOs) 90, 119
normative model of action 113
notes, product information 133

obligation of accessibility 76–7
Office for Disability Issues 26, 33, 92, 112, 242
Office for National Statistics 10
'off-record' conversations 15
older people: doors 149; marginalisation of 33; music 153; parking spots 147; population growth and spending power 51; public environment 142–4; reaching products 154
online and virtual shopping: growing importance of 1; navigation of retail premises 42; symbolises exclusion 164
ontologies 48–9, 52, 53
open method of coordination (OMC) 17, 103, 119–21, 229
operating in retail premises 151–3
operating in the retail premises 165–6
Optional Protocol 71
organised lobbies 120

parking and parking lots: insufficient number of accessible 147; navigation of retail premises 40; public and private transport 146; vulnerable consumers 36
Parliament 109, 172, 211–12, 240
participation facilitation 236–41
participatory design doctrine 47, 52
passive service users 29–31
pathways 36
'patient' 3
pavements, crowded 144
'people first language' 4
'people with disabilities' 4
'people with impairments' 5
personal budgets 31–2, 52
'personal tragedy' 3
perspectives towards accessibility 231–3
physical entrance to the shop 148–51
pictures, product information 134
plastic containers 46
podiums 150
policy decision-making 109
policy discourse, role of: EU instruments 187–9; global regulations 183–6; national policies 189–93; overview 183
policy framework 11
positive discrimination 53n1
postal services 89
potholes 146–7
power relations: personal budgets, impact of 32; professionals and

254 *Index*

disabled users 47–8; unequal 18, 30, 109, 118, 240
'prefer' 180
'pre-reflective' 105
pre-shopping stage 38, 136
priorities 172–3, 178, 190, 200, 237
private business 236–41
private environment 103
private market 44–5, 103, 111–12
private transport 145–8
procurement law 83–4
product accessibility information 136–9, 198–9
product and promotional display 39–40
product catalogues 198
product customer information 133–6
product labelling 81
product ordering 212–14
products waiting to be stocked 40
professionals, disabling *vs.* enabling 46
Professionals Allied to Community (PACs) 29–30
promises, speech mode 115
promotional flyers 129–30
psychological tensions 132
public and renovated public buildings 91
public environment: communication action 103; journey to a shop 141–5; shopping chain 165; vulnerable consumers 36
public institutions 91
public spaces 38, 144
public sphere, communication: awareness 223–5; common goal 217–19; strategic goals 219–22
public transport: accessibility 94, 165; journey to a shop 145–8; vulnerable consumers 36
Public Works Contracts directive 83–4
pubs 193

quantitative advantage, SMEs 110

radio, product information 133
railings 150
railway services 89
ramps, accessible 146, 150
rationalisation of lifeworld 105, 113
reaching products 154–6
real estate staff 41–2
reality domains 8
reasonable accommodation 41, 75, 92
reciprocity 117–18

record-keeping 185
recycling 111
reflective glass 153
regional policy framework 11
research strategy 6–10
retail premises: accessibility 50–1; customer information 38; European single market 82–5
retroductive perspective 8
revolving doors 149
Rights when Travelling by Air directive 82
'right to life' 28
role of business: accessibility 194–6; conclusions 202–4; corporate social responsibility 197–8; expenditures and profit 194–6; overview 193–4; product accessibility information 198–9; training 199–202
routes to shops 131

scent 39, 43, 131
'second class' customer 160
self-recognition 177
semi-structured interviews 9, 15
service arrangement shopping 163
service labelling 81
service points, retail premises 93
services, free movement 77
seven core principles, emancipatory research approach 7
shame 157
shelves 39
shop assistants: attitude, product information 135; awareness and training 41–2, 199–202; informal chats 200; interaction in the shop 42–4, 158–62, 166; mystery shopping observation 13; navigation of retail premises 42
shop information 129–33
shop layout 151–3
shop personnel 136
shopping 197
shopping chain: accessibility 90; customer information 37–8; interaction in the shop 42–4; navigation in retail premises 39–42; overview 36–7
shopping experience 13–14
shopping malls 39
shop premises, inaccessible 36, 165
shops, universal design 50–1
sidewalks, rugged 146

sign language 42, 133–4
sills *see* home environment
Single Equality Act 192
skills 87
small and medium enterprises (SME): financial disadvantages 121; intrusion into 109; lifeworld 110–11; market accessibility and lifeworld 104, 110–11
'small print,' contracts 81
Smart-phones 179, 195
Social Darwinism and Eugenics movement 28
social model of disability 2, 4, 6
social sensitivity, insufficient 153
social status change 34
soft law/legislations 120, 203
solutions 152–3 *see also* coping strategies and solutions
sound recordings 133
spatial distribution 48
'special markets' 33–4
'special' shop assistants 162–4
speech modes 114–16
'Sports'N Spokes 33
stability of product location 155
staff awareness and training 41–2, 199–202 *see also* shop assistants
stakeholders: and disabled customers 214–16; discourse access and power relations 207–16; discursive construction of disabled customers 170; international perspectives 207–12; lifeworld of accessible markets 178–82; national perspectives 212–14; overview 18; perception of disabled people as customers 233–6
Standard Rules on Equalization of Opportunities for Persons with Disabilities 72
standards: accessibility 74, 84, 93–4, 95; ADA and DDA 49; customer vulnerability 35; deviation, equality devaluation 79; user involvement 45; vulnerable consumers 36
State Consumer Rights Protection Authority 88
State Parties (SP) 72–3
statues 148
Statybos Techninių Reikalavimų Reglamentas 147
steering media, transfer from action coordination 106–7
steps 150

stigma: mental health conditions 30; negative impact of diagnoses 3; vulnerable consumers 36
strategic goals 219–22
strategic model of action 113
stress 131–3
Structural Funds directives 84
subordinate research questions 8
subtitles 134, 135
'suffering' 3
sustainable consumption 111
'system' 104–7

'taken-for-granted background assumptions' 105
target of new business 33–4
Technical Regulations for Construction (TRC) 91–2
teleological model of action 113
television 133
'Television services for deaf and visually impaired' 89
temporary unemployment 34
terminology, impact of 3
text messages, product information 134
'the blind' 3
'the disabled' 3
thought control 104
threats, speech mode 115
time, accessibility and common language 48
timing of shopping 144
tourism 197
trade policy developments 110
training: accessibility and common language 48–9; product accessibility 139; product accessibility information 198; role of business 199–202; 'special' shop assistants 163–4
transition, socialist to human rights' values 95
transparency, arguing and CA 119
transport planners 48
traumatic brain injury 42
'travel chain' concept 36–7
travel industry 193
Treaty on the EU 5
Treaty on the Functioning of the European Union (TFEU) 78–80
triangulation 9
trust 115–16, 118
truth-seeking behavior 118

unanimity 118
unchallenged internalisation, common lifeworld 109, 121
unemployment, temporary 34
Unfair Business Practices directive 78–9
Unfair Commercial Practice directive 79, 88
unfair financial practices 160, 166
'unfortunate' 3
UN General Assembly 71
Union of Physically Impaired Against Segregation (UPIAS) 4
United Kingdom Disabled People's Coalition (UKDPC) 7
United Kingdom (UK) 10–11
United States (US) 184–6 *see also specific legislation*
Universal Declaration of Human Rights 72
Universal Design (UD): accessibility 50–1, 74, 90; CRPD 74, 91; excludes disabled people 44–5; overview 17; retail premises 50
unplanned purchases 39
urban design elements/obstacles 142–3
useless eaters 27–9
user-centered design (UCD) 27, 46
user involvement, accessibility 45–8
utilities 87, 89 *see also specific utility*
Utilities directive 84

validity claims 114, 116
value generalisation 105
values, replacement 116
vertical product layout 156
victims of circumstance 4
"Vision for the internal market for industrial products" 78
vision impairments: accessibility and user involvement 45; attitudes, shop assistants 159; doors 149; improper maintenance, public environment 143–4; information about shops 129–31; interaction with informal assistants 157–8; interaction with shop assistants 161; lack of product accessibility information 137; mall maps 151–2; mirrors and reflective glass 153; navigation of retail premises 41; perspective toward disabled customers 171, 175–7; product accessibility information 136; product information 134; public and private transport 145–6; public environment 141–2; public spaces 144; reaching products 155; 'small print,' contracts 81; stress, insufficient shop information 132; 'Television services for deaf and visually impaired' 89
voluntary agreements 188–9
vulnerable consumers: consumers 34–6; legally entrenched 80; perceived *vs.* actual 35; shopping chain concept 34–6, *37*

'want' 179–80, 235
water services 89
'What Is Universal Pragmatics?' 113
wheelchair users: accessibility and user involvement 45; informal assistants, interaction with 157; mall maps 151–2; perception toward 175–6; public and private transport 146; public environment 142; pubs 193; revolving doors 149; shop assistants, interaction with 161–2; stress, insufficient shop information 132; vertical product layout 156
willingness of 'special' shop assistants 163
winter season 143–4
'with' 4–5
within-method triangulation 9
World Health Organization (WHO) 51, 147
World Trade Organisation 118
writing surfaces, retail premises 93

young individuals 35, 42